RACE, REFORM, AND REGULATION OF THE ELECTORAL PROCESS

This book offers a critical reevaluation of three fundamental and interlocking themes in American democracy: the relationship between race and politics, the performance and reform of election systems, and the role of courts in regulating the political process. This edited volume features contributions from some of the leading voices in election law and social science. The authors address the recurring questions for American democracy and identify new challenges for the twenty-first century. They not only consider where current policy and scholarship are headed, but also suggest where they ought to go over the next two decades. The book thus provides intellectual guideposts for future scholarship and policy making in American democracy.

Guy-Uriel E. Charles is a Professor of Law at Duke Law School and the Co-Director of the Duke Center on Law, Race, and Politics. Professor Charles teaches and writes in the areas of constitutional law, civil procedure, election law, law and politics, and race. His articles have appeared in *Constitutional Commentary*, the *Michigan Law Review*, the *Michigan Journal of Race and Law*, the *Georgetown Law Journal*, the *Journal of Politics*, the *California Law Review*, the *North Carolina Law Review*, and others.

Heather K. Gerken is the J. Skelly Wright Professor of Law at Yale Law School, where she specializes in election law, constitutional law, and civil procedure. Professor Gerken is one of the country's leading experts on voting rights and election law, the role of groups in the democratic process, and the relationship between diversity and democracy. Her work has appeared in the *Harvard Law Review*, the *Yale Law Journal*, the *Stanford Law Journal*, the *Columbia Law Review*, *Political Theory*, and *Political Science Quarterly*. Her book, *The Democracy Index: Why Our Election System Is Failing and How to Fix It* (2009), discusses a proposal put into bills by then-Senators Barack Obama and Hillary Clinton and Congressman Steve Israel.

Michael S. Kang is an Associate Professor of Law at Emory University School of Law, where he teaches election law, business associations, and a seminar on law and democratic governance. His research focuses on issues of voting, race, election law, and political science. Professor Kang's articles have been published by the *Yale Law Journal*, *N.Y.U. Law Review*, and the *Michigan Law Review*, among others. He received his J.D. from the University of Chicago Law School and his Ph.D. in government from Harvard University.

Cambridge Studies in Election Law and Democracy

Recent developments have pushed elections scholarship in new directions. As a result, interdisciplinary work has flourished and political scientists and law professors have developed a more sophisticated sense of the relationship between law and politics. This series seeks to create an intellectual roadmap for the field, one that systematically examines the issues confronting both mature and emerging democracies. It will chart those new intellectual paths to spur interdisciplinary work, to identify productive ways in which scholars' research agendas connect to policy makers' reform agendas, and to disseminate this body of work to the growing audience interested in the intersection of law, politics, and democracy.

Race, Reform, and Regulation of the Electoral Process

RECURRING PUZZLES IN AMERICAN DEMOCRACY

Edited by

GUY-URIEL E. CHARLES
Duke Law School

HEATHER K. GERKEN
Yale Law School

MICHAEL S. KANG
Emory University School of Law

CAMBRIDGE
UNIVERSITY PRESS

CAMBRIDGE UNIVERSITY PRESS
Cambridge, New York, Melbourne, Madrid, Cape Town,
Singapore, São Paulo, Delhi, Mexico City

Cambridge University Press
32 Avenue of the Americas, New York, NY 10013-2473, USA

www.cambridge.org
Information on this title: www.cambridge.org/9781107662735

First published 2011
Reprinted 2011
First paperback edition 2012

Race, reform, and regulation of the electoral process : recurring puzzles in American democracy /
edited by Guy-Uriel E. Charles, Heather K. Gerken, Michael S. Kang.
    p.   cm.
Includes bibliographical references and index.
ISBN 978-1-107-00167-1 (hardback)
1. Elections – United States. 2. Voting – United States. 3. African Americans – Suffrage.
4. United States – Race relations – Political aspects. I. Charles, Guy-Uriel E., 1970– II. Gerken,
Heather K., 1969– III. Kang, Michael S., 1973– IV. Title.
JK1965.R33 2011
324.60973–dc22 2010043692

ISBN 978-1-107-00167-1 Hardback
ISBN 978-0-107-66273-5 Paperback

Contents

Figures

Tables

Contributors

Stephen Ansolabehere, Professor of Government, Harvard University

Ronald E. Brown, Associate Professor, College of Liberal Arts and Sciences, Wayne State University

Bruce E. Cain, Heller Professor of Political Science, University of California, Berkeley

Guy-Uriel E. Charles, Professor of Law, Duke Law School, and Co-Director, Duke Center on Law, Race, and Politics

Christopher S. Elmendorf, Professor of Law, University of California, Davis

Edward B. Foley, Robert M. Duncan/Jones Day Designated Professor of Law, Moritz College of Law, Ohio State University

Joshua Fougere, Associate, Sidley Austin LLP

Archon Fung, Professor of Public Policy, Kennedy School of Government, Harvard University

Alan S. Gerber, Professor of Political Science, Yale University

Heather K. Gerken, J. Skelly Wright Professor of Law, Yale Law School

Richard L. Hasen, William H. Hannon Distinguished Professor of Law, Loyola Law School

Jennifer L. Hochschild, Henry LaBarre Jane Professor of Government, Harvard University

Vincent L. Hutchings, Associate Professor of Political Science, University of Michigan

Samuel Issacharoff, Reiss Professor of Constitutional Law, New York University School of Law

James Jackson, Director and Research Professor, Institute for Social Research, Daniel Katz Distinguished University Professor of Psychology, University of Michigan

Michael S. Kang, Associate Professor of Law, Emory University School of Law

Pamela S. Karlan, Kenneth and Harle Montgomery Professor of Public Interest Law, Stanford Law School

Alexander Keyssar, Matthew W. Stirling, Jr., Professor of History and Social Policy, Kennedy School of Government, Harvard University

Nathaniel Persily, Charles Keller Beekman Professor of Law and Political Science, Columbia Law School

Richard L. Pildes, Sudler Family Professor of Constitutional Law, New York University School of Law

David Schleicher, Professor of Law, George Mason University School of Law

Cara Wong, Assistant Professor of Political Science, University of Illinois, Urbana-Champaign

Preface

Fair elections are essential to our democracy. It is critical that current safeguards intended to ensure the integrity of the electoral process evolve to meet the challenges posed by rapid social and economic changes – from rising ethnic diversity and economic inequality to the growing scale of campaign funding. To ensure that our democratic institutions satisfy America's current needs, academic experts and policy practitioners must have a clear understanding of how our elections function, how the obstacles to informed participation are evolving, and how judicial and legislative reform can best foster healthy democracy. *Race, Reform, and Regulation of the Electoral Process* presents the best contemporary research on these questions and charts an agenda for the next generation of scholarship on elections and democracy.

The scholars who contributed to this volume are part of the Tobin Project network of leading academics and policy makers committed to cultivating transformative, interdisciplinary research to address the most important problems for the long-term health, prosperity, and stability of American democracy. This volume is a significant contribution toward that goal, and we are pleased to have played at least a small role in bringing the book to fruition.

The ideas presented here were first shared in February 2009 at a Tobin Project conference: "The Future of Election Law: Policy Challenges and a Research Agenda for Reform." This meeting brought together an extraordinary group of the leading scholars of democracy and elections across the disciplines of law, political science, public policy, and history; esteemed state and federal judges; senior state officials; and the general counsels for both John McCain's and Barack Obama's 2008 presidential campaigns. The research in this book benefited tremendously from the rich exchange of ideas across disciplinary and political boundaries at the conference. The meeting also helped foster the intellectually diverse community necessary to undertake the ambitious research goals laid out herein.

We consider this book to be not the end of a scholarly process, but rather a catalyst for further work and interdisciplinary collaboration. It is our belief that rigorous research and scholarly consensus on an issue of great public importance – the integrity of our elections and democracy – can be a potent force in framing public dialogue and guiding policy reform. We look forward to the continued efforts of those currently engaged in this project and to further collaboration with those committed to achieving a better understanding of these issues.

We are grateful to the scholars, policy makers, practitioners, and donors who have participated in this project. Special thanks are due to Heather K. Gerken, a member of the Tobin Project's steering committee, and Guy-Uriel E. Charles, who together chaired the conference and galvanized the stellar group that contributed to *Race, Reform, and Regulation of the Electoral Process*; co-editor Michael S. Kang, who collaborated with Heather and Guy to formulate the intellectual framework of this volume; the American Law Institute for its generous co-sponsorship of this initiative; and Duke University Law School for providing space for the February 2009 meeting.

The Tobin Project
May 2010

Introduction

The Future of Elections Scholarship

Guy-Uriel E. Charles, Heather K. Gerken, and Michael S. Kang

Race, Reform, and the Regulation of the Electoral Process: Recurring Puzzles in American Democracy is the first volume in Cambridge University Press's Cambridge Studies in Election Law and Democracy series. It offers a critical reevaluation of three fundamental and interlocking themes in American democracy: the relationship between race and politics; the performance and reform of election systems; and the role of courts in regulating the political process. This edited volume features contributions from some of the leading voices in election law and social science. The authors address the recurring questions for American democracy and identify new challenges for the twenty-first century. They consider not just where elections scholarship and electoral policy are headed, but also suggest where scholarship and policy ought to go in the next two decades. The book thus provides intellectual guideposts for future scholarship and policy making.

Most of the democratic reform during the twentieth century – and certainly the most important reform – has related to the central subject of race. Because electoral reform and regulation of the political process have been viewed largely through the prism of race, election law and reform have been framed largely in rights-based terms. Consistent with the civil-rights paradigm, courts emerged as the primary regulatory agents of American democracy and served as the vehicle through which much of the reform of American representative institutions has occurred. During the last fifty years, courts have helped achieve progressive reform on racial equality, and these successes have legitimated the regulatory role of courts in the political process.

As American democracy has matured and racial politics have evolved, however, it may be time to consider these central themes of race, reform, and regulation in different terms. With respect to racial progress, America is increasingly a multiracial society, and even the status of African Americans within American politics has changed. The approach that was effective when black-white relations and de jure discrimination were the dominant paradigms may require retooling as we consider questions of equality going forward. Electoral regulation presents a similar set of questions going forward. As we move away from the civil-rights paradigm and regulation centered largely around race, we may find that courts should play a less central role in regulating politics – something that would require us to develop new regulatory strategies and institutions for policing our democracy. Finally, whereas electoral reform has always faced substantial challenges, those challenges may be more acute when courts are not driving reform and the case for change turns largely on good-governance arguments rather than equality rationales. Here again, the twenty-first century presents new puzzles for those interested in election law and policy.

This volume is divided into three sections, each featuring some of the most profound thinkers in their fields. The first section addresses race and politics in the twenty-first century in the age of Obama. The second section addresses the proper role of courts in the regulation of the political process, particularly as the central focus of election law may be shifting away from the traditional civil-rights paradigm. Finally, the third section addresses the challenges of evaluating election performance and managing electoral reform going forward.

RACE AND POLITICS

Race has long been central to the study of American democracy. The most important democratic reforms of the twentieth century have been driven by concerns over racial equality. Nonetheless, with the election of Barack Obama and continuing challenges to the Voting Rights Act, we are entering a new pivotal period in American law and racial politics. As Jennifer Hochschild points out in her introduction to this section, two important questions face scholars today: (1) Is racial and ethnic stratification changing? (2) What should we do about change or its absence?

Richard Pildes and Pamela Karlan take these questions on directly while offering quite different answers. Pildes argues that times have changed sufficiently to warrant a new approach to voting-rights legislation. He warns against democratic design strategies that may entrench ethnic identities and advocates a dynamic approach to institutional design, one that allows politics to adapt to changes in ethnic and racial identification. In keeping with this view, he argues, those who care about racial equality should now focus on problems – such as felon disenfranchisement and badly run elections – that affect all groups but may have a disproportionate effect on racial minorities.

Karlan, in contrast, emphasizes continuity over change. Insisting on the persistence of racial bloc voting and local discrimination, she argues for a more muscular Voting Rights Act and greater emphasis on policing racial discrimination per se. She argues that Barack Obama's election, far from signifying the obsolescence of traditional voting-rights enforcement, is a timely opportunity for redefining it. She thus calls for courts to imagine the Voting Rights Act not as a strategy for getting us to "normal politics," but as an integral feature of "normal politics."

Vincent Hutchings and his coauthors contribute to this debate by helping identify what we know and don't know about the existing state of racial and ethnic affairs. They negotiate the change/continuity theme by helping us move beyond the black-white paradigm that has dominated racial discourse, by describing the dimensions of intergroup conflict in a multiracial America, and by reminding us of the continued relevance of racial prejudice. As Hochschild points out, this study answers some question and raises many others about interracial rivalries and the notion of linked fate.

COURTS AND THE REGULATION OF THE ELECTORAL PROCESS

One underappreciated legacy of the Voting Rights Act is that most efforts to regulate the electoral process have focused on race and thus been framed in rights-based terms, thereby making courts the central regulatory institutions of American democracy. As American election law has matured, racial politics have evolved, and new regulatory challenges have emerged, some scholars have begun to think of regulation in different terms.

As David Schleicher details in his mapping of "election law's interior," many scholars have begun to think of electoral regulation in structural or institutional terms, and the field has thus taken what Heather Gerken and Michael Kang call an "institutional turn." More than a decade ago, two of this book's contributors, Samuel Issacharoff and Richard Pildes, called on courts and scholars to think of election law in structural rather than rights-based terms. As Schleicher points out, however, in the wake of that important debate, the field's attention turned elsewhere. As a result, in recent years, not much new ground was broken in thinking about the appropriate strategies for regulating the political process. The work here, as Schleicher explains, begins to sketch new paths for research and thus "add[s] to the structural picture" that was partially sketched a decade ago.

Gerken and Kang argue that we should turn away from courts as political regulators and instead focus on strategies that allow us to harness politics to fix politics. They propose a variety of "hard" and "soft" approaches for smoothing the terrain on which reform battles are fought and making genuine reform possible. Pulling together a variety of ideas, including many of their own, Gerken and Kang offer an intellectual framework for future research in this area.

Sam Issacharoff examines electoral regulation from a different angle by analyzing what role courts play in regulating politics in transitional democracies. After examining the use of specialized constitutional courts in other countries, Issacharoff expresses some optimism about the ability of these courts to structure the arena in which political competition takes place. Even though Issacharoff is more optimistic about the role courts can play in this context than Gerken and Kang are in the American context, he too conceives of the courts' role in decidedly structural terms.

Rick Hasen, a long-time foe of the structural approach, nonetheless finds some common ground with Gerken and Kang while indirectly raising questions about Issacharoff's claims. Citing a dramatic increase in election law litigation as cause for alarm, Hasen joins Gerken and Kang in questioning the current reliance on courts as the primary regulators of the political process. Relying on work on the attitudinal model of judging, Hasen is quite pessimistic about the prospect of leaving it to judges to determine the structure of electoral regulations. Hasen is also skeptical, however, of other regulatory approaches, including many of those proposed by Gerken and Kang.

Christopher Elmendorf offers still another angle on the role courts can and should play in regulating electoral politics. The Supreme Court often relies on notions of legitimacy in justifying its regulatory choices. Elmendorf is sympathetic to the normative account one might offer for this practice. But his survey of existing work suggests that the Court is simply mistaken to think that there is a relationship between perceptions of legitimacy and electoral regulation. Elmendorf then considers whether and under what circumstances legitimacy ought to play a role in judicial regulation, identifying empirical and normative work that remains to be done on this question.

ELECTION PERFORMANCE AND REFORM

The last set of papers addresses the challenges of evaluating election performance and managing electoral reform. As Alex Keyssar observes in his introduction, even in the wake of the 2000 election fiasco, the pace of reform in the United States has been remarkably slow. Recent election controversies have revealed the ugly underbelly of our election system and raise serious questions about what we know and don't know about how well our election system is functioning. The papers in this section thus center on two key questions: How do we acquire information to evaluate our election system and why has it been so hard to reform it?

Archon Fung pairs a proposal for evaluating our election system with a strategy for reforming it. Based on the success of sites like fixmystreet.com, Fung has created myfairelection.com, which allows voters to report on problems they encountered when casting a ballot. This real-time, crowd-sourcing solution makes it possible for everyday citizens to monitor how well the election system is working. Were such an approach to catch hold, Fung's idea would not just allow us to identify where problems exist in our system, but make those problems visible to voters even in the absence of the type of electoral disaster we saw in Florida in 2000 and Ohio in 2004.

Joshua Fougere, Steve Ansolabehere, and Nate Persily examine American attitudes toward redistricting and find that most people know very little about how districts are drawn or why districting matters. They thus identify one of the key obstacles to reform: voters' lack of information about basic reform issues. The authors also suggest, however, that when voters are informed about how districting works, they object to the self-dealing inherent in the system and favor a nonpartisan districting process.

Alan Gerber considers the question of voter apathy, examining why voters turn out and how we might encourage them to do so. Reporting on an important methodological advance in the area, Gerber suggests the role that social pressure can play an important role in encouraging people to vote.

Finally, Edward Foley sketches a reform agenda for the next decade, a plan for "state of the art" election law by the year 2020 and describes its key features, including a state-of-the-art election infrastructure and a variety of good-governance reforms. Foley's paper shows us just how much there is to do to improve our election system.

CONCLUSION

Bruce Cain, in his concluding essay, provides a broad overview of the basic questions the field faces in thinking about reform. Cain argues that most reform proposals can be classified as demanding "more democracy" or "less" and insists that the easy assumption that more democracy is better is mistaken. Instead, he shows that election reform inevitably involves a trade-off between important democratic values. Cain then maps the field along these dimensions, offering some concluding thoughts on the papers in this volume and what he calls "the promise of new election law institutionalism."

It is our expectation that this volume will provide readers with a critical basis for appreciating and assessing the capacity and limits of race, reform, and regulation as the central organizing themes for understanding American democracy.

PART I

Race and Politics

Overview: How, If at All, Is Racial and Ethnic Stratification Changing, and What Should We Do about It?

Jennifer L. Hochschild

These chapters on the politics of groups push the reader to consider a difficult but essential question: How, if at all, are old forms of racial and ethnic stratification changing? A broadly persuasive answer would have powerful implications ranging from constitutional design and electoral strategies to interpersonal relationships and private emotions. However, the question is not only difficult to answer for obvious empirical reasons, but also because, for scholars just as for the general public, one's own views inevitably shape what one considers to be legitimate evidence and appropriate evaluation of it. So the study of racial dynamics is exasperatingly circular, even with the best research and most impressive researchers.

Although my concerns about circularity lead me to raise questions about all three chapters, I want to begin by pointing out their quality. Each provides the reader with a clear thesis, well defended by relevant evidence and attentive to alternative arguments or weaknesses in the preferred one. Each chapter grows out of a commitment to the best values of liberal democracy – individual freedom and dignity, along with collective control by the citizenry over their governors – but commitments do not override careful analysis. Each chapter is a pleasure to read and teaches us something new and important.

My observations begin with a direct comparison of Pildes's and Karlan's respective evaluations of the United States' Voting Rights Act and its appropriate reforms. I then bring in Hutchings and his colleagues' analysis of American racial and ethnic groups' views of each other, which provides some of the essential background for adjudicating between Pildes's and Karlan's positions. Underpinning my discussion, and becoming more explicit in the conclusion, is an observation that is not new to me but is nevertheless important: People who identify as progressives are often deeply suspicious of attempts to alter current policies about or understandings of racial and ethnic stratification, whereas people who identify as conservatives are often most eager to see and promote modifications in current practices. There is something deeply ironic here – both in the difficulties of many on the left in recognizing

what has changed and in the difficulties of many on the right in recognizing what
has not.

Richard Pildes argues that it is time for the "next generation" of voting rights legislation to take over from the several-times-renewed Voting Rights Act (VRA) of 1965. In
his view, the VRA succeeded in its initial mission of "getting out in front" of white
public officials' strategies for disfranchising black voters, so much that it is now getting in the way of its own underlying purpose of voting equity. Section 5 of the VRA
is both overinclusive – requiring oversight that is no longer necessary – and underinclusive – not capable of addressing current barriers to citizens' exercise of their right
to vote. Given politicians' tendency to move in only one reform direction at a time,
he urges Congress to largely scrap the old VRA and replace it with a new law that
addresses more contemporary obstacles to voting, such as felon disfranchisement,
outmoded voting technologies, and inefficient or deliberately ineffective electoral
procedures. Although these contemporary obstacles may disproportionately affect
people of color, they are not intrinsically about racial discrimination per se, so the
underlying framework of the old VRA needs to be rethought rather than adjusted.

Pamela Karlan does not quite accuse Pildes of naïveté about continuing racial
discrimination, but such a suggestion hovers around the edges of her essay. She
points to persistent racial bloc voting, especially whites' disproportionate rejection
of Barack Obama's presidential candidacy in locations covered by Section 5 of the
VRA, as well as the possibility of discrimination in local elections and the distinctive
barriers faced by Latinos and Native Americans. For these reasons, among others,
the United States must maintain the old VRA. In fact (Pildes might agree here),
"the government has an obligation to facilitate citizens' exercise of the franchise"
and to become even more vigilant against states and courts' tendency to water down
citizens' voting rights, especially focusing on citizens of color given America's history
of racial stratification. Karlan's most pointed argument is that the VRA does not only
protect individuals' right to vote – a protection that, in her view, we still need –
but also gives minority groups "leverage in demanding accommodation of minority
concerns." Section 5 is what gives that leverage, and therefore it warrants continued
support or even strengthening.

Pildes and Karlan agree on a lot of particular reforms and share an underlying commitment to equality of individual suffrage rights and equity among group
rights. They share the goal of overturning the effects of centuries of discrimination
against black Americans. Nevertheless, the tone of their chapters differs intriguingly.
Karlan worries more about whites' continuing preference for racial domination, or at
least their indifference to its continuation. For example, if Section 5 were repealed,
"the Democratic party might be tempted to spread concentrations of minority voters

among several districts" to promote its highest priority – electing more Democrats – even if this would dilute blacks' political influence. In another example, Karlen points out not only that Southern whites have historically "resist[ed] minority political aspirations," but also that "this backlash phenomenon seems to be alive and well today." Thus we must always remember that "[t]he past is never dead. It's not even past."

In contrast, Pildes implicitly asserts that the past *is* dead, or at least dying, and that our preoccupation with protecting minorities against the evils of twentieth-century-style discrimination is getting in the way of protecting them, and others, against twenty-first-century problems. To put my words into his mouth, racial and ethnic stratification is changing – decreasing in important ways while persisting or even worsening in others. If we cling too tightly to winning the last war, we jeopardize our chances of success in the next one. In his own words, "the voting rights issues we face today are no longer defined by the near-complete exclusion of black voters by a number of readily identifiable state and local governments.... If Congress is serious about protecting the right to vote, it is going to have to go beyond that model." Many of the most serious barriers to voting "tend to impact not only racial minorities, but also the poor and the elderly generally;" thus Pildes calls for laws and policies that are uniform across states and have "universal terms that extend coverage to all voters." In sum, with a few important exceptions, we no longer need laws targeted at specific racial or ethnic groups in particular locations because non-Anglos are often powerful enough to protect their own interests. Instead we need laws to protect newly recognized categories of powerless Americans, a majority of whom might even be white.

In my view, Pildes has the stronger argument; I see more change than continuity in the American racial order since the VRA was formulated and renewed. Some of that change has been for the better. With two exceptions (1976 and 1996), a higher proportion of whites voted for Barack Obama than for any of his Democratic party predecessors in the eleven elections since 1968 (Clayton 2010). Nine states, including three from the old Confederate South, switched from Republican in 2004 to Democratic in 2008, due to a combination of some white support, very strong black and Hispanic support, and changing proportions of groups in the voting public. To put it most simply, Americans have now shown that "a black candidate can win in the majority-white constituency that is the national presidential electorate" (Ansolabehere et al. 2010: 1409).

However, some of the change in the American racial order since the VRA was formulated has been for the worse. The proportion of young non-Anglo men involved with the criminal justice system has skyrocketed; when calculated in 2001, 17 percent of black and 8 percent of Hispanic men, compared with 3 percent of white men, had been incarcerated in a state or federal prison at least once (U.S. Department of Justice 2003) – and the numbers and disproportion have risen since then. Put another way, although blacks comprised 12 percent of the U.S. population in 2008, they accounted for 28 percent of all arrests (Bureau of Justice Statistics 2008: table 4.10.2008). Poor or poorly educated young black men are especially likely to be involved with the criminal justice system, and their families and communities are disproportionately harmed through indirect involvement (Western 2006; Clear 2007). Thus the old issue of felon disfranchisement has taken on new urgency as the prison population has soared in recent decades, and it now arguably has as much or more impact on racial disparity in political representation as do more conventional forms of discrimation against minority would-be voters. I leave it to the experts to answer questions about how exactly to shape voting rights laws to combat these new forms of racial and ethnic stratification. But I am convinced that the problems revealed since roughly 2000 represent broader and deeper challenges to liberal equality than do those persisting from the civil rights era (again, with pockets of exceptions). I urge analysts and activists alike to focus more on developing policies to fight new forms of political inequality than on retaining policies to protect against the old ones.

RACIAL ATTITUDES: THE ANSWERS YOU GET DEPEND ON THE QUESTIONS YOU ASK

One of the most important changes in racial and ethnic stratification in the United States over the past few decades has been the rise in immigration. Demograhic projections show that the United States is on a course to become a majority non-Anglo country by the middle of the twenty-first century (if Hispanics are classified as non-white). I believe this to be historically unprecedented; never before has the majority group in a democratic polity permitted its elected officials to enact laws that will predictably make that group a minority. The United States could, of course, enact a new version of the 1924 Immigration Act in an effort to curtail immigration of the "wrong" kinds of people, but with each passing year since the 1965 Hart-Celler Act, the possibility of this occurring seems less likely.

As many readers also likely realize, the process of immigrant incorporation is difficult, often incomplete, and sometimes nonexistent. As I write, the state of Arizona proposes to implement a draconian law to identify and arrest illegal immigrants (it is appealing a court injunction against implementing most features of the law), and several other states may follow suit. More generally, relations between native-born and foreign-born residents, as well as among nationalities and pan-ethnic or racial groups, can be tense and full of conflict. In this political context, Vincent Hutchings and his colleagues' National Ethnic Politics Survey (NEPS) offers very welcome evidence of the attitudes of Americans with varying racial and immigration statuses.

The NEPS has many virtues, starting with the fact that it is "the first multiracial and multiethnic national study of political and racial attitudes." It includes large samples from five distinct groups (Caucasians, Hispanics, African Americans, Asian Americans, and Afro-Caribbeans). A slight majority of the Afro-Caribbeans and Hispanics, as well as three-quarters of the Asian-American respondents, were immigrants, as were roughly 5 percent of the black and European respondents. The list of questions is extensive and, unlike many surveys, includes an array of political items designed to test important theories within political science.

The chapter by Hutchings and his colleagues reinforces Karlan's view that twentieth-century-style discrimination is alive and well. More than 90 percent of black respondents believe that their group faces at least some discrimination, as do more than 80 percent of Hispanics and Afro-Caribbeans, 70 percent of Asian Americans, and even 40 percent of whites. The question is clearly very broad, but if we consider the responses in relation to one another rather than in absolute terms, all non-European groups report a great deal more discrimination than do non-Hispanic whites. Additional reports on this survey show that approximately one-quarter of (each) blacks and Latinos, compared with about 15 percent of each the other three groups, agree that whites want to keep blacks and Latinos, as a group, down. A majority of the members in every non-European group report that they have faced at least a little discrimination at some time in their life. And as the chapter shows, non-European groups are all more likely to see whites as zero-sum competitors for jobs or political influence than to see each other in the same light, although intergroup competition among non-Europeans is also robust.

Like a law or regulation, perceptions of mistreatment or competition can be overinclusive, underinclusive, both, or neither. But these 2004 results are drearily similar to results from many other surveys conducted in the previous several decades, and also to those of studies using matched testers or aggregate data analysis. The NEPS shows that it would be foolish – and no contributor to this volume is anywhere near that foolish – to argue that racial and ethnic stratification has disappeared in the United States or is on a certain path to extinction.

Nevertheless, the Hutchings et al. analysis would be stronger if the authors addressed the possibility that the degree or kind of racial and ethnic stratification is changing in the United States. I see several directions for development. First, the questions invite reports of illegitimate treatment or hostile relations, but there are no countervailing questions inviting reports of cooperative treatment or productive relations. Respondents can report the absence of discrimination or hostility, but they have no opportunity to express the presence of desirable interactions. Similarly, respondents are asked if "more good jobs (or influence in politics) for [another group] means fewer good jobs for people like me," but not whether "more good jobs (political influence) for another group improves the chances that my group will attain good jobs (political influence)." Respondents can disagree with the idea of zero-sum competition, and generally a majority of them do (mean scores are below 0.5 in Table 3.1). Still, they have no place to report positive-sum perceptions.

Questions focused on successful racial or ethnic relations might, of course, reveal even deeper perceptions of maltreatment, and in any case, because these questions were seldom asked in earlier surveys, one would find it hard to track change over time in positive interactions. Nevertheless, it would be useful to know if people who perceive a great deal of discrimination also see group dynamics as more complex, multifaceted, or even attractive than these items allow them to express (for an example of a study that shows both sets of views, see Baker et al. 2009).

A similar observation has to do with the classic item on "linked fate." The NEPS shows that one-half to two-thirds of all five groups agree that "what happens generally to [respondent's race] people in this country will have something to do with what happens in your life" (Hutchings et al. 2005). These results are in accord with those in other surveys conducted in the past few decades, although the NEPS helpfully extends the question to all five groups – a rare innovation, since most previous surveys asked linked-fate questions only of blacks, or at most of blacks and Latinos. Previous research shows that perceptions of linked fate are associated with a variety of political views and behaviors, so this item reveals a lot about the persistent nature of racial and ethnic stratification. However, the question is asked immediately after the series on zero-sum competition among groups and other questions on racial identity, so there is the risk of a priming effect, the real extent of which we do not know.[1] In addition, the Pew Research Center recently asked roughly the opposite question, with intriguing results. In 2007, 37 percent of black respondents agreed that "blacks today can no longer be thought of as a single race because the black community is so diverse" (no other group was asked this question). Young black adults were more likely than older ones to agree (Pew Research Center for the People and the Press 2007). A year later, young adults were also more likely than older ones to agree that "there is no general black experience in America" (results provided to author by Fredrick Harris, from ABC News et al. 2008). In 2009, approximately one-third of blacks said that middle-class and poor blacks have only a little or almost nothing in common; only 22 percent saw "a lot" in common (Pew Research Center and National Public Radio 2010).

Is the sense of linked fate dissipating, or perhaps was it never as strong as various surveys implied? If so, what does this suggest about contestation against racial and ethnic stratification? Maybe these new items show that many blacks (and perhaps members of other non-European groups) finally have a sufficiently secure status that they can afford to publicly reveal, and perceive in others, personae unconnected with traditional racial politics – political conservative, Japan scholar, venture capitalist, rower, among others. Or maybe these new items mean that the sense of racial solidarity so essential to protect against persistent racism (Shelby 2005) is being lost in the vain pursuit of acceptance by Wall Street brokerages or elite country clubs. There is a third possibility: Perhaps affluent blacks benefit from the lowering of traditional racial barriers, but poor blacks are harmed by the loss of the traditional middle-class African American commitment to lift as we climb (Ford 2009). Whatever the answer – and the right answer will turn out to be as much a matter of political activity yet to come as of interpreting trend lines – public opinion surveys and other types of research need to be open to the possibility that the ways in which we have understood racial and ethnic stratification are increasingly outmoded. We need to analyze the dissolution or transformation of racial ties as much as we need to track linked fate.

Another query for the (perhaps next) NEPS survey originates from the distinctive nature of the 2004 sample. As I noted earlier, a majority of NEPS respondents were immigrants. But the survey was translated only into Spanish, presumably for reasons of expense and logistical difficulty. This means that Latino immigrants who were not comfortable with English could readily participate, but immigrants from other parts of the world who were not comfortable with English could not. Thus the Asian sample may differ substantially from the Latino sample in its members' degree of assimilation to the United States.

More generally, it would be very useful to have more items that emerge from an immigrant's perspective rather than that of a native-born racial minority. For example: What do you find most startling about American racial and ethnic relations? Most problematic? Most gratifying? What benefits do your children receive from living in the United States? What harms do they encounter? What would draw you into political activism? Perhaps nativism differs from discrimination in important ways that new survey items could reveal. Of course, one would need to construct such questions carefully so that they also make sense to native-born residents – but the central point is that since one-quarter of the American population are now immigrants or the children of immigrants, the kinds of issues that we should be studying to understand racial and ethnic stratification may be changing.

Hutchings and his colleagues' chapter inspires a final question, focused more on the results of their analysis than on the survey itself. One of the criteria for a good social science theory, in my view, is that it can explain movement in several directions. Why does political support for, say, intervention in Iraq rise and then fall? Or why do politicians support the president of the opposite party on some occasions but not on others? Racial contact theory has this quality; it can explain high levels of racial antagonism (too little contact, or the wrong kind of contact, among people of different races), low levels of racial antagonism (reasonably favorable contact), and racial amity (a great deal of the right kind of contact among people of different races).

I find it harder, however, to see how group position theory, or several of the others that the NEPS tests, can explain movement in different directions. As Larry Bobo explains its underpinnings, group position theory was developed to explain how "feelings of competition and hostility" emerge from "judgments about positions in the social order" (Bobo 1988). It is of course easy to see why Herbert Blumer in 1958 saw no reason to explore the absence of intergroup hostility and competition, never mind the presence of intergroup sympathy and cooperation. The theory, however, would be richer, and arguably more relevant to what Hutchings et al. characterize as "the nation's increasingly complicated racial atmosphere," if it were extended or modified to show how different beliefs about group position can lead to different racial dynamics. Can group position theory explain feelings of cooperation and amity? Can it explain instrumental political coalitions? Alternatively, if a group's members increasingly diverge in their judgments about their own and other groups' positions in the social order, does group position theory lose its utility?

The degree to which it seems worthwhile to develop more multifaceted theories about race depends on one's view about whether traditional forms of racial and ethnic stratification are changing in important ways. In my view, they are, and I would urge researchers to develop new forms of evidence to test this possibility. Change is not synonymous with improvement, so progressives who rightly remain worried about group-based inequality need not resist the idea that American politics are changing – but the possibility of change does call for innovation in data collection as much as in policy design.

DO AMERICAN MINORITY GROUPS STILL HAVE "AN" INTEREST?

Opinions and perceptions, such as those that Hutchings et al. analyze, work through electoral structures, such as those that Pildes and Karlan evaluate, to produce political and policy outcomes. Determining whether racial and ethnic stratification are changing involves deciding whether minority groups in a majoritarian democracy are getting more or less of what they want and need compared with some point in the past. That decision, in turn, requires measuring a group's interests, which turns out to be increasingly difficult to do.

In some polities at some times – the United States before 1964, South Africa before 1994, Israel at present – it is easy to identify minority interests. At a minimum, they include first-class citizenship, the rights and opportunities to participate in liberal democratic governance, and interpersonal decency and respect. Attaining all of that almost certainly requires governmental intervention in the society and economy. Even after a polity relinquishes legal segregation – the United States after 1964, South Africa after 1994 – a minority group may be so disproportionately poor that its interests remain easy to identify. They include jobs, decent schooling, health care, decent housing, physical safety. The satisfaction of such interests probably also requires extensive policy intervention in the society and economy, although the best policies are probably a little more contestable than in the first stage. But when legal segregation is in the distant past and when a substantial proportion of the group has moved into the middle or even higher end of the income spectrum, it is harder to determine the group's interest.

Arguably, this is where minority groups in the United States are now; whether other countries such as Cuba, Brazil, and the United Kingdom are similarly positioned remains a subject of intense debate. What are group interests beyond the same rights and security as all other residents of the state if one-third or one-half or more of minority group members are in the middle or upper middle class? What are group interests if minority group members marry people outside their group in high and increasing numbers, or if they occupy a proportionate share of the slots in high-status universities, or if a member of the group holds the most powerful and visible elected position in the world? If, as in the United States, a black man is the most important political figure *and* black men are especially likely to be poor, uneducated, jobless, and incarcerated, *and* if blacks are disproportionately victimized by crime committed by other nonwhites, is there any longer a "black interest"? One could ask a parallel question about immigrants, especially since newcomers to the United States tend to have either much less education and remunerative job skills, or much more education and remunerative job skills, than do native-born Americans. As Hutchings et al. show, even if people are upwardly mobile, they may identify their interests with that of their group; and as Karlan shows, even groups that have attained some power may still share an interest in protection against previously dominant groups. Nevertheless, it is harder than it used to be to assume that progressives' social welfare policy preferences are identical to minority groups' interests. One can still endorse those preferences, as I do, but in some places the argument increasingly needs to be made on behalf of a decent society as a whole or on behalf of poor residents of the polity, rather than on behalf of a uniquely disadvantaged group. We must be especially careful not to automatically equate conservatives' social welfare policy preferences with endorsement of minority group subordination; as group dynamics get more complicated, the best policy becomes less self-evident.

This is real progress, and progressives should celebrate it. My final and strongest plea is that we welcome what has changed for the better while simultaneously grappling with what has changed for the worse – in policy design, scholarly theories, data collection, and political action. This peroration comes perilously close to being a cliché, but some clichés are right.

NOTE

1 In most other surveys, the linked-fate question similarly comes after a series of questions about group identity and conflict, so the concern about priming effects is more general.

REFERENCES

ABC News, *USA Today*, Columbia University. 2008. Black Politics Survey. New York: Columbia University, Center for African-American Politics and Society.

Ansolabehere, Stephen, Nathaniel Persily, and Charles Stewart. 2010. "Race, Region, and Vote Choice in the 2008 Election: Implications for the Future of the Voting Rights Act." *Harvard Law Review*. 123 (6): 1386–436.

Baker, Wayne, Sally Howell, Amaney Jamal, Ann Chih Lin, Andrew Shyrock, Ron Stockton, and Mark Tessler. 2009. *Citizenship and Crisis: Arab Detroit after 9/11*. New York: Russell Sage Foundation.

Bobo, Lawrence. 1988. "Group Conflict, Prejudice, and the Paradox of Contemporary Racial Attitudes." *Eliminating Racism: Profiles in Controversy*. Edited by Phyllis. Katz and Dalmas Taylor. New York: Plenum Press: 85–114.

Bureau of Justice Statistics. 2008. *Sourcebook of Criminal Justice Statistics*. Washington DC: U.S. Department of Justice.

Clayton, Dewey. 2010. *The Presidential Campaign of Barack Obama: A Critical Analysis of a Racially Transcendent Strategy*. New York: Routledge.

Clear, Todd. 2007. *Imprisoning Communities*. New York: Oxford University Press.

Ford, Richard. 2009. "Barack Is the New Black: Obama and the Promise/Threat of the Post–Civil Rights Era." *Du Bois Review*. 6 (1): 37–48.

Hutchings, Vincent, Cara Wong, Ronald Brown, James Jackson, and Nakesha Faison 2005. "The National Ethnic Politics Study (NEPS): Ethnic Pluralism & Politics in the 21st Century." American Association of Public Opinion Research, Miami Beach, FL, May 12.

Pew Research Center, and National Public Radio. 2010. A Year After Obama's Election: Blacks Upbeat about Black Progress, *Pew Research Center*. (http://pewsocialtrends. org/assets/pdf/blacks-upbeat-about-black-progress-prospects.pdf).

Pew Research Center for the People and the Press. 2007. Racial Attitudes in America. Pew Research Center. (http://pewsocialtrends.org/assets/pdf/race.pdf)

Shelby, Tommie. 2005. *We Who Are Dark: The Philosophical Foundations of Black Solidarity*. Cambridge, MA: Harvard University Press.

U.S. Department of Justice. 2003. *Prevalence of Imprisonment in the U.S. Population, 1974–2001*. Washington, DC: Department of Justice, Bureau of Justice Statistics. (http://www. prisonpolicy.org/scans/bjs/piuspo1.pdf)

Western, Bruce. 2006. *Punishment and Inequality in America*. New York: Russell Sage Foundation.

1

Voting Rights

The Next Generation

Richard H. Pildes[1]

Today's Voting Rights Act (VRA) (1965), particularly its historically important Section 5, exists in a form and structure little different from the original Act of nearly forty-five years ago. The VRA of 1965 was a justifiably aggressive federal response to the race-based disenfranchisement of African Americans in readily identifiable geographic areas. Although it represented an unprecedented assertion of federal power over states and localities, the Act was in fact carefully and appropriately tailored to the historical context in which it originated. By focusing primarily on race-based denials of voting rights and by targeting its most stringent provisions to those areas with a history of race-based disenfranchisement, the VRA effectively tackled the predominant voting-rights issue of the prior century of American experience: the persistent efforts of mostly Southern jurisdictions to deny minority citizens the right to vote.

As a response to the specific historical conditions that existed in 1965, the VRA was perhaps the most effective civil rights statute enacted in the United States.[2] It represented the last significant step toward universal inclusion of adult citizens in American democracy, and it effectively prevented recalcitrant state and local governments from crafting new laws designed to suppress minority voting. As a policy-making attempt to address contemporary voting-rights problems, however, the VRA – particularly Section 5 – might no longer offer the most effective means of securing access to the ballot box. The issues emerging today – voting technology problems, felon disenfranchisement laws that apply even to those who have completed their sentences, burdensome and unnecessary voter registration requirements – are not confined to jurisdictions with a long history of racially discriminatory voting practices, nor do they necessarily arise from the efforts of state and local governments to target minority voting per se. For this reason, the very statutory structure that rendered the VRA so effective in the initial decades of its existence – its narrow geographic targeting and its focus on *changes* in voting rules and practices – now constrains its ability to protect the right to vote.

As we look to the future of voting rights, one of the choices Congress and voting-reform advocates will face is how to conceive the general form that new voting-rights protections ought to take. In particular, Congress will have to decide if it wishes to continue to adhere to the historically contingent antidiscrimination model of Section 5 of the VRA or is ready to embrace new legislative models that, I want to suggest, better fit the voting rights problems of today.

So far, Congress has proven reluctant to look beyond the existing structure of the VRA, in particular Section 5 of the Act – the "preclearance" provision that requires certain jurisdictions, mostly in the South, to submit proposed changes in voting rules and practices for federal preclearance approval before those changes can be implemented. Given the symbolic significance of the VRA and the fact that racially discriminatory voting practices have not disappeared completely, any proposal to move away from the Section 5 model understandably produces anxiety. Indeed, the last time Congress revisited Section 5, in 2006, Congress reauthorized it without fully addressing whether Section 5 needed to be updated in any profound way to reflect the changes in voting behavior that had taken place since 1965, or even since 1982, when Congress had last addressed Section 5 (Fannie Lou Hamer, Rosa Parks, and Coretta Scott King Voting Rights Act Reauthorization and Amendments Act 2006).

Since 2006, however, the Supreme Court has weighed into the debate in ways that may force Congress' hand. First, the Court's 2009 decision in *Northwest Austin Municipal Utility District Number One v. Holder* (2009) (NAMUDNO) has been widely interpreted as a strong warning to Congress that if Section 5 is not revised to address the Court's concerns, it could be held unconstitutional in a future decision. Even if the Court upholds the constitutionality of Section 5 or avoids confronting that issue, the Court in *NAMUNDO* expressed the kind of skepticism about the justification for Section 5 that might well lead to narrow judicial interpretations of Section 5 going forward. These constitutional issues are prompted by unresolved debates about how different the jurisdictions covered by Section 5's preclearance provisions are from those areas not covered; the Court has raised questions about whether the current pattern of coverage can be justified under the relevant constitutional standard.

Second, the Court's decision a week after *NAMUNDO* in *Ricci v. DeStefano* (2009), which appears to impose a higher standard for demonstrating racial discrimination based on disparate impact than previously required – a decision directed specifically at discrimination claims filed under Title VII of the Civil Rights Act of 1964 – may nonetheless have a significant impact on the VRA. Like Title VII, the VRA protects against voting practices that disparately impact the voting rights of racial minorities. If the disparate impact analysis of *Ricci* takes hold or is expanded, it could thus make it more difficult to establish race-based violations under the VRA, further undermining the Act's practical effect and potentially leading to additional constitutional concerns, particularly if in a later ruling, the Court goes so far as to find disparate-impact doctrines to conflict with the Equal Protection Clause (a question to which *Ricci* begins to open the door).

As Congress reacts to these recent Supreme Court decisions – or, perhaps more likely, to future Supreme Court decisions that might more directly force Congress to address voting issues – it has two legislative models to work from. First, it could tinker at the margins of Section 5, narrowing the Section's geographic scope to target only those jurisdictions with sufficiently egregious race-based voting rights problems to justify continued preclearance oversight. This approach would preserve the basic civil rights model of the VRA and address the constitutional concerns expressed in *NAMUDNO*, but it would further limit the Act's practical effect and do little to address emerging voting rights problems.

Alternatively, Congress could draw on two more recent voting-rights statutes enacted to address contemporary voting-rights concerns: the Help American Vote Act (HAVA) (2002) and the National Voter Registration Act (NVRA) (1993). Both HAVA and NVRA are generally applicable national laws that protect the right to vote *as such* of all citizens nationwide. Because the HAVA model relies on the fundamental constitutional right to vote – a right that was not fully recognized by the Supreme Court at the time the VRA was enacted – rather than on the equal protection concerns of the Fourteenth and Fifteenth Amendments, legislation of this type need not be limited to race-based voting-rights problems, nor tied to jurisdictions with entrenched racially discriminatory voting practices. This model also avoids the constitutional concerns raised by *NAMUDNO* and *Ricci*, even as it *expands* Congress's ability to protect the right to vote.

In this chapter, I will first explain why the VRA model, so effective in the early decades of its existence, may no longer offer an appropriate paradigm for protecting voting rights going forward. Then I will suggest that Congress would be wise, in the wake of the Supreme Court's recent decisions, to think expansively, beyond the existing structure of the VRA, if it wishes to play a proactive role in protecting voting rights moving forward.

If Congress is willing to step up and address the hard questions that the Supreme Court debate over the constitutionality of the VRA now prompts, Congress could ultimately do more to enhance the future of voting rights than by working at the margins of Section 5. In theory, of course, Congress could do both: It could update Section 5, as well as other parts of the VRA, while also enacting additional laws that would provide further protection for the right to vote on a universal, nationwide basis. But as a practical matter, legislative agendas confront various constraints, including ones of focus, energy, resources, and time; realistically, these constraints might mean that Congress will focus on only one type of approach in any future legislative efforts. Furthermore, there are constraints on frameworks of thought as well: An intellectual bias in favor of the status quo might lead Congress and advocates not to think outside the framework of existing approaches enough to pursue the changes that would actually be most meaningful and effective. Thus, my aim is to press the case for thinking about future voting-rights legislation through a model best attuned, I believe, to the voting problems that are central today and most likely to remain so in the immediate years ahead.

THE STRUCTURE OF THE VRA

The VRA (1965) protects the right to vote primarily through two central provisions. The first, Section 2 of the Act, is a nationwide prohibition on voting practices that result in race-based denials of the right to vote. To the extent that Section 2 prohibits voting practices that have a disparate impact on minority voting rights, whether or not those practices are motivated by a discriminatory purpose, the Supreme Court's decision in *Ricci* could lead to a narrower construction of the statute. Such a construction would diminish the practical effect of Section 2. And if the Court follows through on *Ricci*'s suggestion that broad disparate-impact laws conflict with Equal Protection Clause, Section 2 could potentially come under even greater scrutiny.

The second provision, Section 5 of the Act, is the provision most likely to be revisited by Congress in the near future. Section 5 is a more aggressive provision that singles out certain – mostly Southern – jurisdictions and requires them to seek "preclearance" by the federal government before implementing any change to their voting laws or practices.[3] In comparison to Section 2, the preclearance requirements of Section 5 provide for an exceptionally proactive form of federal oversight of state and local voting practices. These provisions essentially place the election systems of covered jurisdictions under a form of federal receivership, putting the burden on state and local governments to prove that a proposed change in voting procedures would not violate the VRA before any such changes – including even slight modifications – may be implemented (Issacharoff et al. 2001). Despite the degree of federal intervention it authorizes, however, Section 5 is in some ways narrower than Section 2. Unlike Section 2, which applies broadly to all voting laws and practices nationwide, Section 5 is more limited in scope and targeted to address a very specific set of regional and cultural conditions.

The scope of Section 5 is limited, or "targeted," in three principal ways. First, Section 5, like much of the VRA, prohibits only denials of voting rights that are racially based. This limitation reflects not only Congress's pressing concern with race-based denials of the right to vote, but also its limited power – at the time the VRA was enacted – to legislate more broadly to protect the right to vote. Until the Supreme Court recognized the right to vote as a fundamental right protected by the Constitution, Congress was limited to regulating only race-based abridgements of voting rights under the Fourteenth and Fifteenth Amendments.[4] The VRA – Section 5 included – thus does not protect the right to vote as such, but instead protects more specifically against racially discriminatory denials or abridgements of the vote.

Second, Section 5 of the VRA narrowly targets particular geographic areas for uniquely aggressive federal oversight. In doing so, it effectively defines in advance which parts of the country have entrenched voting problems that justify the restrictive "preclearance" requirements of Section 5 for the entire authorization period (in the case of the 2006 reauthorization, the next twenty-five years).[5] This second form of targeting is also historically contingent: In 1965 and the decades following, Congress could easily predict that the worst racially discriminatory voting practices were likely to occur in those jurisdictions – mostly in the South – that possessed a long history of denying minority voters access to the ballot box. At that time, patterns of race-based disenfranchisement were clear and ingrained, and geographic targeting enabled the federal government to focus the full extent of its constitutional powers in areas where hostility to the rights of minority voters was most pervasive and deep-seated.[6]

Third, Section 5 is further limited in that it targets only *changes* in existing voting rules and practices for proactive federal supervision. Section 5 requires preclearance approval only of changes to existing practices and does not constrain the operation of baseline, status quo practices (although existing practices would, of course, be subject to the blanket prohibitions of Section 2). Again, this limitation reflects the distinct historical moment at which Section 5 was adopted originally: Prior to 1965, Southern jurisdictions managed to evade federal oversight by crafting new laws and devices to prevent black voters from registering or participating in elections.[7] As soon as one tactic was declared illegal, the state, county, or municipality would simply devise another means of keeping minority voters from the polls. The only way for the federal government to end this kind of manipulation was to get out ahead of these jurisdictions and prevent them from making changes that would impair minority voting rights. By requiring preapproval of any proposed changes to the election system, no matter how trivial, Section 5 effectively ended this game of cat-and-mouse and eventually brought most jurisdictions into compliance with the Constitution.

Thus, the structure of the VRA in general, and Section 5 in particular, reflects a targeted, antidiscrimination approach to voting-rights protection that was crafted to address the specific conditions confronting Congress in 1965. Section 5 set up an aggressive federal oversight structure but one limited in scope to addressing, in a targeted way, the race-based tactics of identifiable state and local governments. Perhaps recognizing that such a targeted provision would need to be updated to remain responsive to ever-changing circumstances, the Congress that enacted Section 5 intended it to be limited in time as well as in scope. Originally enacted for a period of five years, Section 5 was extended, with amendments, for an additional five years in 1970 and then for seven years in 1975. In 1982, however, Congress reauthorized Section 5 for an additional twenty-five years, and it did so again in 2006, extending the provision until 2031 – without making any significant changes to the jurisdictions covered or the nature of the federal oversight provided. The question now is whether the selective-targeting approach of Section 5, crafted to respond to the problems of a specific historical era, remains the most effective means of securing the right to vote today.

THE INHERENT LIMITATIONS OF THE SECTION 5 MODEL

It should be clear from the preceding discussion that Section 5 rests on at least two critical assumptions: first, that Congress can identify, as much as 25 years in advance, areas of the country where systematic racially discriminatory voting practices are unusually likely to arise and, therefore, where pro-active federal intervention is necessary; and second, that these discriminatory practices are likely to result from *changes* to existing voting rules and practices. At the time of the VRA's enactment, these assumptions were reasonable. Under the historical conditions of 1965 and for some years after, the narrow targeting features of Section 5 were both easy to apply and exceedingly effective.

Today, however, we face a set of circumstances and voting problems less predictable and not necessarily confined to areas with a longstanding history of racially discriminatory voting practices. The changes in voting practices over the last decades – brought about in part by the VRA itself – have rendered the structure and logic of Section 5 less well suited to addressing the nature and scope of voting rights problems today. The preclearance provision is now inherently limited, or is likely to be limited by future Court decisions, in at least three ways.

First, although race-based denials of voting rights certainly persist, the voting rights issues we face today are no longer defined by the near-complete exclusion of black voters by a number of readily identifiable state and local governments.[8] Instead, some of the most significant voting-rights problems we see today arise in so-called battleground states or in otherwise close elections, where political parties have an incentive to manipulate voting practices in their favor. Those settings can change dramatically from election to election. Consider, for instance, the 2004 elections. In the presidential race, the most widespread reports of voter problems occurred in Ohio – a state not covered by Section 5's preclearance provisions, but a pivotal battleground state in the election (Tokaji 2005). Similarly, at the state and local levels, the 2004 elections produced intensive voting-rights litigation in Washington State, Puerto Rico, and San Diego,[9] none of which are subject to the preclearance provisions of the VRA. This pattern was also in evidence, of course, in the most significant voting controversy in recent years – the disputes over the highly contested 2000 presidential election results in Florida. Although Florida is partially covered by Section 5, the counties that sparked the greatest voting-rights conflicts during the 2000 election were not among the state's five "covered" jurisdictions and thus not subject to the Act's heightened preclearance scrutiny.[10]

The fact that Section 5 was of no relevance in any of these major voting-rights controversies should give us pause. But it should also appear perfectly logical. Premised

as it is on predictable and geographically confined patterns of race-based disenfranchisement, the Section 5 model simply is not equipped to address voting-rights
problems that cluster around something as fluid and unpredictable as where elections today turn out to be most competitive and where the stakes are therefore the
highest. The location of competitive races with small margins of victory changes
election to election, and there is little way to base national legislation on ex ante
predictions of where federal, state, and local elections are likely to be close over any
significant period of time. When the geographic targeting of Section 5 was crafted,
Congress confronted distinct areas that systemically denied minority voting rights,
whether or not elections were competitive. As these areas have diminished, and
competitiveness has become a better predictor of large-scale voting-rights violations,
the Section 5 model has become both under- and overinclusive.

Second, we now confront voting-rights problems of a fundamentally different
nature than those envisioned by Section 5. For the most part, the problems emerging
today cannot be tied to the systematic discriminatory actions of state and local governments in predictable, geographically limited areas. Consider the problems that
have garnered the most attention in recent years: concerns about voting technology;
lack of clear standards for identifying a valid vote; ballot design confusions; long
lines at polling places; partisan administration of voting laws; incompetent administration at the precinct level; and burdensome voter registration and identification
requirements (Tokaji 2006). These problems are not confined to any particular jurisdictions, and in some cases do not represent predictable or systematic problems at
all. As with closely contested elections, Section 5 is a poor fit for these emerging
problems, for they cannot be accurately identified in advance and they are less likely
to be unique to particular areas that can be targeted for more intensive oversight
than at the time the model of Section 5 was designed.

Importantly, some of these new problems have in fact been dealt with through
Section 5's preclearance requirements, but in a way that presents further complications for the viability of this model. For instance, in May, the Department of Justice
refused to preclear a Georgia law requiring verification of voter citizenship prior to
elections, based on the disproportionate impact the law would likely have on black
and Hispanic citizens (Letter from King 2009). But voter registration, verification,
and identification laws are cropping up all over the country, and they should be
dealt with in a uniform way, whether or not they arise in jurisdictions currently
covered by Section 5. Ultimately, it is far more difficult today to tailor a geographically targeted provision to areas that can be predicted in advance to be unique in
the voting problems they generate. Although there might be a readily identifiable
partisan dimension to the debates over these laws, they cannot be said to have
a similarly identifiable *geographic* dimension, particularly not one that correlates
with other voting-rights issues in a way that identifies specific jurisdictions that are
systematically infringing upon voting rights, and justifies the selective oversight of
Section 5.

Finally, it is not clear that targeting *changes* in voting rules and practices is the best way to protect the right to vote today. In contrast to conditions in 1965, when Congress confronted states and localities intentionally crafting new rules and devices to evade federal oversight, some of the most significant barriers to voting today are actually *existing* laws and *outdated* practices. Felon disenfranchisement laws, for instance, are responsible for the disenfranchisement of a significant proportion of African-American males in this country (Issacharoff et al. 2001). Most of these laws are not recent enactments, nor do they reflect changes in rules or practices associated with voting itself. Rather, the laws are problematic precisely because they were enacted many years ago, when felony conviction rates were lower and the laws had a less significant effect on the voting rights of the population as a whole. Because these laws involve no changes to voting rules or practices, they simply do not fall within the purview of Section 5. Nor could they be brought within the scope of Section 5 without thoroughly disrupting the preclearance model. The entire notion of preclearance is premised upon the existence of some change or new enactment to be preapproved.

Section 5 is similarly unhelpful when it comes to problems with existing voting technology and existing election administration that is incompetent or structurally designed to be controlled by partisan actors. In these cases, the problem is not a *change* in voting procedures, but rather the failure to act to modernize voting administration. Problems with faulty ballots and poor election administration arise primarily from preservation of the status quo, whether that involves a failure to update voting technology, to create nonpartisan administration structures, or to train election officials properly.

Thus, for at least these three reasons, the targeted provisions of Section 5, which conformed well to the historical conditions following the VRA's enactment, are less well adapted to the voting-rights problems we face today. Indeed, one of the practical limitations of Section 5 is suggested by the greater difficulties Congress and academic experts face, as compared to earlier eras, in identifying particular jurisdictions that are systematically more likely than others to adopt racially discriminatory voting rules and practices.[11]

This is not to say that there are no longer any unique, identifiable jurisdictions with entrenched patterns of racially discriminatory voting practices. On the state level, Mississippi continues to generate more minority voting-rights problems than any other state (Lawyers' Commission for Civil Rights 2006). And Native Americans today face obstacles to voting similar to those faced by African Americans at the time of the VRA's enactment (McCool 2006). If Congress focused a renewed Section 5 more narrowly on smaller jurisdictional units, such as counties rather than states, it might be better able to identify in advance those jurisdictions with the deeply ingrained, race-based voting-rights problems that justify Section 5 coverage.[12] Yet such a solution fails to get to the root of the problem. Rather than expanding protection to address the widespread voting-rights issues emerging today, it would simply retain the already limited status quo in a narrower form capable of protecting fewer and fewer voters. Any legislation that aims to seriously grapple with the limitations of Section 5 will have to go further and look to other legislative models more targeted to twenty-first-century problems.

ADDITIONAL PRESSURE FROM THE SUPREME COURT

As the congressional reauthorization of Section 5 in 2006 demonstrates, Congress did not reexamine the basic conceptual or policy structure of this provision when it reauthorized the Act. Absent significant external pressure, Congress is unlikely to do so. Although all the inherent limitations of Section 5 discussed above existed in 2006, one significant thing has since changed: The Supreme Court has entered the debate with two decisions that put further pressure on the model of voting rights protection reflected in Section 5 and, to some extent, in Section 2 of the Act as well.

The first of these decisions, *Northwest Austin Municipal Utility District Number One v. Holder* (NAMUDNO 2009), directly addresses the VRA. Prior to 2006, many academics had suggested that Section 5 would face serious constitutional scrutiny from the Supreme Court if Congress did not revisit the coverage formula and other elements of the Act when reauthorizing it in 2006. As it becomes harder to marshal evidence demonstrating that, absent federal oversight and control, covered jurisdictions are more likely than noncovered areas to engage in widespread discriminatory voting practices, it becomes harder to persuade a skeptical Court that a geographic pattern of federal oversight established at least forty years ago continues to be constitutionally defensible today. In fact, before the 2006 reauthorization, some scholars, including myself, urged Congress to take a more serious look at Section 5, in part to forestall its invalidation on constitutional grounds (Pildes 2006).

In its first confrontation with these issues, the Court in *NAMUDNO* avoided resolving the constitutional issues, but in a way that left doubt lingering over how the Court would ultimately rule. The Court avoided the constitutional question by finding a way, through statutory interpretation, to give the particular jurisdiction all the relief it claimed to want (*NAMUNDO* 2009). In doing so, however, Chief Justice Roberts, writing for the Court, spoke directly of the "federalism costs" imposed by Section 5 and suggested that because the "evil that § 5 is meant to address may no longer be concentrated in the jurisdictions singled out for preclearance," serious questions existed concerning whether Congress had exceeded its constitutional authority by reauthorizing the provision in 2006 (*NAMUNDO* 2009). Rather than concurring separately to express support for Section 5's continued constitutionality, all the Justices joined the 8–1 opinion (with only Justice Thomas in dissent). Given this, the *NAMUDNO* opinion may be seen as a warning to Congress: Either modernize Section 5 or risk seeing it struck down in a future decision.

The second decision, *Ricci v. DeStefano*, involved a different civil rights statute, Title VII of the Civil Rights Act. Title VII, which deals with discrimination in the employment context, imposes liability for employment decisions that involve disparate *treatment* or disparate *impact* based on race and other protected classifications. In *Ricci*, the City of New Haven argued that it could legitimately reject the results of a promotional exam it had given to city firefighters because failing to reject those results would have left the city vulnerable to challenge under Title VII. The exam results would have disproportionately excluded black candidates from promotion; had the city certified the exam results, it argued, it therefore would have been subject to potential disparate-impact liability (*Ricci* 2009). To determine whether the city was justified in rejecting the exam, the Court had to determine whether the city had a "strong basis in evidence" to believe that it would be subjected to disparate impact liability had it certified the test results (*Ricci* 2009).

Although *Ricci* addressed a different statute than the VRA, the Court's treatment of disparate-impact issues under Title VII must be taken seriously by those concerned about the future of voting rights. The concept of disparate impact plays a key role in Section 2 and Section 5, both of which prohibit actions that have a disparate impact upon the voting rights of minority citizens. *Ricci*'s disparate impact analysis is important for the VRA in two respects. First, by narrowly defining what constitutes a legitimate disparate impact case, *Ricci* could make it more difficult to prove a violation of the VRA, thereby further diminishing the Act's practical effect. In applying the "strong basis in evidence" standard, the *Ricci* majority stated that a threshold showing of a statistical disparity alone – even a showing of "significant" statistical disparity – is "far from a strong basis in evidence that the city would have been liable" under the disparate impact provision of Title VII (*Ricci* 2009). Instead, to demonstrate a strong basis in evidence for a disparate impact claim (let alone to win one), the Court indicates that more must be examined, including whether the city might nonetheless have legitimate reasons for implementing the policy, in spite of its impact (*Ricci* 2009). This is now a demanding standard; it generates reason to believe the Court may be similarly more demanding in the VRA context. The Court may well start insisting more demandingly on proof of disparate impact "plus" – a requirement of more than just a racially disparate impact – before it will find a state or local voting law in violation of the VRA. Such a heightened standard would affect both the targeted provisions of Section 5 and the general, nationwide provisions of Section 2. The result would be to further limit the practical effectiveness of the race-based model of voting-rights legislation.

Second, *Ricci* could potentially raise additional constitutional questions for the entire VRA, although this concern is more speculative. *Ricci* identifies a potential collision course between Title VII, which requires employers to take remedial, race-conscious action to avoid employment policies that produce unjustifiable disparate impact, and the Equal Protection Clause, which forbids the government from using race except in a narrowly cabined circumstances. Although the Court did not directly address this issue, Justice Scalia concurred separately to speak to the constitutional question, noting that it was "not an easy one" but would have to be confronted eventually (*Ricci* 2009).

A similar potential collision course underlies the VRA. The VRA requires state and local governments to avoid disparate racial impacts in the voting area, whereas the Constitution's general prohibition on race-based decision making is being construed more and more by the Court to apply to all race-based public actions, whether in the affirmative action context or not. Indeed, Justice Kennedy has already raised this concern in several of his VRA opinions. *Ricci* is only likely to increase this tension in the VRA context.

Justice Scalia's concurrence implies that the issue might be resolved through doctrine that distinguishes among the kinds of disparate impacts that federal laws make illegal. Laws that invoke disparate impact as "an evidentiary tool used to identify genuine, intentional discrimination" would pass constitutional muster (*Ricci* 2009). In contrast, statutes that bar disparate impact standing alone, without any connection to a discriminatory purpose, would be unconstitutional. If this were where the *Ricci* decision is heading, the consequences for the VRA would be twofold: an increased vulnerability to constitutional challenge and ever-narrower constructions of the Act as a whole to avoid constitutional problems.

Taken together, *NAMUDNO* and *Ricci* thus give Congress strong reason to act to update voting-rights policy. Congress, however, might well do nothing unless the Court actually holds Section 5 unconstitutional, either on its face or in a series of important as-applied decisions. The Court's opinion in *NAMUDNO* confirms that Section 5 will be vulnerable to constitutional challenges, and, in fact, if Georgia decides to appeal the DOJ's preclearance decision on its voter verification law, that challenge could come sooner rather than later. Although the effect of *Ricci* could prove more attenuated, given the differences between the VRA and Title VII, it too could raise additional constitutional complications and is likely to further diminish the Act's already limited practical effect by imposing a heightened disparate impact standard. These decisions, and *NAMUDNO* in particular, could force Congress to take a hard look at Section 5 and create an opportunity to craft legislation better tailored to the voting-rights problems we face today.

THE FUTURE OF VOTING RIGHTS

If Congress decides to take charge of this issue – either in response to *NAMUDNO* and *Ricci*, or, more likely, after further Supreme Court decisions force Congress' hand more directly – it should start by recognizing that the history of voting-rights legislation provides us with two possible models: the targeted, antidiscrimination approach of Section 5 of the VRA; and the broader, right-to-vote approach of more recent federal legislation, such as the Help America Vote Act of 2002 and the National Voter Registration Act of 1993. Indeed, the choice between these two models may prove to be the most important decision for the future of voting rights.

Of course, if Congress responds to *NAMUDNO* or another Court decision, it will likely be tempted to try to preserve Section 5 by simply adjusting the formula used to determine the jurisdictions subject to preclearance. As discussed above, the symbolic significance of the VRA and the notion that legislation to protect voting rights must hew to the civil rights, antidiscrimination approach means that any departure from the Section 5 model is difficult, both intellectually and politically. If Congress renews debate over Section 5, we will likely see mobilization in defense of preserving some form of the status quo, just as we did during the 2006 reauthorization debates.

To be sure, Congress might be able to construct a constitutionally viable Section 5 by focusing its coverage on smaller jurisdictional units and narrowly targeting those areas where systematic race-based voting problems or preclearance denials persist. But I have argued that the geographic targeting of Section 5 is part of what limits the practical effectiveness of the Act (or any modestly modified version) today, and this solution would narrow its geographic reach even further. More importantly, this approach would do nothing to address the fundamental limits inherent to the Section 5 model: The fact that the major voting-rights problems are no longer as satisfactorily addressed by the targeted features of Section 5 as they were in the past. If Congress is serious about protecting the right to vote, it is going to have to go beyond that model and confront the hard questions it avoided in 2006.

If Congress and reformers are willing to think outside the box of the VRA and consider alternative models, they need not look far for models that track today's voting-rights problems. In the past twenty years, Congress has quietly worked its way into a new approach to voting-rights legislation, reflected in recent enactments like the NVRA and HAVA. In contrast to the targeted, antidiscrimination model of the VRA, these statutes embody a much broader substantive right-to-vote model that seeks to protect the right to vote *as such* by regulating the way the election process functions for all citizens. HAVA's (2002) provisions, for instance, create uniform, nationwide rights and standards – such as the right to a provisional ballot, statewide registration databases, and financial incentives for improved voting technology – that are not specifically targeted only at race-based discrimination in voting, at changes in laws, or at certain pre-identified jurisdictions.

This model is possible now because of changes in the Supreme Court's view of Congress's powers under the Fourteenth Amendment. If, as we see in *Ricci*, the Court is narrowing the power of government to take certain race-conscious steps to eliminate racially disparate impacts of the policies, the Court at the same time has expanded Congress's power to protect the right to vote as a fundamental constitutional right under the substantive standards of the Fourteenth Amendment. Whether Congress had such power was unclear, at best, in 1965. By now, however,

Supreme Court doctrine has entrenched the right to vote as a fundamental constitutional right, as cases like *Bush v. Gore* (2000; Pildes 2004) confirm. As a result,
Congress has constitutional power to legislate to protect against arbitrary or unfair
voting practices generally, whether or not they involve racial discrimination. This
relatively new authority enabled Congress to enact the uniform, national standards
of HAVA and NVRA, and it could be used more broadly to address many of the
voting-rights issues emerging today.

Accepting the legislative model of universal laws like HAVA would allow Congress
to shift focus from the geographically targeted, selective federal oversight model of
Section 5 and concentrate instead on developing voting-rights legislation of uniform
national scope. It would also allow Congress to move away from Section 5's pro-
phylactic targeting of changes in voting rules and to focus instead on establishing
an appropriate baseline for election practices nationwide. This, in turn, could bring
some much-needed uniformity to our decentralized election system and ensure that
elections are conducted in conformity with basic national standards. HAVA and the
NVRA themselves were both relatively limited in scope – HAVA to voting technology
and provisional ballots, NVRA to registration issues. But the model of voting-rights
legislation they represent nonetheless constitutes a major breakthrough in national
voting-rights policy. Such laws provide a conceptual model for creating the uniform,
national laws necessary to protect voting rights today.

Of course, national standards are not appropriate for every aspect of the electoral
process, and when it comes to state and local elections in particular, the boundary
between which aspects ought to be regulated nationally rather than locally is a
difficult question. But HAVA demonstrates that national policy can impose uniform
standards without dictating precisely how these standards must be met at the state
level. In the realm of voting technology, for instance, HAVA sets national standards
and offers incentives for states to replace certain equipment, but it does not require
states to adopt any particular technology. Uniform, national standards can thus retain
flexibility and allow for state-based experimentation where appropriate. National
goals can be established, without command-and-control impositions of identical
means to reach those goals required in every state.

Moreover, a number of the pressing voting-rights issues of today do seem well
suited to national regulation, if they are going to be regulated at all. For instance, the
forms of identification necessary to protect against voter fraud – currently a subject
of heated debate in state legislatures – might be most effectively resolved through
national legislation. There seems to be little need or justification for state variation
in this area, and consistent national standards would make it easier for voters moving
from state to state to secure access to the ballot. Under the VRA, establishing this kind
of national consistency would not be possible. Under Section 5, of course, the same
voter ID law might be illegal in states covered by the preclearance requirement
while being legal in others. And because voter ID laws tend to impact not only
racial minorities but also the poor and the elderly generally, even the nationwide

prohibitions of Section 2 might treat the same laws differently in different states. An ID requirement in Georgia that disproportionately impacts the state's large African-American population might violate Section 2, whereas the same requirement in a state without a significant minority population might disenfranchise poor and elderly whites without actually violating the prohibitions of the Act. Of course, it is possible that uniformity might eventually be achieved through constitutional litigation. But states have passed, or are in the process of passing, numerous and varied laws regarding voter identification, registration, and verification standards, and it would take years for all of these to work their way through the courts. Instead, Congress could use the HAVA model to legislate uniform, national voter identification requirements and resolve the issue at the federal level rather than awaiting costly case-by-case resolution in the courts.

There are also a number of ways in which the HAVA model would allow Congress to legislate beyond the limits not only of Section 5, but the VRA more generally. Although Section 2 of the Act is not targeted geographically or focused on changes in voting practices, it is limited to protecting against voting-rights violations that are racially discriminatory. As noted earlier, this limitation reflects not only the massive race-based voting problems that the 1965 Congress confronted, but also Congress's belief at that time that it lacked the constitutional authority to protect the right to vote more broadly. In contrast, more recent legislation like HAVA and NVRA draw on Congress's now-recognized power to enforce the fundamental constitutional right to vote, whether or not the abridgments at issue involve the element of racial discrimination. These statutes thus sweep more broadly than the VRA, covering all forms of voting-rights denials without forcing Congress to provide evidence of racially discriminatory impact or purpose.

Although racial discrimination unfortunately remains a concern in American elections, there are a number of reasons why legislation that is not tied to a race-based, antidiscrimination model might actually be better able to protect the right to vote of voters in general and minority voters in particular. First, in the context of modern politics, where large-scale voting rights violations tend to cluster around highly contested elections, it is often difficult to untangle racial considerations from partisan concerns. Voter ID laws, for instance, are highly partisan when voted on in legislative bodies – typically supported by Republicans, eschewed by Democrats – but they do have a racial impact in places with significant minority populations, and some charge that they are in fact racially motivated. The VRA model requires courts to separate the racial motivations from the partisan ones to determine which actually "caused" the voting practice to be adopted. This problem will only be heightened if the Supreme Court, following the line of analysis in *Ricci*, continues to construe disparate impact statutes more narrowly by requiring a showing of something closer to discriminatory intent to prove a violation of the VRA. With disparate impact largely off the table, litigants would have to show that voter ID laws, even those with a statistical disparate impact, were motivated primarily by race rather than politics.

As long as black voters remain predominantly Democratic, however, it will be nearly impossible in many contexts to separate race from politics for these purposes. Particularly if close elections continue to produce most large-scale voting-rights violations, it is likely only to become harder for courts to separate political motivation from racial discrimination. And as the lines between these considerations continue to blur, there is greater risk that courts will find laws and practices to be motivated primarily by politics and therefore not violations of the VRA. A more general law based on the HAVA model could avoid this stew of problems by prohibiting laws that impinge on access to the ballot box without sufficient countervailing justification; such a standard would not require litigants to prove, or courts to judge, whether laws like these "really" reflect or amount to racially discriminatory voting rules. Counterintuitively, perhaps, such general laws might actually afford better protection to minority voters than the antidiscrimination model of the VRA.

Such general laws would also reduce incentives to racialize conflicts over voting policies. Under the VRA, most challenges to a voting law or practice must necessarily be cast in racial terms; otherwise, the VRA is of no relevance. Yet it is far from clear that requiring all voting challenges to be framed as a form of racial discrimination is helpful or desirable, particularly when alternative means of addressing voting-rights violations are available.

As I noted at the outset, the HAVA/NVRA model and the existing VRA model are not logically or inherently exclusive. In addition, there are some issues, like vote dilution, that can only be addressed effectively through legislation that singles out minority voting rights for protective regulation. Language assistance requirements also seem best dealt with through targeted legislation intended to assist only those voters with unique language assistance needs.

These kind of issues aside, though, the more far-reaching question is how Congress and others ought to think about the general form that future voting-rights legislation ought to take. For the reasons described here, my analysis suggests that future national legislation to protect the right to vote will have the greatest practical effect if designed in the model of nationwide laws that apply uniformly throughout the country and universal terms that extend coverage to all voters.

NOTES

1 I would like to thank Laura Trice for her assistance with this chapter.
2 See Pildes 1995 for a summary of studies on the effectiveness of the Act.
3 For detailed discussion of the structure and justification of Section 5, see *South Carolina v. Katzenbach* (1966), which upheld the constitutionality of this provision, and *Allen v. State Bd. of Elections* (1969), which defined the scope of voting practices that Section 5 covers.
4 In several Reconstruction-era cases, for instance, the Supreme Court construed national voting-rights laws as applying only to racially based denials of the vote, on the grounds that to read the statutes more broadly would call into question whether Congress had legislated beyond the limited authority that the Fifteenth Amendment

grants Congress. See, e.g., *United States v. Cruikshank* (1875); *United States v. Reese* (1875).

5 Coverage is determined by a formula specified in Section 4 of the VRA. 42 U.S.C. § 1973b(b) (2009). States currently covered as a whole are Alabama, Alaska, Arizona, Georgia, Louisiana, Mississippi, South Carolina, Texas, and Virginia. See Procedures for the Administration of Section 5 of the Voting Rights Act of 1965, as Amended, 28 C.F.R. app. pt. 51.In addition, selected counties in California, Florida, New York, North Carolina, and South Dakota are covered, as well as certain townships in Michigan and New Hampshire. Id. See also U.S. Department of Justice Civil Rights Division website, Section 5 Covered Jurisdictions, http://www.usdoj .gov/crt/voting/sec_5/covered.php (accessed August 12, 2009).

6 For a detailed history of the original Voting Rights Act, see generally Davidson and Grofman 1994.

7 This history is recounted in detail in *South Carolina v. Katzenbach* (1966).

8 Native American voters, however, face exclusionary barriers to voting resembling those of the pre-VRA world. See McCool 2006.

9 For details of these election disputes, see Issacharoff et al 2001, 199–205.

10 *Bush v. Gore* arose from controversy surrounding recounts in Palm Beach, Miami-Dade, Broward, Volusia, and Nassau counties, none of which are covered by Section 5. See *Bush v. Gore* (2000); U.S. Department of Justice Civil Rights Division website, http://www.usdoj.gov/crt/voting/sec_5/covered.php (accessed August 12, 2009).

11 For a discussion of recent studies, see Pildes 2006.

12 For the suggestion that an amended Section 5 should be targeted at counties rather than states, see Grofman 2006. See also Pitts 2005 (noting that thirty-seven of the forty DOJ objection letters since 2000 under Section 5 have addressed local, not state, voting changes).

REFERENCES

Allen v. State Bd. of Elections, 393 U.S. 544 (1969).

Bush v. Gore, 531 U.S. 98 (2000).

Davidson, Chandler, and Bernard Grofman, eds. *Quiet Revolution in The South: The Impact of the Voting Rights Act 1965–1990*. 1994.

Fannie Lou Hamer, Rosa Parks, and Coretta Scott King Voting Rights Act Reauthorization and Amendments Act of 2006, Pub. L. 109–246, 120 Stat. 577 (2006).

Grofman, Bernard, and Thomas Brunell. "Extending Section 5 of the Voting Rights Act: The Complex Interaction between Law and Politics." In *The Future of the Voting Rights Act*, 311–39, edited by David Epstein, Richard H. Pildes, Rodolfo O. de la Garza & Sharyn O'Halloran. 2006.

Help America Vote Act, Pub. L. No. 107–252, 116 Stat. 1666 (2002).

Issacharoff, Samuel, Pamela S. Karlan, and Richard H. Pildes. *The Law of Democracy: Legal Structure of the Political Process*. 2007.

Lawyers' Commission for Civil Rights Under Law, National Commission on the Voting Rights Act, Protecting Minority Voters: The Voting Rights Act at Work, 1982–2005. (2006).

Letter from Loretta King, Acting Assistant Attorney General, Civil Rights Division, U.S. Dep't of Justice, to The Honorable Thurbert E. Baker, Attorney General of Georgia (May 29, 2009), *available at* http://www.usdoj.gov/crt/voting/sec_5/ltr/l_052909.php.

McCool, Daniel, Susan M. Olson, and Jennifer L. Robinson, eds. *Native Vote: American Indians, the Voting Rights Act, and the Right to Vote*. 2006.

National Voter Registration Act, 42 U.S.C. § 1973gg (2000).

Northwest Austin Municipal Utility District Number One v. Holder, 129 S. Ct. 2504 (2000).

Pildes, Richard H. The Politics of Race: Quiet Revolution in the South. *Harvard Law Review* 108 (1995): 1359.

Pildes, Richard H. The Constitutionalization of Democratic Politics. *Harvard Law Review* 118 (2004): 48–50.

Pildes, Richard H. The Future of Voting Rights Policy: From Anti-Discrimination to the Right to Vote. Howard Law Journal 49 (2006): 752–4.

Pitts, Michael J. Lets Not Call the Whole Thing Off Just Yet: A Response to Samuel Issacharoff's Suggestion to Scuttle Section 5 of the Voting Rights Act. *Nebraska Law Review* 84 (2005): 612.

Ricci v. DeStefano, 129 S. Ct. 2658 (2009).

South Carolina v. Katzenbach, 383 U.S. 301 (1966).

Tokaji, Daniel P. Early Returns on Election Reform: Discretion, Disenfranchisement, and the Help America Vote Act. *George Washington Law Review* 73 (2005): 1220–39.

Tokaji, Daniel P. The New Vote Denial: Where Election Reform Meets the Voting Rights Act. *South Carolina Law Review* 57 (2006): 689.

United States v. Cruikshank, 92 U.S. 542 (1875)

United States v. Reese, 92 U.S. 214 (1875).

Voting Rights Act, Pub. L. 89–110, 79 Stat. 437 (1965) (codified as amended at 42 U.S.C. §§ 1971, 1973 to 1973bb-1).

2

The Reconstruction of Voting Rights

Pamela S. Karlan[1]

In 1883, in the *Civil Rights Cases*, the Supreme Court wrote:

> When a man has emerged from slavery, and by the aid of beneficent legislation has shaken off the inseparable concomitants of that state, there must be some stage in the progress of his elevation when he takes the rank of a mere citizen, and ceases to be the special favorite of the laws, and when his rights as a citizen, or a man, are to be protected in the ordinary modes by which other men's rights are protected.[2]

The distinction between "special favoritism" and the "ordinary modes" of rights protection is a recurring question in American constitutional law. Consider just two recent examples: In *Romer v. Evans*,[3] the Supreme Court confronted a Colorado initiative ("Amendment 2") that foreclosed the adoption of antidiscrimination provisions that would forbid discrimination on the basis of sexual orientation. Colorado defended the enactment on the grounds that it did nothing more than deny "special rights" to gay people.[4] The Supreme Court rejected that argument:

> We find nothing special in the protections Amendment 2 withholds. These are protections taken for granted by most people either because they already have them or do not need them; these are protections against exclusion from an almost limitless number of transactions and endeavors that constitute ordinary civic life in a free society.[5]

Similarly, in *Grutter v. Bollinger*,[6] although the Supreme Court upheld the University of Michigan Law School's use of race-conscious admissions policies, it emphasized that such policies must have "a termination point,"[7] and expressed an "expect[ation] that 25 years from now, the use of racial preferences will no longer be necessary."[8] In the area of voting rights, the special rights/ordinary favoritism question has reemerged with special salience in light of the confluence of two events: the 2006 reauthorization of the preclearance and bilingual election materials provisions of the Voting Rights Act[9] and the 2008 election of Barack Obama.

The first case to challenge the constitutionality of the 2006 reauthorization, *Northwest Austin Municipal Utility District Number One v. Holder*[10] was ultimately resolved on statutory grounds, but along the way the challenger drew attention to the confluence, opening its reply brief at the jurisdictional stage with the sentence: "The America that has elected Barack Obama as its first African-American president is far different than when § 5 was first enacted in 1965."[11] And although it did not reach the constitutional question, the Chief Justice's opinion for the Court devoted substantial space to describing the changes wrought over the forty years since the Act's original passage and suggested that those changes might render the Act's continued constitutionality a "difficult constitutional question."[12] The Court's opinion thus fits into the long-standing position of conservative lawyers, scholars, and policy makers who have argued that the special protections of federal law provided by the Voting Rights Act – most immediately, of Section 5, but in the longer term of Section 2, which forbids nationwide and permanently the use of election practices that have a racially disparate impact regardless of whether the plaintiffs can prove a discriminatory purpose – are no longer necessary. Minority voters, these critics argue, can participate on an equal footing with all other citizens, and if they lose out in the process, well, that's simply how politics works.

Liberal and progressive scholars and policy makers must respond to the conservative attack by advancing a more fine-grained understanding of what President Obama's election signifies. To be sure, President Obama's election marks a transitional moment in American democracy. But to paraphrase the perhaps apocryphal prayer by an elderly black preacher often invoked by the Reverend Martin Luther King, Jr., although we ain't what we was, we also "ain't what we ought to be, and we ain't what we're gonna be."[13] In what follows, I identify three tasks for us to undertake. The first is empirical: Scholars need to develop a more precise picture of the state of racial politics than a snapshot of the presidential inauguration can provide. That picture should consider both the regional variation in the full integration of minority citizens into the electoral process and the distinctive problems of non-black racial and ethnic minority voters, particularly Latinos and Native Americans. The second task is conceptual: Scholars should develop a more affirmative vision of the right to vote, one in which the government takes an active responsibility for ensuring that all citizens have full access to the political process, instead of one where constitutional and legal constraints operate primarily to set bounds on the permissible reasons for excluding people from the franchise. The final task is doctrinal: Scholars must explain why the Voting Rights Act and other progressive legislation *are* "ordinary modes" of protecting rights to which courts should defer, rather than exceptional statutes that should trigger judicial skepticism.

THE EMPIRICAL DEBATE: BLACK, WHITE, AND BROWN, RED AND BLUE

Nineteen sixty-five marked not only the year the Voting Rights Act was passed, but also the first time a majority of respondents to a Gallup poll indicated their

willingness to consider voting for a black presidential candidate.[14] For some scholars
and commentators, the realization of this willingness in Barack Obama's election
suggests that the Voting Rights Act – or at least its special preclearance provisions
that require federal approval for changes in covered jurisdictions' voting laws – is
no longer necessary. Echoing Professor Richard Hasen's trenchant observation that
"Bull Connor is dead,"[15] they argue that the Voting Rights Act responds to a bygone
era. The linchpin of their claim is that racial polarization within the political process
has disappeared, or at least has lessened to the extent that it no longer impairs the
ability of minority voters to elect candidates of their choice. Abigail and Stephan
Thernstrom, for example, wrote that Obama's election proved that "there are no
longer any meaningful racial barriers to voting or holding office in America."[16]

A half-century ago, the greatest novelist of the American South, William Faulkner,
reminded us that "[t]he past is never dead. It's not even past."[17] In thinking about
the lessons to be drawn from the 2008 election, it is important to keep Faulkner's
observation in mind.

First, as an empirical matter, the 2008 election hardly disproved the existence
of racial bloc voting, especially in the southern jurisdictions that have been the
primary focus of voting rights litigation and the special provisions of Section 5.
Exit polling data showed that Obama received less than one-third of the white vote
in seven of the nine fully covered southern states[18] – a significantly lower share
of the white vote than he received in the rest of the country – not to mention a
night-and-day difference from the support he received from black voters. More fine-
grained analysis using county-level data suggests that across covered jurisdictions,
only nineteen percent of white voters voted for Obama (as opposed to 44 percent
of white voters in noncovered jurisdictions).[19] This minuscule support cannot be
attributed simply to partisan politics. In Alabama, Mississippi, and Louisiana, Obama
received a smaller share of the white vote total than John Kerry had in 2004.[20] And
the difference in relative white and black vote shares that Obama received in the
primaries was equally striking.[21]

Second, whatever the ability of an extraordinarily well-financed major-party candidate to win an election when *all* the objective indicators pointed toward the victory of
the Democratic nominee, whoever he or she might be, we should be quite cautious
about extrapolating to the prospects of minority-supported candidates at the local
or even state levels. For far too long, much of the scholarly attention to the Voting
Rights Act and the state of minority political power has focused on the national or
congressional level, with scant attention being devoted to politics at the local and
county level.[22] One central project going forward will be to document these realities,
to see whether and to what extent minority voters are participating fully and electing
the candidates of their choice in the more quotidian arena of local politics.

At the same time that liberal and progressive scholars focus on the local level,
we should also direct greater attention to the distinctive barriers faced by minority
groups other than African Americans. Latinos constitute a fast-growing share of the

electorate in jurisdictions across the country, and although some of the barriers facing Latino communities parallel those confronted by African Americans – for example, the use of at-large elections or retrogressive redistricting – some are distinctive: for example, failure to implement the bilingual ballot provisions of Section 203 in a way that safeguards their right to participate.[23] In 2004, Section 203 jurisdictions saw a far higher rate of provisional ballots than other jurisdictions.[24] What accounts for this disparity, which resulted in fewer voters from Section 203 jurisdictions actually having their votes counted? Is it the failure to handle Latino names appropriately in the registration matching process mandated by the Help America Vote Act?[25] Is it the failure to provide adequate training or assistance at the polls? Latino communities may also be especially vulnerable to claims of discriminatory annexations or failures to annex given their rapid growth in unincorporated areas.

Similarly, the 2006 reauthorization process for the Voting Rights Act revealed that Native Americans, particularly in South Dakota, remain victims of widespread discrimination. There has been relatively little scholarship devoted to the distinctive issues that may arise with respect to their voting rights claims.[26]

In short, if all politics is local, as Tip O'Neil famously observed, voting-rights scholars and policy makers must get local as well. The legislative record from the 2006 reauthorization contains extensive local material that can be mined for a variety of purposes and provides a useful starting point.

A VOTING IN THE AFFIRMATIVE: DEVELOPING A DIFFERENT CONCEPTION OF THE RIGHT TO VOTE

The Constitution and the United States Code are honeycombed with provisions regarding political participation. The most explicit protections of the franchise, however, are phrased almost entirely in the negative – that is, they simply prohibit particular forms of disenfranchisement. The Fifteenth Amendment, for example, forbids denial of the right to vote "on account of race"; the Nineteenth, "on account of sex"; and the Twenty-Fourth, "by reason of failure to pay any poll tax." At the statutory level, Section 2 of the Voting Rights Act prohibits the use of voting qualifications, prerequisites, standards, practices, or procedures only to the extent that their use "results in a denial or abridgement of the right of any citizen of the United States to vote on account of race or color, or [membership in a language minority group]."[27]

Still other constitutional provisions simply bootstrap off states' decisions about the franchise; for example, the right to vote in congressional elections is protected for individuals who have "the qualifications requisite for electors of the most numerous branch of the State legislatures."[28] In a similar vein, the Uniformed and Overseas Citizens Absentee Voting Act[29] protects the voting rights of members of the armed forces and U.S. citizens now living overseas to the extent that they would otherwise have been qualified to vote under state law.[30] In light of the express constitutional language, the Supreme Court long ago declared itself "unanimously of the opinion that the Constitution of the United States does not confer the right of suffrage upon any one."[31]

That the right to vote is expressed in negative terms is not entirely surprising. The entire Constitution is characterized by negative rights. Even the Fourteenth Amendment, the centerpiece of the First Reconstruction, largely acts to restrict government action: "[N]or shall any State deprive any person of life, liberty, or property, without due process of law; nor deny to any person within its jurisdiction the equal protection of the laws." This conception can work well enough when the right at issue can fairly be framed as a right to be left alone: The right to privacy, for example, can be vindicated in large part simply by telling the government to stay out of our bedrooms, away from our e-mail, and off our property.

A negative conception, however, does not work nearly so well when the ability to exercise a right depends on governmental action. If the government holds a monopoly over a particular resource, then citizens are dependent on the government for their ability to exercise rights dependent on access to that resource. The decision to conduct elections on official ballots[32] has important consequences for the right to vote. A citizen who is handed an official ballot written in a language she does not understand is effectively denied the right to vote.[33] A citizen who lives in a county that uses antiquated voting machines that frequently break down may effectively be prevented from voting by the press of other responsibilities that make it impossible for him to wait in line for hours to cast a ballot.[34] Similarly, laws that require citizens to present government-issued identity documents to cast their ballots[35] prevent individuals from voting unless the government acts affirmatively to provide those documents; if the government imposes burdensome prerequisites to obtaining the necessary documentation, this will bar people from the polls.

What would it mean to develop an affirmative conception of the right to vote, one in which the government has an obligation to facilitate citizens' exercise of the franchise? One concrete context involves voter registration. There is a bedrock principle of the Fourteenth Amendment with respect to other government-recognized or -created entitlements that the kind of notice the government must give someone before it deprives her of life, liberty, or property should be the sort that "one desirous of actually informing" the individual "might reasonably adopt." A "mere gesture" is not enough.[36] If voting-rights doctrine were to begin from the presumption that all citizens of voting age are entitled to vote,[37] and were to treat the right to vote as a kind of liberty or property that was inherent in the very notion of citizenship, this understanding might lay the groundwork for claims that the government must take affirmative measures to make sure that citizens are included on the voting rolls. Here, the experience of other countries could prove instructive. The United States uses a decentralized system that places the burden on individual citizens to register and leaves to individual states the responsibility for updating voting rolls to respond to changes in address among a highly mobile population. By contrast, in Canada, for example, the national government for many years conducted a "door-to-door enumeration" before every federal election, to make sure that all eligible citizens were able to participate; it moved away from this system only once it had developed a national database with systematic updating.[38] In many other nations, official identity documents – provided, in contrast to identity documents issued by the federal and state governments, at no charge to individual citizens – are in themselves sufficient to permit individuals to vote.

More broadly, treating voting as an affirmative right of citizenship could also help reframe the way courts, legislatures, and the public think about the relationship between voter participation and vote fraud. The most important governmental interest at stake in voting cases is ensuring the integrity of the electoral process. In recent years, there has been a shift in popular and judicial framing of the primary threat to electoral integrity. From roughly the 1960s through the mid-1990s, the focus of judicial and legislative efforts was on "false negatives" – that is, on the wrongful exclusion of citizens who should be entitled to vote. This concern prompted the passage of the Voting Rights Act of 1965 and its periodic extensions and amendments, as well as the National Voter Registration Act of 1993. Since the turn of the century, however, there has been a significant shift toward fear of "false positives" – specifically, the casting of ballots by ineligible individuals such as noncitizens, nonresidents, or the dead.[39] Since the 2000 election, the public, elected officials, and the courts have often assumed that there is an inevitable tradeoff between making it easier for citizens to vote and increasing the likelihood of fraud. The first major federal voting-rights statute of the twenty-first century, the Help America Vote Act (HAVA),[40] was infected from the start by its pairing of the goal of making it "easier to vote" with a desire to make it "harder to cheat."[41] So although HAVA required states to set up statewide voter registration databases, it required maintaining their accuracy through a "matching" program that led many states to remove voters from the rolls, ostensibly to prevent fraud but in reality on the basis of inaccuracies, glitches in data entry, and the like.[42]

The arena where this participation/fraud tradeoff has played out most recently is voter identification laws.[43] In *Crawford v. Marion County Election Board*,[44] the Supreme Court upheld a draconian Indiana voter ID requirement.[45] The analysis of the state's interests adopted by a majority of the Court[46] is instructive. They saw essentially two compelling interests. The first was in deterring or detecting actual vote fraud at the polls. The latter was in maintaining public confidence in the integrity of elections.

Whereas preventing fraud has long counted as a compelling government interest,[47] Justice Stevens's opinion announcing the judgment seemed remarkably unconcerned by the lack of any evidence that such fraud was an actual problem. The record, he acknowledged, "contain[ed] no evidence of any [in-person, voter-impersonation] fraud actually occurring in Indiana at any time in its history."[48] Indeed, Justice Stevens recognized that there were only "scattered instances of in-person voter fraud" anywhere in the United States.[49] His opinion harkened back to an "infamous example," but it involved Boss Tweed and the New York City municipal elections of 1868[50] – an episode far removed in time and place from twenty-first-century Indiana. Perhaps, as with his experiences learning to drive in the old days and living through Prohibition,[51] Justice Stevens's experiences as a Republican in Chicago had made him particularly attuned to the risk of vote fraud.

Ultimately, Justice Stevens turned away from the risk of actual fraud and identified furthering the state's interest "in protecting public confidence" as an "independent" factor justifying ID requirements.[52] In its earlier decision in *Purcell v. Gonzalez*,[53] the Court had elaborated on this point:

> Confidence in the integrity of our electoral processes is essential to the functioning of our participatory democracy. Voter fraud drives honest citizens out of the democratic process and breeds distrust of our government. Voters who fear their legitimate votes will be outweighed by fraudulent ones will feel disenfranchised. "The right of suffrage can be denied by a debasement or dilution of the weight of a citizen's vote just as effectively as by wholly prohibiting the free exercise of the franchise." *Reynolds v. Sims*, 377 U.S. 533, 555 (1964).[54]

The Court's rhetorical move in *Purcell* and *Crawford* is strongly reminiscent of its approach in *Bush v. Gore*,[55] where it also wrapped what was a structural decision with deep partisan undertones in the mantle of individual rights and the iconic commitment to one-person, one-vote.[56] Its equation of state denial of the right to vote with voters' *private* decisions not to participate represents a breathtaking expansion of the concept of vote dilution. By treating the case as involving a tradeoff between the rights of two classes of individual voters, the Court subtly shifted the terms of analysis from one focusing on whether particular restrictive practices can be justified to one that presupposes that some level of vote denial or dilution is inherent in the system. Under this pessimistic perspective, the only question was which group of voters should be excluded.

However, the hypothesis that *some* group of voters will be kept from the polls – and implicitly, that as between voters who have the necessary documents and voters who lack them, the former group is more deserving of protection – has been sharply undercut by research conducted by Stephen Ansolabehere and Nathaniel Persily. They found that fears of fraud "do not have any relationship to a [citizen's] likelihood of intending to vote or turning out to vote."[57] Other available evidence suggests that the number of qualified citizens who face exclusion at the polls exceeds many times over whatever fraud is actually prevented.[58] One future empirical project that may help reframe the question of voter confidence and the right to vote might look at the actual reasons otherwise eligible citizens give for not turning out. I suspect that there are other structural explanations such as voters' sense that the outcomes are foreordained through gerrymandering and other forms of incumbent protection or logistical barriers such as inconvenient polling places and long wait times to vote. Reframing the nature of the right to vote might also involve drawing analogies about the purported tradeoff from other areas of constitutional law. In the criminal justice system, for example, it is well understood that requirements such as proof of guilt beyond a reasonable doubt may occasionally result in acquitting guilty people. But the system bears that risk in order to protect the innocent – hence the phrase "better a hundred guilty men go free than that one innocent person be convicted." By recognizing that voting, like physical freedom, is a fundamental constitutional right, perhaps we can move toward a similar perspective with respect to the franchise.

In reframing the conception of the right to vote, liberals should also build upon the emerging recognition that the fundamental right to vote, while it is an important symbol of an individual's full membership in our political community, is a structural/ aggregative right as well as an individual one.[59] Voting is instrumental: It determines how political power gets allocated. If punitive offender disenfranchisement statutes bar over one million African Americans from voting, their disenfranchisement is not just their own business: It deprives the black community as a whole of political power and can skew election results sharply to the right, creating legislative bodies hostile to civil rights and economic justice for the franchised and disenfranchised alike. If four-hour lines to vote in urban precincts in Ohio deter voters there from casting their ballots, their absence can swing a presidential election, thus impairing the political interests of voters across the country. Although we stand by ourselves in the voting booth casting a secret ballot, no one really votes alone. Recognizing that the right to vote is not only an affirmative right but also a collective right may also offer at least a starting point for rethinking fundamental questions about who deserves representation and how our representative institutions should be constructed. The Second Reconstruction embraced a commitment to ensuring that members of traditionally excluded racial and ethnic minority groups, such as African Americans, Latinos, and Native Americans, achieve representation on elective bodies. That representation has been accomplished largely through the use of geographic districts, making lemonade out of the sorry fact that the United States remains deeply residentially segregated. But the use of geographic districts does nothing to enhance the electoral prospects of female candidates or candidates representing numerical minorities who do not live in discrete communities. Moreover, it can make it more difficult for liberal, progressive, and moderate white voters to elect candidates. One of the striking facts about the emergence of democracies in the former Soviet bloc, in South Africa, and in the developing world is that although all these nations have adopted features of the U.S. Constitution such as a bill of rights and judicial review, *none* has adopted our system of winner-take-all single-member districts as the sole means of electing national and provincial legislatures. Instead, they have all adopted systems that are more explicitly proportional. After its last election, in which the number of parliamentary seats garnered by different parties differed wildly despite relatively close vote totals, even the United Kingdom seems open to considering changes to produce electoral results that better track the electorate's preferences. There is a traditional Korean saying that one should never let one's skill exceed one's virtue. Forty-five years after the Reapportionment Revolution, gerrymander-ers' technical skill in manipulating district lines exceeds the power of our current legal doctrine to assure fair elections. Part of the task of reconstructing voting rights must be to develop new principles to address this distortion.

Whereas some activists and legislators have suggested the need for a new consti-tutional amendment recognizing the affirmative right to vote, my own view is that the existing constitutional provisions are sufficient. A better tactic, it seems to me, lies in reviving – as conservatives have done for their own ends – Charles Black's approach to constitutional reasoning from the structure and relationship of consti-tutional provisions.[60] The federalism revolution of the later Rehnquist Court relied on this approach in using the language in the Tenth and Eleventh amendments to expand state sovereignty and to constrain congressional power to vindicate civil rights. It is time for liberals and progressives to make similar arguments with respect to the contours of the right to vote. The entire Constitution presupposes free and fair elections in which all qualified citizens can participate. The individual amendments that have expanded the electorate should be read to express a more general principle. The decision in the Seventeenth Amendment to take the selection of U.S. senators away from the state legislatures should be seen as fundamentally inconsistent with a decision to turn the selection of U.S. representatives into the province of the state legislatures, as the current hands-off approach to redistricting has done. The decision in the Twenty-Fourth Amendment to abolish poll taxes should be seen as reflecting a fundamental commitment to eliminating barriers to registration and to ensuring that wealth plays less of a role in our politics.

JUST POLITICS: THE VOTING RIGHTS ACT AS "ORDINARY" LEGISLATION

The prior generation of liberal and progressive scholars grew up in the era of the Warren Court. Their view of questions of political and racial justice was highly court-centered: The Supreme Court played *the* central role in the Reapportionment Revolution[61] and was the key player in striking down a series of discriminatory practice ranging from the notorious Tuskegee gerrymander,[62] to discriminatory literacy tests,[63] to the poll tax.[64]

During the Warren Court era, the courts performed a critical role precisely because minority citizens were effectively disenfranchised. But times have changed in an important way: The success of the Voting Rights Act in effectively enfranchising minority citizens has transformed blacks and Latinos from "the wards of the Equal Protection Clause"[65] into its shapers, most formally through their participation in congressional efforts to enforce the Fourteenth Amendment.

There is a long-standing debate in equal protection theory. Partisans of what has come to be known as the antidiscrimination or anticlassification rationale see the central meaning of the clause as lying in a prohibition on the government distinguishing among individuals on the basis of impermissible criteria, of which race is the epitome. Under this approach, "at the heart of the Constitution's guarantee of equal protection lies the simple command that the Government must treat citizens as individuals, not as simply components of a racial, religious, sexual or national class."[66] By contrast, supporters of the "antisubordination" principle[67] see the clause as essentially a prohibition on the creation or perpetuation of disadvantaged classes.

Part of the argument liberal scholars need to make is that, to the extent that we have made significant strides in fully integrating minority citizens into the political process, courts ought to defer to that process's judgments about how best to achieve equality. Although he was dead wrong at the time to argue against judicial intervention – precisely because the political process was so infected by sclerotic malapportionment and disenfranchisement – Felix Frankfurter's position that "[i]n a democratic society like ours," the most complete relief for inequality in the political process may "come through an aroused popular conscience that sears the conscience of the people's representatives"[68] may be right today.

The Voting Rights Act of 1965 as amended makes two fundamental political choices: 1) to recognize claims resting on the disparate racial impact of challenged practices as well as claims of intentional discrimination; and 2), to protect the inherently group-based right to elect representatives as well as the individual right to participate. These choices reflect straightforward congressional responses to restrictive judicial constructions of both the Constitution and prior versions of the Voting Rights Act, most strikingly in *City of Mobile v. Bolden,*[69] *Reno v. Bossier Parish School Board,*[70] and *Georgia v. Ashcroft.*[71] The 1982 amendments to Section 2 adopting the disparate impact test are "[a]rguably . . . the first formal political compact in the history of the United States to which a fully enfranchised black electorate has given its consent."[72] Congress's choice of language about "class[es]" of citizens and "members" of groups was quite deliberate. Both supporters and opponents of the Act understood that it was what Justice Clarence Thomas later described it to be: "[A] device for regulating, rationing, and apportioning political power among racial and ethnic groups."[73] But *all* election laws serve as a device for regulating, rationing, and apportioning political power among groups. What the Voting Rights Act has done goes far beyond channeling the analysis in voting rights litigation. It changed the political context as well. First, it has given minority communities a critical bargaining chip:

> Black political leaders were able to deploy their newly won federal statutory rights to gain powerful leverage in the complex, hard-nosed negotiations with state and local legislatures over the structures of electoral systems, including the boundaries of Congressional districts. . . .

> [T]he greatest victories legal action has achieved for black plaintiffs, for black and white communities, and for American democracy came not from judicial decrees, but from fairly negotiated compromises between black and white political leaders. Court involvement had its optimal effect when it struck down systematically unfair

electoral structures and provided something approaching a level bargaining table. The remedial deals that were products of genuinely mutual respect and the spirit of give and take are the ones that have lasted the longest and have generated the most satisfaction. None of these deals was loved by all or intended to last forever, but that actually contributed to the sense of fairness the participants came away with. These provisional arrangements are subject to being brought back to the table at any time, either by the next census, by municipal annexations, or simply by the passage of time and the turning of the world.[74]

Since all political deals take place in the shadow of the law, the negotiations among politicians in covered jurisdictions are inflected by the Act's standards. The minority community's ability to "appeal" relatively costlessly to federal authorities in Section 5-covered jurisdictions increases its leverage in demanding accommodation of minority concerns. This is particularly true when it comes to redistricting. In the absence of Section 5's nonretrogression requirement, the Democratic Party might be tempted to spread concentrations of minority voters among several districts, rather than to preserve or create majority-minority seats: Such a strategy would increase the probability of Democrats winning elections, and minority voters' only alternative to voting for white-sponsored Democratic candidates in so-called "influence" districts would be to stay home, thereby potentially throwing the election to even more objectionable Republican candidates. Section 5's nonretrogression principle forecloses that particular strategy, at least in part, and requires white Democrats to offer more of the potential electoral gains from redistricting to their minority colleagues.

Moreover, Section 5 provides political cover. It enables political actors in covered jurisdictions to blame federal authorities for adopting voting-related practices that benefit minority voters, rather than having to take full responsibility for those changes. Whereas the anticommandeering jurisprudence of *New York v. United States*[75] and *Printz v. United States*[76] may rest on the view that clear lines of responsibility are important for political accountability, when it comes to protecting the voting rights of minority citizens, there may be a countervailing consideration. As an historical matter, white voters in the South have tended to resist minority political aspirations and to punish politicians they see as catering to minority interests.[77] This backlash phenomenon seems to be alive and well today: One of the factors behind the way Texas Republicans redrew the state's congressional map during the long-running post-2000 redistricting process was to eliminate the seats of white Democrats in order to "marginalize Democrats as the black-and-brown party and drive white voters to the Republican side of the political divide."[78] Thus, even when officials know that avoiding retrogression in the adoption of new voting practices is the right thing to do, they may be deterred from doing so by the political consequences. Section 5 provides them with a justification for doing the right thing.

In short, the Voting Rights Act has given minority citizens the ability – as well as the obligation – "to pull, haul, and trade to find common political ground,"[79] and they have found themselves on a far higher ground and a far more level playing field than the Supreme Court would have provided. Like all other electoral politics, Voting Rights Act-inflected politics may be a bit grubby. But this is "ordinary politics" of the kind we should also perhaps celebrate.

The framers of the Fourteenth and Fifteenth Amendments – mindful of a Supreme Court that had all too recently produced *Dred Scott v. Sandford*[80] – "were not content to leave the specification of protected rights to judicial decision."[81] Particularly in the area of political regulation, it is appropriate for Congress to play a leading role. The Supreme Court has recognized that the allocation of political power often involves situations where courts are ill-equipped to confront those issues without congressional guidance. In *Vieth v. Jubelirer*,[82] for example, all nine Justices acknowledged that excessive partisan gerrymanders raise serious constitutional questions and all nine located the constitutional infirmity at least in part in the equal protection clause.[83] And yet, a majority of the Court refused to adjudicate the plaintiffs' challenge to Pennsylvania's congressional redistricting. Justice Scalia, in a plurality opinion for himself, Chief Justice Rehnquist, and Justices O'Connor and Scalia would have held political gerrymandering claims nonjusticiable altogether, because "no judicially discernible and manageable standards for adjudicating political gerrymandering claims have emerged."[84] Justice Kennedy, concurring in the judgment, was unwilling to foreclose the possibility that such standards might emerge in the future, but he explained that "[t]he lack . . . of any agreed upon model of fair and effective representation" made it difficult for courts to determine, "by the exercise of their own judgment," whether a particular plan unconstitutionally "burden[s] representational rights."[85]

But although the plurality thought *courts* could not provide a remedy for partisan gerrymanders, it recognized that "the Framers provided a remedy" – at least for gerrymandered congressional districts – in the elections clause of Article I, Section 4.[86] Although the clause locates initial control over congressional elections in the state legislatures, it provides that "Congress may at any time by Law make or alter such Regulations."[87] Since 1842, Congress has used this power to impose a particular theory of representation on the states by requiring the use of geographically defined single-member districts to elect Representatives.[88] The decision to use such districts reflects, among other things, a commitment to a form of proportionality in which one faction or party cannot capture a state's entire congressional delegation (as might be true under an at-large system), and a preference for geographically contiguous groups over groups whose members are not geographically discrete.[89] Thus, Congress has a special role to play in ensuring fair representation in federal elections.

Arguably, that role should carry over to ensuring fair representation in state and local elections as well.[90] The Reconstruction Amendments parallel, in an important sense, the allocation of power under the elections clause: Congress can override the states' initial decisions if the intervention safeguards the equal protection, due process, and antidiscrimination values expressed by the amendments. The Voting Rights Act involves an area – regulation of the political process – that raises important issues of political fairness that are not fully determined by the sweeping commands of Sections 1 of the Fourteenth and Fifteenth Amendment and that can be particularly within the expertise of politicians. Part of the reason the Supreme Court has grappled with the justiciability of political gerrymandering claims for nearly forty years is precisely because the issue calls on courts to decide among hotly contested principles of political philosophy. To give just one example that bears on the most recent amendment to Section 5 responding to *Georgia v. Ashcroft*, people active in and knowledgeable about politics differ vociferously about whether, in crafting electoral districts, political fairness is better ensured by drawing each district to be as competitive as possible (which increases both the chances that any individual voter will cast a decisive ballot and the risk that small changes in electoral preferences can produce grossly disproportionate legislative bodies) or by drawing districts that are predictably controlled by identifiable blocs of voters (which can produce proportional representation of the blocs within the legislative body but which results in larger numbers of voters casting essentially meaningless, or "wasted," votes).[91] Thus, at least with respect to apportionment, any regulation of the process demands choosing among theories of representation: If the Court cannot do this in the first instance, then Congress should perhaps have more leeway to make initial choices. And the Court should not then deploy special scrutiny to deprive minority citizens of the benefits their fuller participation has achieved.

Seeing the Voting Rights Act as an "ordinary mod[e]" of protecting minority citizens' rights, rather than as an extraordinary deviation from normal legislation, allows liberals and progressives to argue that the Supreme Court should approach the Act not with heightened skepticism, but with its usual presumption that Congress has legitimately used its enumerated powers. This shift in perspective seems especially critical if, as I hope, we are entering into an era where liberals and progressives will often wield the levers of political power.

NOTES

1 Kenneth and Harle Montgomery Professor of Public Interest Law, Stanford Law School. I thank Debo Adegbile and Viola Canales for helpful suggestions. Some of the material in this chapter has appeared, in somewhat different forms, in Goodwin Liu, Pamela S. Karlan, and Christopher H. Schroeder, *Keeping Faith with the Constitution* (Washington, DC: American Constitution Society 2009); Samuel Issacharoff and Pamela S. Karlan, "Groups, Politics, and the Equal Protection Clause," *University of Miami Law Review* 58 (2003): 35; Pamela S. Karlan, "Bullets, Ballots, and Battles on the Roberts Court," *Ohio Northern Law Review* 35 (2009): 445; and Pamela S. Karlan, "Voting Rights and the Third Reconstruction," in *The Constitution in 2020*, ed. Jack Balkin and Reva Siegel (New York: Oxford University Press 2009), 159.
2 109 U.S. 3, 25 (1883).
3 517 U.S. 520 (1996).
4 Ibid., 626.
5 Ibid., 631.
6 539 U.S. 306 (2003).

7 Ibid., 342.
8 Ibid., 343.
9 Fannie Lou Hamer, Rosa Parks, and Coretta Scott King Voting Rights Act Reauthorization and Amendments Act of 2006, Public Law 109–246, U.S. Statutes at Large 120 (2006): 577, codified at U.S. Code 42 (2006), § 1973c (preclearance) and § 1973aa-1a (bilingual ballot materials).
10 129 S. Ct. 2504 (2009).
11 Appellant's Brief Opposing Motions to Affirm at 1, Northwest Austin Mun. Util. Dist. No. 1 v. Mukasey, No. 08–322 (filed Dec. 2008).
12 Northwest Austin, 2511–13.
13 Martin Luther King, Jr., "Response to Award of the American Liberties Medallion (May 20, 1965)," American Jewish Committee, http://www.ajc.org/site/apps/nl/content3.asp?c/ijITI2PHKoG&b/843719&ct/1052923 (accessed March 9, 2010).
14 Jeffrey M. Jones, "Some Americans Reluctant to Vote for Mormon, 72-Year-Old Presidential Candidates," Gallup, http://www.gallup.com/poll/26611/ Some-Americans-Reluctant-Vote-Mormon-72YearOld-Presidential-Candidates.aspx (accessed March 9, 2010).
15 Richard L. Hasen, "Congressional Power to Renew the Preclearance Provisions of the Voting Rights Act After Tennessee v. Lane," *Ohio State Law Journal* 66 (2005): 177, 188. Hasen himself in fact supported the renewal of the Act.
16 George Will, "Voting Rights Anachronism," *Washington Post*, January 18, 2009, B07 (quoting the Thernstroms).
17 William Faulkner, *Requiem for a Nun* (New York: Random House 1951), 92.
18 Kristen Clarke, "The Obama Factor: The Impact of the 2008 Presidential Election on Future Voting Rights Act Litigation," *Harvard Law and Policy Review* 3 (2009): 59, 70.
19 Stephen Ansolabehere, Nathaniel Persily, and Charles Stewart III, "Race, Region, and Vote Choice in the 2008 Election: Implications for the Future of the Voting Rights Act," *Harvard Law Review* 123 (2010): 1385, 1416–17.
20 Ibid., 1414.
21 Clarke, "The Obama Factor," 73–5.
22 Ibid., 79–81 (suggesting distinctions between the 2008 presidential election and more local races).
23 The most extensive study of the issues facing language minorities generally is James Tucker, *The Battle over Bilingual Ballots: Language Minorities and Political Access under the Voting Rights Act* (Burlington, VT: Ashgate Press 2009).
24 Samuel Issacharoff, Pamela S. Karlan, and Richard H. Pildes, *The Law of Democracy: Legal Structure of the Political Process*, 3d ed. (New York: Foundation Press 2007), 1126 (summarizing a 2004 report by the federal Election Assistance Commission).
25 See pages xx below (describing that process and the problems).
26 One notable exception is Laughlin McDonald, *American Indians and the Fight for Equal Voting Rights* (Norman, OK: University of Oklahoma Press 2010).
27 Voting Rights Act, U.S. Code 42 (2006), § 1973(a).
28 U.S. Constitution, art. I, § 2.
29 Uniformed and Overseas Citizens Absentee Voting Act, U.S. Code 42 (2006), §§ 1973ff et seq.
30 Ibid., § 1973ff-6(1), (5).
31 Minor v. Happersett, 88 U.S. 162, 178 (1875).
32 For a discussion of this history, see Issacharoff, Karlan, and Pildes, *The Law of Democracy*, 205–08 (discussing the ballot and state gatekeeping).

33 As I discuss further, the bilingual ballot provisions are one of the few strongly affirmative voting rights currently provided by federal law.

34 In a similar vein, a recent report by the Overseas Voting Foundation suggests that more than one in five voters who sought to cast their ballots in 2008 pursuant to the Uniformed and Overseas Citizens Absentee Voting Act did not have their votes counted because their ballots were sent to them too late to meet the Election Day deadline. Kat Zambon, "More Than One in Five Military and Overseas Voters Disenfranchised in 2008: New Report Explains Challenges, Offers Solutions," electionlineWeekly, http://www.pewcenteronthestates.org/uploadedFiles/wwwpew centeronthestatesorg/Reports/Electionline_Reports/electionlineWeekly02.12.09.pdf (accessed May 9, 2010).

35 Indiana Code Annotated section 3–11-8–25.1(a), for example, requires generally that a voter who "desires to vote an official ballot at an election shall provide proof of identification," and section 3–5-2–40.5(4) clarifies that "[p]roof of identification" is satisfied only by a document that "was issued by the United States or the state of Indiana."

36 Mullane v. Central Hanover Bank and Trust Co., 339 U.S. 306, 315 (1950).

37 I leave aside here the question whether some citizens should affirmatively be excluded (for example, for conviction of a crime or because of a mental disability). I discuss those questions elsewhere. Pamela S. Karlan, "Convictions and Doubts: Retribution, Representation, and the Debate Over Felon Disenfranchisement," *Stanford Law Review* 56 (2004): 1147 (discussing the exclusion of individuals convicted of a crime); Pamela S. Karlan, "Framing the Voting Rights Claims of Cognitively Impaired Individuals," *McGeorge Law Review* 38 (2007): 917 (discussing the voting rights of persons with mental disabilities).

38 Elections Canada, "Description of the National Register of Electors," Elections Canada, http://www.elections.ca/content.asp?section/ins&document/national&dir/ nre&lang/e&textonly/false (last visited February 9, 2009).

39 David Schultz, "Less Than Fundamental: The Myth of Voter Fraud and the Coming of the Second Great Disenfranchisement," *William Mitchell Law Review* 34 (2008): 483.

40 Help America Vote Act, U.S. Code 42 (2006) §§15301–15545.

41 Daniel P. Tokaji, "Voter Registration and Election Reform," *William and Mary Bill of Rights Journal* 17 (2008): 453, 470 (quoting Rep. Steny Hoyer).

42 Justin Leavitt, Wendy R. Weiser, and Ana Muñoz, *Making the List: Database Matching and Verification Processes for Voter Registration* (New York: Brennan Center for Justice 2006), 1–22, http://www.policyarchive.org/handle/10207/bitstreams/8767.pdf (accessed May 9, 2010).

43 For a general discussion of these laws, see Spencer Overton, "Voter Identification," *Michigan Law Review* 105 (2007): 631.

44 553 U.S. 181 (2008). I served as one of the lawyers for the petitioners.

45 I discuss Crawford more extensively in Karlan, "Bullets, Ballots, and Battles."

46 There was no opinion for the Court, but on this point, Justice Scalia's opinion (joined by Justices Thomas and Alito) agreed with Justice Stevens's opinion announcing the judgment (which was joined by Chief Justice Roberts and Justice Kennedy). See Crawford, 553 U.S. at 209 (Scalia, J., concurring in the judgment).

47 Dunn v. Blumstein, 405 U.S. 330, 345 (1972) (terming "prevention of such fraud . . . a legitimate and compelling government goal").

48 Crawford, 553 U.S. at 194.

49 Ibid., 195 n.12.
50 Ibid., 195 n.11.
51 Scott v. Harris, 550 U.S. 372, 390 n.1 (2007) (Stevens, J., dissenting) (arguing that his colleagues would have reacted differently to the videotape of a police pursuit if they had "learned to drive" – as implicitly he had – "when most high-speed driving took place on two-lane roads rather than on superhighways"); Granholm v. Heald, 544 U.S. 460, 494–97 (2005) (Stevens, J., dissenting) (explaining his position on interstate wine shipment as based in part on his "recollection" of the historical context in which Prohibition and its repeal occurred).
52 Crawford, 553 U.S. at 197.
53 549 U.S. 1 (2007).
54 Ibid., 4.
55 531 U.S. 98 (2000).
56 Pamela S. Karlan, "Equal Protection: Bush v. Gore and the Making of a Precedent" in *The Unfinished Election of 2000*, ed. Jack N. Rakove (New York: Basic Books 2001).
57 Stephen Ansolabehere and Nathaniel Persily, "Vote Fraud in the Eye of the Beholder: The Role of Public Opinion in the Challenge to Voter Identification Requirements," *Harvard Law Review* 121 (2008): 1737, 1739.
58 Spencer Overton, *Stealing Democracy: The New Politics of Voter Suppression* (2006).
59 Heather K. Gerken, "Understanding the Right to an Undiluted Vote," *Harvard Law Review* 114 (2001): 1663; Pamela S. Karlan, "The Rights To Vote: Some Pessimism About Formalism," *Texas Law Review* 71 (1993): 1705.
60 Charles L. Black, Jr., *Structure and Relationship in Constitutional Law* (Baton Rouge: Louisiana State University Press 1969).
61 E.g., Baker v. Carr, 369 U.S. 186 (1962); Wesberry v. Sanders, 376 U.S. 1 (1964); Reynolds v. Sims, 377 U.S. 533 (1964).
62 Gomillion v. Lightfoot, 364 U.S. 339 (1960).
63 Lousiana v. United States, 380 U.S. 145 (1965) (striking down a state requirement that aspiring voters interpret a section of the state constitution before being registered).
64 E.g,, Harman v. Forssenius, 380 U.S. 528 (1965); Harper v. State Bd. of Elections, 383 U.S. 663 (1966).
65 Owen M. Fiss, "Groups and the Equal Protection Clause," *Philosophy and Public Affairs* 5 (1976): 107, 147.
66 Miller v. Johnson, 515 U.S. 900, 911 (1995) (internal quotation marks omitted).
67 Fiss, "Groups," 108.
68 Baker v. Carr, 369 U.S. 186, 270 (1962) (Frankfurter, J., dissenting).
69 446 U.S. 55 (1980).
70 528 U.S. 320 (2000).
71 539 U.S. 461 (2003).
72 James U. Blacksher, "Dred Scott's Unwon Freedom: The Redistricting Cases As Badges of Slavery," *Howard Law Journal* 39 (1996): 633, 663.
73 Holder v. Hall, 512 U.S. 874, 893 (1994) (Thomas, J., concurring in the judgment). For diverse discussions of the legislative history of the 1982 amendments, see Blacksher, "Dred Scott's Unwon Freedom"; Thomas M. Boyd and Stephen J. Markman, "The 1982 Amendments to the Voting Rights Act: A Legislative History," *Washington and Lee Law Review* 40 (1983): 1347; Armand Derfner, "Vote Dilution and the Voting Rights Act Amendments of 1982" in *Minority Vote Dilution*, ed. Chandler Davidson (Washington, DC: Howard University Press 1984) 61; Abigail Thernstrom, *Whose Votes Count?: Affirmative Action and Minority Voting Rights* (1987).

74 Blacksher, "Dred Scott's Unwon Freedom," 660 and 686.

75 505 U.S. 144 (1992).

76 521 U.S. 898 (1997).

77 V.O Key, Jr., *Southern Politics in State and Nation* (New York: A.A. Knopf 1949); Laughlin McDonald, "The Counterrevolution in Minority Voting Rights," *Mississippi Law Journal* 65 (1995): 271, 308.

78 Editorial, "The Ghettoization of Texas Democrats," *Austin American-Statesman*, January 16, 2004, A16.

As I have explained elsewhere, to the extent that the Voting Rights Act has caused the political realignment of the South, the causal connection is not so much that the creation of majority-minority districts has deprived other Democratic candidates of sufficient support, but that the very enfranchisement of black voters created the opportunity for the Republican "southern strategy." Pamela S. Karlan, "Loss and Redemption: Voting Rights at the Turn of a Century," *Vanderbilt Law Review* 50 (1997): 291, 314–20.

79 Johnson v. DeGrandy, 512 U.S. 997, 1020 (1994).

80 60 U.S. (19 How.) 393 (1857). The central purpose of the Fourteenth Amendment's first sentence – "All persons born or naturalized within the United States, and subject to the jurisdiction thereof, are citizens of the United States and of the State wherein they reside" – was to overturn Dred Scott's holding that blacks could not be citizens.

81 Michael McConnell, "Institutions and Interpretation: A Critique of City of Boerne v. Flores," *Harvard Law Review* 111 (1997): 153, 182, 176. For other recent discussions of the understandings of the framers of the Fourteenth Amendment regarding Congress's power under the enforcement clauses, see William E. Nelson, *The Fourteenth Amendment: From Political Principle to Judicial Doctrine* (1988); Cass R. Sunstein, *The Partial Constitution* (1993).

82 541 U.S. 267 (2004).

83 Ibid., 292, 293 (plurality opinion) (expressing an assumption that severe partisan gerrymandering is "incompatib[le] . . . with democratic principles" and "unlawful"); ibid., 313–14, 316 (Kennedy, J., concurring in the judgment); ibid., 319 (Stevens, J., dissenting); ibid., 347–52 (Souter & Ginsburg, JJ., dissenting); ibid., at 365 (Breyer, J., dissenting).

84 Ibid., 281 (plurality opinion).

85 Ibid., 307 (Kennedy, J., concurring in the judgment).

86 Ibid., 275 (plurality opinion).

87 U.S. Constitution, art. I, § 4.

88 Vieth, 541 U.S. at 276 (plurality opinion).

89 Rosemarie Zagarri, *The Politics of Size* (Ithaca: Cornell University Press 1987); Samuel Issacharoff, Pamela S. Karlan and Richard H. Pildes, *The Law of Democracy: Legal Structure of the Political Process*, Rev. 2d ed. 1156–1160 (New York: Foundation Press 2002); Branch v. Smith, 538 U.S. 254 (2003) (discussing the single-member district requirement of United States Code 2 (2006) § 2c.

90 Although the elections clause does not speak directly to state or local elections, one of the rationales voiced in support of the clause in the ratifying debates resonates here as well. A delegate at the Massachusetts convention warned that state legislatures might often be tempted to "make an unequal and partial division of the states into districts for the election of representative," and that "[w]ithout these powers in Congress, the people can have no remedy." The elections clause, however, would "provid[e] a remedy, a controlling power in a legislature, composed of senators and representatives

of twelve states, without the influence of our commotions and factions, who will hear impartially, and preserve and restore to the people their equal and sacred rights of election." Vieth, 541 U.S. at 276 (plurality opinion) (quoting 2 Debates on the Federal Constitution 27 [J. Elliot 2d ed. 1876]).

91 For one recent exchange on this issue, compare Nathaniel Persily, "In Defense of Foxes Guarding Henhouses: The Case for Judicial Acquiescence to Incumbent-Protecting Gerrymanders," *Harvard Law Review* 116 (2002): 649, with Samuel Issacharoff, "Gerrymandering and Political Cartels," *Harvard Law Review* 116 (2002): 593 and Samuel Issacharoff, "Why Elections?" *Harvard Law Review* 116 (2002): 684.

3

Explaining Perceptions of Competitive Threat in a Multiracial Context

Vincent L. Hutchings, Cara Wong, James Jackson,
and Ronald E. Brown

The United States has undergone a dramatic demographic transformation in the last several decades. For example, as recently as 1980, the U.S. census reported that White Americans represented over 79 percent of the total national population. Most of the remaining fraction of Americans was of African descent (11 percent). Hispanics and Asian Americans were a much smaller share of the population at 6 percent and 1 percent, respectively.[1] In the ensuing twenty years, however, increased immigration and relatively high birth rates have resulted in a surprisingly rapid growth in the number of Hispanic and Asian Americans and a concomitant decline in the proportion of Whites. According to the most recent census, Whites now represent 69 percent of the national population whereas Hispanics account for almost 13 percent and Asian Americans – the fastest-growing ethnic/racial group in the country – make up almost 4 percent. The share of Blacks in the population has held fairly steady over the past twenty years at 12 percent, although their rate of increase remains much smaller than is the case for Asians and Hispanics.

As the racial environment in this country has grown increasingly complex, the old Black-White binary perspective on American race relations is being joined by, and perhaps replaced with, a newer racial dynamic. That is, in addition to the traditional political divide between Whites and African Americans over such hot-button issues as affirmative action and bussing, the nation is increasingly confronted with contentious disputes over the rights of language minorities and immigration issues. For example, in May 2006, more than 1 million mostly Hispanic immigrants marched in several large cities to protest what they perceived as punitive immigration reform measures pending before Congress.[2] In addition to the protests, organizers also called for immigrant employees to stay home on the day of the march to protest what they viewed as increasingly prevalent and negative stereotypes about immigrant workers. Many businesses throughout the country reported being affected by the boycott.

Another interesting element in this increasingly complicated racial environment is that Hispanics and Asians are not just clashing with Whites as they seek economic and political clout, but also with African Americans. This conflict among racial and ethnic minority groups has mostly played out on the local level. For example, on the political front, Blacks and Hispanics expressed different political preferences in the 2005 New York City mayoral contest pitting Mayor Michael Bloomberg against former Bronx Borough President Fernando Ferrer. Interestingly, Bloomberg is a Republican yet he garnered 47 percent of the Black vote, a normally staunch Democratic constituency. Ferrer, who is of Puerto Rican descent, retained the support of most Hispanics (62 percent) but because of the lack of support among Whites (31 percent) and tepid support among Blacks, he lost by a substantial measure to the incumbent (Saul and Colangelo 2005). Similar political battles between Blacks and Hispanics have occurred in Los Angeles, Houston, and Miami. Blacks (and Hispanics) have also clashed with Asian Americans. Perhaps the most infamous example occurred in Los Angeles in the early 1990s, when a Korean-American liquor store proprietor fatally shot fifteen-year-old Latasha Harlins for allegedly stealing a $1.79 bottle of orange juice. Not long after this incident, the L.A. riots unfolded after the not-guilty verdict in the trial of four White officers accused of beating Black motorist, Rodney King. Korean-owned shops were apparently targeted during the unrest that involved a multiracial group of participants including Hispanics (43 percent), Blacks (34 percent) and Whites (14 percent) (Nasser 1992). In spite of the generally Democratic leanings of racial minority groups, tensions and disagreements over immigration remain high.

A number of theoretical perspectives have been developed to account for the racial attitudes that likely emerge from the nation's increasingly complicated racial atmosphere. As detailed more fully further in this chapter, however, we argue that the group position perspective offers the most comprehensive explanation. In this work, we seek to elaborate on, and test the empirical implications of, the group position theory of racial attitudes. Specifically, we examine the scope and determinants of perceptions of racial group competition among a broad national sample of Americans including Whites, Blacks, Hispanics, Asian Americans, and Afro-Caribbeans. We believe this is the first such scholarly examination of these groups and these issues at the national level. Although our results are generally consistent with the group position model, our findings diverge in important ways from other work in this literature.

THEORETICAL BACKGROUND

Scholars have offered a number of theoretical explanations to account for intergroup conflict (see, e.g., Adorno et al. 1950; Allport 1954; Blumer 1958; Kinder and Sears 1981; Sniderman and Carmines 1997). Most of these theories have been developed with Whites, or superordinate groups in general, in mind. However, more recently, a number of researcher have sought either to adapt existing theories or to develop new ones that recognize and attempt to explain the views of racial minority group members (Bobo and Hutchings 1996; Sidanius and Pratto 1999; Kaufmann 2003;

Oliver and Wong 2003; McClain et al. 2006). In this paper, we examine the effects of several different theoretical perspectives on perceptions of zero-sum competition among both Whites and racial minorities.

Classical Prejudice

The classical prejudice explanation for intergroup conflict is most closely associated with the work of Gordon Allport (1954). According to Allport, interracial hostility is primarily borne out of particular psychological dispositions rather than objective material conditions. That is, individuals come to view members of another racial or ethnic group as competitors because of socially learned feelings of aversion and the preadult acquisition of negative out-group stereotypes. From the perspective of this influential model, feelings of intergroup hostility are not the rational byproduct of clashing group interests or individuals' particular social circumstances, but rather a consequence of cultural ideas about, and emotional responses to, out-group members.

In the view of this model, feelings of competitive racial threat are similar to, and likely a consequence of, prejudiced and stereotypical attitudes (Sears and Kinder 1985). As a result, this theory would predict that individuals who embrace negative out-group stereotypes should also endorse the view that success for out-group members comes at the expense of in-group members.

Although, as indicated earlier, this theory was developed to explain White attitudes about African Americans, there are some reasons to believe that it should also apply to emerging minority groups such as Hispanics and Asian Americans. For example, a variant of the classical prejudice model, symbolic racism, has been extended beyond the Black-White divide and successfully applied to issues of immigration, Native American rights, and language policy (Sears et al. 1999; Bobo and Tuan 2006). Moreover, the classical prejudice explanation need not apply only to Whites' attitudes about racial minorities but can also be applied to the racial attitudes of racial minority groups themselves. Sniderman and Piazza (2002), for instance, find some limited evidence that prejudice influences the attitudes that Blacks have about Whites and Jews. Further, McClain and her colleagues (2006) report that negative stereotypes about Blacks influence the views that Latinos in North Carolina have about perceptions of commonality with African Americans. For all of these reasons, it is conceivable that racial prejudice will influence perceptions of racial group competition for Whites as well as minorities.

Neighborhood Context and Interracial Contact

Another explanation for intergroup hostility locates the source more in an individual's immediate surroundings than in psychological disposition. Actually, there are at least two seemingly inconsistent expectations about how one's racial environment might influence perceptions of competitive racial threat. An extensive literature in political science and sociology has found that increases in Black population size (usually measured at the county or metropolitan level) are associated with greater racial conservatism among White Americans (Key 1949; Giles & Buckner 1993; Glaser 1994; Taylor 2000). The link between Black population density and racial conservatism has often been characterized as "the threat hypothesis." That is, Whites' negative racial attitudes increase in the face of larger minority populations because these larger numbers spark Whites' racial fears as well as resentments over the prospect of competition for scarce local resources.

A competing view about the effects of racial context holds that interracial proximity leads to greater racial tolerance rather than increased interracial hostility (Oliver and Wong 2003; Welch, Sigelman, Bledsoe, and Combs 2001). According to this perspective, racial animosity is largely a consequence of ignorance. As individuals from different racial and ethnic groups come to interact more with one another, negative stereotypes break down (Allport 1954). This perspective is known as the contact theory and has been shown to apply to both Whites and racial minorities (Oliver and Wong 2003). Indeed, Oliver and Wong (2003) argue that the power threat hypothesis and the contact theory can be reconciled in that the former generally measures context at the larger aggregate level of the county or metropolitan area. This is important because Blacks and Whites, for example, are often in close proximity to one another at the county level even as they remain separate in their own segregated communities. Contact theory, on the other hand, highlights the importance of direct interracial interaction. This is more likely to occur in smaller geographic units such as the neighborhood. It is at this level, they argue, that racial context should lead to more tolerant attitudes.[3]

Assuming that the expectations of the contact theory take precedence when measuring more compact geographic units, we expect that individuals who live in less racially segregated communities will also be less likely to adopt a zero-sum attitude about interactions with out-groups. Additionally, individuals who report more interracial friendships should also be less likely to view other racial groups as competitive threats. Oliver and Wong (2003) do not test these propositions directly in their analyses of the 1992–1994 Multi-City Study of Urban Inequality as they rely on census tract data on the neighborhood racial characteristics of their respondents. Still, implicit in their analyses is the notion that greater neighborhood racial diversity affects attitudes about interracial hostility through the mechanism of meaningful and positive contact across racial lines. If true, then presumably self-reports of the racial make-up of one's friendship networks and neighborhood racial composition should capture much of what is gauged with more objective measures. Finally, although we do not consider this possibility here, it should also be the case that the expectations of the power threat hypothesis kick in at more expansive levels of racial context. That is, at the metropolitan or county level, greater racial diversity should lead to heightened levels of competitive racial threat.[4]

Group Identity

A third explanation for intergroup conflict posits the importance of in-group identity. Most of the research on the relationship between group identity and racial attitudes has been done with respect to White attitudes about Blacks. In general, researchers have found only a small and inconsistent linkage between higher levels of in-group identity among Whites and negative racial attitudes toward African Americans. Adherents to the prejudice explanation for racial conflict have interpreted this to mean that Whites' racial attitudes are not significantly driven by a need to protect their racial group interests (Sears, Van Laar, Carrillo, and Kosterman 1997). Thus, in-group identity should have limited influence among Whites, although whatever effects it does produce should lead to greater hostility rather than less.

What little research there is on the effects of group identity among racial minorities suggests that these attitudes are likely to promote greater tolerance rather than increased hostility (Gurin, Hatchett, and Jackson 1989; Davis and Brown 2002; Kaufmann 2003; McClain et al. 2006). Among Blacks, for example, a number of studies have found that greater support for the sentiment that what affects the racial group will also affect the individual ("linked fate") is associated with *less* animosity directed at Whites (Gurin et al. 1989; Herring, Jankowski, and Brown 1999; Davis and Brown, 2002). Similarly, both Kaufmann (2003) and McClain and her colleagues (2006) find that a greater sense of linked fate among Latinos translates into increased perceptions of commonality with African Americans. The explanation for this latter finding seems to be that as Latinos move away from ties to their country of origin and instead adopt a broader quasi-racial group identity, they view their groups' circumstances as similar to that of Blacks and thus perceive them more as fellow travelers rather than competitors. In light of this emerging literature on Blacks and Latinos, this model leads one to expect that for these groups, and perhaps other racial minorities, greater levels of group identity should be associated with lower levels of interracial conflict.

Group Position Theory

The final theory we examine in this chapter is the group position theory. Herbert Blumer introduced this theory in 1958, and it maintains that intergroup hostility is not simply the product of negative affect or stereotypes about salient out-groups. Bobo and Hutchings (1996) expound upon the underpinnings of this theory in some detail:

> [According to the group position model] *feelings of competition and hostility emerge from historically and collectively developed judgments about the positions in the social order that in-group members should rightfully occupy relative to members of an out-group.* The core factor in Blumer's model is the subjective image of where the in-group *ought* to stand vis-à-vis the out-group (Bobo and Hutchings 1996, p. 955, italics in original).

Blumer lists four elements as important to the development of a sense of group position. The first element is the belief in in-group superiority or at least a strong sense of in-group preference. This concept is in many ways analogous to the concept of group identity discussed earlier in the chapter. The second element in the group position framework is the view among in-group members that out-group members are different and alien. This perception is akin to notions of negative stereotyping and prejudice discussed earlier. The third element is a sense among the in-group members that they are entitled to certain rights, resources, and privileges. Finally, this model maintains that in-group members fear that out-group members desire a larger, and illegitimate, share of the in-group's rights and privileges.

As with most other theories addressed in this chapter, the group position model was originally designed to explain White attitudes about African Americans. Bobo and Hutchings (1996) however, demonstrated that the theory could be extended to racial minorities in their study of Los Angeles. In addition to applying the theory to non-White groups, Bobo and Hutchings also explored an important, albeit implicit, proposition of the model, namely that perceptions of racial alienation are a primary determinant of perceptions of competitive racial threat. By racial alienation, Bobo and Hutchings meant that, given the history of race relations in the United States, some racial group members were more likely to feel a sense of racial group entitlement even as others were more apt to feel that their group had been disenfranchised and discriminated against. In the context of the multiracial setting of their analyses, they argued that racial minority group members, perhaps especially native-born African Americans, were most likely to express such feelings of alienation, *but whatever group one belonged to, such feelings should be highly predictive of perceptions of zero-sum competition.*

In addition to broadening our scope beyond negative affect and stereotypes, the group position theory has the advantage of incorporating elements from some of the other theories we examine in this paper. That is, as with the classical prejudice model, the group position theory anticipates an important role for negative out-group stereotyping and concerns with maintaining social distance as predictors of intergroup hostility. Similarly, in-group preference or group identity is also an important element of the group position theory. However, unlike some recent work on the racial attitudes of racial minorities, the group position model expects heightened levels of group identity to be associated with greater racial hostility. This is because individuals who identify more strongly with their group should also feel a greater sense of threat when out-groups are perceived as encroaching on their groups' "territory." Finally, with respect to the effects of the racial environment on intergroup attitudes, the group position theory is much more consistent with the power threat hypothesis than contact theory. That is, as others have argued, part of the reason that larger minority populations are theorized to produce greater racial conservatism is that such cues trigger a sense of competitive threat among the dominant group. As a result, although meaningful interracial contact may ameliorate perceptions of competitive threat to a degree, the group position model would not expect them to have a significant impact on these attitudes.

DATA AND METHODS

In order to fully explore the determinants of intergroup hostility, we designed the National Politics Study (NPS). The primary goal of the NPS is to gather comparative data about individuals' political attitudes, beliefs, aspirations, and behaviors at the beginning of the twenty-first century. Our survey went into the field in September 2004, shortly before the presidential elections, and concluded a few months later, in February 2005. All of the 3,339 interviews were conducted over the telephone. The interviews were conducted in either English or Spanish, depending on the preference of the respondent, and the overall response rate was 31 percent.

We believe that the NPS is the first multiracial and multiethnic national study of political and racial attitudes. Unlike previous efforts to study these issues, we have not focused on a single city (Bobo and Hutchings 1996; McClain et al. 2006), a single state (Bobo and Tuan 2006), or a small group of cities (Oliver and Wong 2003).[5] Instead, our study is based on a national sample of individuals, aged eighteen years or older, from a variety of different racial and ethnic groups. Specifically, we interviewed 756 African Americans, 919 non-Hispanic Whites, 404 Caribbean Blacks, 757 Hispanics, and 503 Asian Americans.[6]

There are two additional advantages that the NPS represents relative to previous multiracial surveys. First, the NPS does not concentrate solely on attitudes about racial minority groups, but also focuses on the views that other racial and ethnic groups have about Whites. That is, both the 1992 Los Angeles County Social Survey (LACSS) that serves as the dataset for the Bobo and Hutchings (1996) article on interracial tensions in Los Angeles, and the 1992–1994 Multi-City Study of Urban Inequality (MCSUI), which serves as the primary dataset for Oliver and Wong's (2003) study of intergroup prejudice, exclude questions about hostility directed at Americans of European descent. We believe that it is important to examine all sides of the complicated racial debate in this country if we are to fully understand the determinants of intergroup conflict.

A second advantage of the NPS has to do with its timing. Although both the LACSS and the MCSUI represent important, and indeed groundbreaking, efforts to catalog and ultimately explain the racial views of a diverse group of Americans, their proximity to the Los Angeles riots may have influenced responses. The fact that the LACSS was fielded in L.A. County and it was also one of the cities represented in the MCSUI survey simply amplifies this concern. In short, it is possible that the level of racial conflict reported in these studies is at least partially a result of the heightened racial tensions of the time. That the NPS was fielded over ten years after these studies allows researchers to ascertain with greater confidence the overall levels and determinants of perceptions of competitive racial threat in the absence of any national, high-profile, racialized incident.

The NPS included multiple measures of the concepts discussed above. Our primary dependent variable, *perceptions of competitive threat*, was measured with two items originally developed in 1992 for the LACSS (see Bobo and Hutchings 1996). The questions were worded as follows: "More good jobs for [INSERT GROUPS] means fewer good jobs for people like me;" and "The more influence [INSERT GROUPS] have in politics the less influence people like me will have in politics." Respondents from each of our five racial/ethnic groups were only asked about the remaining four groups in random order. Response options ranged from "strongly agree" to "agree" to "disagree" to "strongly disagree." Although we present some initial results of each item separately, for most of the rest of this chapter, these items are combined into a scale. This variable, as with all other primary independent variables in our analyses, was recoded onto a 0–1 scale. Higher values on this scale correspond to greater support for the concept of zero-sum competition.[7] The specific wording of all of our independent variables is described below.

RESULTS

Mapping the Distributions of Zero-Sum Competition

In Table 3.1, we present the mean scores on each of the two racial conflict measures, as well as the scale of the two items. The respondents' race or ethnicity is shown on the horizontal axis and the race of the target group on the vertical axis. The first column presents the results for the Whites in our sample. With respect to the job competition item, we find that a small, although by no means trivial, fraction of Whites endorse the view that more good jobs for other racial and ethnic groups means less for their group. On average, about 20 percent of the Whites in our sample endorse this view. Interestingly, no significant distinctions are made across groups for White respondents: Blacks, Hispanics, Asian Americans and Afro-Caribbeans are all treated more or less the same when it comes to Whites' beliefs about competition over jobs. Furthermore, these results are somewhat lower than what Bobo and Hutchings (1996) report for Los Angeles. In their study, they found that about 28 percent of the Whites in their sample endorsed the notion of zero-sum competition, with Asians typically perceived as the most threatening and Blacks as the least threatening.

Among African Americans, as shown in the second column of Table 3.1, perceptions of competitive racial threat are markedly different than for Whites. For one thing, Blacks are about twice as likely as Whites to agree that more good jobs for other racial groups come at the expense of people like them. Additionally, there is far more variance shown among Blacks with respect to which groups they view with the greatest suspicion. Among Blacks, the most troublesome competitors, by far, are Whites. On average, about half of African-American respondents indicate that

TABLE 3.1. *Mean scores on the zero-sum competition scale by respondents' race and race of target group*

	Respondents' race					
Target groups	White	Black	Latino	Asian	Afro-Caribbean	F-Stat.
Job Competition						
Whites	–	.50	.42	.36	.50	19.3*
Blacks	.18	–	.31	.28	.32	31.6*
Hispanics	.20	.38	–	.27	.38	46.4*
Asian Americans	.19	.40	.32	–	.38	54.7*
Afro-Caribbeans	.19	.33	.30	.26	–	29.6*
Political Competition						
Whites	–	.57	.53	.58	.55	2.6*
Blacks	.18	–	.38	.40	.34	73.6*
Hispanics	.19	.37	–	.37	.35	55.9*
Asian Americans	.18	.37	.36	–	.36	69.3*
Afro-Caribbeans	.18	.32	.35	.35	–	58.5*
Zero-Sum Scale						
Whites	–	.54	.47	.47	.53	8.4*
Blacks	.18	–	.34	.34	.33	67.5*
Hispanics	.20	.38	–	.32	.36	63.6*
Asian Americans	.18	.38	.34	–	.37	81.7*
Afro-Caribbeans	.18	.32	.32	.31	–	54.3*

Notes: * $p \leq .05$.

Whites are their competitors in the job market. In contrast, only about one-third of them express similar sentiments when it comes to Afro-Caribbeans. Although still relatively high, this lower level of perceived threat makes sense because Blacks and Afro-Caribbeans share the same racial identification even if their cultural values are sometimes at odds. Hispanics and Asian Americans fall somewhere between these two poles at .38 and .40, respectively. These figures are roughly comparable to what Bobo and Hutchings (1996) report in their study of intergroup conflict in Los Angeles.

Latinos, as represented in the third column of Table 3.1, adopt views much more similar to Blacks than to Whites. As with African Americans, Latinos perceive relatively high levels of zero-sum conflict with other groups. The levels are not quite as high as for Blacks, however. Still, Whites are again identified as the most threatening group, with all other groups scoring some ten or more points lower. Among Asians, as presented in the fourth column, Whites are also viewed as the most threatening, but the effects are considerably reduced relative to Blacks and, to a lesser extent, Latinos, at least in the realm of job competition. In the case of both Latinos and Asians, the share of respondents who see group relations in zero-sum terms is analogous to results from the LACSS.

Afro-Caribbeans represent an interesting case for the study of perceptions of competitive racial threat. This is because although they are racially indistinguishable from African Americans, their immigrant background and different cultural affinities have, at times, brought them into conflict with Black Americans (Waters 1999). As a result, it is not at all clear whether they should view the world in a manner similar to other Blacks or if their perspective is more similar to groups with larger immigrant populations such as Asians and Latinos.[8] Results for Afro-Caribbeans are presented in the fifth column of Table 3.1. As it turns out, this group perceives relations with other racial groups in ways almost identical to African Americans. As with other Blacks, about half of Afro-Caribbeans indicate that more good jobs for Whites means fewer good jobs for people like them. Slightly more than one-third adopts a similar position with respect to Hispanics and Asian Americans. And, not surprisingly, other Blacks are seen as the least threatening group, although approximately one-third endorsed this view.

The middle portion of Table 3.1 presents the results for the item on political competition. The most remarkable difference between this item and the jobs question is that perceptions of zero-sum competition are generally higher. White respondents represent an exception to this rule because, again, slightly less than 20 percent indicate agreement with the notion that other racial groups represent competitive threats to their group. Blacks also make little distinction between the two items when the target groups are other racial minorities. However, with respect to Whites, fully 57 percent of African Americans identify this group as a competitor to their racial group. Latinos are also more likely to view Whites as competitors in the political arena, with 53 percent endorsing this view. Latinos also view the remaining groups as greater threats with respect to politics, but the increase is not as large as with Whites.

As with other racial minority groups, Asian Americans are also far more concerned with Whites in the political arena than in the job market. Fifty-eight percent of Asians – the highest percentage among all groups in Table 3.1 – regard greater political influence for Whites as coming at the expense of Asian Americans. The remaining groups are also viewed as more threatening in the political arena, but as with Blacks and Latinos, Asian Americans are clearly making a distinction between their concern with the political power of White Americans and their perceptions of other racial groups. Finally, Afro-Caribbeans adopt a view very much equivalent to that of African Americans. Slightly more than half consider Whites to be a serious competitor for political influence, with slightly more than a third adopting similar beliefs about other racial groups.

The zero-sum competition scale, shown at the bottom of Table 3.1, captures the overall reactions to these items for the racial groups in our study. In general, Whites are least likely to agree that other groups are their competitors, and Blacks and Afro-Caribbeans are the most likely to see Whites as their main source of competition. Asian Americans and Latinos fall somewhere between these two groups, but their views are generally closer to African Americans and Afro-Caribbeans than they are to Whites. Additionally, although there are some interesting differences between perceptions of job and political competition, the overall pattern is about the same for both items as reflected in the scale. For these reasons, all of our subsequent analyses rely on the zero-sum competition scale.

Determinants of Zero-Sum Competition

Now that we have determined the absolute levels of support for the proposition of competitive racial threat, we turn to assessing the best explanations for these attitudes. To answer these questions, we have developed measures of all the theoretical concepts describe earlier in this paper. We measure racial prejudice with two items, one tapping notions of social distance and the other negative out-group stereotypes.[9] Group identity is measured with the traditional linked fate item as well as a question tapping whether it is more important to respondents "being American, being [RESPONDENT RACE], or are both equally important to you?"[10] The concept of racial context was measured with two items. The first asks simply, "How would you describe the ethnic mix of your current neighborhood where you live? Would you say it is mostly White, mostly black, mostly Hispanic, mostly Asian, or mixed?" Respondents who indicate that their own racial group is predominant in their neighborhood receive a value of 1, and all other responses are coded zero. The second measure of racial context asks, "How would you describe the ethnic mix of your group of friends? Would you say your friends are mostly White, mostly Black, mostly Hispanic, mostly Asian, or mixed?" Respondents who indicate that their friends are either mostly "mixed" or mostly from a racial group other than their own are coded 1 with all other responses coded zero. Finally, the concept of racial alienation was measured by asking respondents how much discrimination they believed their group encounters in the United States and how strongly they agreed or disagreed with the following question: "American society just hasn't dealt fairly with people from my background."[11] As with all of the other primary independent variables, responses were re-coded onto a 0–1 scale to ease the interpretation of coefficients across variables. All subsequent analyses also control for education, age, gender, and household income.[12]

We turn first to an examination of the results of our analyses for Whites, as shown in Table 3.2. A number of our hypotheses are supported for Whites, with perhaps the greatest explanatory power captured in the prejudice measures. Without exception, Whites who reject interracial marriage in principle (about 20 percent) are also more likely to view other racial groups as competitive threats. The magnitude of this effect across racial groups ranges from 10 to 16 points. Interestingly, the negative stereotype item is most significant in the case of African Americans and Afro-Caribbeans, the two racially Black groups. This is probably due to the fact that the stereotype about laziness has historically been applied most strongly to Blacks (Schuman, Steeh, Bobo, and Krysan 1997). This variable is only marginally significant when Latinos

TABLE 3.2. *Determinants of perceptions of zero-sum competition for whites*

Target groups	Blacks	Latinos	Asians	Afro-caribbeans
Intercept	.04	.13**	.12**	.09*
	(.04)	(.04)	(.04)	(.04)
Prejudice				
Interracial Marriage	.10***	.16***	.14***	.14***
	(.02)	(.03)	(.02)	(.02)
Negative Stereotypes	.19***	.06+	−.02	.11**
	(.03)	(.04)	(.04)	(.04)
Group Identity				
Linked Fate Perceptions	.03	.02	.01	.03+
	(.02)	(.02)	(.02)	(.02)
Racial Identity	.08**	.11**	.08**	.09**
	(.03)	(.03)	(.03)	(.03)
Racial Context				
Segregated Neighborhood	.00	−.00	.01	.00
	(.01)	(.02)	(.01)	(.01)
Racially Mixed Friends	−.03*	−.03	−.03+	−.02
	(.01)	(.02)	(.02)	(.02)
Racial Alienation				
Opportunity Structure	.05*	.09**	.07**	.05*
	(.02)	(.03)	(.03)	(.03)
Perceived Discrimination	.11***	.11***	.13***	.10**
	(.02)	(.03)	(.03)	(.03)
Adjusted R sq.	.23	.21	.21	.22
N	833	830	830	831

Notes: * $p \leq .05$; ** $p \leq .01$; *** $p \leq .001$ for two-tailed test. Models also control for education, age, gender, and household income.

are the target group, and the size of the coefficient is less than one-third that for African Americans.

The group identity measures, particularly racial identity, also contribute significantly to attitudes about competitive racial threat. The sizes of the coefficients are smaller compared to the indicators of prejudice, but they are consistent across all racial groups and all positive. Thus, although previous work has found only sporadic and relatively weak support for the idea that Whites' racial attitudes are affected by group identity, we find moderately strong support for its influence. We find little support for the racial context variables. Although Whites who indicate that they have a racially diverse group of friends are somewhat less likely to endorse zero-sum perceptions, the effects are relatively mild and inconsistent across groups. Residence in racially homogenous neighborhoods has essentially no effect on the dependent variable. This effect seems to run counter to the findings of Oliver and Wong (2003), although they relied on more objective measures rather than the subjective measures we utilize here.

TABLE 3.3. *Determinants of perceptions of zero-sum competition for blacks*

Target groups	Whites	Latinos	Asians	Afro-Caribbeans
Intercept	.04	.20**	.11	.14*
	(.07)	(.07)	(.07)	(.07)
Prejudice				
Interracial Marriage	.00	.13***	.04	.07+
	(.04)	(.04)	(.04)	(.04)
Negative Stereotypes	.16***	.04	.05	.11**
	(.04)	(.05)	(.05)	(.04)
Group Identity				
Linked Fate Perceptions	.09**	.06*	.05	.05+
	(.03)	(.03)	(.03)	(.03)
Racial Identity	.13**	.03	.10*	.07+
	(.05)	(.05)	(.05)	(.04)
Racial Context				
Segregated Neighborhood	.01	−.02	−.02	−.00
	(.02)	(.02)	(.02)	(.02)
Racially Mixed Friends	−.04+	−.03	−.01	−.01
	(.02)	(.02)	(.02)	(.02)
Racial Alienation				
Opportunity Structure	.21***	.07+	.11**	.05
	(.04)	(.04)	(.04)	(.04)
Perceived Discrimination	.17**	.08	.10+	.03
	(.06)	(.06)	(.06)	(.05)
Adjusted R sq.	.18	.07	.06	.07
N	698	694	696	694

Notes: * $p \leq .05$; ** $p \leq .01$; *** $p \leq .001$ for two-tailed test. Models also control for education, age, gender, and household income.

The racial alienation items also work as anticipated. Indeed, although the magnitudes are somewhat smaller compared to the prejudice items, the alienation measures are the most consistent predictors in the model. Each measure is related to each target group with coefficients ranging from 5 points to 13 points. Clearly, a significant determinant of perceptions of racial group competition is, at least for Whites, the sense that one's racial group has not fared as well as it should have in America. Interestingly, this sense of racial disenfranchisement has a much more consistent effect than was demonstrated in the Bobo and Hutchings (1996) examination of Los Angeles. They found that racial alienation only affected perceptions of zero-sum competition when the target group was Blacks. It is unclear whether these broader effects are due to the larger national sample or to the greater salience that Hispanics and Asian Americans have taken on since the 1990s.

Table 3.3 presents our results for African Americans. Here, the results seem to differ somewhat, depending on the target group. In the case of Whites, the most powerful explanatory variables are both measures of racial alienation. The coefficients on the opportunity structure item and the perceived discrimination item are .21 and .17, respectively. This translates into a roughly 20 percent shift in support of the view that Whites represent a competitive threat as one moves from the least to the most alienated. The next most influential variable is the stereotype measure. Recall that, in the case of Whites, this measure does not ask about the group's propensity to be lazy but rather whether Whites want to keep minorities down. Blacks who subscribe to this view are significantly more likely to view Whites as competitors.

Group identity also plays an important role in shaping views about competitive racial threat with Whites. Unlike some previous research, however, we find that higher levels of group identity are associated with more insular racial views rather than the reverse. Although contrary to some recent work, this finding is very much in keeping with the theoretical expectations of the group position model.

When the target group is Latinos, we find that racial alienation plays a much smaller role. Although the opportunity structure item achieves borderline statistical significance, the magnitude of this effect is much smaller than was the case for Whites. Further, in contrast to the situation with Whites, the social distance prejudice measure turns out to be a strong predictor of the view that Latinos' success comes at the expense of Blacks. The negative stereotype item has no effect here. The group identity items are also less powerful compared to when Whites were the target group, but the results are significant for the linked fate item and, again, positive. Finally, the racial context measures fall well short of statistical significance. These findings may differ from the MCSUI results because of the broader sample on which we rely.

The effects for Asian Americans are, in some respect, closer to what we uncovered for Whites. Here we find that Blacks who believe that the opportunity structure has been closed to their group or who believe that their group has faced discrimination are most inclined to view Asians as competitors. The only other significant variable is the linked fate item that, again, suggests that higher levels of group identity are associated with a greater likelihood of viewing Asians as a competitive threat.

When Afro-Caribbeans are the target group, as shown in the last column of Table 3.3, almost all of the predictors appear to be muted. This is not unexpected because of all the groups in our study, Afro-Caribbeans are the most closely aligned with African Americans. And, as we saw in Table 3.1, Blacks seem the least concerned with encroachments from this group. Still, although the racial alienation measures are predictably weak for this group, we do find that the stereotype measure predicts support for the view that more for this group means less for African Americans. Interestingly, the group identity measures also achieve borderline significance, although again, they suggest that higher levels of identity are associated with greater concern about the implications of success for other groups.

In Table 3.4, we examine the effects of our predictor variables on the racial attitudes of Hispanic Americans. For this group, the largest and most consistent predictor variables are the racial alienation measures, especially the item about the opportunity structure in America. Further, as with Blacks, the effects of these variables are

TABLE 3.4. *Determinants of perceptions of zero-sum competition for Latinos*

Target groups	Whites	Blacks	Asians	Afro-Caribbeans
Intercept	.16*	.14*	.25***	.22***
	(.07)	(.07)	(.06)	(.06)
Immigrant	.01	.06**	.07**	.07**
	(.03)	(.02)	(.02)	(.02)
Prejudice				
Interracial Marriage	−.02	.04	−.01	.02
	(.04)	(.04)	(.04)	(.04)
Negative Stereotypes	.11**	.12**	−.05	−.01
	(.04)	(.04)	(.05)	(.05)
Group Identity				
Linked Fate Perceptions	.04	−.01	−.01	.00
	(.03)	(.03)	(.03)	(.03)
Racial Identity	.14**	.04	.05	.03
	(.05)	(.05)	(.05)	(.05)
Racial Context				
Segregated Neighborhood	.02	.04+	.04	.05*
	(.02)	(.02)	(.02)	(.02)
Racially Mixed Friends	−.02	−.01	−.03	−.02
	(.02)	(.02)	(.02)	(.02)
Racial Alienation				
Opportunity Structure	.17***	.12***	.10**	.10**
	(.03)	(.03)	(.03)	(.03)
Perceived	.10*	.03	.02	.02
Discrimination	(.05)	(.04)	(.04)	(.04)
Adjusted R sq.	.12	.10	.09	.09
N	692	689	688	688

Notes: * $p \leq .05$; ** $p \leq .01$; *** $p \leq .001$ for two-tailed test. Models also control for education, age, gender, and household income.

especially strong when the target group is White Americans, as shown in the first column. Only when Whites are the reference group do both variables achieve statistical significance. Negative stereotypes about Whites and racial identity also play an important role in structuring perceptions of competitive racial threat, but the racial context variables again fail to achieve statistical significance.

When the target group is African Americans, racial alienation still plays a prominent role in organizing Latino perceptions of intergroup conflict. Negative stereotypes about Blacks also play a significant role here, although interestingly, group identity does not. Finally, whether or not one was born in this country also contributes to perceptions of competitive threat. As Kaufmann (2003) also found, immigrants are more likely to view Blacks as competitors than Latinos who were born in this country.

TABLE 3.5. *Determinants of perceptions of zero-sum competition for Asians*

Target groups	Whites	Blacks	Latinos	Afro-Caribbeans
Intercept	.26**	.08	.15*	.22**
	(.08)	(.08)	(.08)	(.08)
Immigrant	.07**	.13***	.11***	.11***
	(.03)	(.03)	(.03)	(.03)
Prejudice				
Interracial Marriage	.06	.09*	.05	.04
	(.05)	(.05)	(.05)	(.05)
Negative Stereotypes	.03	.16**	.12*	.01
	(.06)	(.06)	(.06)	(.07)
Group Identity				
Linked Fate Perceptions	.08*	.06+	.07*	.06+
	(.03)	(.03)	(.03)	(.03)
Racial Identity	.06	.01	.03	.04
	(.05)	(.05)	(.05)	(.05)
Racial Context				
Segregated Neighborhood	.06	−.01	.01	−.02
	(.05)	(.05)	(.04)	(.04)
Racially Mixed Friends	−.04	.00	−.00	−.02
	(.02)	(.02)	(.02)	(.02)
Racial Alienation				
Opportunity Structure	.28***	.09**	.10**	.07*
	(.04)	(.04)	(.04)	(.04)
Perceived Discrimination	.01	−.03	−.09+	−.06
	(.05)	(.05)	(.05)	(.05)
Adjusted R sq.	.19	.13	.12	.08
N	412	411	413	411

Notes: * p ≤ .05; ** p ≤ .01; *** p ≤ .001 for two-tailed test. Models also control for education, age, gender, and household income.

In the case of Asian Americans and Afro-Caribbeans, Latinos attitudes are structured almost entirely by measures of racial alienation and immigrant status and nothing else. The one exception occurs for the neighborhood racial composition variable. In the case of Afro-Caribbeans, this variable achieves statistical significance, which is in keeping with the general thrust of Oliver and Wong (2003) but not their specific findings. That is, although they find that Latinos – at least in Los Angeles – are more likely to adopt negative stereotypes about Blacks when their neighborhoods become more racially isolated, they do not find this to be the case for perceptions of competitive threat.[13] In any case, the effects are not especially large relative to the effects of alienation and prejudice, but they do mirror the borderline effects found when Blacks are the target group.

The results for Asian Americans are presented in Table 3.5. Once again, the most consistent predictors are for the racial alienation items, especially the indicator of attitudes about the opportunity structure. When Whites are the target group, this variable is more than three times the size of any of our other primary independent variables. Linked fate perceptions also play an important role in shaping Asian attitudes about other groups. As with African Americans, higher levels of linked fate are associated with a greater propensity to view Whites as competitors for scarce resources. The only other significant variable when Whites are the target group is immigration status. Asian Americans who were not born in this country are more likely to view relations with White Americans as zero-sum.

With Blacks as the target group, the only other variables aside from the alienation item to achieve statistical significance are the prejudice variables, the measure of immigration status, and, to a limited extent, the linked fate item. For Asian Americans, both opposition to interracial marriage in principle and the acceptance of negative stereotypes about African Americans contribute to the perception that greater success for Blacks comes at the expense of Asians. In the case of immigration status, the effects are particularly large. Indeed, immigration status is a consistently significant variable across racial groups, but the effects are particularly large for Blacks. This finding may reflect some of the tensions that Asian immigrant group have had with African Americans in a number of cities across the country (Kim 2000).

Results similar to African Americans are uncovered when Latinos and Afro-Caribbeans are the target groups. Immigration status is an important predictor, as are linked fate perceptions and, at least in the case of Latinos, negative stereotypes. Racial context variable again fails to achieve statistical significance. The one noteworthy departure from previous results is the effects of perceived discrimination. Although the effects are of only borderline significance, the coefficient is negative when Latinos are the target group, suggesting that alienated Asians are *less* likely to view Latinos as competitors. This finding runs counter to our theoretical expectations, but its singular nature suggests that we should not read too much into this result.

In our last table, we examine the determinants of zero-sum perception among Afro-Caribbeans. Once again, we find that the most consistent effects occur for the measures of racial alienation, particularly the opportunity structure item. Also, similar to all other groups in our analyses, racial alienation is most strongly triggered when Whites are the target group. No other variable comes close to matching the magnitude of this effect for Afro-Caribbeans. In addition to racial alienation, we also find that the racial diversity of one's friendship network influences perceptions of competitive threat. As with Whites in Table 3.2, Afro-Caribbeans who socialize with a more diverse group of friends are also less likely to view Whites as competitors. Negative stereotypes and immigration status also contribute to perceptions of competitive threat, although these effects are of only borderline statistical significance.

The second column of Table 3.6 presents the results for other Blacks as the target group. Given that all Caribbean Americans in our sample racially identify as Black,

TABLE 3.6. *Determinants of perceptions of zero-sum competition for Afro-caribbeans*

Target groups	Whites	Blacks	Latinos	Asians
Intercept	.19+	.41***	.34***	.30**
	(.10)	(.09)	(.09)	(.09)
Immigrant	.07+	.13***	.10**	.08*
	(.04)	(.04)	(.04)	(.04)
Prejudice				
Interracial Marriage	−.02	.06	.01	.04
	(.06)	(.05)	(.06)	(.06)
Negative Stereotypes	.11+	.02	.11+	.02
	(.06)	(.06)	(.07)	(.07)
Group Identity				
Linked Fate Perceptions	.00	.02	−.00	−.04
	(.05)	(.04)	(.04)	(.04)
Racial Identity	−.08	−.14*	−.15*	−.06
	(.08)	(.07)	(.07)	(.07)
Racial Context				
Segregated Neighborhood	.05	.02	.02	.02
	(.04)	(.03)	(.03)	(.03)
Racially Mixed Friends	−.08*	−.03	.02	−.02
	(.04)	(.03)	(.04)	(.04)
Racial Alienation				
Opportunity Structure	.20***	.04	.12*	.12**
	(.05)	(.05)	(.05)	(.05)
Perceived Discrimination	.10	−.08	−.08	−.01
	(.07)	(.07)	(.07)	(.07)
Adjusted R sq.	.10	.07	.06	.02
N	354	355	353	354

Notes: $+ p \leq .10$ * $p \leq .05$; ** $p \leq .01$; *** $p \leq .001$ for two-tailed test. Models also control for education, age, gender, and household income.

we do not expect the same effects for our independent variables. As anticipated, the racial alienation items fall short of statistical significance (similar effects occurred for Blacks when Afro-Caribbeans were the target group) for this group. Similarly, the prejudice items and racial context measures have no effect. In the case of racial identity, the effects run counter to what we have uncovered with other groups. The negative, and statistically significant, coefficient on this variable indicates that respondents who identify with their racial group are also less likely to view other Blacks as competitive threats. Only in the case of immigrant status are results consistent with the results of previous groups. Here we find that Afro-Caribbeans born outside the United States are more likely to view other Blacks as competitors for their group.

In the case of Latinos and Asian Americans, very little achieves statistical significance beyond the alienation variables. When Asians are the target group, the one exception is the immigrant status variable. Once again, Afro-Caribbeans born outside the United States are more apt to view the out-group as succeeding at the expense of their group. This is also true in the case of Latinos. Interestingly, for this group, the racial identity measure is also significant and has a negative sign. This may be due to the fact that many Afro-Caribbeans hail from parts of the world that are also heavily populated by Hispanics.

CONCLUSION

This work has sought to describe and explain perceptions of intergroup conflict among a multiracial national sample of Americans. In general, we found that such perceptions varied across groups, although a majority – or near-majority – of racial minority group members perceived relations with Whites in zero-sum terms. We examined four distinct, although not necessarily competing, theoretical perspectives to account for these attitudes: the classical prejudice model; the group identity model; the racial context hypothesis; and the group position model. Although we found some support for each of the theories we examined, the group position model provided the most consistent and comprehensive explanation.

Building on the work of Bobo and Hutchings (1996), we argued that an important implication of the group position model was that individuals who felt that their racial or ethnic group had been alienated by society should feel most threatened by the economic and political success of other groups. Our measures of racial alienation turned out to be highly predictive of perceptions of competitive racial threat for Whites, Blacks, Latinos, Asian Americans, and Afro-Caribbeans. In the case of Whites, both measures – attitudes about the nation's opportunity structure for their group and perceptions of discrimination against the in-group – were predictive of perceptions of zero-sum competition with racial minorities. For other groups, the measures were somewhat more uneven. For example, in the case of Black respondents, neither measure worked very well when the target groups were Latinos or Afro-Carribeans. In the case of Latino respondents, perceptions of discrimination were only significant when Whites were the target group. In the case of Afro-Caribbeans, perceptions of discrimination never achieved conventional levels of statistical significance. We suspect that much of this unevenness is a result of the applicability of the concept to the relevant target group and the length of time each group has had to develop socially constructed grievances in the United States. That is, it is not surprising that a sense of group position should not characterize relations between African Americans and Afro-Caribbeans, given the significant overlap in these identities. Similarly, the particular grievance regarding discrimination should be applied less often to other racial minority groups because they are likely not seen as the primary source of discrimination. For racial minorities, this distinction is reserved for Whites, and for this target group, the racial alienation measures are typically more consistent and more powerful.

Both racial prejudice and group identity also demonstrated an important influence on perceptions of competitive racial threat. This was particularly true for White respondents, for whom the racial prejudice measures were usually the most powerful predictors. Still, these results are not inconsistent with the group position model. As indicated earlier in this chapter, this theory anticipates a role for negative out-group stereotypes and in-group preference in structuring attitudes about intergroup conflict. However, the classical prejudice model is usually interpreted as dismissing the importance of group interest concerns. Our results undermine this view of prejudice. Further, although contrary to some previous work, we find that in-group preference works very much as anticipated by the group position model. Individuals who express greater levels of group identification are also more likely to view other groups as competitors. We found that this was true both of Whites and racial minorities. The one exception to this pattern was among Afro-Carribeans. We found that, alone among the groups in our sample, their sense of competition with other Blacks and Latinos decreased as their level of group identification increased. Interestingly, even among Afro-Caribbeans, this relationship did not occur when either Whites or Asian Americans were the target group.

We found little support for the contact hypothesis in our analyses. Almost without exception, we found that the racial make-up of one's neighborhood or friendship network had no effect on perceptions of zero-sum competition. Our results run counter to the findings of Oliver and Wong (2003), although their work is based on objective measures of racial context whereas we relied on more subjective measures. In future versions of this research, we hope to incorporate additional objective measures or racial context to sort out the discrepancies between these two sets of findings.

Aside from the support and extension of the group position model, our analyses also demonstrate that the increasing complexity of racial politics in this country has not diminished. A significant fraction of Whites, and at times a majority of Blacks, Latinos, Asians, and Afro-Caribbeans, continue to view race relations in zero-sum terms. Moreover, a sense of racial alienation is overwhelmingly embraced by racial minorities and contributes mightily to perceptions of intergroup conflict.[14] The growing number of immigrant groups may complicate our discussion of racial politics, but we see no evidence that the color line will be any less problematic in the twenty-first century than it was in the twentieth century.

NOTES

1　In this paper we use the terms "Black" and "African American" interchangeably. Similarly, we also use the terms "Hispanic" and "Latino" to describe the same population. "White" describes all Americans of European ancestry.

2 According to some reports, as many as 600,000 people marched in Los Angeles, 400,000 in Chicago, and somewhat smaller turnouts were recorded in San Francisco, Houston, and other location throughout the country.

3 Oliver and Wong (2003) recognize that self-selection may account for some of these effects. That is, individuals predisposed to be racially tolerant may be more likely to seek out interracial neighborhoods in which to live. Although they find some support for this among Whites in their data, this does not apparently explain the positive effects of interracial contact among Blacks and Latinos.

4 In later versions of this work, we plan to geo-code the survey data so that we can examine the effects of broader, and objectively defined, racial contexts on perceptions of racial competition.

5 Kaufmann (2003) relied on a 1999 *Washington Post*/ Henry J. Kaiser Family Foundation/Harvard University survey in her examination of Latino attitudes about African Americans. Although this survey contained a significant number of Latinos (2,417) and Whites (1,802), it included only 285 Black respondents. Additionally, the survey included a small national sample, but was primarily based on a variety of state level samples including California, Texas, Florida, Illinois, New York, and Washington, D.C.

6 Unlike in the U.S. Census, respondents were not asked whether or not they considered themselves Hispanic before the racial question. Instead, the Hispanic category was treated as a mutually exclusive option alongside the traditional racial categories. Afro-Caribbeans were identified by asking respondents if they consider themselves to be of "Caribbean or West Indian descent," or if they or any of their ancestors are "from any of the following countries: Bahamas, Belize, Bermuda, Guyana, Haiti, or Panama?" These latter countries were singled out because we have learned from prior surveys that sometimes individuals from these countries do not consider themselves to be from the Caribbean. Only respondents who had previously identified themselves as Black and answered affirmatively to either of the two items mentioned above were classified as Afro-Caribbean.

7 As with all other attitudinal variables in our analyses, those few respondents who indicated "don't know" or "refuse" were re-coded into the midpoint.

8 Fifty-two percent of the Afro-Caribbeans in our sample were born outside of the United States, compared to 55 percent of Hispanics and 75 percent of Asian Americans. Only 3 percent of African Americans and 6 percent of Whites indicated that they were born outside of the United States.

9 Attitudes about social distance were measured by asking respondents how strongly they agreed or disagreed with the following statement: "I would approve if someone in my family married a person of a different racial or ethnic background." Negative stereotypes were measured by asking respondents "where would you rate [RACIAL/ETHNIC GROUP] in general on a scale of 1 to 7 where 1 indicates lazy and 7 means hard working and 4 indicates most [RACIAL/ETHNIC GROUP] are not closer to one end or the other." Both items have been re-coded onto a 0–1 scale so that higher values indicate greater racial prejudice. Since the laziness variable has less historic applicability to Whites, we have substituted a more relevant negative stereotype for this group: the belief that Whites are racially prejudiced. Specifically, this item asks, "On the whole, do you think that most White people want to see [R RACE, except Whites fill in "racial and ethnic minorities"] get a better break, do they want to keep [R RACE, except Whites fill in "racial and ethnic minorities"]

down, or don't they care one way or the other?" Responses are re-coded on to 0–1 scale.

10 The linked fate question asks, "Do you think what happens generally to [R RACE] people in this country will have something to do with what happens in your life?" Respondent who indicate that the answer is "yes" to this question are then asked if it affects them "a lot, some or not very much?" Responses to this question were re-coded onto a 0–1 scale, with higher values indicating greater support for linked fate. For the racial identity item, responses were also re-coded on to a 0–1 scale, with priority given to ones racial identity coded as "1."

11 Specifically, the questions on perceptions of discrimination asks, "Now I would like to ask you about how much discrimination or unfair treatment you think different groups face in the U.S. Do you think the following groups face a lot of discrimination, some, a little, or no discrimination at all?" Response options range from "a lot" to "some" to "a little" to "none."

12 In the case of Hispanics, Asian Americans, and Afro-Caribbeans, we also control for immigrant status. Kaufmann (2003) has shown that Latino immigrants are less likely than others to view their interests as being in common with Blacks.

13 Oliver and Wong (2003) measure these attitudes exactly as we have in the NPS.

14 For example, we found that 80 percent of Blacks either strongly agreed or agreed with the notion that America has not dealt fairly with their group. Comparable percentages among Whites, Latinos, Asians, and Afro-Caribbeans were 15 percent, 47 percent, 47 percent, and 54 percent, respectively. Similarly, more than 90 percent of Blacks believed that their group faced at least some discrimination in the United States. About 41 percent of Whites, 84 percent of Hispanics, 71 percent of Asian Americans, and 81 perent of Afro-Caribbeans view their groups as experiencing at least some discrimination.

REFERENCES

Adorno T. W., E. Frankel-Brunswick, D. J. Levinson, and R. N. Sanford. 1950. *The Authoritarian Personality*. New York: Harper & Row.

Allport, Gordon W. 1954. *The Nature of Prejudice*. Garden City, NY: Doubleday Anchor.

Blumer, Herbert. 1958. "Race Prejudice as a Sense of Group Position." *Pacific Sociological Review* 1: 3–7.

Bobo, Lawrence D., and Vincent L. Hutchings. 1996. "Perceptions of Racial Group Competition: Extending Blumer's Theory of Group Position to a Multiracial Social Context." *American Sociological Review* 61: 951–72.

Bobo, Lawrence D., and Mia Tuan. 2006. *Prejudice in Politics: Group Position, Public Opinion, and the Wisconsin Treaty Rights Dispute*. Cambridge, MA and London: Harvard University Press.

Davis, Darren W., and Ronald E. Brown. 2002. "The Antipathy of Black Nationalism: Behavioral and Attitudinal Implications of an African American Ideology." *American Journal of Political Science* 46: 239–52.

Giles, M. W., and M. A. Buckner. 1993. "David Duke and Black Threat: An Old Hypothesis Revisited." *Journal of Politics* 57: 221–8.

Glaser, James M. 1994. "Back to the Black Belt: Racial Environment and White Racial Attitudes in the South." *Journal of Politics* 56: 21–41.

Gurin Patricia, Shirley Hatchett, and James Jackson. 1989. *Hope and Independence: Blacks' Response to Electoral and Party Politics*. New York: Russell Sage Foundation.

Herring, M., T. B. Jankowski, and R. E. Brown. 1999. "Pro-Black Doesn't Mean Anti-White: The Structure of African-American Group Identity." *Journal of Politics* 61: 363–86.

Kaufmann, Karen M. 2003. "Cracks in the Rainbow: Group Commonality as a Basis for Latino and African-American Political Coalitions." *Political Research Quarterly* 56(2): 199–210.

Key, V. O. 1949. *Southern Politics in State and Nation.* Knoxville, TN: University of Tennessee Press.

Kim, Claire Jean. 2000. *Bitter Fruit: The Politics of Black-Korean Conflict in* New York City. New Haven, CT: Yale University Press.

Kinder, Donald R., and David O. Sears. 1981. "Prejudice and Politics: Symbolic Racism versus Racial Threats to the Good Life." *Journal of Personality and Social Psychology* 40: 414–31.

McClain, Paula D., Niambi M. Carter, Monique L. Lyle, Jeffrey D. Grynaviski, Shayla C. Nunnally, Thomas J. Scotto, J. Alan Kendrick, and Gerald F. Lackey. 2006. "Racial Distancing in a Southern City: Latino Immigrants' Views of Black Americans." *Journal of Politics* 68(3): 557–584.

Nasser, Haya El. 1992. "Hispanics Arrested Most During L.A. Riots, Says Studies." *USA Today*, June 18, 11A.

Oliver, J. Eric, and Janelle Wong. 2003. "Intergroup Prejudice in Multiethnic Settings." *American Journal of Political Science* 47(4): 567–82.

Saul, Michael, and Lisa Colangelo. 2005. "*I'll Never Run Again, Says Mike: Will Turn to Charity When Term is Over.*" New York Daily News November 10.

Schuman, Howard, and Charlotte Steeh, Lawrence D. Bobo, and Maria Krysan. 1997. *Racial Attitudes in America: Trends and Interpretations.* Rev. Ed. Cambridge, MA: Harvard University Press.

Sears, David O., Colette Van Laar, Mary Carrillo, and Rick Kosterman. 1997. "Is It Really Racism? The Origins of White Americans Opposition to Race-Targeted Policies." *Public Opinion Quarterly* 61(1): 16–53.

Sears, David O. et al. 1999. "Cultural Diversity and Multicultural Politics: Is Ethnic Balkanization Inevitable?" pg. 35–79 in *Cultural Divides: Understanding and Overcoming Group Conflict* (35-79), ed. D. A. Prentice and D.T. Miller. New York: Russell Sage Foundation.

Sears, David O. and Donald R. Kinder. 1985. "Whites' Opposition to Busing: On Conceptualizing and Operationalizing Group Conflict." *Journal of Personality and Socical Psychology* 48: 1148–61.

Sidanius, Jim, and Felicia Pratto. 1999. *Social Dominance: An Intergroup Theory of Social Hierarchy and Oppression.* New York: Cambridge University Press.

Sniderman, Paul M., and Edward G. Carmines. 1997. *Reaching Beyond Race.* Cambridge: Harvard University Press.

Sniderman, Paul M., and Thomas Piazza. 2002. *Black Pride and Black Prejudice.* Princeton, NJ: Princeton University Press.

Taylor, Marylee C. 2000. "The Significance of Racial Context." In *Racialized Politics: The Debate about Racism in America* (118–36), ed. D. O. Sears, J. Sidanius and L. Bobo, Chicago: University of Chicago Press.

Waters, Mary C. 1999. *Black Identities: West Indian Immigrant Dreams and American Realities.* New York: Russell Sage Foundation.

Welch, Susan, Lee Sigelman, T. Bledsoe, and Michael Combs. 2001. *Race & Place: Race Relations in an American City.* Cambridge: Cambridge University Press.

PART II

Courts and the Regulation of the Electoral Process

Overview: Mapping Election Law's Interior

David Schleicher

This chapter is full of innovative and highly individual work. While each piece is valuable on its own, together they form something of a cross-section of contemporary work in election law, providing us with an opportunity to see the interests and ambitions of the field as a whole. After a decade in which theoretical engagement took a bit of a back seat to studying the machinery of elections, the pieces in the chapter reveal a field in which scholars are once again asking big questions about how law interacts with and shapes the practice of democracy. Each piece builds on methodological insights of election law's first generation of theoretical work, which was created to understand how the Supreme Court addresses, and should address, problems like legislative self-dealing and limits on minority representation. But they apply them to new problems, taking the study of election law outside of the confines of the courthouse or even outside of the country, examining questions ranging from how to change the process through which election laws are created in the first place to what form judicial review of election law should take in transitional democracies. Further, they each incorporate new ways of thinking about the bodies that either regulate or are regulated by election law, adding to previous models ideas about how voters develop political opinions, how opinions affect the perceived legitimacy of elections, and how courts decide election cases. If the first generation of work in the field provided both a methodology for studying election law and a map of the coastline of the possible issues election law scholars could address, the papers in this section reveal a field ready to explore a vast interior of possible topics.

Before launching into this bout of navel-gazing, though, it is worth it to discuss – very briefly – the history of the study of the field of the "law of democracy" or election law.

When the field was created in the 1990s, its ambitions were very, very big indeed. It was decidedly not simply an effort to study election law rules, but rather a deeper inquiry into the role law plays in self-governance. In an article summing up the state of the field near the end of the decade, two of its leading figures, Samuel

Issacharoff and Rick Pildes, stated: "Ultimately our concern is with the structural aspects of constitutional law, not the regulatory arcana of elections. Approaching the law of democracy from this vantage point makes the field not a derivative and limited domain but a body of ideas that reflect the meaning and assumptions of constitutional law itself" (Issacharoff and Pildes 1999: 1183).

However, the goal was not to incorporate the law of democracy into general constitutional law, but to *remove* the study of the legal aspects of self-governance from general constitutional law, because applying ordinary methods in constitutional challenges to election rules caused the Supreme Court to develop deeply inconsistent, theoretically unmoored election law jurisprudence. "The conventional frameworks of individual rights, compelling state interests, First Amendment freedoms, and the ubiquitous debate over the legitimacy of judicial review all made their predictable, and most often uninformative, appearances" (Ibid.). Instead, these scholars sought to create a field that was able to understand how law, and particularly constitutional law, shaped and should shape how we elect our leaders and how we think about politics.

And so they did. Pam Karlan, Michael Klarman, Richard Niemi, Daniel Ortiz, Issacharoff, Pildes, and others (and, a little later, some of their students like Heather Gerken and Guy Charles) generated a body of scholarship that criticized the Supreme Court's election law jurisprudence and its reliance on the logic of individual rights. (For excellent summaries of this work, see Charles 2005: 1115–1141; Charles 2007: 650–656.) First, they argued that election law cases fundamentally are about groups seeking to aggregate their voices and thereby influence government, not individuals seeking to avoid government sanction. Second, courts engaging in judicial review in election cases are differently situated than they are in ordinary constitutional cases, because election laws govern the selection of the legislatures that promulgate them and thus put courts reviewing them in an arguably promajoritarian rather than countermajoritarian role. Looking at issues like standing in election cases, racial gerrymandering, and ballot access, they argued that, despite its rhetoric, the Supreme Court reviews election law cases not with individual rights in mind, but as a method of regulating the structure of politics. As Karlan stated, the "Court deploys the Equal Protection Clause not to protect the rights of an identifiable group of individuals, particularly a group unable to protect itself through operation of the normal political processes, but rather to regulate the institutional arrangements within which politics is conducted" (Karlan 2001: 1346). The scholars of the "structural turn" argued it should do so with theoretical clarity about how its jurisprudence fits into and will improve democratic outcomes.

The central piece in the field from this period is Pildes and Issacharoff's well-known article, *Politics as Markets: Partisan Lockups of the Democratic Process*, which provided a compelling and universal model for analyzing all election law claims for their harms to the responsiveness of legislators to democratic pressures (Issacharoff and Pildes 1998: 643). They argued that courts should review election laws passed by legislatures in much the same way as antitrust regulators reviewed acts undertaken by monopolists, asking whether laws had unjustifiable anticompetitive effects. This work mushroomed into a research project in which scholars used "politics as markets" style of reasoning to examine virtually every election law rule in an ever-more economically and politically sophisticated manner (see, e.g., Issacharoff and Karlan 1999: 1705; Pildes 1999: 1605; Issacharoff 2001: 275; Pildes 2004: 142; Schleicher 2006: 163). It was also challenged on theoretical grounds by a group of scholars, including Dan Lowenstein, Rick Hasen, and Nate Persily, who developed a critique based on the difficulties of judges and other putatively independent bodies using political theory to create a body of constitutional law, particularly one that was not connected closely to the Constitution's text (Lowenstein 2000: 264; Persily 2002: 649; Hasen 2004, 130).

This was big, heady stuff. However, although there has been much innovative work in the field, the last decade or so has not seen the same fireworks.[1] Instead, it has been as much about "regulatory arcana" as it has been about big theoretical questions about the Constitution and the meaning of self-governance. Anyone who has participated in the field over the last decade has heard far more than they ever expected to hear about things like the promise and perils of optical scan voting machines, or the methods by which challenges can be offered to disputed ballots in during recounts. Even the big arguments of the decade, like Issacharoff's titanic *Harvard Law Review* debate with Persily over how the Supreme Court should address partisan gerrymandering, were more about the application of relatively settled theoretical models to new problems than they were about carving out a new conception of what election law does and can do (Issacharoff 2002a: 593; Persily 2002: 649; Issacharoff 2002b, 649).

Why did this change occur? There are two major reasons. The first is *Bush v. Gore*, which generated an incredible amount of popular and scholarly attention for issues in election law, but also revealed the frailties of the machinery of American democracy. Faced with a visibly crumbling election system, a sharply divided population, and ever-more litigious political party operations, it just seemed more important to understand the arcana than it might have seemed in 1999.

But his is not the only reason. The "problem" is that the scholars of the structural turn in election law scholarship largely succeeded in their scholarly aims. Although the Supreme Court has not accepted its logic (or has only done so intermittently), and while there are still disagreements about some of its implications, the work generated a clear, consistent, and normatively attractive theory of election law jurisprudence and applied it to virtually every type of election law problem. Similarly, those opposed to the "politics as markets" approach and the structural turn in election law generally – like Hasen and Lowenstein – created a consistent critique of this work that also was able to address a range of topics in election law and the Court also has only listened intermittently.) For many of big issues addressed by the Supreme Court, the scholarship had fleshed out the issues as well as they could be fleshed out, and the sides were clearly drawn. The question was where the field should go next.

The papers in this section represent efforts to break new theoretical ground in the study of election law, to move the discussion beyond the stasis and niggling details it found itself stuck in for much of the 2000s. Reading them, one is reminded of the comparison Paul Krugman drew between economic modeling and the history of cartography during his well-known Ohlin lectures.[2] (Krugman 1995, 1–6, 66–81). Premodern maps included detailed information about the interiors of countries and continents, both about topography and populations. Even though some of the information was untrue, and they weren't scientific about where everything was exactly, these premodern maps contained a great deal. When map makers first developed the tools of modern cartography, they were able to use them to sketch coastlines extremely accurately. But once they did so, they were no longer willing to use the rough-and-ready style of map making that preceded them. The result was maps with detailed coastlines and empty interiors. The new technology had led to both increases and decreases in understanding. It was only later, when the new tools could be applied to the interior of continents, that maps again contained the information that the premodern maps had, but now had that information with a greater degree of accuracy.

Krugman notes that the history of economic modeling worked in roughly the same way. Once economists decided to mathematize and systematize their work, a great deal of premathematic economic reasoning had to be abandoned, not because it was wrong, but because it could not be rendered in a formal fashion easily. Only later, when mathematical advances and computers made modeling certain things easier, did economists return to areas with problems like agglomeration economics or the relationship between monopolistic competition and international trade. However, when they did, they did with far greater accuracy than the economists who worked in these areas before the modeling revolution.

"Politics as Markets" and the related work created a similar map. In order to get traction on how law integrates with political processes and the values underlying American democracy, they had to exclude a great deal. The central moves – for example, the analogy between courts and market regulators, the focus on representation as the goal of elections – provided a clear way to study one type of problem, specifically how the Supreme Court should address anticompetitive election laws generated by self-interested legislatures. Focusing on a single type of problem inside the broader world of regulation of democratic processes with a single set of tools, the scholarship was able to get analytical purchase on how election rules shaped incentives among parties and voters and how rules could be used by insiders to generate antidemocratic outcomes. The method drained away the confusing rights-talk of courts and the mishmash of political theories that undergirded much discussion of election law. Doing so was necessary to create a framework for understanding the effects of election law on American politics. But they were also necessarily parsimonious, using simplified versions of who regulates elections, what goals electoral competition serves, and how voters behave, in order to be able to provide predictive and normative force (see Pildes 1999, 1606; Schleicher 2006, 163). Much like the maps of the early modern period, they provided clear guidance about how to understand the shore, but left much of the interior unmapped.

These papers suggest ways to fill in the map of interior of election law. Each uses a new technology or methodology to suggest a way to add to the structural picture drawn in the field's earlier days. These build on the analysis provided by work of the 1990s (including Rick Hasen's contribution, which builds on his critique of those earlier models). But they draw on strands from the political science and economic literature about elections – about voter ignorance, party behavior, and the like – that could not fit into the early structural analysis, which needed parsimony in order to cover the range of election law topics. They also tackle questions that are different in kind from the ones addressed in the 1990s.

Election law scholarship has been largely "juriscentric," studying how courts, usually the Supreme Court, address constitutional challenges to already-passed election laws that entrench parties or incumbents or deny protected rights. In "The Institutional Turn in Election Law Scholarship," Heather Gerken and Michael Kang address, a problems in election law's interior: How election laws, particularly anti-competitive or otherwise suspect laws, are formed in the first place and how the process of generating election laws can be improved. They propose an "institutional turn," consisting of a number of "hard" and "soft" suggestions about how the tools of election law analysis – an understanding how laws can shape individual and political party incentives and therefore channel political competition – can be used to make it possible for election reform to get passed by legislatures rather than imposed by courts.

The paper consists largely of a summary of a large and fascinating research project – led by Gerken and including substantial work by scholars like Kang, Chris Elmendorf, Ned Foley, and Sam Hirsch – that has examined how to create an attractive political atmosphere for political reform. The "hard" suggestions are laws that could be used to shape political incentives in ways that favor election reform, like requiring districting to be done in a formalized competitive process, as suggested by Hirsch, or to be voted on directly by voters, as suggested by Kang. The soft approaches are informational. Gerken's "Democracy Index" proposal, endorsed by President Obama, among others, would create a ranking of state election law systems along a number of objective criteria, giving voters a metric to assess the performance of their elected state election regulators (Gerken 2009, 7). Similarly, they promote "shadow institutions," like advisory commissions and "amicus courts," that would provide information to political actors and regulators about how they should behave and provide information to voters by creating a contrast between the actual behavior of actors and these idealized shadow institutions.

The key to the "institutional turn" is not only that it focuses on a different moment in the election law development process than much of the traditional work in the field, but that it promotes a somewhat different conception of how voters form their preferences. Following Anthony Downs, much of the election law work has used an implicit model of voters with static and preexisting preferences about policies, and understood election law as governing the ways in which candidates and parties compete for the allegiance of these voters. However, election law rules, particularly the existence of a party label on the ballot, are central in how people form preferences (Gerken 2009; Schleicher 2010, 40). Gerken and Kang's proposals for new institutions are as focused on the problem of how election law rules shape voter preferences (and therefore shape new election law rules) as they are on the behavior of institutional figures.

In this way, Gerken and Kang understand election law not only as a weapon in an existing political conflict, but as constitutive of how politics functions. Elsewhere, I have called this the "public good" theory of election law, in which election laws – much like the role sidewalks play in generating retail competition in a city – play the role of establishing the possibility of political competition and its structure (Schleicher 2010, 44).[3] This complements, rather than replaces, the idea of courts serving as competition regulators by suggesting that election law, whether created by legislatures or courts, has an important role to play in both setting the ground rules for and policing the conduct of political competitors, and that in both roles, courts and legislators can promote informed participation by voters and representation.

Election law's focus on the U.S. Supreme Court has not only moved attention away from the law-generating part of election law, but also has had an important effect in limiting the scope of the discussion. The Supreme Court did not address many election law cases before *Baker v. Carr*, which came after the central aspects of American politics had been settled. In "Constitutional Courts and the Boundaries of Democracy," Samuel Issacharoff takes up an issue he first raised in his work titled *Fragile Democracies*, namely what constitutional limits on election laws look like in places where the basic structure of democracy is less well established (Issacharoff 2007, 1405). In this essay, he discusses how constitutions and constitutional courts in countries transitioning to democracy address the common problem that, after the constitution is passed, a period of one-party rule is likely. He argues that new democracies often give their constitutional courts (or specialized election courts) powers far beyond American courts, allowing them to decide central questions like whether a constitution provides for a presidential or parliamentary system, whether the president should be impeached, or minimum vote threshold for getting seats in parliament. Further, these courts make decisions in these cases that go against the interests of dominant coalitions. Issacharoff argues that constitutional framers understand that power will shift in the post-framing period, but are unsure of how to constrain whomever becomes the new majority. Thus, new constitutions are necessarily and intentionally incomplete, and the framers provide constitutional courts with extensive power to use constitutional law to shape politics in a way that will avoid majoritarian abuses.

This generates several major questions, particularly why do most countries give courts, rather than some other institution, this power and why does it seem to work? After all, courts, armed with pens and robes, not purses or swords, lack the capacity of other institutions. From an American perspective, the questions answered by foreign constitutional courts often seem ineluctably political, far beyond the abilities of judges. However, as Issacharoff shows, new democracies (and notably constitutional framers who know they are soon to be in the minority) put these political questions in the hands of courts, and doing so seems to have frequently succeeded in providing some degree of social stability and protection for minority groups.

Although there are no clear answers to these difficult questions, Issacharoff provides a few suggestions which point to a somewhat different understanding of the role courts play in modern democracies. Issacharoff argues that constitutional courts can use their power "to alter the dynamics of the institutional constitutional balance." Giving courts the ability to structure election law rules gives them the power to protect minorities substantively because it gives them the power to structure how political competition unfolds.[4] Issacharoff's study of foreign courts is thus bound up with the work of scholars like Arend Lijiphardt and Donald Horowitz about what substantive election rules and constitutional rules should be drafted in transitional societies to reduce interethnic conflict (Lijphardt 1977, 25; Horowitz 1985, 569). While they argue that changing election law rules ex ante can reduce conflict – be it the proportional representation and federalism of Lijiphardt and the consociationalists or Horowitz's "centripetal" ideas for using tools like single-transferable voting systems to create incentives for cross-ethnic political coalitions – Issacharoff's essay shows that countries frequently leave the decision about what will reduce conflict and constrain majoritarian abuses for courts to decide after the transition occurs. Thus, courts can do more than act as electoral regulators ensuring that laws do not inhibit competition; they can help define the terms of political competition by creating rules shaping how many parties will compete, where parties will compete, and what the spoils of political competition will be. These decisions can impede majorities because they change the political incentives for all political actors. These courts review election law rules not only to protect competition from legislative entrenchment and venality, but as a way to ensure the creation of particular types of electoral competition in service of constitutional values. As Issacharoff notes at the end of his fascinating piece, there surely will be important implications for this work, not only internationally but domestically, as we have spent little time considering the interaction between structural constitutional law and forms of political competition (for an exception, see Levinson and Pildes 2006, 1315).

Rather than look at a different setting from the original structural work, in "Empirical Legitimacy and Election Law," Christopher Elmendorf turns to a separate normative justification for the caring about competition in election law: legitimacy.

Whereas the early political scientists of the competitive model of elections, particularly Joseph Schumpeter, were centrally concerned with the question of what type of elections (and whether elections) produced definitive results that were accepted by voters, election law scholarship has largely avoided the question of what types of rules produce legitimacy, or rather the perception of legitimacy among the citizenry (Schumpeter 1942, 272; Schleicher 2006, 178). The reason legitimacy lies in election law's interior probably derives from a combination of Downs's formalization of the competitive model of party competition in static terms that did not incorporate legitimacy concerns (Schleicher 2008, 155) and the American focus of election law scholarship, as there are only rarely the type of serious questions about the legitimacy of American elections that there are in other countries.

Even so, Elmendorf notes that the Supreme Court regularly invokes the importance of legitimacy in justifying its decisions in election law cases, ranging from Justice Scalia's argument in *Bush v. Gore* that counting ballots in advance of determining whether they were legally cast would undermine "the public acceptance democratic stability requires"[5] to claims that the appearance of corruption is a justification for limiting speech rights in campaign finance cases. Indeed, the Supreme Court's decision to make the right to vote fundamental for equal protection purposes was premised on the claim that "unjustified discrimination in determining who may participate in political affairs . . . undermines the legitimacy of representative government."[6]

Elmendorf argues that there is a strong argument in certain situations for allowing legitimacy concerns – for instance, promoting rules that are likely to stave off a politics that will lead to illiberal revolution – to trump otherwise important democratic values, like representation or equal access. This, however, is not the situation in which courts invoking legitimacy find themselves today. Instead, when the Supreme Court refers to promoting legitimacy it means something like promoting election rules that will "keep a moderately satisfied populace moderately satisfied." While he is unsure whether such arguments should trump other values, Elmendorf argues that electoral legitimacy might generate important public goods, like promoting greater compliance with governmental decisions or reducing the risk of constitutional crises. That said, Elmendorf surveys the empirical work studying popular perceptions of election rules like campaign finance reform or antifraud policies like voter identification requirement. His finding is stark: There is virtually no clear connection between any election law rule and perceptions of legitimacy, public trust, or willingness to vote. This is an amazing result – the Supreme Court's frequent and repeated invocations of legitimacy in election law cases have little or no empirical backing.

However, Elmendorf notes that some research suggests that changing simple barriers to voting, like poll worker incompetence, distant polling places, and complicated voting technology, increases confidence in electoral institutions. Elmendorf argues that these are the types of rules about which the Court has not rendered opinions, leaving them to vicissitudes of politics. If we expand the scope of values we think courts should promote in election law cases, even inside competitive models of politics, this will almost necessarily entail searching out new the types of cases to explore. This piece provides us with an idea about where to begin that search.

Just as scholars are using new tools and new ideas to explore ideas left untouched by the early "politics as markets" work, the critics of that approach have developed their critique using new methods. Rick Hasen's work, particularly his book *The Supreme Court and Election Law: Judging Equality from Baker v. Carr to Bush v. Gore* (2003), was the fullest-fledged critique of the politics as markets scholarship, favoring "judicial modesty" and rights protection to broader notions of courts as electoral regulators. One of the central points of *The Supreme Court and Election Law* is that judges are political, and we should not trust them to be neutral election regulators. In "Judges as Political Regulators: Evidence and Options for Institutional Change," Hasen calls on positive political theory, and particularly on the well-known and well-developed attitudinal model of judges, that has found statistically significant relationships between the political party that appoints a judge and that judge's decisions across a number of types of decisions. Hasen's work with John Matsusaka on judicial decisions about the "single-subject rule," a state constitutional rule that limits voter initiatives to one subject, suggests that just such a relationship exists in election cases, validating his concern about the politics of judges in election cases (although others, notably Michael Gilbert, have found that legal variables have a more significant effect in single-subject rule cases [Gilbert 2009].) Bringing positive political theory to bear on the critique of the structural model is an important and useful step. The argument in favor of federal courts as structural election regulators has never been that they are pure of the taint of politics, but rather that courts are comparatively better situated than state legislatures to police excesses in self-dealing and are likely to make decisions in election cases regardless, and therefore should do so in a coherent way. Positive political theory may provide a metric by which we can compare judicial and legislative competence in election law cases.

Hasen is not only skeptical of judges acting as as election regulators, but also of the type of institutional reforms proposed by Gerken and Kang. He argues that proposals that rely on shaming judges, like Ned Foley's proposal for amicus courts, may not work in the face of political judges, and that proposals to shame administrators, like the Democracy Index, may not work in the face of shameless politicians. Although he does not reject these proposals, he argues there is little evidence of their effectiveness.

Such is the nature of the frontier. Election law scholarship has begun to explore issues that it has not traditionally addressed – the ones addressed in this chapter, the difference between state, local, and federal elections, how election law integrates with other constitutional commitments, like the separation of powers, and many, many others. As it does so, inevitably there will be uncertainty. Our well-developed rhetoric and differences about the traditional topics of election law will adapt in time, but it will take much work and much ingenuity. Election law's interior still needs to be mapped. These articles, however, should serve as guides.

At least we won't be talking about optical scan machines.

NOTES

1 This leaves to the side the vast amount of innovative work during this period that has been done studying the Voting Rights Act. This is addressed elsewhere in this volume.
2 Perhaps only I'm reminded. Alas.
3 As Downs's model is based on Hotelling's analysis of retail competition along a strip, the metaphor is not entirely accidental (Hotelling 1929, Downs 1957).
4 This echoes Daryl Levinson's recent work on how democratic delegation can generate stability in constitutional commitments generally (Levinson 2010, 16–20).
5 *Bush v. Gore*, 531 U.S. 1046, 1046–47 (2000) (Scalia, J., concurring).
6 *Kramer v. Union School District*, 395 U.S. 621 (1969).

REFERENCES

Guy-Uriel Charles, Democracy and Distortion, *Cornell Law Review* (2007) 92.
Guy-Uriel Charles, Judging the Law of Politics, *Michigan Law Review* 103 (2005) 1115–41.
Anthony Downs, An Economic Theory of Democracy (1957) 115–22.
Heather Gerken, The Democracy Index: Why Our Election System Is Failing and How to Fix It (2009) 7.
Michael D. Gilbert, How Much Does Law Matter? Theory and Evidence from Single Subject Adjudication, available at http://papers.ssrn.com/sol3/papers.cfm?abstract_id=1433796.
Rick Hasen, The Supreme Court and Election Law: Judging Equality from Baker v. Carr to Bush v. Gore (2003).
Donald Horowitz, Ethnic Groups in Conflict (1985) 569.
Harold Hotelling, Stability in Competition, *Economic Journal* 39 (1929) 41.
Samuel Issacharoff, Private Parties with Public Purposes: Political Parties, Associational Freedoms, and Partisan Competition, *Columbia Law Review* 274 (2001) 275.
Samuel Issacharoff, Gerrymandering and Political Cartels, *Harvard Law Review* 116 (2002a) 593.
Samuel Issacharoff, Why Elections? *Harvard Law Review* 116 (2002b) 684.
Samuel Issacharoff, "Fragile Democracies," Harvard Law Review 120 (2007) 1405.
Samuel Issacharoff and Pamela S. Karlan, "The Hydraulics of Campaign Finance Reform," *Texas Law Review* 77 (1999) 1705.
Samuel Issacharoff and Richard H. Pildes, Election Law as Its Own Field of Study: Not by 'Election' Along, *Loyola Los Angeles Law Review* 32 (1999) 1183.
Samuel Issacharoff and Richard H. Pildes, Politics as Markets: Partisan Lockups of the Democratic Process, *Stanford Law Review* (1998) 643.
Pamela S. Karlan, Nothing Personal: The Evolution of the Newest Equal Protection from Shaw v. Reno to Bush v. Gore, *North Carolina Law Review* 79 (2001) 1346.
Paul Krugman, Development, Geography, and Economic Theory (Ohlin Lectures) (1995) 1–6, 66–81.
Daryl Levinson, Parchment and Politics: The Positive Puzzle of Constitutional Commitment, available at http://papers.ssrn.com/sol3/papers.cfm?abstract_id=1577749.

Daryl J. Levinson and Richard H. Pildes, *Separation of Parties, Not Powers, Harvard Law Review* 199 (2006) 2315.

Arend Lijphardt, Democracy in Plural Societies: A Comparative Exploration (1977) 25.

Daniel Lowenstein, The Supreme Court Has No Theory of Politics, in Daniel K. Ryden, ed, *The US Supreme Court and the Electoral Process* (2000) 260–3.

Nathaniel Persily, In Defense of Foxes Guarding Henhouses: The Case for Judicial Acquiescence to Incumbent-Protecting Gerrymanders, *Harvard Law Review* 116 (2002) 649.

Richard H. Pildes, Foreword: The Constitutionalization of Democratic Politics, *Harvard Law Review* 118 (2004) 142.

Richard H. Pildes, The Theory of Political Competition, *Virginia Law Review* 85 (1999) 1605–6.

David Schleicher, "Irrational Voters, Rational Voting," *Election Law Journal* 7 (2008) 155.

David Schleicher, 'Politics as Markets' Reconsidered: Natural Monopolies, Competitive Democratic Philosophy and Primary Ballot Access in American Elections, *Supreme Court Economic Review* 14 (2006) 163, 176.

David Schleicher, "Irrational Voters, Rational Voting," Election Law Journal 7 (2008) 155. David Schleicher, "What if Europe Held and Election and No One Cared?" Harvard International Law Journal 52 (forthcoming 2010) 40, 44, available at http://papers.ssrn.com/sol3/papers.cfm?abstract_id=1525015.

Joseph Schumpeter, Capitalism, Socialism and Democracy (1942) 270–3.

4

The Institutional Turn in Election Law Scholarship

Heather K. Gerken and Michael S. Kang

One of the central problems for election reform – and a central concern of elections scholarship – is political self-interest.[1] Political lock-ups and lock-outs (Issacharoff and Pildes 1998; Cain 1999) – efforts by incumbents to entrench themselves – lead to a set of electoral rules and institutions that range from the silly to the perverse. The result is not only bad policy, but a system that is unusually resistant to change.

Political self-interest is, however, a double-edged sword (Kang 2006; Gerken 2007). Scholars familiar with its perverse consequences in the elections arena tend to lament its existence, but political self-interest is also the engine that fuels a vibrant political system. The key in the arena of election reform is to figure out how to align the interests of partisans with the interest of voters, to redirect political energies into healthier channels. The key is to harness politics to fix politics.

Stated in these terms, the idea seems unobjectionable, even banal. Of course, one thinks, we should be attentive to partisan self-interest in thinking about reform. But even though most agree with the basic idea, scholars have not been sufficiently attentive to all of its implications. This is an idea worked out in the "apps," an idea whose significance becomes apparent only when one digs into the questions of institutional design and election reform that are the bread-and-butter of election law scholarship. We believe that the field should shift its emphasis in several ways. There are many arenas where the notion of harnessing politics to fix politics has not been fully worked out. Here we attempt to identify the limitations of current scholarship and chart the paths we think it ought to take in the future. Because the applications matter a good deal here, we briefly reference a number of projects that fit into the research agenda we are outlining.

The vast majority of scholarship in election law has fallen into a fairly narrow category of cases – those having to do with partisan gerrymandering (and, relatedly, the use of the Voting Rights Act to pursue a partisan agenda). Now that the leaders of the field have written in detail (and well) on the topic, partisan gerrymandering is a subject that may be close to being written out. But there are other areas where a structural lens, which enables us to think more systematically about political self-interest, has not yet been put to full use. For example, election administration questions, which tend to be cast in rights-based terms, might be recast if we were more attentive to the notion of harnessing politics to fix politics. Similarly, campaign finance reform – structural almost by virtue of statutory command[2] and riven with questions of political self-interest – has also not been systematically cast in these terms.[3]

Two caveats are worth stating at the outset of the project. First, in some ways the field of election law is almost entirely about the problem of political self-interest. Indeed, the work of the field's founding generation provides the core intellectual tools that we will use in this chapter to map current scholarship. We don't claim that this is a path not traveled. Our goal is simply to chart where the next road should lead the second generation of election law scholars. We assume that it is possible to argue for more emphasis to be placed on this important idea – to suggest that there are still new directions to take it – without downplaying the significance of the work that has already been done on this question. Our contribution, then, stems not from coming up with the idea or recognizing its significance for election law questions, but in offering what we hope will be a set of new ideas about where we go next.[4] We will describe what we think of as the beginning of an "institutional turn" in elections scholarship. Our goal is to describe set of institutional interventions and new political structures that would align leadership incentives properly with the public interest but nonetheless promote democratic participation and engagement with the central questions of election law.

Second, what we offer in this chapter is necessarily abbreviated and inadequately footnoted. Needless to say one might well require a book-length treatment to cover all the ideas we discuss in this chapter. For that reason, the sketch we offer is necessarily that – a sketch.

POLITICAL SELF-INTEREST AS A SOLUTION, NOT JUST A PROBLEM

Perhaps the most common lament in elections scholarship is that politicians prevent us from having the politics we deserve. Because we leave the regulation of politics *to* politics, elected officials often set the rules by which they are elected. The foxes are guarding the henhouse.

A trouble with much election law scholarship is that this phrase tends to be the punch line to the story, not the starting point for the analysis. It is all too easy to show why politics caused this or that reform to fail. The bigger challenge is figuring out a better strategy. To the extent that academics and policy makers think about solutions to the problem of political self-interest, the proposed cure is often to retreat from the political process. Often these proposals involve taking power away from politicians and giving it to an independent, often technocratic set of decision makers who are insulated from the distorting effect of partisanship. It is no surprise then that scholars are so attracted to courts as solutions to political entrenchment: They are all too familiar with the challenges involved in getting reform passed through other channels. Political self-interest – which largely takes the form of partisan competition, incumbency, and local self-interest – generates tides that run against reform. It seems easier to ask courts – formally outside of the political system – to solve these problems for us.

It is not hard to imagine why election law scholars have such a strong impulse to look to neutral decision makers like courts to cure what ails us. Once one has diagnosed politics as the disease, it is hard to imagine it as the source of a cure.[5] Moreover, because legal scholarship is normatively inflected, legal scholars who find the notion of self-interest morally distasteful are reluctant to sing its praises in this context. The problem, of course, is that full-blown nonpartisan bureaucracies do not spring, as did Athena, from the head of a god. They have to be created by somebody, usually a political somebody, and we thus find ourselves back to the problems of outwitting the foxes. Perhaps calls from the moral high ground will eventually persuade politicians to do the right thing. But we are reluctant to ask reformers to keep fighting this same fight in the vague hope that something will eventually take.

Put simpler, we have a "here to there" problem in election reform (see Gerken 2009a). We spend a great deal of time thinking about what's wrong with our election system (the "here") and how to fix it (the "there"). But we spend almost no time thinking about how to get from here to there – how to create an environment in which reform can actually take root. Reform advocates work tirelessly to help specific projects blossom. But they are fighting this battle on difficult terrain, and almost no one is thinking about how to change the terrain itself. We've spent too much time identifying the journey's end and not enough time figuring out how to smooth the road that leads there.

In some ways, it is surprising that academics have spent so little time solving the "here to there" problem. After all, most arguments for election reform depend on a single premise: Process shapes substance. Academics are quick to tell you that the structure of our political process (campaign finance law, redistricting rules) helps determine the substance of our policies (who gets elected, what gets passed). But they do not apply that lesson to election reform. The structure of our political process also determines what kind of election reform gets passed. Or, in the case of the United States, it creates an environment where precious little gets passed. In our view, we should take a step back and figure out how to create an environment that is more receptive to change generally. It is time to think less about the end game and more about the interim strategies and institutional tweaks that will help us get from here to there. Indeed, in our view, smoothing the path for reform ought to be at the top of the agenda for academics and reformers.

If the work of reformers is to be something other than a Sisyphean task, process should be our main focus, and smoothing the path for change ought to be at the top of the reform agenda. "Here to there" proposals may seem modest when compared to typical reform proposals, like calls for public financing or nonpartisan election administration. But these wide-ranging reform proposals have been met with a deafening silence. We have plenty of ideas about what kind of change we want. What we need is an environment in which change can happen. We are not just skeptical that courts will step in to fix these problems. We also have faith that the political environment can be changed to make it more receptive to reform.

The promising solution, in our view, is to harness politics to fix politics. Pam Karlan and Sam Issacharoff have argued that money in politics is like water. It will exert a hydraulic pressure on the campaign finance system; when regulations block one channel, money will simply find a new outlet (Issacharoff and Karlan 1999). As one of us has argued, however, the hydraulics of campaign finance is simply part of a broader hydraulic effect. Political energy, like money, will find its own level; it cannot be cabined effectively with legal regulations (Kang 2005). The key to any hydraulics argument, of course, is that although it may be impossible to suppress political energies, it may be possible to *redirect* them into healthier channels. (In our view, as we note later, the focus should be on creating incentives for elites to pull the public into these debates). Unfortunately, there is less work on the possibility of redirection than there ought to be no matter what normative vision you prefer. Some of the seminal work on redirecting political energies has been done by Sam Issacharoff and Rick Pildes. Their most noteworthy contribution is "Politics as Markets," where the two call for a "structural approach" to election law that emphasizes the role of "second-order regulations" in creating a healthy political marketplace (Issacharoff and Pildes 1998). The article had a profound effect on the field, including our own work.

Our primary complaint about the decade of scholarship that has followed "Politics as Markets" is that election scholars, unsurprisingly, continue to look to the courts for structural solutions. The two of us differ regarding the degree to which courts are capable of engaging in structural analysis in a serious way,[6] but we agree that courts are generally not the institutions best suited for structural analysis, nor have they shown a great deal of interest in engaging with the structural dimensions of voting. Judges may decide political cases badly, at least in part, because they possess liabilities that compromise their judgment and few assets to help them manage politics astutely. Lifetime tenure insulates federal judges from politics and democratic input, while the judiciary is equipped with few compensatory resources for understanding politics empirically. When judges are required to decide political cases, they appear to fall back on their personal attachments, as figures of the establishment, in favor of both major-party duopoly and their respective partisanship (see Hasen 1997; Cox and Katz 2002; Pildes 2001). Moreover, judges uncomfortable with the relentlessly instrumental analysis demanded by a structural approach (combined with their discomfort with the political ramifications of their actions) often prefer to render highly formalistic opinions in the cadence that is conventionally juridical – the language of individual rights (see Karlan 1992).

In our view, there are more promising institutional paths for redirecting political energies and checking incumbent entrenchment. Indeed, the natural extension of a structural approach's focus on process, with its concomitant attentiveness to political leadership, is the development of nonjudicial institutions that would deploy politics as the remedy for politics. These process-oriented solutions may prove more consistent and durable in the long run than reliance on courts or other watchdogs. Process-oriented solutions do not depend on the vigilance, good faith, and neutrality of courts, independent commissions, or nonpartisan election overseers. Nor do they place such democratically vulnerable adjudicators in the difficult position of deciding political disputes or dividing up spoils. Instead, process-oriented reforms may be naturally self-maintaining once set into motion.

AN INSTITUTIONAL TURN: HARD AND SOFT APPROACHES

Looking beyond courts for process-oriented solutions, we advocate the development of nonjudicial institutions along at least two different directions – "hard" and "soft" approaches. Both "hard" and "soft" approaches aspire to harness the political self-interest of elites and allow "ambition . . . to counteract ambition" in the Madisonian tradition. Both hard and soft approaches rearrange elite incentives and reshape the political process in healthier directions, not by insulating election law from politics, but by redirecting the existing politics that control election law. Although bound together by their institutional, process-oriented outlook, hard and soft approaches aim to achieve the same goals by different mechanisms.

Hard approaches attempt to change the politics of election law by reforming the "hard" lawmaking institutions through which election law is made. The hard approach is to reconfigure existing lawmaking institutions or to create new institutions that produce new, better incentives for political leaders. It changes "the rules that govern the composition, powers, or voting mechanisms of the relevant institutions" (Gersen and Vermeule 2007, 681). For instance, one of us has proposed that any statewide redistricting plan must receive popular approval through direct democracy, against a competing plan proposed by the opposition, as a requisite for enactment. Such an approach would not mandate what criteria ought to guide the redistricting, let alone ensure a politically neutral process. But the change in the institutional pathway for lawmaking would create the right kinds of incentives for legislators, as they would have to consider the necessary approval of the median voter for enactment, rather than simply trying to maximize political self-advantage when drawing district lines.

Along similar lines, one of the most promising new proposals for negotiating the same redistricting morass is Sam Hirsch's proposal for citizen-based districting commissions, which would deploy a baseball-arbitration-style redistricting process that challenges the political parties to put forward better plans than the last proposal. We particularly admire two elements of Hirsch's proposal. First, he resists the notion that we should try to take politics out of redistricting.[7] Second, he relies on an iterative decision-making process that puts the creative energies of the political parties to work for the public, forcing them to find ways to connect partisan self-interest with the public good.

Even though political scientists have written at length about the significance of intraparty conflict, legal scholars have not yet fully absorbed the insights from that literature.[8] Reform depends as much on changing the balance of power *among* political leaders as on changing the balance of power *between* political leaders (as a class) and the voters. In thinking about institutional solutions to current problems, it is important to focus not just on empowering voters, but empowering political leaders within a party who will push for election reform against other intraparty factions (see Kang 2005). After all, parties are diverse coalitions containing proreform and antireform elements. Hard approaches that alter the paths of lawmaking through new institutions can give proreform elements critical leverage in intraparty fights.

By contrast to hard approaches, "soft" approaches reform the politics of election law by changing elite incentives without changing the hard lawmaking pathways. That is, soft approaches work through existing institutions but aim to change the politics around them and thus the incentives flowing through them. Soft approaches draw to a degree on Joseph Nye's notion of "soft power," or the ability to obtain "the outcomes one wants by setting the agenda and attracting others . . . rest[ing] on the ability to shape the preferences of others to want what you want" (e.g., Nye 2008, 29). Soft approaches persuade lawmakers to assume more public-regarding preferences by creating public demand for them to do so.

A good example of a soft approach is the Democracy Index, which would rank states and localities based on how well their election systems perform, thereby creating an incentive for election officials to pay attention to performance. The Index would not create national performance standards. It would take power away from partisan officials. It would not even endorse a set of best practices for administering elections. Instead, it should push in the direction of better performance, less partisanship, and greater professionalism. The Democracy Index harnesses mass electoral pressures in the service of accountability in the otherwise obscure policy domain of election administration.

Another example of a soft approach, and one of the most promising proposals for reform in recent years, is what one of us has termed "shadow institutions" (Gerken 2008) – private institutions that mimic public ones. They represent a nonpartisan cognate to the decidedly partisan "shadow cabinets" that exist in Great Britain and elsewhere. Composed of members of the leading opposition party, the shadow cabinet provides a standing alternative to the party in power. It gives the opposition a platform to critique the government and showcase competing policy proposals.

In a system where political self-interest is the central obstacle to reform, creating nonpartisan shadow institutions may be one of the most promising strategies available for getting traction with reform.[9] In the short term, shadow institutions can give the public a baseline for evaluating the decisions of partisan decision makers. They can thus help shame those in power into doing better, tamping down on overtly partisan decisions. In the long term, shadow institutions raise awareness of the need for more substantial reform. Whenever an institution's decision deviates from its shadow's, someone – a journalist, reformer, or member of the losing side – will draw attention to that fact. A shadow institution, by its mere presence, reminds us that we can do better and pressures lawmakers in those public-regarding directions. It also defeats the naysayer's favorite challenge to any reform proposal – that it can't be done. Showing that something does work is more persuasive than vouching that it can.

Here's a specific example. One of us has proposed creating "shadow" districting commissions for the 2010 districting cycle (Gerken 2008; 2009b). The price tag for this proposal would be quite small. The relevant census data can be downloaded from the Census Bureau for free, and districting software costs roughly as much as a flat-screen television. Even though the shadow districting plan would have no legal effect, it would exercise soft power in the debate. If the majority party in the legislature created a plan designed to maximize its own advantage, the opposing party could use the shadow commission's plan to show partisan bias. If the legislature created safe seats for all incumbents, reformers could point to the plan as evidence that the legislature had insulated its members from political competition. In each instance, arguments would be based on what's achievable in the real world instead of abstract claims about what's possible in the ideal.

Shadow districting commissions would be an inexpensive soft approach for improving existing practices in the short term and jump-starting debate in the long term. In the immediate future, the districting plans offered by shadow commissions should reduce legislators' incentive to engage in the type of shamelessly self-interested line drawing we so often see today. Legislators never like bad publicity. They can thus help shame those in power into doing better, tamping down on the most egregiously partisan decisions. As to the long haul, debates over the competing plans should raise public awareness about the problems associated with legislative self-interest in districting.

Along the same lines, consider Ned Foley's proposal for "amicus courts" (another shadow institution) (Foley 2008). Foley's view is that states should set up specialized courts for adjudicating election disputes. In thinking about the "here to there" question, however, he realized that it would be difficult to get such a proposal put in place. He then began to ask himself how we could get what he terms "reform without legislation" (Foley 2008, 62). His answer? Creating "shadow courts" to issue decisions in election disputes and submit those decisions to existing courts in the form of amicus briefs.

Foley's idea, inspired in part by the www.factcheck.org site set up by the Annenberg Public Policy Center, could influence post-election adjudication in two useful ways. First, we would expect existing judges to pay a good deal of attention to what a bipartisan group of experts had to say about the cases before them. Election law can be a fiendishly complex subject, and judges are often grateful for a helping hand. Second, the mere existence of the shadow courts could create a terrain that is more receptive to reform. As Foley writes, "if and when an actual court deviates from an amicus opinion of the shadow court – and the actual court's decision appears to be motivated by mere partisanship – this deviation might generate some momentum" for the creation of the type of specialized courts that Foley believes we need (Foley 2008, 62). By modeling how a well-functioning court should function, Foley suggests, the shadow court increases the likelihood that this reform will actually take root.

In addition, we think there are a number of institutions that combine hard and soft approaches and could prove promising sites for election reform efforts. For instance, Archon's Fung's citizen-based election monitoring (see http://myfairelection.com) and a Democracy Index (Gerken 2009a) similarly would harness politics to fix politics. Each of these would offer voters a readily accessible yardstick for judging election performance, thus making the problems that infect election administration salient to voters and giving politicians an incentive to pay attention (see Gerken 2009a). So, too, Chris Elmendorf's (2005) proposals for advisory electoral reform commissions, and his jointly authored call for citizen redistricting and reform commissions (Elmendorf and Gerken 2004; Gerken 2005) would offer the public the decision-making shortcuts they need to wade through the debate over election reform. These new institutions are promising precisely because they identify and cultivate self-interest instead of trying to bypass it.

One need not depend entirely on private institutions to change direct political self-interest in healthier channels, of course. For instance, Rick Pildes has suggested investing election reform resources in a single state. Noting that it is not only difficult to pass election reform at the national level, but that national reform will often be too general to be meaningful, Pildes writes that they will be "feel-good, credit-claiming exercises, at least until there's a concrete experience at the state level." Pildes thus argues that foundations should choose a single state to serve as the "poster child" for election reform (he suggests Ohio). Pildes suggests that this focused effort might result in the passage of a comprehensive package of reforms.

The benefit of Pildes' strategy is twofold. First, passing reform at the state level allows reformers to take advantage of the ways in which well-funded initiative campaigns can pressure legislators to do the right thing (a dynamic that cannot be reproduced at the federal level). Second, the state-level reform could serve as a model for, and build momentum behind, national reform. After all, there is no such thing as a silver bullet in election reform. We are much more likely to see noticeable results from a package of reform than from the type of piecemeal change that typically gets passed today.

Needless to say, now that democracy has been "constitutionalized" (Pildes 2004a) it would be foolish to ignore the role the courts play in monitoring politics. Judicial decisions that shape the law of politics are themselves an important institution that constrains and influences the interactive process among political actors going forward. In the future, however, we think that scholars should do their best to reframe traditional legal questions to push the courts to manage politics in more productive ways rather than viewing litigation as one-off resolutions of discrete disputes. One way to do that, of course, is to encourage the courts to think in structural terms, as per Pildes and Issacharoff. A structural approach explicitly asks courts to think of second-order arrangements and to be attentive to the currents generated by political self-interest when they are creating the legal rules that govern politics.[10]

Surprisingly, the approach that is less developed in the literature involves tweaking the *litigation* process to push politics in the right direction. One of us emphasizes in previous work that courts have a prime opportunity to channel ongoing political conflict when they decide election law cases (Kang 2005). When courts decide election law cases, they usually step into the middle of what was likely a political conflict between competing actors that has spilled from the political forum into a judicial one. Although courts and commentators focus mainly on the legal rights and principles implicated by a given case, they should consider just as prominently the ex ante political incentives created by handing victory to one side or the other. In the context of party regulation, one of us argues that courts should strike down state regulation of party internal affairs because of the resulting effect on party actors and how they handle their affairs. Rejection of judicial intervention there would force feuding party rivals to compromise politically rather than seek a legal trump against each other that they can enforce in court. In other words, the shape of the election law made by courts influences the incentives for political players and in the best cases encourages them to engage in political compromise before they ever head for the courthouse.

Even though the basic insight that bargaining takes place in the shadow of the law is well known (and often closely analyzed by election law scholars ex post), surprisingly few commentators think about how to put that insight to work for reform. Sam Hirsch's paper on the New Jersey redistricting process provides an excellent example of the strategy we envision (although he is less explicit than he might be in describing it for reasons that, we suspect, have to do with the fact that he is a practicing lawyer with clients) (Hirsch 2002). Hirsch describes the way in which the Democratic Party in New Jersey built a coalition with legislators who represented racial minorities in order to push through a districting plan featuring a number of coalition districts (usually the preferred districting strategy of Democrats seeking to reconcile the mandates of the Voting Rights Act with the desire to gain legislative seats). Although Hirsch does not discuss how the Democratic Party's lawyers thought about the effort, it is not hard to imagine the way in which the threat of litigation (specifically, the fact that majority-minority districts represented the default option under the Voting Rights Act) led the lawyers advising the Democrats to conclude that the best way to protect their plan from challenge would be to win the support of as many minority legislators as possible. The result of this effort was an impressive coalition among whites, African Americans, and Latinos in the districting process, something that plainly influenced the court reviewing the challenge that followed.

One of us has proposed building on this model by encouraging courts explicitly to look to decision-making proxies in assessing the legality of a districting plan under the Voting Rights Act (Gerken 2006). Thus, just as the Supreme Court in *Georgia v. Ashcroft* seemed to place great weight on the testimony of John Lewis and the support of minority legislators in upholding a challenge districting plan, so too courts should explicitly look to the support of leaders of the minority community – legislators, community groups, and the like – in assessing whether a redistricting plan is in the best interests of the group. Although there are questions concerning judicial capacity to carry out this type of analysis,[11] judicial scrutiny in this direction might unleash a healthy competition among party lawyers in trying to prove the bona fides of their community support, encouraging them to build and document community support, bring new voices into the districting process, and create more channels for community input into the districting process.

Or take our proposal that we develop a "procedural solution" to partisan gerrymandering,[12] asking the Court to calibrate its standard of review to the kind of districting process used. Under this proposal, courts would closely scrutinize a districting plan produced by self-interested legislators. But it would grant deference to – even create "safe harbors" for – districting processes with sound credentials and thus create incentives for legislators to improve the districting process on their own. For instance, the Court might grant lower scrutiny to any districting plan the legislature chooses, provided it has been approved via a subsequent referendum. Or the Court might grant lower scrutiny for any plan that has been "blessed" by appropriate stakeholders (e.g., plans endorsed by good governance groups or by citizens via deliberate polling or citizen commissions). If legislators knew that they could guarantee adoption of their districting plan only by obtaining the blessings of the relevant stakeholders, they would have every incentive to build new coalitions and pay attention to constituencies that have been shut out of the districting process thus far. There is a massive amount of political energy devoted to redistricting, and this kind of procedural solution would redirect those energies into more productive channels without removing districting entirely from the democratic process. Here again, such an approach would realign the interests of elected officials with those of the people they represent.

Thinking of litigation as part of a larger dynamic, iterative process would help us help courts do a better job when they intervene in the political process, and it's odd that election law scholars tend to underplay these possibilities. After all, we are essentially proposing that scholars think of litigation in the same dynamic fashion that most scholars think about politics.

Constitutional law scholars are often chastened for being insufficiently attentive to the rise of the Fourth Branch and the insights of administrative law, and we think the same can be said of election law scholars (for exceptions, see Issacharoff

2004; Elmendorf 2005; Gerken 2006). Rick Hasen (1999) correctly identified the first generation of elections scholarship as being the product of two parents – constitutional law and political science. Perhaps political science might find a better genetic partner to sire the second generation of election law scholarship. Administrative law offers a rich line of scholarship that election scholars have yet to draw upon in a systematic fashion, and it would help move the field away from the limits of a rights-based approach. In our view, for instance, some of the best recent work on Section 5 of the Voting Rights Act has analyzed it with an administrative law frame rather than a civil rights frame. After all, the difficult problems we've recently witnessed in the Voting Section are ill-suited for a rights-based solution, but epitomize a set of issues with which administrative law scholars are intimately familiar.

The benefits of shifting to an administrative law paradigm should be clear. To begin, administrative law – with its focus on systematic analysis, quantitative proof, and the proper supervision of agency decision making – would push courts and scholars toward the structural questions they ought to be answering (and, we might note as an aside, may provide a more comfortable format for courts to think structurally than the direct structural approach advocated by many). Consider, for instance, the way we adjudicate most election administration cases, pitting the right of an individual against the vast interests of a state trying to run an election (Issacharoff and Pildes 1998). Little wonder that plaintiffs' claims get short shrift. Perhaps courts would do better to evaluate election administration decisions as election *administration* decisions, analyzing the process that produced them, the reasoning behind them, and the costs and benefits they generate. As one of us has recently argued (Gerken 2009a), the long-term health of election administration depends almost entirely on the professionalism of the bureaucrats who run it. Courts could do a great deal to promote professional norms within election administration by treating election bureaucrats as generic bureaucrats.

The insights of administrative law extend further, in our view. If you are thinking about the dilemma posted by the Voting Rights Act – how to regulate racial politics as we transition from entrenched racism to normal politics – the flexibility inherent in an administrative law approach has much to commend it (Gerken 2006). Indeed, a shift to an administrative law paradigm would mitigate some unfortunate tendencies in election reform and academic circles.

One unfortunate tendency among reformers and academics addressing these questions is to adhere to the civil rights paradigm in which someone – the Department of Justice, the Court – takes the role of the knight in shining armor to protect racial minorities. Two problems have arisen from this model, both of which could have easily been predicted by a scholar of administrative law. The first is that the DOJ's armor can easily be tarnished by politics.[13] Whereas the civil rights model does not provide an easy solution to the problem, administrative law scholarship has many insights about dealing with the dilemma of agency capture. The second problem is that even when the DOJ or the Court is willing and able to play the knight's role, the civil rights model's heavy reliance on courts to protect minority voters has become an increasingly unwieldy strategy for making the fine-grained contextual judgments required in this changing political environment. Here again, the rights model falls short (Issacharoff 2004; Pildes 2004a).

An administrative law approach to election law might also redirect the energies of scholars to thinking about soft power, not hard law, as the source of change in the way we administer elections. Scholars and reformers tend to assume that change comes from without – from top-down legislation, from pressure created by reform groups, or from judicial mandates. One of the most important pressures for improvement, however, comes from within, the professional norms that bind together a set of bureaucrats (Gerken 2009a). Strong and stable professional norms help for two reasons. First, it turns out that peer pressure can be just as effective in the workplace as it is in high school. When professional identity becomes intertwined with particular practices, peoples' own sense that they are doing a good job depends on conforming to these norms. For those of us trying to suppress memories of high school, it's nice to know that the herd instinct can do a bit of good in the world. Second, professional norms don't just offer a model of behavior, a script for being good at one's job; they also offer us decision-making shortcuts. No one has the time to think through the practical and moral considerations involved in every decision they make. Administrators need shorthand to guide their behavior. A professional consensus on best practices can represent a pretty sensible heuristic for figuring out the right choice. Thus, an administrative law approach would suggest that the efforts of reformers and academics alike should be directed toward creating and diffusing professional norms among election administrators.

Finally, most of this chapter has been devoted to identifying areas where we think there's more to write. We will end by identifying one area where we think the debate has largely run its course: the rights/structure, is-competition-the-right-theory-for-regulating-politics debate. Although we, like many in the field, accept many of the basic insights of the Pildes and Issacharoff's model, we think that the differences between the two camps has been exaggerated, for reasons identified by Guy Charles (2002) within the election law tribe and by Larry Tribe (1999) outside of it. As to the debate about competition (the mediating theory Issacharoff and Pildes have chosen for their structural approach), we recognize that competition is a value that can promote many larger goals (Pildes 2004b). In our view, the most attractive path for future scholarship lies not in debating these extremes, but in finding a pragmatic third way that blends the best of both arguments.

An idea that has been central to our own work, for instance, blends participatory and elite-centered conceptions of democracy (Gerken 2006; Kang 2008). We believe that the deeply contested questions about representation that are embedded in electoral regulation ought to be decided not by elites, but by members of the relevant community. We are also cognizant, however, of the useful role that elites play in generating political energy – the way they can serve as "conversational entrepreneurs" within the polity (Bennett 2003, 36–37). This, of course, brings us back to the basic premise that animates this work – it is possible to harness politics to fix politics.

CONCLUSION

This chapter briefly surveys some of the basic lines of analysis that, we think, election law scholars ought to take in the future. Although it now looks like a bit of a laundry list, we think that the trends and possibilities we have identified above suggest what is – or ought to be – an institutional turn in election law scholarship. An institutional turn would move our attention away from the courts toward a new set of private and public institutions, away from big reform proposals toward the more modest institutional tweaks that will make bigger and better reform possible in the long run. Were the field to take an institutional turn, scholarship and reform proposals would sound in the cadence of administrative law, not civil rights. Even within the confines of the judiciary, scholars should be more attentive to its institutional limits, moving away from direct demands for structural analysis toward encouraging the court to do structure in the more comfortable guise of administrative law and developing a more dynamic, iterative account of litigation that connects political self-interest to reform goals. All of these changes would be knit together by a common idea: That the solution to many of our democratic woes is not to isolate the regulation of politics from politics, but to harness politics to fix politics.

NOTES

1 We use the phrase "political self-interest" because it encompasses both partisan politics and the other political interests that may drive elites, such as incumbency and local or intraparty competition.
2 We owe this phrase to Bob Bauer.
3 See Kang (2007a) who argues for an extension of the structural frame from partisan gerrymandering to problems, such as campaign finance, where it has been less discussed.
4 Even here, we will be drawing on the ideas of others and of our own, all with an aim to show how they form the basis for a broader research agenda.
5 Unless one thinks like an immunologist, as one of us has suggested (Gerken 2007).
6 Compare Gerken (2004) with Kang (2007b).
7 See Gerken (2007) who proposes that we should not quarantine election reform from politics, but inoculate it against politics by introducing some politics into the reform process; Kang (2006) for an emphasis on the importance of politics to successful reform.
8 For a fuller development, see Kang (2005; forthcoming). For early examples to think in these terms, see Lowenstein (1993) and Garrett (2002).
9 For an excellent, in-depth analysis of one type of shadow institution, the advisory election reform commission, see Elmendorf (2005).

10 See, e.g., Kang (2005) for the view that litigation over the constitutionality of party regulation as part of an ongoing, iterative political process in which party actors compete for advantage across multiple venues, including courts.

11 See, e.g., Kang (2006) who questions whether the court accurately discerned the politics of *Georgia v. Ashcroft*.

12 This proposal builds on Issacharoff (2004).

13 See, e.g., Pitts (2007) who describes recent controversies surrounding allegedly partisan nonenforcement of Section 5 of the Voting Rights Act.

REFERENCES

Bennett, Robert W. 2003. *Talking It Through: Puzzles of American Democracy*. Ithaca, NY: Cornell University Press.

Cain, Bruce. 1999. "Garrett's Temptation." *Virginia Law Review* 85: 1589.

Charles, Guy. 2002. "Constitutional Pluralism and Democratic Politics." *North Carolina Law Review* 80: 1103.

Cox, Gary and Jonathan Katz. 2002. *Elbridge Gerry's Salamander: The Electoral Consequences of the Reapportionment Revolution*. New York: Cambridge University Press.

Elmendorf, Christopher. 2005. "Representation Reinforcement through Advisory Commissions: The Case of Election Law." New York *University Law Review* 80: 1366.

Elmendorf, Christopher and Heather Gerken. 2004. "Next Time, Start with the People." *Balkinization* (Nov. 10).

Foley, Edward. 2008. "Let's Not Repeat 2000." *Legal Times* XXXI.62 (April 21).

Garrett, Elizabeth. 2002. "Is the Party Over? Courts and the Political Process." *Supreme Court Review* 2002: 95–152.

Gerken, Heather. 2004. "Lost in the Political Thicket." *University of Pennsylvania Law Review* 153: 503.

———. 2005. "Citizens Must Drive Electoral Reform." *Roll Call* (Nov. 15).

———. 2006. "A Third Way for the Voting Rights Act: Section 5 and the Opt-In Approach." *Columbia Law Review* 106: 708.

———. 2007. "The Double-Edged Sword of Independence." *Election Law Journal* 6: 184.

———. 2008. "Out of the Shadows: Private Redistricting Can Help Overcome Lawmakers' Partisanship." *Legal Times* XXXI.18 (May 5).

———. 2009a. *The Democracy Index: Why Our Election System Is Failing and How to Fix It*. Princeton, NJ: Princeton University Press.

———. 2009b. "Getting from Here to There in Election Reform: A Trio of Ideas." *Election Reform Agenda Conference*. University of Iowa.

———. 2010. "Keynote Address: Getting from Here to There in Redistricting Reform." *Duke Journal of Constitutional Law and Policy* 5: 1–15.

Gersen, Jacob and Adrian Vermeule. 2007. "Chevron as a Voting Rule." *Yale Law Review* 115: 676.

Hasen, Richard. 1997. "Entrenching Duopoly." *Supreme Court Review* 1997: 331.

———. 1999. "Introduction: Election Law at Puberty: Optimism and Words of Caution." *Loyola LA Law Review* 32: 1095.

Hirsch, Sam. 2002. "Unpacking Page v. Bartels: A Fresh Redistricting Paradigm Emerges in New Jersey." *Election Law Journal* 1: 7.

Issacharoff, Samuel. 2004. "Gerrymandering and Political Cartels." *Harvard Law Review* 116: 593.

_____. 2004. "Is Section 5 of the Voting Rights Act a Victim of Its Own Success." *Columbia Law Review* 104: 1710.

_____ and Pamela Karlan. 1999. "The Hydraulics of Campaign Finance Reform." *Texas Law Review* 77: 1705.

_____ and Richard Pildes. 1998. "Politics as Markets." *Stanford Law Review* 50: 643.

Kang, Michael. 2005. "The Hydraulics and Politics of Party Regulation." *Iowa Law Review* 91: 131.

_____. 2006. "De-Rigging Elections." *Washington University Law Review* 84: 667.

_____. 2007a. "To Here from Theory." *Texas Law Review* 87: 787.

_____. 2007b. "When Courts Won't Make Law." *Ohio State Law Journal* 68: 1097.

_____. 2008. "Race and Democratic Contestation." *Yale Law Review* 117: 734.

_____. 2011. "Sore Loser Laws and Democratic Contestation." *Georgetown Law Journal* forthcoming.

Karlan, Pamela. 1992. "Rights to Vote: Some Pessimism about Formalism." *Texas Law Review* 71: 1705.

_____. 2004. "Ashcroft and the Retrogression of Retrogression." *Election Law Journal* 3(1): 21.

Lowenstein, Daniel Hays. 1993. "Associational Rights of Major Political Parties." *Texas Law Review* 71: 1741.

Nye, Joseph S. Jr. 2008. *The Powers to Lead*. New York: Oxford University Press.

Pildes, Richard. 2001. "Democracy and Disorder." *University of Chicago Law Review* 68: 695.

_____. 2004a. "The Constitutionalization of Democratic Politics." *Harvard Law Review* 118: 28.

_____. 2004b. "Competitive, Deliberative, and Rights-Oriented Democracy." *Election Law Journal* 3: 685.

_____. 2007. Proposal for Tobin Project Working Group Meeting, "Getting from Here to There in Election Reform," Tobin Project, Democratic Institutions Working Group, Cambridge MA (unpublished paper; on file with author).

Pitts, Michael J. 2007. "Defining 'Partisan' Law Enforcement." *Stanford Law and Policy Review* 18: 324.

Tribe, Laurence. 1999. "The Supreme Court 1998 Term – Comment: Saenz Sans Prophesy: Does the Privileges or Immunities Revival Reveal the Future – Or Expose the Hidden Structure of the Present?" *Harvard Law Review* 113: 110.

5

Judges as Political Regulators

Evidence and Options for Institutional Change

Richard L. Hasen

INTRODUCTION

A major theme of election law scholarship over the last decade has been that judicial oversight of the devices of democracy is desirable to foster adequate political competition. Under this view, politicians' self-interest should preclude them from deciding the conditions for their own future races, such as the location of legislative districts. Apart from the merits or problems with this approach, the reality is that courts increasingly are called upon to engage in political regulation. Election law litigation has more than doubled in the last decade.

Turning to judges as political regulators can be problematic in two ways. First, judges, like politicians, might act in self-interest to favor their past or present political party or to keep themselves in office. Second, apart from self-interest, judges come to these cases with their own world views and might not apply "neutral" principles in deciding election law cases. If either of these two concerns has merit, then the role of judges as political regulators needs further examination. Under what circumstances should judges decide issues of political regulation? What changes in the structure of adjudication or legislative drafting could be made to minimize the problems with judicial regulation of politics? Are there other institutions that may be designed for the regulation of politics?

This chapter does not answer these questions, but sets forth some of the evidence bearing on them as well as an agenda for future research. The first part briefly describes the case for judicial intervention in politics and describes the litigation explosion in the election law area in the last decade. The second part discusses the literature and open questions regarding how judges decide political regulation cases. It draws upon, among other things, a study on judges and the "single subject rule" applicable to initiatives. The third part considers whether changes in legislative drafting or institutional design could improve the field of political regulation. In particular, it considers whether "New Institutionalist" proposals may be relied upon to lessen the public's dependence upon judges as political regulators.

THE NORMATIVE ARGUMENT FOR, AND POSITIVE EVIDENCE REGARDING, THE USE OF JUDGES AS POLITICAL REGULATORS

One of the enduring debates in the field of election law is the extent to which courts should set the rules for political competition. Rick Pildes and Sam Issacharoff put forward the leading argument for the "political markets" approach to election law in a 1998 law review article, "Politics as Markets" (Issacharoff & Pildes 1998). According to their argument, courts should aggressively police election laws to prevent politicians' self-dealing. The authors see an inherent problem with politicians setting the rules for future political competition, such as through passage of campaign finance rules, redistricting plans, and limits on ballot access for third parties and independent candidates. They suggest an aggressive judicial response. Most provocatively, using an analogy to antitrust and the need to break up "political cartels," Issacharoff has advocated that courts declare all redistricting adopted by partisan elected officials as presumptively unconstitutional (Issacharoff 2002).

Scholars in the political markets camp want courts to focus more on the proper functioning of the political market and less on a traditional "balancing" of the rights of those challenging election laws against the state's interests purportedly furthered by the challenged election law. The analysis is not moored to traditional constitutional analysis; these scholars are mostly unconcerned which provision of the Constitution a court would use to engage in this political regulation.

Against the structuralist approach of the political markets school are scholars who assert that judicial modesty is in order in election law cases. According to some in this school, judicial intervention is necessary only to protect "core" equality rights, such as the right to cast a ballot that will be counted. Remaining "contested" questions, such as which factors are appropriate for redistricting, should be left to the political process, not the courts (Hasen 2003). Skeptics of the political markets approach believe that judges do not have a comparative institutional advantage in political regulation compared to politicians themselves (Persily 2002), that there is no widely-accepted normative baseline for courts to use in promoting "appropriate" political competition (Lowenstein 2007), and that aggressive court regulation may have unintended negative consequences.

A third group of election law scholars contends that the rights-structure debate is overblown, and they seek to narrow the differences between the two approaches. They argue that even the rights approach implicitly takes structure into account in setting forth certain minimum democratic requirements to be enforced by courts, and that structuralist approaches are favored, fundamentally, to help voters or groups of voters (Charles 2005; Dawood 2008).

However the scholarly debate gets resolved, the political markets approach thus far has received a frosty exception at the Supreme Court. Though isolated opinions

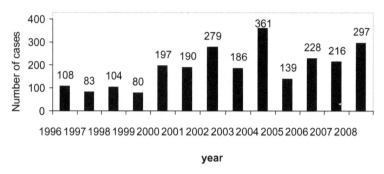

FIGURE 5.1. Election Challenge Cases by Year (1996–2008) (Hasen 2009)

of Supreme Court Justices sometimes seem to embrace this approach (*Randall v. Sorrell*, 2006, Breyer, J.),[1] a Supreme Court majority appeared to reject it in a 2007 case, holding that it is not the Court's job to promote political competition as a constitutional matter (*New York State Board of Elections v. Lopez Torres* 2008). Persily (2009) notes that many of the recent Supreme Court cases have given the Court an opportunity to embrace the political markets approach but the Court has not taken the bait.

The academic debate over the proper role of judges in regulating politics remains unsettled and is likely to remain so going forward. But the facts on the ground show that, for good or bad, judges increasingly are called upon to decide election law disputes. The number of such disputes nationally averaged 96 cases per year in the 1996–1999 period, and they more than doubled, to an average of 237 cases per year, in the 2001–2008 period (Hasen 2009) (see Figure 5.1).

Election law cases in recent years have gone to state court more often than federal court, though the most recent numbers show a move toward parity between state and federal courts. As Figure 5.2 shows, state court cases have made up a majority of election challenge cases heard in the courts in every year but one in the last twelve years. In the early 2000s, more than 80 percent of the election challenge cases were

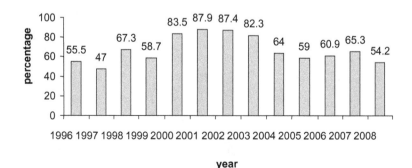

FIGURE 5.2. Percentage of Election Challenge Cases in State Courts (1996–2008) (Hasen 2009)

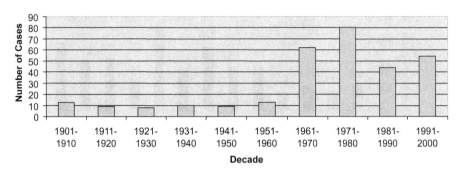

FIGURE 5.3. Supreme Court Election Law Cases through the Twentieth Century

heard in state courts. The figure has dropped somewhat, standing at 54 percent of cases, in 2008 (see Figure 5.2).

At the Supreme Court level, the amount of election litigation has remained at a high level since the 1960s, when the average number of cases rose sixfold from the pre-1960 period (from an average of ten to an average of sixty cases per decade) (Hasen 2003) (see Figure 5.3).

The reasons for the explosion in election law litigation across the American legal system since 2000 are uncertain. One theory posits that election law has become part of a "political strategy" followed by politicians in an effort to manipulate the rules of the game to get elected and to win in the event of an election recount or contest (Hasen 2005). It is also possible that *Bush v. Gore* (2000), the Supreme Court's opinion ending the disputed 2000 presidential election, spurred more litigation by creating new equal protection claims.[2] Other factors may be at work as well; election litigation might be a manifestation of the increased party polarization in American politics.[3] Further research on the causes of the election law litigation explosion is in order.

Thus, regardless of the merits of the debate over rights versus structure, the fact is that courts have become ever more involved in political regulation than before. The question is whether such a change is positive or negative, and if it is negative, what can be done to lower the amount of political regulation engaged in by courts.

PROBLEMS AND PITFALLS OF USING JUDGES
AS POLITICAL REGULATORS

To lawyers, legislators, and others, it may seem odd to refer to judges as "political regulators."[4] After all, judges are not expressly labeled "political regulators" like commissioners of the Federal Election Commission (FEC), members of a redistricting commission, or officials at the Department of Justice charged with determining whether voting changes in "covered jurisdictions" should be precleared pursuant to

Section 5 of the Voting Rights Act. Yet judges and not members of these bodies have set the basic rules for political competition in the United States; indeed, the latter group of regulators is restrained by, and takes cues from, the Supreme Court's political regulation decisions. As the FEC crafts rules limiting "coordinated" spending, for example, it must take account of the Supreme Court-created First Amendment limits on the ability of government to regulate election-related spending. A redistricting commission drawing new lines for state legislative districts must comply with Supreme Court requirements of equipopulous districts (one person, one vote), constitutional limits on the use of race in redistricting (racial gerrymandering), and the requirements of Section 2 of the Voting Rights Act as it has been interpreted in numerous complex opinions of the Supreme Court. DOJ officials ruling on preclearance requests must consider both the congressionally mandated language in Section 5 of the Voting Rights Act and the Supreme Court's shifting interpretations of Section 5.

Courts do more than provide ground rules for election law administrative action. They also directly decide election law disputes across a wide spectrum of cases (including campaign finance, redistricting, voting rights, ballot access, initiative law, and term limits) and are often the final arbiter in deciding contested elections.[5]

Though courts play a crucial role in these election law cases, some scholars have raised questions about how judges decide such cases. Chief complaints are that judges might decide cases in line with self-interest, or be subconsciously biased, or decide cases on ideological grounds.[6] By "self-interest" I mean that judges might decide cases to favor of their past or present political party or to keep themselves in office. The second problem, that of ideological decision making, recognizes that judges come to these cases with their own world views and might not apply "neutral" principles in deciding election law cases even if they can avoid self-interest problems. Of course, both of these problems inhere in any system of political regulation. My point in this part of the chapter is to show that these problems may apply to judges acting as political regulators as well.

In considering the self-interest point, there is a vast political science literature on how judges, especially Supreme Court Justices, decide cases. One of the leading theories is the "attitudinal model" that posits that Justices decide cases in line with their personal ideologies (Segal & Spaeth 1993). Some scholars in the positive political theory camp have refined the attitudinal model to argue that Justices seek to put in place their preferred policy positions to the extent they may do so without being reversed by Congress or others (McNollgast 1995). That is, these scholars argue that judges make decisions within the context of institutional constraints and the possibility of reaction to court decisions by other political actors including legislatures, agencies, and executives.

As applied to Supreme Court Justices, the attitudinal model has been criticized on a number of grounds, including the fact that ideology is not always a reliable predictor of judicial votes (Cross 2009). Others, such as Posner (1993, 3) argue that "trying to change the world plays no role in [the judge's utility] function," but that judges gain utility from the mere consumption value of voting.

Even if the attitudinal model accurately describes the behavior of U.S. Supreme Court Justices, who have life tenure and whose decisions are not easily undone, it might not apply (or apply in the same way) to the other judges who decide the vast majority of election law cases. For example, lower court federal judges, who face the possibility of Supreme Court reversal, have different constraints in deciding election law cases. The model is open to even sharper skepticism as applied to state court judges, who face factors other than the possibility of reversal by the U.S. Supreme Court. Many also run as candidates in elections, some of them partisan elections. Elected judges may have an incentive, at least in theory, to curry favor with either voters or members of their own political party (Hasen 1997). Incentives may also differ for judges who must face reappointment by a governor, legislature, or judicial commission.

As political scientists debate the question of judicial motivation as a general matter, election law scholars have turned to judicial decision making in election law cases in particular, looking for evidence of judges acting in their self-interest or at least appearing to be swayed subconsciously in election law cases by sympathy for particular litigants or positions.

An important recent study by Cox and Miles (2008) examined how federal judges decided cases brought under Section 2 of the Voting Rights Act, which was intended to expand political opportunities for minority voters. The authors made three central findings, two of which are relevant to this study.[7] First, judges appointed by Democratic presidents were significantly more likely than judges appointed by Republican presidents to find for minority plaintiffs in Section 2 cases. Second, the authors "show that a judge's race influences her voting pattern even more than her political affiliation. After controlling for other factors, an African-American judge is more than *twice as likely* as a non-African-American judge to vote for section 2 liability" (Cox and Miles 2008, 4).

Evidence of potential ideological skew in election law cases also comes from state and federal courts deciding challenges to the recent controversial voter identification laws. Hasen (2007a, 42) noted that the entire U.S. Court of Appeals for the Seventh Circuit split almost perfectly along party lines in voting whether to rehear *en banc* a 2–1 decision upholding Indiana's voter identification law, a law described by the (Democrat-appointed) dissenting judge as "a not-too-thinly-veiled attempt to discourage election-day turnout by certain folks believed to skew Democratic." Similarly, on the Michigan Supreme Court, the state justices (who are elected in partisan elections) split 5–2 along party lines over whether the Michigan voter identification law violated the state constitution(Hasen 2007a, 42, n201).[8]

Not all the evidence demonstrates a partisan split on courts in election law cases. Kopko (2008) examined decisions of state courts in 2004 ballot access cases involving Green Party candidate Ralph Nader's attempts to secure a place on the presidential ballot. Democrats opposed Nader, fearing his presence on the ballot could take votes away from Kerry. Looking at "Nader's ballot access claims in fifteen states, and accounting for factors that could influence partisanship in the judicial decision-making process, [Kopko found] that a judge's partisan affiliation is not a statistically significant determinant of a judge's case vote." Instead, Kopko found the decision of the state election authority to grant ballot access as a significant determinant of the judge's ruling (Kopko 2008, 302).

No doubt much more work is necessary to consider the circumstances in which party affiliation is a good predictor of judicial voting in election law cases and, to the extent it is, to consider whether self-interest or more subconscious motivations explains the split.

Matsusaka and Hasen (2010) offer additional findings that shed some more light on the question of judicial motivation. The research considers the single-subject rule applicable to voter initiatives. The rule requires that voters not be presented with initiatives embracing more than one "subject." Judicial application of the single-subject rule therefore requires judges to decide whether particular initiatives have more than one "subject," however the state defines "subject." Unlike issues such as voter identification, single-subject challenges present an issue without an obvious partisan valence.

Lowenstein (1983) argued that when judges are forced to make highly subjective decisions, it is hard for their reasoning not to be influenced by their belief systems, values, and ideologies. Matsusaka and Hasen (2010) found strong support for this claim. They examined votes of state appellate court judges on single-subject cases in five states during the period 1997–2006 (more than 150 cases and more than 700 individual votes). They found that judges are more likely to uphold an initiative against a single-subject challenge if their partisan affiliations suggest they would be sympathetic to the policy proposed by the initiative. More importantly, they found that partisan affiliation was extremely important in states with aggressive enforcement of the single-subject rule – the rate of upholding an initiative jumped from 42 percent to 83 percent when judges agreed with the policy than when they disagreed – but not very important in states with restrained enforcement. This evidence suggests that placing judges in a position with significant discretion could well lead to an increase in arbitrary or political decisions.

These results suggest that whether consciously or subconsciously, judges decide at least some election law cases in systematically different ways depending upon their ideology and background, wholly apart from partisan considerations. For this reason, political reformers should be cautious before encouraging more political regulation cases into the courts.

Finally, one might consider whether there is more or less judicial partisanship, self-interest, or subconscious bias on state courts or federal courts. Given the track records of both sets of courts in election law cases in recent years, it is not clear that one forum is better from the point of view of fair political regulation rather than the

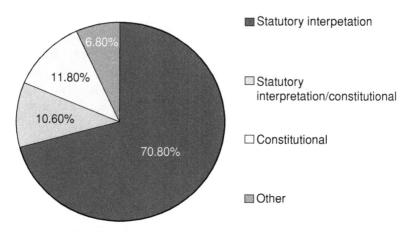

FIGURE 5.4. 2008 Election Challenge Cases (by type of case) (Hasen 2009)

other, despite the fact that rational models of judging suggest that judges with life tenure should behave differently than judges who must run for periodic election (sometimes in partisan contests) or be considered for reappointment. If judges on state and federal courts reach the same results in election law cases, it suggests that the institutional approach of positive political theory may be overstating the extent to which judges worry about responses of other institutional actors to judicial decisions.

MINIMIZING THE NEED FOR JUDGES AS POLITICAL REGULATORS

If it is correct that judges cannot be counted on to decide election law cases in a wholly neutral way, at least some of the time, election law scholars should consider alternative ways of resolving (or better, ex ante avoiding) election law disputes. This part of the chapter considers whether changes in legislative drafting and institutional design could improve election law dispute resolution, and sets forth an agenda for future research. Improved legislative drafting can clarify the law so that fewer election law disputes arise, and those that do arise are resolved quickly and without controversy. Institutional design changes may be used both to induce legislators to draft clearer election law statutes and, more directly, to avoid self-interested and ideological judicial decision making in election law cases.

Reducing Election Law Disputes through Clearer Legislative Drafting

Though election law disputes raise quite a variety of problems, the bulk of such cases involve questions of statutory interpretation. In 2008, for example, more than 81 percent of state election law cases involved either statutory interpretation questions (70.8 percent) or a mix of statutory and constitutional issues (10.6 percent) (see Figure 5.4).

Though statutory interpretation questions can arise regardless of the clarity of the law, there is no doubt that gaps and ambiguities in the law increase both the potential for litigation and the variance in how courts decide disputes arising under applicable statutes. Given this point, one way to lessen the public's dependence on judges as political regulators is for the legislature to draft clearer statutes that fill in gaps and resolve ambiguities.

Ideally, state legislatures and Congress should establish periodic "election law audits" (Hasen 2005; Martinez 2005) to review existing election laws and make suggestions for commonsense improvements in clarity and coverage. For such audits to work, reformers will have to consider appropriate mechanisms for both choosing the personnel to conduct such audits and for having the recommendations from such audits voted on by state legislative bodies or Congress.

Institutional Design Changes

Calling for clearer election law statutes to minimize the frequency of election law litigation raises a classic "Here to There" problem in election law (Gerken 2009; Kang 2009): If those who must enact reform are motivated by self-interest and ideology, how will reform get enacted? Election law audits will not be ordered simply because reformers think they are a good idea. Interest group politics, busy legislative agendas, and forces of inertia work against the establishment of such audits and the adoption of audit recommendations into law. The best chance for reform may come at times when one party controls the legislative process and believes reform is in the party's interest. It might be that states with unified party control of the legislature and governor's office would be most likely to agree to proposed election law changes (Palazzolo & Ceaser 2005; Hasen, forthcoming).

Apart from such relying on political self-interest to lead directly to election law reform, some election law scholars have advocated institutional design reform to create the conditions for reform indirectly. If these efforts are successful, they could lower the amount of election law litigation and reliance upon judges as political regulators.

This recent trend in election law scholarship, which I have dubbed "The New Institutionalism" (Hasen, forthcoming), proposes new institutions or mechanisms, such as amicus courts and electoral advisory commissions, to prod existing institutions into election law reform. For example, Heather Gerken (2009) has proposed the formulation of a "Democracy Index," which would rank states upon a series of election administration criteria. Gerken argues that the ranking system will create the right incentives for jurisdictions to move toward professionalized and nonpartisan election administration, which in turn can lower the amount of election law litigation.

The key to New Institutionalist proposals like Gerken's is harnessing the power of *embarrassment* to foster election reform. There is certainly something to this idea. Consider, for example, how Florida reacted after the 2000 election debacle in that state. The state legislature, following the controversial decisions of the Florida Supreme Court and machine breakdowns responded by (1) eliminating the "protest" phase for election challenges; (2) changing the conditions for when a manual recount is triggered; (3) requiring recounts to be conducted jurisdiction-wide, with a look at both undervotes and overvotes; (4) and requiring the use of written standards for judging the intent of the voter in ballots examined during an election contest (Jones 2006). It also eliminated all punch-card balloting machines that raised all kinds of judicially reviewable issues about voter intent.[9]

Embarrassment, however, does not guarantee that states will perform periodic "election law audits." As Hasen (2007a, 18) noted, despite the fact that there were more than twenty lawsuits brought challenging one or another aspect of California recall law in 2003 (when Governor Gray Davis was recalled and replaced by Arnold Schwarzenegger), the California legislature has done nothing to fix the obvious contradictions and problems with the California Elections Code. My favorite example is the internal code contradiction on the rules for nominating someone to be a replacement candidate in the event voters choose to recall a sitting governor. The recall rules state that the "usual nomination rules shall apply" to recall elections. And the first of the "usual nomination rules" provides that the rules do not apply to recall elections. The California Secretary of State then applied the rules (which normally apply to primary elections) requiring that candidates wishing to run for governor in the recall provide only 65 signatures and $3,000, leading to the unwieldy 2003 election and ballot featuring 135 candidates for governor, including the child actor Gary Coleman, watermelon-smashing comedian Gallagher, and a porn star.

The California example suggests that attempts at embarrassment of election administrators or legislators through bad publicity may not always work, even to resolve some high-salience disputes. For this reason, it is not clear that legislators would pay attention to blue-ribbon advisory commissions established to recommend changes to election law (Elmendorf 2006). More direct methods of change may be required, such as a "citizens commission" with the power to bypass the legislature and put election reforms directly on the ballot subject to a popular vote (Gerken 2007). The question then, of course, is how to mandate creation of such a commission.

Further study is necessary to understand when and how embarrassment affects the actions of election administrators and legislators considering election law changes. At this point, the mechanics of embarrassment have been posited but not well tested. Figure 5.5 illustrates the implicit causal mechanism beneath the Gerken Index.

According to the model, new information generated by the Index has both a direct and indirect effect on state and local election administrators. Directly, the Index provides new information that may trigger both rational and emotional responses in the administrators to the new information. Indirectly, the new information may

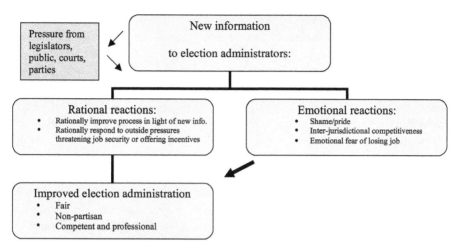

FIGURE 5.5. State and Local Election Administrators' Potential Response to New Information Generated by the Democracy Index (Hasen, forthcoming)

trigger rational and emotional responses in other people and entities that hold influence over election administrators. Thus, legislators, the public, courts, and political parties react to the information contained in the Index and then may pressure or encourage election administrators to act in certain ways.

Election administrators (as well as outsiders, such as legislators and the public) react rationally to information provided by the Index to improve election administration. Jurisdictions learn of their strengths and deficiencies relative to other jurisdictions, and explore the reasons for relatively low rankings. Some problems will require additional funds, which are easier to justify (and demand) in the presence of comparative data. Other problems will require revamping of machinery, organizational management, chains of command, or public relations. Election administrators also rationally respond to threats to job security and incentives for better performance from legislators, the public, and others.

Election administrators also respond emotionally to the rankings. They may feel shame in not being highly ranked, or not ranked highly against a relevant peer group. They may feel pride at being ranked highly, and determined to keep a high ranking. Similarly, the rankings may engender interjurisdictional competitiveness, just as the U.S. *News* rankings trigger competitive behavior among competing law schools. Finally, election administrators may react emotionally out of fear of losing their jobs because of disapproval of legislators, the public, and others, or – to the extent that the administrators are elected – to competitors who run against them in future elections.

If Gerken is right that the Index may spur the development of nonpartisan election administration (a point about which the evidence is still out), this result may take some of the pressure off judicial political regulation. It may be that courts will defer more to state election officials when those election officials are nonpartisan or are perceived to be nonpartisan by the public or the courts. It also may be that there is less litigation (or litigation that goes all the way to a judicial opinion) in states with such nonpartisan election officials,[10] perhaps because such legislators are more apt to make neutral and fair decisions. Professionalism plausibly will lessen the chances of administrative errors, themselves the source of election law litigation. These hypotheses too must be tested.

Though the Democracy Index focuses on improving election administration at the administrative level, some New Institutionalists seek to harness the potential for embarrassment to improve *judicial* decision making in election law cases more directly. For example, Ned Foley (2008) would convene an amicus court comprised of equal numbers of retired Democratic judges, Republican judges, and Independents to consider high-profile election law cases being considered before real courts. The amicus court would submit its proposed decision in the form of an amicus brief to the actual court.

According to Foley, the amicus court could indirectly influence courts to decide cases fairly:

> Unanimity among the amicus judges would show how to resolve the case without partisanship. But even a divided ruling from the Amicus Court, given its independent tiebreaker, would cast a salutary shadow over the actual court's deliberations. If the actual result differed from the Amicus Court's, the divergence would be questioned. To avoid such scrutiny, the actual judges might follow the Amicus Court's outcome and reasoning. In this way, without government power, the Amicus Court could promote fairness – and the perception of fairness – in resolving election disputes.
>
> Over time, if the Amicus Court develops a strong reputation for nonpartisan fairness, candidates might feel compelled to accept its judgment, pledging not to seek a contrary ruling from an actual court. The Amicus Court then would become a kind of alternative arbitration panel for election litigation, much like labor arbitration developed to settle union-management disputes. This scenario is most likely to occur if the Amicus Court's members, in addition to having blue-ribbon resumés, display judicious temperament in striving for consensus rulings grounded in the objective requirements of law.

The underpinnings of Foley's arguments are quite similar to Gerken's. The amicus court provides information about "the objective requirements of law." The judges rationally may use this information as an aid to decision. Emotionally, judges may also feel shame if they deviate from the neutral amicus court's requirements and feel pride if they follow the amicus court. The public gains a new tool to evaluate the fairness of judges, an objective baseline, much like how the Index would allow the public and legislators to evaluate the competence and fairness of election administrators.

We have no experience with this type of institutional design, and some judges on the actual courts might not give much credence to such amicus briefs, especially if they are viewed by conservative judges as coming from a project with a liberal agenda. (*Ryan v. Community Futures Trading Comm'n* 1997, Posner, J.; *Jaffee v. Redmond* 1996, Scalia, J., dissenting).

Some New Institutionalist proposals to improve judicial decision making in election law cases propose new judicial bodies. One possibility is the establishment of a special election law court. Other countries, such as Mexico,[11] have dedicated courts that can develop expertise on complex aspects of state or federal election laws. The question is whether such courts can overcome some of the conscious or subconscious biases sometimes seen in existing courts that decide election law disputes.

To achieve neutrality, the "election law court" might be comprised of two judges from different partisan backgrounds who pick a third "neutral" judge to sit with them. This approach yielded a unanimous result in the recent *McCain v. Obama* simulation,[12] but it is unclear whether the method would produce such clear and unanimous results if the case involved a real-world dispute. In any case, assuming the outcome of a case before the election law court could still be appealed to the U.S. Supreme Court, it is not clear that the self-interest and ideology problems could necessarily be solved. They simply may be shifted to a higher court.

CONCLUSION

To a great degree, judges remain the "black boxes" of political regulation. We send a great many election law disputes into the box for decision, and decisions emerge at the conclusion of each case. It is time to rethink the paradigm of great reliance on judges in the field of political regulation as we continue to explore how judges decide election law disputes.

The appeal of judges as political regulators is that they are considered to be neutral decision makers, somehow above politics, who can rely on neutral principles of the law to reach unbiased results. The reality, well understood by lawyers but rarely acknowledged, is that judges sometimes come to cases with their own conscious or subconscious biases favoring or opposing various candidates, parties, and interests.

If judges are going to continue playing a major role in political regulation, we should stop pretending that neutral decisions will magically emerge from the judicial black box. Instead, we should consider ways to improve the process so that judges are called on to make fewer decisions, and the decisions that they make be mediated through institutions that will cabin both administrative and judicial discretion. Further research is necessary to identify the best ways to accomplish a limitation

on discretion and judgment throughout the administrative and judicial systems of
political regulation. In the meantime, reformers should think twice before proposing
an expansion of the role of the judiciary in deciding election law disputes.

NOTES

1   Compare to Hasen (2007b) who noted that the Court plurality was not consistent in
    its focus on competition even within the *Randall* case itself.
2   But see Smith and Shortell (2007; noting that the rise in litigation related to presi-
    dential elections began in 2000, before *Bush v. Gore*).
3   See Jacobson (2000), documenting a marked rise in polarization in Congress and in
    American public opinion).
4   Cf. Cain (1999, 1119; stating the field is better defined as "political regulation" rather
    than "election law").
5   When it comes to federal elections, Congress may exercise authority superior to the
    courts to determine disputes involving presidential and congressional elections. See
    U.S. Const. Art I, § 5 ("Each House shall be the judge of the elections, returns and
    qualifications of its own members"); Amend XII (setting out rules for counting of
    Electoral College votes).
6   In addition, judges might lack expertise to decide certain election law issues. I return
    to this point in the third part of the chapter, in discussing potential institutional
    changes in political regulation.
7   The third set of findings relates to the amount of Section 2 liability over time and
    across jurisdictions. These findings are not relevant to the issues discussed in this
    chapter.
8   In the U.S. Supreme Court's review of the challenge to Indiana's voter identification
    law, the Justices split 6–3 on its constitutionality. Six Justices appointed by Republican
    presidents voted to uphold the law. Two Justices chosen by a Democratic president
    and one Justice (Souter) chosen by a Republican president voted to strike down the
    law as unconstitutional (*Crawford v. Marion County Election Board*, 2008).
9   This did not end the matter. Facing new public lack of confidence in electronic
    voting machines following a dispute over a close congressional election in Sarasota
    County, Florida, the state chose to ban such machines in favor of other systems such
    as those using optically scanned paper ballots (Vartabedian 2008).
10 Aside from considering whether the method of selecting election officials affects
    the amount of election law litigation, scholars should examine variations in the way
    that election officials do their jobs and interpret statutes. In the 2008 election, for
    example, the Ohio Attorney General sought to mediate election law disputes before
    they had to be resolved through a judicial decision (Niquette 2008). Alternative
    dispute resolution could keep more election law cases out of the courts, or at least
    resolved before judicial decision.
11 See Eisenstadt (2004).
12 For details on the simulation and the unanimous court decision, visit http://moritzlaw
    .osu.edu/electionlaw/electioncourt/. The simulation is a project of Election Law@
    Moritz, at the Ohio State University College of Law. Another example is that of
    the three-judge courts set up by statute to deal with certain Voting Rights Act,
    redistricting, and campaign finance cases. See Solimine 1996 and Solimine 2007.
    These cases go on direct appeal to the U.S. Supreme Court.

REFERENCES

Bush v. Gore, 531 U.S. 98 (2000).

Cain, Bruce E. 1999. Election law as its own field: A political scientist's perspective. *Loyola of Los Angeles Law Review* 32: 1105.

Charles, Guy-Uriel. 2005. Judging the law of politics. *Michigan Law Review* 103: 1099.

Cox, Adam B. and Thomas J. Miles. 2008. Judging the voting rights act. *Columbia Law Review* 108: 1.

Crawford v. Marion County Election Board, 553 U.S. 181 (2008).

Cross, Frank B. 2009. *The Theory and Practice of Statutory Interpretation*. Stanford, CT: Stanford University Press.

Dawood, Yasmin. 2008. The antidomination model and judicial oversight of democracy. *Georgetown Law Journal* 96: 1411.

Eisenstadt, Todd A. 2004. Settling election disputes: What the United States can learn from Mexico. *Election Law Journal* 3 (3): 530.

Elmendorf, Christopher S. 2006. Electoral commissions and election reform: An overview. *Election Law Journal* 5 (4): 425.

Foley, Edward B. 2008. Let's not repeat 2000: A special political tribunal could help resolve election conflicts without mistrust. *Legal Times* (April 21). http://moritzlaw.osu.edu/library/documents/Foley-LegalTimes-4–21-08.pdf (accessed April 5, 2010).

Gerken, Heather K. 2007. The double-edged sword of independence: Inoculating electoral reform commissions against every day politics. *Election Law Journal* 6 (2): 184.

———. 2009. *The Democracy Index: Why Our Election System Is Failing and How to Fix It*. Princeton, NJ: Princeton University Press.

Hasen, Richard L. 1997. High court wrongly elected: A public choice model of judging and its implications for the voting rights act. *North Carolina Law Review* 74: 1305.

———. 2003. *The Supreme Court and Election Law: Judging Equality from Baker v. Carr to Bush v. Gore*. New York: New York University Press.

———. 2005. Beyond the margin of litigation: Reforming U.S. election administration to avoid electoral meltdown. *Washington and Lee Law Review* 62: 937.

———. 2007a. The untimely death of *Bush v. Gore. Stanford Law Review* 60: 1.

———. 2007b. The newer incoherence: Competition, social science, and balancing after *Randall v. Sorrell. Ohio State Law Journal* 68: 849.

———. 2009. The democracy canon. *Stanford Law Review* 62: 69.

———. Forthcoming. Election administration reform and the new institutionalism. *California Law Review*.

Issacharoff, Samuel. 2002. Gerrymandering and political cartels. *Harvard Law Review* 116: 593.

Issacharoff, Samuel and Richard H. Pildes. 1998. Politics as markets: Partisan lockups of the democratic process. *Stanford Law Review* 50: 643.

Jacobson, Gary C. 2000. Party polarization in national politics: The electoral connection. In *Polarized Politics: Congress and the President in a Partisan Era* ed. Jon R. Bond and Richard Fleisher. Washington, DC: CQ Press.

Jaffe v. Redmond, 518 U.S. 1 (1996).

Jones, Clifford A. 2006. Out of Guatemala? Election law reform in Florida and the legacy of *Bush v. Gore* in the 2004 presidential election. *Election Law Journal* 5 (2): 121.

Kang, Michael S. 2009. From here to theory in election law. *Texas Law Review* 87: 787.

Kopko, Kyle C. 2008. Partisanship suppressed: Judicial decision-making in Ralph Nader's 2004 ballot access litigation. *Election Law Journal* 7 (4): 301.

Lowenstein, Daniel H. 1983. California initiatives and the single subject rule. *UCLA Law Review* 30: 936.

———. 2007. Competition and competitiveness in American elections. *Election Law Journal* 6 (3): 278.

Martinez III, Ray. 2005. Greater impartiality in election administration: Prudent Steps Toward Improving Voter Confidence. *Election Law Journal* 5 (3): 235.

Matsusaka, John G. and Richard L. Hasen. 2010. Aggressive enforcement of the single subject rule. *Election Law Journal* 10: 399.

McNollgast 1995. Politics and the courts: A positive theory of judicial doctrine and the rule of law. *Southern California Law Review* 68: 1631.

New York State Board of Elections v. Lopez Torres, 552 U.S. 196 (2008).

Niquette, Mark. 2008. Voter-registration lawsuit against Brunner is dropped. *Columbus Dispatch* (October 21). http://www.dispatch.com/live/content/local_news/stories/2008/10/21/dismissed.html?sid=101 (accessed April 5, 2010).

Palazzolo, Daniel J. and James W Ceaser, eds. 2005. *Election Reform: Politics and Policy*. Lanham, MD: Lexington Books.

Persily, Nathaniel. 2002. Reply: In defense of foxes guarding henhouses: The case for judicial acquiescence to incumbent-protecting gerrymanders. *Harvard Law Review* 116: 649.

———. 2009. Fig leaves and tea leaves in the Supreme Court's recent election law decisions. *Supreme Court Review*, 2008, 89.

Posner, Richard A. 1993. What do judges and judges maximize? (The same thing everyone else does). *Supreme Court Economic Review* 3: 1.

Randall v. Sorrell, 548 U.S. 230 (2006).

Ryan v. Community Futures Trading Comm'n, 125 F.3d 1062 (7th Cir. 1997).

Segal, Jeffrey A. and Harld J. Spaeth. 1993. *The Supreme Court and the Attitudinal Model*. New York: Cambridge University Press.

Smith, Charles Anthony and Christopher Shortell. 2007. The suits that counted: The judicialization of presidential elections. *Election Law Journal* 6 (3): 251.

Solimine, Michael E. 1996. The three-judge district court in voting rights litigation. *University of Michigan Journal of Law Reform* 30: 79.

———. 2007. Institutional process, agenda setting, and the development of election law on the Supreme Court. *Ohio State Law Journal* 68: 767.

Vartabedian, Ralph. 2008. Electronic voting is facing a recall. *Los Angeles Times* (January 29). http://www.latimes.com/news/nationworld/nation/la-na-natvote29jan29,1,1372072,full.story (accessed April 5, 2010).

6

Empirical Legitimacy and Election Law

Christopher S. Elmendorf

INTRODUCTION

Worries about public confidence in the basic institutions of the political order have been a recurring theme of the Supreme Court's constitutional election law jurisprudence. They seem to inform the Court's articulation of constitutional rights; its understanding of the state interests that may justify burdens on such rights; and the development of prudential limitations on judicial involvement in electoral disputes, such as the political question doctrine. To date, however, the Court's confidence-minded decisions have turned entirely on judicial guesswork about the functional relationships of interest. The Court has simply assumed, for example, that campaign-contribution restrictions will inspire confidence among citizens who would otherwise believe the electoral process corrupted by moneyed interests. The Court has also relied on rank conjectures about the consequences of perceived corruption of the electoral process. In *Purcell v. Gonzalez* (2006), for example, the Court posited that "honest citizens" who believe that voter fraud is common will be "drive[n] out of the democratic process."

The jurisprudence of public confidence is on a collision course with recent developments in political science. Findings from new survey research cast doubt on some of the Supreme Court's most important conjectures, while also hinting at the possibility that seemingly unexceptional features of the electoral practices may prove constitutionally vulnerable – if the Court is serious about the idea that constitutional political rights derive their shape in part from what the citizenry deems important to the legitimacy of the political order.

Professor of Law, University of California at Davis. For refining my thinking about the topics treated in this paper, I am indebted to the participants in the Constitutional Law and Legal Theory Colloquium at the University of Texas School of Law (Mitch Berman and Larry Sager especially); to the participants in a Tobin Project/ALI conference on "The Future of Elections Scholarship" at Duke Law School; to the editors of this volume (Mike Kang especially); and to Ned Foley and Thad Kousser.

The first part of this chapter examines the role of public confidence and related ideas in the Supreme Court's election law jurisprudence, and concludes with some thoughts on the normative force of positive (empirical) legitimacy as a criterion for judicial decision in constitutional cases. The second part reviews political science findings on the relationship between electoral arrangements and empirical legitimacy. The third part offers suggestions for the courts. If the Supreme Court is serious about safeguarding public confidence in the basic institutions of the political order, it would do well (1) to specify more precisely the confidence-related values it means to privilege; (2) to review state and local election laws more deferentially than national laws; and (3) to recognize a compelling state interest – sufficient to justify substantial burdens on previously recognized constitutional rights – in bona-fide regulatory experiments with confidence-minded electoral reforms.

THE ROLE OF PUBLIC CONFIDENCE IN THE SUPREME COURT'S THINKING ABOUT ELECTION LAW

This part begins with a look at the rhetoric of legitimacy and public acceptance in constitutional election cases. I then address the Court's concern for the judiciary's reputation as impartial and politically neutral. I conclude with some observations about the normative pull of positive legitimacy in the adjudication of constitutional election law disputes.

Legitimacy and the Appearance of the Electoral Process

Explaining his vote to stay the Florida recount following the presidential election of 2000, Justice Scalia wrote:

> The counting of votes that are of questionable legality does in my view threaten irreparable harm to petitioner Bush, and to the country, by casting a cloud upon what he claims to be the legitimacy of his election. Count first, and rule upon legality afterwards, is not a recipe for producing election results that have *the public acceptance* democratic stability requires (*Bush v. Gore* 2000, 1047).[1]

This statement is unmatched for the vigor and transparency with which it embraces "public acceptance" as a guiding norm for judicial superintendence of the electoral process, but it nonetheless fits comfortably with much that came before it. In *Kramer v. Union Free School District No. 15* (1969), the canonical case that consolidated the fundamental status of the right to vote, the Warren Court asserted that the right is fundamental for equal protection purposes because, inter alia, "[a]ny unjustified discrimination in determining who may participate in political affairs or in the selection of public officials *undermines the legitimacy of representative government*" (262).

Kramer's use of the word *legitimacy* is susceptible to two interpretations, with quite different implications for how judges should adjudicate constitutional challenges to election laws. The Court might have meant positive or empirical legitimacy – whether citizens *in fact* believe that the system of democracy as it then exists legitimizes the government's rule, morally obligating them to comply with duly enacted laws and official orders made under those laws. Or the Court might have meant normative legitimacy – whether the political system comports with a privileged philosophical account of the characteristics it ought to have in order to be worthy of citizens' respect and obedience. Although the Court has never undertaken to explain the sense in which it used the world *legitimacy* in *Kramer*, it has repeatedly disclaimed that its election law jurisprudence rests on any normative "theory of democracy" (Gerken 2002; Ortiz 2004). Some such theory is essential for any jurisprudence of normative legitimacy.[2] On the other hand, the Court has never referenced the empirical literature on positive legitimacy in explaining what facets of the political process enjoy constitutional protection. This would seem essential if the grounding of political rights on positive legitimacy is to be more than nominal.

Notwithstanding *Kramer*'s ambiguity, there are good reasons to suspect that worries about positive legitimacy have informed the Court's articulation of constitutionally privileged interests in election law cases, reasons that go beyond the occasional blurt, such as the previously quoted statement by Justice Scalia explaining his vote to stay the Florida recount. The Court's consistent attention to "appearances" in elaborating constitutional political rights speaks to a concern for positive legitimacy (though it is also susceptible to other interpretations). And the Court's treatment of "public confidence" as a value that can justify regulatory burdens on otherwise protected rights suggests, to this observer, that the same concerns are probably at work when the Court is giving content to political rights whose footing in constitutional text and history is doubtful at best.

Perhaps the most clear-cut example of the Court's recourse to appearances in elaborating constitutionally privileged interests occurred in *Shaw v. Reno* (1993) and subsequent cases about the "excessive" use of race in designing electoral districts. The *Shaw* Court found a bizarrely shaped majority-minority district unconstitutional on the ground that the district's uncouth design sent a message that the legislator elected from it was only supposed to represent African-American voters rather than all of his or her constituents (648). As Pildes and Niemi (1993) wrote, "what distinguishes 'bizarre' race-conscious districts [unconstitutional under *Shaw*] is the *signal they send out* that . . . race has become paramount and dwarfed all other, traditionally relevant criteria" (501).[3]

Consider also how the Court has treated partisanship in electoral reform. All nine Justices in *Vieth v. Jubelirer* (2004) agreed in principle that "too much" partisanship in redistricting would be unlawful, even as four concluded that the "how much is too much" question was not judicially manageable. Kennedy's concurrence is especially telling. Though unable to conjure a manageable standard for judging run-of-the-mill partisan gerrymanders, Kennedy refused to join the plurality's political question holding because he thought that at least some imaginable cases of partisanship in redistricting would violate the Constitution and could be identified by the courts as such. He offered this example:

> If a State passed an enactment that declared "All future apportionment shall be drawn so as most to burden Party X's rights to fair and effective representation, though still in accord with one-person, one-vote principles," we would surely conclude the Constitution had been violated (*Vieth v. Jubelirer* 2004, 312).

The offense in Kennedy's example is that the partisanship is *transparent* – loudly proclaimed on the face of the statute – as well as brutal. That it is the transparency of some partisan gerrymandering (and what this portends for positive legitimacy) that kept Kennedy in the game is suggested by the penultimate paragraph of his opinion:

> The ordered working of our Republic, and of the democratic process, depends on a sense of decorum and restraint in all branches of government, and in the citizenry itself. Here, one has the sense that legislative restraint was abandoned. That should not be thought to serve the interests of our political order. Nor should it be thought to serve our interest in demonstrating to the world how democracy works. Whether spoken with concern or pride, it is unfortunate that our legislators have reached the point of *declaring* that, when it comes to apportionment: "We are in the business of rigging elections" (*Vieth v. Jubelirer* 2004, 316–7).[4]

Consider also *Crawford v. Marion County Election Board* (2008), which dealt with voting requirements enacted on a straight party-line vote. Justice Stevens, who wrote the lead opinion, recognized that although some partisan self-seeking in the design of voting requirements is inevitable, bare partisanship (meaning that the requirements serve no neutral public purpose at all) would be unconstitutional.[5] His reservation of the unconstitutional-because-of-partisan-purpose rule for voting requirements that lack a disguising fig leaf of public purpose is at least arguably consistent with an emphasis on delegitimating appearances.[6] The judicial objective is not to sniff out illicit motives and then to restore the legal landscape to the form it would have taken absent their distorting influence (this being the standard project of intent-based equal protection jurisprudence; see, for example, Klarman 1997) but instead to negate only those rules that cannot be rationalized except with reference to bad motives, and which as such are transparently partisan. "Intelligent voters," Stevens has written, are sure to "resent . . . political manipulation of the electorate for no public purpose" (*Vieth v. Jubelirer* 2004, 322, quoting *Davis v. Bandemer* 1986, 177).

Also consistent with an emphasis on delegitimating appearances, though not explained in these terms, are the cases establishing a firm constitutional rule against conditioning political participation (voting, ballot position, and even appointment to public office) upon payment of a fee or ownership of property (*Harman v. Forssenius* 1965; *Harper v. Va. State Board of Elections* 1966; *Cipriano v. City of Houma* 1969; *City of Phoenix v. Kolodziejski* 1970; *Turner v. Fouche* 1970; *Bullock v. Carter* 1972; *Lubin v. Panish* 1974; *Hill v. Stone* 1975; *Chappelle v. Greater Baton Rouge Airport Dist.* 1977; *Quinn v. Millsap* 1989). In deciding these cases, the Court required no proof that the fee-based regime had substantial adverse effects on political participation by or representation of poor people. What the money-or-property-condition cases achieve is in some ways symbolic: They prevent the state from establishing rules for political participation that facially – that is, transparently – and disproportionately burden a class of citizens susceptible to political alienation (c.f. Pildes 1998, 744–6).[7]

To be sure, the appearances cases do not compel the conclusion that the justices' beliefs about what contributes to positive legitimacy are substantially influencing the Court's elaboration of constitutional political rights. It could be the case, as Pildes (1998) has suggested, that these cases instead represent an effort at taste-shaping – using law's normativity to reinforce those values that the justices believe should define us as a people. This is not the same as protecting the empirical legitimacy of the political order. To see the difference, consider the problem of funny looking, majority-minority districts. On the taste-shaping view, the problem is that these districts signify that it is "okay" for race to be the dominant criterion in district design, when in fact – on the right normative approach to redistricting – racial representation should be a secondary consideration at best. On the positive-legitimacy understanding, by contrast, the problem is not that such districts convey an inherently bad message, but rather that they expose and exacerbate a conflict between two groups of citizens with very different and strongly felt views about the proper, legitimate role of race in electoral institutions. The Court in the *Shaw* line of cases undertook to structure the electoral process in a manner that both groups could regard as tolerably legitimate; the accommodation it reached was to allow districts to be designed for racial purposes so long as the district designers honored, or appeared to honor, other goals as well.

In my view, the weight that the Court has given to public confidence in justifying *burdens* on otherwise protected interests – the topic I shall take up next – suggests that the Court's attention to appearances in deciding what interests are constitutionally privileged in the first instance reflects a concern for positive legitimacy. The elaboration of constitutional political rights has occurred in a discretionary, common-law-like manner, without much regard for constitutional text or time-of-enactment history. Given the subjectivity of this undertaking, it would be odd for the concerns that feature prominently in cases about the justification of burdens on otherwise protected rights to have had no pull on the justices' thinking about what interests undergird the political rights themselves. That the concern for citizens' understandings of legitimacy is only implicit on the rights-elaboration side of the equation probably reflects the justices' doubts about whether express recourse to this consideration can be squared with conventional understandings of legality in the project of rights elaboration, rather than a conviction that positive legitimacy is unimportant in defining the content of political rights.[8]

The Court has made no bones about justifying burdens on the exercise of constitutional rights in terms of the state interest in citizens' acceptance of the legitimacy of the political order. Thus, in *Buckley v. Valeo* (1976), the Court upheld the constitutionality of federal campaign contribution limits enacted after Watergate, stating:

> Of almost equal concern as the danger of actual quid pro quo arrangements is the impact of the appearance of corruption stemming from *public awareness* of the opportunities for abuse inherent in a regime of large individual financial contributions. . . . Congress could legitimately conclude that *the avoidance of the appearance of improper influence is . . . critical . . . if confidence in the system of representative government is not to be eroded to a disastrous extent* (*Buckley v. Valeo* 1976, 27).

In subsequent campaign finance cases, the Court recognized that the absence of evidence of actual corruption does not mean that citizens do not perceive the system to be rife with opportunities for abuse, and reiterated that combating this perception is adequate grounds for restricting citizens' First Amendment right to make monetary contributions to political campaigns (e.g., *Nixon v. Shrink Missouri Government PAC* 2000).

A similar idea informs the new generation of cases concerning administrative barriers to voting.[9] In *Purcell v. Gonzalez* (2006), a unanimous Court per Justice Kennedy opened its analysis with these words:

> A State indisputably has a compelling interest in preserving the integrity of its election process. *Confidence in the integrity of our electoral processes is essential* to the functioning of our participatory democracy. Voter fraud drives honest citizens out of the democratic process and *breeds distrust* of our government. Voters who fear their legitimate votes will be outweighed by fraudulent ones will *feel disenfranchised* (*Purcell v Gonzalez* 2006, 6; internal citations and quotation marks omitted).

Whatever one makes of Justice Kennedy's supposition that "honest citizens" who imagine fraud to be rampant will cease voting,[10] it cannot be gainsaid that this passage bespeaks a powerful concern with how citizens see, experience, and subjectively evaluate the political process. The refrain continued in *Crawford*. Justice Stevens, who wrote the lead opinion, deemed the Indiana photo ID requirement facially justified by, inter alia, the state's interest in "protecting public confidence 'in the integrity and legitimacy of representative government'" (1620, quoting Brief for State Respondents, No. 07-25, 53). Stevens acknowledged that this interest was "closely related to the State's interest in preventing voter fraud," but he insisted that "public confidence" was of "independent significance" because it "encourages citizen participation in the democratic process" (1620, quoting Brief for State Respondents, No. 07-25, 53).

The Appearance of Judicial Impartiality

The Supreme Court's evolving role as overseer of the political process has long been informed by the justices' concern for public confidence in the courts themselves.

The Court undertook to constitutionalize the electoral process against the better judgment of Justice Frankfurter, who warned that this project would inevitably result (for want of clear textual and historical guidance) in judges "mak[ing] their private views of political wisdom the measure of the Constitution" (*Baker v. Carr* 1962, 301–2). This, in turn, would "give the appearance, if not reflect the reality, of [judicial] involvement with partisan politics. . . ." (*Baker v. Carr* 1962, 301–2). The price to be paid would come in the coin of judicial authority, which "ultimately rests on sustained public confidence in [the Court's] moral sanction," a "feeling [which] must be nourished by the Court's complete detachment, in fact and in appearance, from political entanglements. . . ." (*Baker v. Carr* 1962, 267).

Though the Court rejected Frankfurter's position on the justiciability of malapportionment claims, his warnings have not gone unheeded. The "manageable standards" prong of the political question doctrine today embodies Frankfurter's anxiety about the courts being perceived as just another partisan actor (Fallon 2006) – a concern that reaches its zenith when the question at bar bears directly on the distribution of political power. Writing for a four-justice plurality in *Vieth v. Jubelirer*, Justice Scalia asserted the fuzzy standards proposed by the dissenters for adjudicating partisan gerrymandering claims were "unmanageable" within the meaning of the political question doctrine because judicial application of so loose a test in cases with such high partisan stakes would inevitably bring "partisan enmity . . . upon the courts" (2004, 301). Justice Kennedy, concurring, posited that firm "rules to limit and confine judicial intervention" were necessary in partisan gerrymandering cases, lest the courts end up "assuming political, not legal, responsibility for a process [the design of electoral districts] that often produces ill will and distrust" (*Vieth v. Jubelirer* 2004, 307).

The Court's concern for the appearance of judicial impartiality is equally evident from the election cases where it does intervene. Commentators attribute the rigidity of doctrines like "one person, one vote" to the felt necessity of bright-line rules for the resolution of legal questions that substantially affect the distribution of political power.[11] And even when the Court *says* it is applying an open-ended balancing test in election law cases, it tends to *produce* fairly crisp rules for the lower courts to apply (Elmendorf 2007, Elmendorf and Foley 2008). This tendency is not limited to the constitutional context. The Court's interpretations of the Voting Rights Act and the Help America Vote Act also manifest a desire to avoid getting involved in high-stakes political conflicts without a clear rule of decision to apply (Elmendorf 2010).

Worries about the appearance of judicial partiality also crop up in many nonelectoral contexts. Thus, the "requirements due process" have been held to "sometimes bar trial by judges who have no actual bias and who would do their very best to weigh the scales of justice equally between contending parties," if the judge's participation would not "'satisfy the appearance of justice'" (*In re Murchison* 1955, 136, quoting *Offutt v. United States* 1954, 14). As well, because "[t]he legitimacy of the Judicial Branch ultimately depends on its reputation for impartiality and nonpartisanship," there are judge-made, separation-of-powers limits on the political branches' author-ity to assign nonjudicial tasks to Article III judges" (*Mistretta v. United States* 1989, 407). The fear is that the courts' reputation would be put at risk if "borrowed by the political Branches to cloak their work in the neutral colors of judicial action" (Id. 407).

Does Positive Legitimacy Have Normative Force?

Frankfurter's stated concern for judicial authority seems adequate to explain the Supreme Court's efforts to protect the appearance of judicial impartiality, but why should the Court give any weight to how the public perceives – and consequently evaluates the legitimacy of – the electoral process? It is helpful to think about this problem from two perspectives: (1) crisis interventions meant to forestall illiberal con-stitutional revision or revolution; (2) quotidian maintenance of the political order. If civil war, rule by strongman, or religious or ethnic persecution is an imminent possibility, most judges who are themselves committed to liberal democracy will probably do what they can to restore public confidence in the extant constitutional order, if it is relatively liberal. They will be acting, though, more as statespersons than as judges (Issacharoff 2010). Fealty to precedent and conventional sources of legal meaning will be abandoned if the stakes are high enough.

These are not, of course, the circumstances in which federal judges find them-selves today, and it would be a huge stretch to say that revolution was a realistic possibility even during the birth years of the Supreme Court's modern jurispru-dence of political rights, the tumultuous 1960s. The Court's efforts to bolster (or to clear space for the legislature to bolster) public confidence in the political order are more sensibly understood as "ordinary maintenance" – keeping a moderately satisfied populace moderately satisfied, as opposed to talking the people back from the precipice of illiberal revolution.

I am not sure that it makes sense for the courts to define constitutional political rights with an eye to performing this sort of maintenance, or to allow otherwise recognized rights to be limited by legislation that does such maintenance, but I do think that reasonable judges could settle on this approach, for at least three sets of reasons. The first owes to the procedural fairness/compliance hypothesis developed by Tom Tyler and others (Tyler 2006). It has been shown in many different contexts that persons who accept the basic legitimacy or fairness of a decision-making body are more likely to comply voluntarily with adverse decisions and freely contribute to collective efforts. Perceived "procedural fairness" fosters compliance in settings ranging from the workplace to the courtroom (Tyler 2006). It has also been established that people who in some sense "trust" their government (or a particular governmental body, such as a police department) are more willing than the untrust-ing to help out with the government's undertakings, be that fighting a war (Levi 1997), investigating crimes (Sunshine and Tyler 2003), or paying taxes (Scholz and

Pinney 1995; Scholz and Lubell 1998). There is some evidence that declining trust in government leads to rising homicide rates (LaFree 1998; Roth 2009).[12] And trust in government depends, in part, on fair procedures (Hibbing and Theiss-Morse 2002).

This body of research suggests a conjecture about the electoral process: Elections that are perceived to be fair will induce losing candidates and their supporters to voluntarily accept the government's right to rule, to freely comply with duly enacted laws and orders, and to maintain a spirit of civic voluntarism (Gonzalez and Tyler 2008). Though there is precious little empirical evidence about the consequences of perceived electoral fairness for prosocial behavior,[13] the hypothesis may be plausible enough to inform judges who believe they cannot delay decision until all the data are in.

The hypothesized relationship between citizens' perceptions of electoral fairness and prosocial behavior suggests that there could be a very important ("compelling") state interest in even ordinary maintenance of public confidence in the electoral process, one that might justify regulatory burdens on constitutionally protected interests. Moreover, judges who doubt that legislators will update the electoral process to propitiate "low confidence" citizens might well decide to treat constitutional political rights (such as the right to vote on equal terms with others) as tools for bringing low-confidence citizens back into the mainstream. The contours and reach of the right would come to depend on these citizens' legitimacy judgments.

In point of fact, the Supreme Court has regularly expressed skepticism about whether elected officials can be trusted with regulating the ground rules of political competition (e.g., *Davis v. Federal Election Commission* 2008, 2773-74; *Randall v. Sorrell* 2006, 248-49; *Tashjian v. Republican Party of Connecticut* 1986, 224). The justices seem to believe, not unreasonably, that the normal processes that render the government responsive to citizen concerns are unreliable in this domain because incumbent office holders and then-dominant political parties are loath to change any rules that provide them with a competitive edge. Moreover, as noted previously, the justices seem to think that citizens who doubt the "fairness and integrity" of the electoral process will simply cease participating. If this is so, growing public dissatisfaction with election procedures would perversely reduce the ballot-box pressure on incumbent representatives to enact meliorative reforms. Some external corrective would be necessary, one that judges schooled in "representation reinforcing" theories of judicial review should be happy to provide (Ely 1980).

Judges who do not accept the fairness/compliance rationale for a jurisprudence of positive legitimacy in ordinary times might converge on this approach for another reason: precaution. If it is effective, a jurisprudence of positive legitimacy should help keep the times ordinary, reducing the likelihood (however remote) of a constitutional crisis pregnant with illiberal potential. Such precautions will seem ludicrous to many observers of the contemporary American scene, but as Rick Pildes has shown, a working majority on the Supreme Court has in recent years been extremely attuned to the risks of democratic instability or breakdown (Pildes 2002a). Notice too that even if an ordinary-times jurisprudence of positive legitimacy does nothing to forestall potentially illiberal crises, the precedents established during ordinary times could provide helpful cover for judges who opt for radical confidence-building measures at a moment of true crisis. Though the crisis-confronting justices may be acting more as statespersons than as judges, it will be easier for them to act in this way – and to rebuff accusations of lawlessness – if they can justify their interventions in terms of long-established precedents.

Finally, some judges may see in the positive-legitimacy approach to constitutional political rights a mean of partly resolving the tension between, on the one hand, how the public expects judges to decide constitutional cases and, on the other hand, the practical imperative to reach results that fit with citizens' self-understanding as participants in a contemporary democracy and the judge's own sense of what is minimally acceptable. The text of the Constitution says little about the democratic process, and the Framers had conceptions of democracy that were quite different from ours. An election law jurisprudence that relied on conventional arguments from the constitutional text and time-of-enactment history would not reliably generate outcomes that are palatable today (Gardner 1997). Yet neither will it do for judges simply to read contemporary democratic theory into the Constitution; the public is adamant that judges not rely on their personal policy preferences, and the public wants judges to reason from traditional sources of legal meaning (Scheb and Lyons 2000; Scheb and Lyons 2001).

In some legal domains, judges have tried to thread the needle – keeping constitutional law congruent with contemporary political morality while honoring norms of legality – by defining rights in terms of the consensus practices of the states. Thus, criminal punishments are likely to be deemed "cruel and unusual" within the meaning of the Eighth Amendment only if most of the states have abolished the punishment in question. There are traces of such thinking in the Supreme Court's election law jurisprudence, but the Court has not really embraced a state-consensus approach for electoral purposes, and arguably for good reason. With respect to political rights, a substantial consensus of state practices could reflect an underlying societal consensus, but it might also indicate that the political faction that happens to be in power in most states has found that the practice in question helps insulate its hold on power.

The state-consensus approach to constitutional rights seems best suited to prominent moral issues (capital punishment, abortion, etc.), where state law is likely to reflect the strongly felt views of the state's citizenry. Some election law problems may fit into this category (for example, whether felons who have completed their prison sentence should be allowed to vote), but many others have obscure technical dimensions (for example, whether the rules for translating votes into legislative representation result in a legislature whose political makeup shifts "symmetrically" with underlying changes in public opinion[14]). The more technical or low-profile the question, the less likely it is that typical state practices will correspond to real preferences of average citizens.

The state-consensus approach is also in some tension with constitutional election law's traditional concern for political minorities. The First Amendment protects political dissent (see, e.g., *Board of County Commissioners, Wabunsee County, Kansas v. Umbehr* 1996).[15] Poor people were among the early beneficiaries of the Supreme Court's constitutionalization of the right to vote (see, e.g., *Harper v. Va. Bd. of Elections* 1966). Third-party and independent candidates were given access to the ballot so that citizens dissatisfied with the status quo could air their grievances at the polls (see, e.g., *Williams v. Rhodes* 1968). To make constitutional law a vehicle for consolidating the majority view with respect to questions about the electoral process is to betray this history and would probably grate against many judges' self-understanding of their role in ensuring that all citizens have access to the political process.

The notoriously ad hoc nature of constitutional election law likely reflects both the problems with relying on the state-consensus technique in this domain and the difficulty of reasoning from constitutional text and time-of-enactment history to outcomes that are palatable today. Murky arguments from murky precedents have accordingly become the judicial technique of choice. A reasonable judge who is working in this tradition might well decide, however, that it would be better to tie textually unmoored political rights to positive legitimacy. This move would be risky, because opponents of the judge's decisions would probably attack him or her for disregarding norms of legality. Murky arguments from precedent are a well-established part of our legal tradition; the justification of textually doubtful rights in terms of their practical consequences for public support for the political order is not. The judge who would make this move cannot be sure whether political and legal elites will come to accept it. (This may explain why *Kramer*'s statement that the right to vote is fundamental because "the legitimacy of representative government depends on it" remains today, forty years later, just a pregnant suggestion in the jurisprudence of political rights.)

But tying political rights to empirical legitimacy would also have advantages for judges who wish to keep the political rights jurisprudence relevant and respectable in the present day. By making the grounds for judicial decision more transparent, it would bolster the judge's argument that she is not simply importing her own political preferences under the guise of interpreting the Constitution. The elaboration of constitutional political rights in terms of positive legitimacy would also resonate with one of the central purposes of the Constitution: forging a political order that enables the citizens governed by it to coexist peaceably notwithstanding their very different ideas about some very fundamental matters.[16] To be sure, it is not the role of the courts to function as an ongoing constitutional convention, updating the document as new fissures or tensions within the citizenry become apparently. But when there is ambiguity about the meaning of precedents (or text, or structure), the judge might say, it is reasonable for her to resolve the open question with reference to positive legitimacy, in light of the Constitution's overarching purposes. This need not turn the Constitution into a malleable thing that responds to every latest fad in thinking about the electoral process. It would be easy enough to hold that only those practices with a demonstrable and substantial influence on citizens' apprehension of the legitimacy of the political order are subject to attack, and that the attack will necessarily fail unless the asserted right has some further footing in precedent, in constitutional text, or in constitutional structure.

Notice also that in contrast to the typical-state-practices approach, a positive-legitimacy approach to political rights would direct the courts' attention to citizens who are alienated, rather than to the views of current majorities. This is in keeping with the traditions of the modern Court's political rights jurisprudence. And importantly, the positive legitimacy approach would help the Court to explain that its solicitude for the fringes is not just a matter of conferring "special favors" on undeserving groups, but of protecting the essential interest of all citizens in a political order characterized by peaceful political transitions, uncoerced compliance with duly enacted law, and civic voluntarism.[17]

In summary, whatever one makes of the hypothesized connection between electoral legitimacy and prosocial behavior, or of the precautionary case for privileging "public confidence," a judge who is uncomfortable with ad hocery but wants to protect minorities' access to the political process (or to ensure that constitutional law does not become divorced from current understandings of democratic fairness) may be drawn to the positive legitimacy approach. It creates space for her to do these things while abjuring reliance on her own, personal views of political justice, and while honoring the originating purposes of the Constitution itself.

THE SUPREME COURT VS. POLITICAL SCIENCE: EVIDENCE ABOUT
THE EFFECTS OF ELECTION LAWS AND PRACTICES ON
"PUBLIC CONFIDENCE" IN THE POLITICAL ORDER

As noted above, the Supreme Court's confidence-oriented interventions in the electoral process have been based entirely on conjecture about the functional relationships of interest. Those functional relationships have attracted the attention of empirically minded political scientists, and an emerging body of research casts doubt on the justices' conjectures. This part of the chapter surveys the principal empirical findings, setting up the discussion in the following part of how legitimacy-minded courts ought to proceed.

Two caveats before we begin. First, the studies reviewed here employ a wide range of dependent variables, everything from confidence that "your vote with be counted as intended," to confidence in whether the last election was "conducted fairly," to "external efficacy" (the belief that one can influence the political process), to confidence in particular governmental bodies (such as Congress), to measures of "public trust" in government generally, to journalists' perceptions of corruption, and more. This variety reflects the lack of consensus among political scientists about how to define and measure positive legitimacy. Second, some of the studies try to explain election law effects on the beliefs or views of citizens generally, whereas others investigate effects on groups that have lower-than-average regard for the electoral process or political system (e.g., citizens who voted for the losing side).

Campaign Finance Regulations and the "Appearance of Corruption"

The Supreme Court upheld campaign contribution limits on the theory that they protect the political process from the appearance of corruption (see *Buckley v. Valeo* 1976). A nascent body of empirical research suggests, however, that stringent campaign finance laws may have precisely the opposite effect.

Several researchers have tried to shed light on how campaign finance restrictions affect public perceptions of corruption by studying the perceptions of journalists. The thinking here is that journalists' beliefs will filter through to the citizenry at large. An early, cross-sectional analysis of American states by Alt and Lassen (2003) found a negative, statistically significant correlation between campaign finance restrictions and an index of journalists' perceptions of state government corruption. But this correlation could reflect the propensity of states with a "clean" political culture to adopt campaign finance restrictions, as opposed to the supposedly dampening effect of these restrictions on perceived corruption. Subsequent work by Rosenson (2009) employed instrumental variables to attack the direction-of-causation problem and found that more stringent campaign finance laws actually increase journalists' perception of corruption. This result proved robust to various conceptualizations of stringency, to different measures of journalists' perceptions of corruption, and to different approaches to instrumenting regulatory stringency.

State-level variation in campaign finance laws was also exploited by Primo and Milyo (2006) who, using panel data, studied the effect of election laws on "external efficacy" as measured by the National Election Studies (NES) survey.[18] The authors found that state campaign disclosure requirements have a significant positive influence on political efficacy; that contribution restrictions that apply only to organizations have a significant positive effect on one measure of external efficacy (but not on another); that contribution restrictions that apply to individuals as well as organizations do not improve external efficacy; and that public funding worsens external efficacy. Public funding comes across in a better light – positively and significantly correlated with "confidence that the last election was conducted fairly" – in a recent comparative study of twenty-eight nations (Birch 2008). But that analysis was purely cross-sectional, leaving one to wonder whether public funding for candidates and parties bolsters public confidence in electoral fairness, or whether public funding is instead just a common incident of the electoral process in countries where elections tend not to be rigged.

Persily and Lammie (2004) observed that the explosion in soft-money contributions to political campaigns during the 1990s (whose subsequent ban the Supreme Court upheld on an "appearances" theory) occurred at the same time as NES measures of trust in government were trending upwards. To date, however, political scientists have yet to incorporate campaign contributions and expenditures, campaign finance laws, or other election law variables into sophisticated, dynamic models of trust in government. (Recent work in this vein shows that intertemporal variation in the NES measures of trust in government is largely caused by the prominence of foreign policy and crime on the public's issue agenda, economic performance, congressional approval, presidential approval, and scandals (Hetherington and Rudolph 2009)).

In summary, save for disclosure requirements and contribution limits on organizations, no type of campaign finance regulation has been shown to enhance "public confidence" in studies that control for possible endogeneity. The best evidence to date suggests that stringent contribution limits and public financing probably worsen the appearance of corruption. Though causal links have not been established, "scandal" seems a likely mechanism.[19] The tighter the regulation of campaign finance, the more pressure there will be to evade the law, and news stories about big-money interests that wield influence while skating or breaking the law may well be more common and do more to capture the public's imagination – and to damage public confidence – than stories about the lawful influence of big money under lax regulatory regimes.

Voter ID, "Electoral Integrity," and Voter Participation

The Supreme Court has suggested that voter ID requirements advance a powerful state interest not only in preventing actual voter impersonation, but also in safeguarding "public confidence in the integrity of the electoral process" (*Crawford v. Marion County Election Board* 2008, 1620). The Court linked the importance of this interest to its presumed effect of "encouraging citizen participation in the democratic process" (*Id.*; see also *Purcell v. Gonzalez* 2006). Ansolabehere and Persily (2008) used three national, election-time surveys to plumb the relationships among voter identification, perceived vote fraud, and voter participation. They found no correlation between respondents' perceptions about the extent of vote fraud or vote theft, and whether the respondent intended to or did vote in the election.[20] Ansolabehere and Persily's data also suggest that there is no connection between perceptions about the extent of voter fraud or vote theft and either (1) whether the respondent was asked to show photo identification at the polls, (2) the fraction of voters in the respondent's state who were asked for photo ID at the polls, or (3) the facial stringency of the state's voter identification requirements. Ansolabehere and Persily's static analysis cannot rule out the possibility that voters in states with restrictive voter identification practices would have had more-dire-than-average perceptions about vote fraud if the state's ID requirements had not been so tight, but this seems to me a very unlikely explanation of their findings.[21]

That said, the Supreme Court's intuition that perceived electoral integrity can enhance voter participation is not completely bereft of empirical support. In a cross-national study, Birch (2005) found a strong positive correlation between respondents' confidence that "the last election was conducted fairly" and whether they voted in that election. This result held even controlling for political efficacy and overall satisfaction with democracy, and was more pronounced in advanced than in nascent democracies.[22] The Birch and Ansolabehere/Persily results might be reconciled by positing that what drives would-be voters out of the process is not their perception about the extent of vote fraud as such, but rather their take on the culpability of the state. Citizens who believe that the electoral process has been set up and administered in good faith will participate; citizens who believe that the government itself has rigged the game will drop out. (Alternatively, Birch's findings may reflect a psychological effect of the act of voting on perceptions of electoral integrity, rather than an effect of perceived electoral integrity on the likelihood of voting.)

Barriers to Voting

Do tangible barriers to voting undermine "the legitimacy of representative government," as the *Kramer* Court posited? Primo and Milyo's (2006) study of the impact of campaign finance law on political efficacy casts some doubt on this idea. As controls, Primo and Milyo included dichotomous variables that capture the presence or absence of poll taxes, literacy tests, and "easy voter registration" (same-day or no registration). Poll taxes were found to have a significant negative correlation with one measure of external efficacy, but not the other. None of the other barriers-to-voting variables proved significant.[23] Primo and Milyo's study does not, however, address the possibility that barriers to voting have a differential impact on the political efficacy of those citizens who find the barriers hardest to surmount. (Alvarez and Hall 2009 found that about ten percent of Americans think voter registration in their state is difficult).

A number of scholars have begun to investigate citizens' confidence that their ballots will be counted as intended. The early results indicate that this species of confidence is responsive to poll worker competence (Atkeson and Sanders 2007; Hall et al 2009), polling-place convenience (Stein et al 2008),[24] whether voting technology is easy to use (Atkeson and Sanders 2007; Stein et al 2008),[25] and, rather more equivocally, whether voting technology leaves a "paper trail" that can be used to audit election results (Atkeson and Saunders 2007; Alvarez et al 2008; Llewellyn et al 2008; but see Bullock et al 2005; Stein et al 2008; Stewart 2009).[26] Persons who vote absentee have considerably less confidence than in-person voters that their ballot will be counted correctly (Alvarez et al 2008; Atkeson and Saunders 2007). One study has shown that voters' experiences at the polling station affect not only their judgments about the likelihood that their ballots will be counted correctly, but also their beliefs in the overall fairness of the electoral process (Hall et al 2009).

Voters' confidence that their ballots will be counted as intended is highly responsive to election outcomes. The results of the 2006 elections, which ended one-party (Republican) control of the national government, chopped sixteen percentage points off the "confidence gap" between Republicans and Democrats (Republicans had been and remained more confident) (Llewellyn et al 2008). State and local government winner effects appear to be less pronounced, though voters who identify with a locally dominant party are more likely to have confidence in the counting of their vote (Llewellyn et al 2008). Research on the 2008 elections revealed that Democrats in states won by Obama and Republicans in states won by McCain were more confident than their co-partisans elsewhere. Analogous winner effects have been found in all manner of empirical studies concerning the effect of elections on trust or legitimacy (Anderson et al 2005).

A limitation of most extant research on voters' confidence that their ballot will be counted as intended is that it proxies poll worker competence, the ease-of-use of voting technology, and related items with independent variables constructed from respondent perceptions.[27] It could be the case that a certain class of dour respondents is predisposed to believe that their votes are unlikely to be counted correctly, and that the pessimism of these respondents also clouds their perceptions of poll workers and voting technology.[28] Beliefs about the legitimacy or trustworthiness of the political system have been shown to color subsequent evaluations of societal conditions, public policies, and branches of government (Anderson et al 2004; Anderson and Tverdova 2003; Chanley et al 2000; Craig et al 2006; Sigelman et al 1992; Weatherford 1984). They probably distort perceptions of the voting process as well.

All that said, if it turns out that tangible features of the voting experience itself (wait times, technology choice, ballot length, poll worker competence, etc.) substantially determine citizens' confidence in the integrity of elections, this would have important implications for constitutional election law – if the right to vote is fundamental because of its role in producing governmental legitimacy. The Court has long been dismissive of voter claims that it sees as raising issues of mere convenience, in contrast to "absolute" or "severe" barriers to the exercise of the franchise.[29] Empirical research on the relationship between the quality of citizens' voting experiences and their confidence in the electoral process could put pressure on the Court to take these claims seriously – or to abandon the idea that the right to vote is fundamental because of its legitimating properties.

The Structure of Representation and Governance

The modern Supreme Court has been of two minds about judicial elaboration and enforcement of the structural provisions of the Constitution. Some structural commitments, such as the guarantee of "republican government" found in Article IV, have long been treated as nonjusticiable (*Pacific States Tel. & Tel. Co. v. Oregon* 1912; *Baker v. Carr* 1961). Others, such as Article II, Section 2's implied limit on congressional authority to appoint or remove officers charged with the implementation of statutes, and Article I's implied limit on the power of the states and Congress to establish qualifications for service in Congress, have been enforced with bright-line rules (*Buckley v. Valeo* 1976; *Bowsher v. Synar* 1986; *U.S. Term Limits, Inc. v. Thornton* 1995). Still others, such as the restrictions on the domain of congressional authority implied by Article I and the Tenth Amendment, have been the subject of ongoing judicial equivocation (*Maryland v. Wirtz* 1968; *Nat'l Leage of Cities v. Usery* 1976; *Garcia v. San Antonio Metro. Transit Auth.* 1985; *Gregory v. Ashcroft* 1991), or have gone unenforced for want of agreement on the contours of the limitation and manageable standards for its implementation. Such has been the fate of the implied constitutional limitation on partisan gerrymandering, a limitation whose existence is now broadly accepted (*Vieth v. Jubelirer* 2004; *League of United Latin American Citizens v. Perry* 2006).

Does the empirical literature on the legitimacy of representative government shed any light on the payoff (or lack thereof) from judicial enforcement of one or another conceptualization of the structural provisions of the Constitution? To date it offers only suggestive hints. There is a growing body of cross-national comparative scholarship on the consequences of horizontal and vertical separation of powers for public confidence in the system of democracy. A consistent finding is that losing voters – citizens who voted for a party that is not part of the governing coalition – express more confidence in nations that are organized as federations of states and that have separated powers or consociational structures at the national level (Anderson and Guillory 1997; Anderson et al 2005). This interesting result may be quite relevant to the work of constitution drafters. But it hardly follows that more aggressive enforcement of the separation of powers or states' rights by U.S. judges would result in greater public confidence in our system of democracy. Comparative results obtained through the use of binary, qualitative independent variables to measure large structural differences (e.g., is the system federal or not?) cannot shed much light on the consequences of marginal, judge-made adjustments to the practice of federalism in the United States today.[30] Further complicating matters, aggressive enforcement of some conceptualizations of the separation of powers could make it harder for the government to forestall or abate economic crises, or to address other pressing policy problems.[31] And economic performance – especially bad economic performance – has a powerful impact on public trust in government (Hetherington and Rudolph 2009).

The losers' consent literature does have implications for the development of judicially enforceable limits on partisan gerrymandering. Justice Breyer was right to suggest, in his dissenting opinion in *Vieth v. Jubelirer* (2004), that partisan gerrymandering is most problematic when it results in a minority party by vote share winning a majority of seats in the legislature *and sustaining its majority position over multiple election cycles*. Although it not yet known whether "minority rule" as such has a special sting for citizens who support out-of-power parties, it is well established that losers' consent plummets when the same people are on the losing side election after election (Anderson et al 2005). Oscillation in party control of government helps sustain buy-in from the losers in any given election.

Greater proportionality in the translation of votes into seats may also enhance losers' consent. This intuition draws support from a comparative study of citizen satisfaction with European democracies (Anderson et al 2005). There is also evidence from the United States that persons who feel they have "no say in what government does" are particularly supportive of proportionality (Karp 2007),[32] though it remains to be seen whether proportionality-enhancing reforms have a material effect on these citizens' support for the political system. Whatever the results of further research, however, it is extremely unlikely that the Supreme Court will make proportionality an anchoring value in its partisan gerrymandering jurisprudence. As Justice Stewart once wrote, "the Court has sternly set its face against the claim, however phrased, that the Constitution somehow guarantees proportional representation" (*Mobile v. Bolden* 1980, 79). Here again we see a point of tension between the Court's practice and the emerging social science of empirical legitimacy.

It is common for proponents of judge-made limits on partisan gerrymandering to decry the small number of competitive seats in the U.S. House of Representatives. But the empirical literature on citizens' satisfaction with the political system raises a cautionary flag about increasing the number of seats that both Democrats and Republicans have a good shot at winning. The greater the frequency of politically homogeneous constituencies, the more citizens will be able to "vote for a winner" in congressional elections. Brunell (2008) has shown that citizens who supported the winner in congressional elections have more confidence not only in their own representative but in Congress as an institution; they also express a greater sense of political efficacy.[33] On the other hand, Anderson and LoTempio (2002) found no effect of voting for the winning congressional candidate on overall trust in government; their results suggest that the presidential race is what counts. Further work is necessary to sort out whether and under what conditions being a congressional district winner can soften "loser effects" at the presidential level or at the level of party control of Congress. But if Brunell's findings hold up, they suggest that reformers seeking to increase the overall responsiveness of Congress to swings in public opinion should try to do this by creating additional moderate districts that are politically homogenous, rather than by creating districts that combine equal numbers of very conservative and very liberal voters with a small, balance-tipping pool of moderates.

Direct Democracy

The Supreme Court has shown little interest in direct democracy. It has deemed the alleged incompatibility between initiated legislation and Article IV's guarantee of republican government a nonjusticiable political question (*Pacific States Tel. & Tel. Co. v. Ore.* 1912). It has refused to create special equal protection doctrines to protect minorities from the majoritarian excesses feared by some critics of direct democracy,[34] and it has extended no deference to initiated measures that revise political arrangements favored by incumbent politicians for reasons of self-interest.[35]

Political scientists, by contrast, have long been curious about direct democracy and in recent years they have tried to understand its impact on citizens' sense of political efficacy, confidence in government, and voting behavior (Smith and Tolbert 2007). Initial studies found a positive correlation between frequency of ballot-initiative use at the state level and internal and external political efficacy (Bowler and Donovan 2002; Hero and Tolbert 2004; Smith and Tolbert 2004).[36] But more recent work, covering longer time periods and a wider range of surveys, suggests that the overall effect of direct democracy on citizen efficacy is negligible, and that direct democracy may exacerbate the "efficacy gap" between knowledgeable and less informed citizens (Scholzman and Yohai 2008; Dyck and Lascher 2009).[37] There also appears to be a negative relationship between frequency of ballot-initiative use and citizen confidence in state elected officials and state and local government (Dyck 2009), though the direction of causation has not been investigated. Notice too that the ballot initiative could decrease trust in state "government" – understood as the officials who have been elected to govern – while simultaneously increasing citizens' sense of allegiance to the state's political order as a whole, given the check that the ballot initiative arguably represents on shirking or self-dealing by the voters' elected agents. There is as yet no evidence bearing on this hypothesis.

In sum, it is too soon to draw even preliminary conclusions about the likely relationship between ballot-initiative use and empirical legitimacy, let alone to infer implications for judicial review by legitimation-minded courts.

Political Conflict over the Electoral Process

The Supreme Court seems wary of – and inclined to police – political conflict over election results as well as election law. The justices are alert to the possibility that incumbents' personal or partisan self-interest will distort lawmaking and administration in this area, and if *Bush v. Gore* is any indication, they are uneasy leaving the resolution of disputed elections to political bodies even when Congress has so provided.[38] Contributing to their eagerness to settle the 2000 presidential election may have been an intuition that the election's outcome would be easier for the losers to stomach if determined by a politically neutral, black-robed body, rather than by partisan majorities in Congress or partisan actors in Florida. Or perhaps the justices feared that if they stayed their hand, the ensuing fight over the election's result would generate more public scrutiny of the mechanics of the electoral process (aided and abetted by conspiracy theorists or partisan elites with an axe to grind), which in turn would undermine citizens' confidence in the system.

Political scientists have yet to investigate whether high-visibility elite conflicts over election results (or electoral reform) affect ordinary citizens' perceptions of the legitimacy of the electoral process, but there is some basis for suspecting a negative and potentially substantial effect. This hypothesis draws from two bodies of literature, one on the role of partisan cues in shaping voter opinion about public policy alternatives, and the other on Americans' desire for a nonfractious "politics of good faith." As to the first: Citizens typically have nonexistent or weak opinions about most issues of public policy (Zaller 2002). But when partisan officials stake out visible positions on a policy question, many citizens follow suit, taking their cue from the leaders of the party with whom the citizen identifies (Bartels 2002; Zaller 2002; Lenz 2009). It follows that if partisan elites make prominent, visible attacks on the electoral system, party members will probably come to see the system as vulnerable or flawed and thus lose confidence in it.[39]

More so than in other policy domains, partisan conflicts over electoral reform and electoral dispute resolution seem to devolve into attacks on good faith. Each side portrays the other as jeopardizing basic democratic values, or the integrity of the electoral process, in the hopes of tilting the playing field to its advantage. Hibbing and Theiss-Morse (2002) have shown that many Americans want their elected leaders to govern nonconflictually, on the basis of the leaders' good-faith understandings of the public interest. For many – perhaps most – voters, it is much more important that their representatives behave in this way than that they enact particular policies favored by the voter. Hibbing and Theiss-Morse did not study electoral reform as such. But under their model of "stealth democracy," high-profile, highly partisan conflict over election results and electoral reform would seem almost uniquely destructive of public confidence in both electoral institutions and political elites because of its tendency to draw the good faith of elected officials into doubt, while raising questions about the fairness or efficacy of the very process which is supposed to enable citizens to hold those officials to account.

Summary

The evidence to date suggests that the boldest conjectures in the Supreme Court's jurisprudence of public confidence – on the relationship between campaign contribution limits and perceptions of corruption, and the impact of voter identification requirements on the perceived integrity of elections and the consequent propensity of "honest voters" to withdraw from the political process – are quite likely off the mark. Conversely, matters that the Court has treated as constitutionally inconsequential, such as the user-friendliness of the voting process, may significantly affect citizens' confidence in the electoral system.

Taken as a whole, the empirical literature on the relationship between election law and positive legitimacy flashes a strong cautionary signal, but it is more helpful as a warning than as a directive guide for judicial action. Basic issues of measurement remain unresolved (different researchers use very different measures of "legitimacy" or "confidence");[40] as do questions about causation (many of the studies are cross-sectional, and even results based on time-series data are subject to doubt because electoral reforms are not adopted at random). Prominent early findings have been undermined by later, more comprehensive studies (for example, concerning the effect of direct democracy on political efficacy). And the foundational hypothesis about the effect of perceived electoral legitimacy on prosocial behavior has received very little empirical attention. Under these circumstances, what is a judge to do?

STRATEGY FOR A LEGITIMATION-MINDED SUPREME COURT

Given the limits of the existing literature on election law and positive legitimacy, and the unreliability of "common sense" as a guide in this domain, legitimacy-minded justices cannot hope to achieve much good with decisive rulings that authorize (or deem out of bounds) one or another contested form of electoral regulation. The wiser course is to try to enable and induce further, more probative research, and to structure doctrine so that lower courts can respond flexibly to new information.[41] How might this be done?

The first and most important step, in my view, is for the Court to define the constitutionally privileged value or values more clearly. As things now stand, "public confidence" may well be a placeholder for several distinct concerns. The *Buckley* (1976) opinion speaks of preventing "confidence in *the system of representative government* [from being] eroded to a *disastrous extent*," suggesting that the underlying concern is illiberal revolution (27, emphasis added). Justice Scalia's explanation of the stay in *Bush v. Gore* (2000) invokes "the public acceptance democratic stability requires" (1047), which perhaps suggests a more modest concern with smooth, peaceful transitions.[42] Justice Stevens's and Justice Kennedy's opinions about the importance of protecting public confidence in "electoral integrity" arguably suggest that the ultimate objective is encouraging voter participation, not protecting public confidence for its own sake or for the sake of political stability (*Purcell v. Gonzalez* 2006; *Crawford v. Marion County Election Board* 2008).

A statement from the Court about which legitimacy-related values it cares to protect, and why, would be enormously helpful to political scientists, whose research could then be designed to produce better grist for the judicial mill. If the Court were to declare, for example, that the Constitution requires electoral systems to be reasonably designed to maintain "public acceptance" of the electoral process insofar as such acceptance promotes voluntary compliance with duly enacted law or enables newly elected officials to implement the program on which they campaigned, this would shift the research agenda away from such recently fashionable questions as "confidence that your vote will be counted as intended" and toward more basic and behavioral questions about legitimation and its consequences.[43] Survey-based measures of "public confidence" would be credited by the courts only to the extent that litigants demonstrate a relationship between the survey items and the values the Supreme Court prioritized.

Beyond clarifying the values to be protected, the Court should also acknowledge that the public interest in a better understanding of how election laws affect positive legitimacy weighs in favor of a two-tiered jurisprudence of political rights, with one set of rules for federal elections and another for state and local elections. The courts should be somewhat more deferential to the states, because it is the fact of variation at the state and local level that has allowed researchers to make some headway in understanding how electoral arrangements affect public confidence. The germ of such a two-tiered approach to political rights may be found in the Court's malapportionment jurisprudence, which affords more leeway to the states in drawing districts for state and local elections than for congressional elections (Brown v. Thomson 1983). To justify this deference, the Court pointed to the distinctive state interest in maintaining congruity between local government boundaries and state legislative districts, given the traditional role of local governments in implementing state programs. The collective, national interest in state-level variation as a source of information about the effect of election laws on constitutionally privileged values is different, but the constitutional dimension of this interest suggests that it should weigh heavily in the balance.

Going one step further, the Court should recognize that there is a "compelling state interest" in allowing the states to carry out bona-fide programs of electoral experimentation, designed to enhance whatever legitimacy-related values the Court decides to privilege. Recognition of this interest would allow states to put in place – on a trial basis – otherwise impermissible regulatory burdens on political rights, such as the right to make unlimited expenditures on political campaigns or the right to vote on equal terms with others. Recognition of this interest would be a way of limiting the damage, as it were, from earlier decisions that established or extended political rights haphazardly (on the basis of the raw or unspoken conjectures), while also making it difficult for incumbent lawmakers to invoke public confidence as a pretext for burdening political rights for reasons of personal or partisan self-interest.

The success of this venture would depend on the development of workable standards for identifying bona-fide programs of regulatory experimentation.[44] Judges surely do not want to regularly adjudicate disputes between plaintiffs' social scientists and defendants' experts about whether a purportedly experimental regulation of the political process was established pursuant to a bona-fide program of regulatory experimentation. But neither would it be necessary for judges to make first-order evaluations of the reasonableness of a state's "experimental" program or to pass on the good faith of the legislators or administrators who created it. One of the hallmarks of the Supreme Court's political rights jurisprudence has been the creation of strong presumptions to avoid "battles of the experts" in every case (Elmendorf 2007).[45] A court might hold as a matter of law that a putative regulatory experiment is not a bona-fide experiment unless (1) the state first convened an advisory panel of political scientists, using a selection process that is either blind to the members' political affiliations or that expressly balances partisan membership; (2) the state delegated to the panel authority to design and propose regulatory experiments, within bounds established by the state legislature;[46] (3) the panel determined that it was possible to conduct a meaningful regulatory experiment within the confines set by the legislature, and proposed one or more such designs; and (4) the regulatory measures challenged by the plaintiff were chosen from the menu furnished by the advisory panel, and implemented pursuant to its guidelines.[47] Regulatory experiments that emerge from this process would enjoy a strong presumption of permissibility; other ostensible experiments would be deemed presumptively *faux* as a matter of law.

The strategy I have sketched in this part presumes that self-conscious and transparent efforts by courts to promote positive legitimacy would not be intrinsically self-undermining. But perhaps some citizens would take offense at this, seeing it as a diversion from the proper state (or judicial) purpose of ensuring that the electoral process is *normatively* legitimate. If enough citizens were to react in this way, positive legitimacy would suffer from the problem of obliquity: The goal could be reached only as the incidental byproduct of otherwise-oriented action – more specifically, through reforms designed for normative legitimacy.[48] This possibility strikes me as unlikely. Judicial opinions tend to be low visibility. If the public were to tune in, I suspect that most contemporary Americans would, on reflection, deem positive legitimacy a proper object of state action, given (1) the fact of good-faith normative disagreement on "live" questions about political reform, and (2) the hypothesized relationship between positive legitimacy and prosocial behavior. But the risk is at least worth acknowledging.

CONCLUSION

It is commonly thought that elections help secure the positive legitimacy of the political order, leading citizens who may vehemently disagree with the current course of public policy to accept the government's right to rule, to comply voluntarily with duly enacted laws, and to channel their disagreements toward the next election. The Supreme Court's constitutional election law jurisprudence seems motivated, at least in part, by a desire to ensure that American elections perform this function. As yet, however, the Court's legitimacy-minded interventions have been predicated on judicial surmise about the relationship between election law and positive legitimacy. Recent research by political scientists has cast doubt on some of the Court's suppositions while also suggesting that features of the electoral process that the Court has treated as inconsequential may have significance for empirical legitimacy. It will not be long before this body of work is regularly cited in legal briefs. This will put pressure on the courts either to clarify the sense in which the exigencies of empirical legitimacy inform the substance of (and limitations upon) constitutional political rights, or else to abandon the notion that citizens' legitimacy-related beliefs or behaviors have doctrinal relevance. In recognition of the moment at hand, I have sought in this chapter to clarify why a reasonable judge might want to make

constitutional election law responsive to social science findings about positive legitimacy; to summarize the relevant empirical findings to date; and to outline a path
forward for the courts.

NOTES

1 Though Scalia wrote only for himself, there is no indication that the other Justices
   who voted to grant the stay disagreed with his explanation of it. They may well
   have declined to join Scalia's opinion because of the custom of not issuing opinions
   in connection with a stay, rather than out of substantive disagreement with Justice
   Scalia's argument. Cf. *Bush v. Gore* (2000, 1046) ("Though it is not customary for
   the Court to issue an opinion in connection with its grant of a stay, I believe a brief
   response is necessary to Justice STEVENS' dissent.") (Scalia, J., concurring in the
   grant of the stay).
2 Under a jurisprudence of positive legitimacy, by contrast the citizenry's own, evolving
   understanding of legitimacy (or its behavioral correlates) would furnish the requisite
   polestar.
3 Whether this message actually bothered white or other voters is not something the
   Court bothered to investigate. It bears noting that the Court has since said that
   the constitutional harm in *Shaw* was not the district shape as such, but rather that
   race "predominated" over all other legitimate criteria in the design of the district at
   issue. See *Miller v. Johnson* (1995). However, "district shape" – the *publicly visible*
   manifestation of racial gerrymandering – continues to be a very significant factor,
   integral both to the threshold showing that plaintiffs must make in a *Shaw* claim (see
   Hunt v. Cromartie 2002) and the "narrow tailoring" analysis triggered by a showing
   of racial predominance (see *Bush v. Vera* 1996).
4 In this and other judicial opinions quoted in the text, I have added italics for emphasis.
5 Justice Scalia, concurring, agreed that illegitimacy of purpose would render a voting
   requirement unconstitutional. Like Stevens, Scalia evidently took a restrictive view
   of the illicit-purpose standard because he did not even bother to assess whether the
   Indiana law might be unconstitutional because of the reason for its enactment.
6 To say that Stevens's "sole purpose" test is arguably consistent with an emphasis on
   appearances is not to say that it is the right test for a court concerned with positive
   legitimacy. The sounder course is probably to focus on whether citizens perceive
   that partisan purposes have predominated over other, legitimate ends.
7 This is not to say that the rule against express money or property conditions on the
   franchise serves no instrumental purpose, for it does take off the table one particularly
   convenient and probably effective way for legislatures to discourage voting by poor
   people.
8 Undertheorized analogical arguments from precedent – the bread and butter of the
   Court's political rights jurisprudence – are standard fare in constitutional adjudication. By contrast, expressly elaborating a textually and historically uncertain "right"
   in terms of contemporary understandings of legitimacy would be a large departure
   from standard interpretive practices.
9 On the implications of Buckley for such cases, see DeLaney (2008).
10 Regarding the empirical evidence on point, see *infra* Part II.B.
11 See, e.g., Elmendorf (2007) (discussing judicial preference for clear rules in the
   "electoral mechanics" cases); Pildes (2002b) (discussing judicial preference for clear
   rules in vote-dilution cases under the Voting Rights Act).

12 The Roth and LaFree studies do not employ sophisticated statistical techniques to assess the counterhypothesis – for which there is some evidence (see Hetherington and Rudolph 2009) – that crime causes declining trust. But the impressive historical narrative in Roth's study, which tracks murder rates across all of American history and draws on comparative data from other countries and ages as well, gives considerable force to his hypothesis that the murder rate is driven in large measure by trust in government and beliefs about the legitimacy of political institutions.

13 Gonzalez and Tyler (2008), who advanced this conjecture and sought to provide supporting evidence, were unable to provide evidence *from studies of the electoral process* about what reforms would enhance citizens' sense of electoral fairness, or about whether "electoral fairness" as such is itself enough to induce prosocial behavior in marginalized citizens. The only directly relevant evidence they cited concerns the statistical correlation between direct democracy, "happiness," and tax compliance in Switzerland, and these findings have been cast into doubt by subsequent research. See Dorn et al (2007) (arguing, on the basis of a new dataset, that earlier findings on direct democracy and happiness were an artifact of the researchers' failure to control for the respondent's language).

14 The possible uses of "symmetry" as a standard for judging partisan gerrymandering were explored by several justices in *League of United Latin American Cities v. Perry* (2006).

15 See, e.g., *Bd. of County Comm'ners, Wabunsee County, Kan. v. Umbehr* (1996), which holds that the First Amendment protects independent contractors from termination or nonrenewal of at-will government contracts in retaliation for criticism of the government.

16 The original Constitution infamously incorporated highly unprincipled compromises on slavery and on representation for small states in the Senate.

17 Note in this regard that there is some public support for basing judicial decisions on concern for the general welfare, and also for judicial attentiveness to public opinion (Scheb and Lyons 2001).

18 The authors' dependent variable is noisy, because the relevant NES questions refer to "the government" rather than "state government," but use of this variable allowed Primo and Milyo to construct a fifty-year time series.

19 Hetherington and Rudolph (2009) show that prominent scandals negatively impact public trust in government in subsequent time periods.

20 Curiously, respondents who admitted being "not sure" about the extent of voter fraud or vote theft were less likely to vote.

21 I think it unlikely because pressure for the enactment of stringent voter identification requirements seems to have come from party elites rather than from outpourings of citizen anger triggered by high-profile instances of fraud.

22 Other researchers have uncovered a positive relationship between political efficacy and voter turnout in American elections (Rosenstone and Hansen 1993), and it is not farcical to hypothesize that widespread fraud (or a perception thereof) would tend to undercut honest citizens' sense that the elected officials are responsive to people like them.

23 The coefficient on "easy registration" was significant (and positive) in a supplemental analysis the authors did of *relative* trust in state and federal government during 1996. Primo and Milyo offer no explanation for this seemingly odd result. Perhaps easy voter registration symbolizes for some voters that the state government (which sets registration rules) is competent and cares about people like them.

24 Stein et al (2008) found, in a study of voters in a Texas county who were given a choice of voting technologies, that voter ratings of the polling place itself (tapped mostly with questions about convenience) was nearly significant at the 5% level in explaining voter's confidence that their ballot will be counted correctly.

25 Stein et al (2008) found that voter ratings of the usability of the voting technology powerfully explain voter confidence ballots will be counted correctly. The effect of the voter's rating of the "usability" of the voting technology was approximately eight times as large as the effect of the voter's evaluation of the polling place. Atkeson and Sanders (2007) found that voter ratings of whether they "enjoyed" their voting method were positively correlated with confidence that their ballot would be counted correctly, and that voter assessments of whether the ballot itself was "confusing" were negatively correlated with voter confidence.

26 Llewellyn et al (2008) found, using a national survey, that voters who used electronic machines were significantly less confident, following the election, than voters who used paper ballots, but that this negative effect of electronic voting machines on voter confidence did not occur in the case of electronic machines that provided a paper printout; Atkeson and Saunders (2007), in survey of voters in two congressional districts, found that voter confidence is positively and significantly correlated with voters' perception that the voting technology they used creates a "paper receipt that can validate election results"; and Alvarez et al (2008), in a national survey, found that voters who used a paper ballot expressed the most confidence that their ballots would be counted correctly, and that electronic-machine voters expressed the least confidence. But Stewart (2009), also employing a national survey, found that voters who used electronic and optical scan voting were about equally confident that their ballot would be counted correctly, whereas voters who used old "legacy" voting equipment, or who voted in polling places with multiple technologies, were more confident. Similarly, Bullock et al (2005), in a study of Georgia voters, found that voting technology does not explain voter confidence. Stein et al (2008), in study of Texas voters given a choice between electronic or paper voting technology, found that more than 80 percent chose electronic machines, and that voting technology was not significantly related to voter confidence that their ballots will be counted correctly. (It is of course conceivable that paper [or electronic] technology might have had a negative impact on voter confidence *if* voters uncomfortable with the technology were required to use it.)

27 An exception is Stewart (2009) who used an objective measure of voting machine type.

28 Related to this, Persily and Lammie (2004) demonstrate that beliefs about governmental corruption are highly correlated with individual characteristics of the respondent.

29 Compare, for example, *Rosario v. Rockefeller* (1973), which sustained a lengthy advance enrollment requirement for voting in partisan primaries on the theory that the plaintiff was at fault for not registering in time, with *Kusper v. Pontikes* (1973), which struck down an even longer advance enrollment requirement (so long as to force the diligent plaintiff to sit out an election). See also *Crawford v. Marion County Election Bd* (2008), where Justice Stevens's "lead opinion" strongly suggests that Indiana's photo ID requirement for voting should be upheld as applied to any voter for whom it does not represent a very substantial impediment to voting. For examples of lower court cases that turn on the "voter fault" norm, see Elmendorf (2008, 657, note 67).

30 The federalism findings reported in Anderson et al (2005) are based on a study of European democracies in which the presence of a federal structure is coded with a dummy variable (133, table 7.2).

31 Cf. Bowsher v. Synar (1986), which invalidated innovative structural provisions of a deficit reduction act on separation-of-powers grounds.

32 It should be noted that Karp (2007) finds ideology (liberal-conservative) to be an even stronger factor in explaining support for proportionality-enhancing reforms.

33 Blais and Gélineau (2007), using Canadian data, similarly found that "partial winners" – voters whose local choice for MP was elected, but whose party did not obtain control of the government – were nearly as satisfied as "full winners."

34 Whether the Court has been de facto suspicious of initiated legislation is open to debate. Eule (1990) maintains that it has; Judge O'Scannlain pointedly disagrees (*Bates v. Jones* 1997, 852–5).

35 See, e.g., *California Democratic Party v. Jones* (2000), in which a seven-justice majority held California's blanket primary unconstitutional, notwithstanding that nearly 60% of the voters – including a majority of registered Democrats and Republicans – had voted for the initiative. Justice Stevens, in a dissent joined by Justice Ginsburg, wrote that he would have "give[n] some weight" to that expression of popular preference (601).

36 See also Frey and Stutzer (2004) who, using Swiss data, found that liberal provisions for direct democracy are correlated with self-reported happiness, whereas frequency of use of the ballot initiative is not. But Dorn et al (2007), using a new dataset, argue that Frey and Stutzer's results on direct democracy and happiness reflect a failure to control for respondents' language.

37 Dyck and Lascher also observe that the positive correlation between frequency of initiative use and external efficacy found in earlier studies could be an artifact of strategic behavior by ballot initiative proponents. At times and places characterized by high levels of efficacy, initiated legislation is a more feasible route to policy change (this follows from the fact that confused or uncertain voters tend to vote "no" on ballot initiatives).

38 Note also that the lower courts, seeking to curtail political shenanigans around close elections, the have created a due process jurisprudence that limits the states' ability to apply new state law – and novel constructions of existing state law – retroactively in resolving disputed elections (Pildes 2001).

39 One might expect partisan attacks to have an equal and opposite effect on the confidence of citizens who identify with the defending party. Attacks by Democratic leaders, for example, on partisan electoral reforms pushed through by a Republican-controlled legislature might cause self-identified Republicans to think that the electoral system is calibrated just right. However, this seems to me unlikely. Partisan attacks on the electoral process seem generally to be met with a partisan counterpunch in which the attacking party is accused of putting political self-interest ahead of sound policy. In this environment, partisan attacks may ultimately result in a generalized sense of wariness or unease about the electoral process among supporters of the defending party, at least in a federal regime where national elections are run by the states and largely pursuant to state law. (Have the other guys rigged the game in states where they're in power? Did they corrupt my own state's electoral machinery when they were last in power here? What might they do next, should they win the next election?).

40 Note the wide variation in the choice of dependent variables in the studies reviewed here. For more on the measurement debate, see Citrin 1974; Miller 1974a; 1974b; Muller and Jukam 1977; Erber and Lau 1990; Weatherford 1992; Canache et al 2001; Cook and Gronke 2005. .

41 Note that the strategy outlined here could be adapted to serve most any other functional, system-level property (something other than positive legitimacy) that might be designated as a basis for constitutional political rights.

42 See also Justice Scalia's dissent in *Rutan v. Republican Party (1990)*, where he argued that patronage fosters "political stability and facilitate[s] the social and political integration of previously powerless groups" (107).

43 An exemplar is Nadeau and Blais (1993), who, following an election in which the preeminent question was whether Canada should enter a free-trade agreement with the United States and Mexico, investigated whether citizens agreed that "as a result of this election, . . . the Canadian people gave the Conservative government the right to implement the Free Trade Agreement." In other words, they investigated whether the election performed its legitimation function.

44 Note that some regulatory programs may only be meaningfully testable through collaborations among similarly situated states, with some of the collaborating states being assigned at random to a "treatment" group and others serving as the control.

45 A good example is the doctrinal test applied to signature requirements for ballot access. As the Court explained in *Storer v. Brown* (1974), the constitutional standard is whether "a reasonably diligent independent candidate [can] be expected to satisfy the signature requirements, or [whether] the unaffiliated candidate will succeed in getting on the ballot [only rarely]" (742). But the Court also signaled that signature requirements of 5% or less of the "available pool" of potential signers are almost always permissible, and that requirements "approaching 10%" should trigger heightened scrutiny (742–3; Elmendorf 2007, 345–53). In *Munro v. Socialist Workers Party* (1986), the Court noted that the doctrinal framework for judicial superintendence of ballot access was designed to avoid "endless court battles over the sufficiency of the evidence" (195, internal quotation marks omitted).

46 The legislature might, for instance, decide that it wishes to experiment, or *not* to experiment, with certain types of regulations.

47 For a general account of conditions under which courts should rely on expert advisory panels, see Vermeule (2009).

48 I am indebted to Mitch Berman (personal communication) for raising this issue.

REFERENCES

Alt, James E. & David D. Lassen. 2003. The Political Economy of Institutions and Corruption in American States. *Journal of Theoretical Politics* 15: 341.

Alvarez, R. Michael & Thad E. Hall. 2009. How Hard Can It Be? Do Citizens Think It Is Difficult to Register to Vote? *Caltech/MIT Voting Technology Project Working Paper* 48.

Alvarez, R. Michael, Thad E. Hall, & Morgan H. Llewellyn. 2008. Are Americans Confident Their Ballots Are Counted? *Journal of Politics* 70: 754.

Anderson, Christopher J., Shaun Bowler, Todd Donovan, André Blais, & Ola Listhaug. 2005. *Losers' Consent: Elections and Democratic Legitimacy*. Oxford: Oxford University Press.

―――― & Christine A. Guillory. 1997. Political Institutions and Satisfaction with Democracy, *American Poliical Science Review* 91: 66.

_____ & Andrew J. LoTempio. 2002. Winning, Losing, and Political Trust in America. *British Journal of Political Science* 32: 335.

_____, Silvia M. Mendes, & Yuliya V. Tverdova. 2004. Endogenous Economic Voting: Evidence from the 1997 British Election. *Electoral Studies* 23: 683.

_____ & Yuliya V. Tverdova. 2003. Corruption, Political Allegiances, and Attitudes Toward Government in Contemporary Democracies. *American Journal of Political Science* 47: 91.

Ansolabehere, Stephen & Nathaniel Persily. 2008. Vote Fraud in the Eye of the Beholder. *Harvard Law Review* 121: 1737.

Atkeson, Lonna Rae & Kyle L. Saunders. 2007. The Effect of Election Administration on Voter Confidence: A Local Matter? *PS-Political Science & Politics* 4: 655.

Baker v. Carr, 369 U.S. 186 (1962).

Bartels, Larry M. 2002. Beyond the Running Tally: Partisan Bias in Political Perceptions. *Political Behavior* 24: 117.

Bates v. Jones, 131 F.3d 843 (1997).

Birch, Sarah. 2008. Electoral Institutions and Popular Confidence in the Electoral Process: A Cross-National Analysis. *Electoral Studies* 27: 305.

_____. 2005. Perceptions of Electoral Fairness and Voter Turnout. Paper presented at the 2005 Annual Meeting of the American Political Science Association in Washington, DC.

Blais, André & François Gélineau. 2007. Winning, Losing, and Satisfaction with Democracy. *Political Studies* 55: 425.

Board of County Commissioners, Wabunsee County, Kansas v. Umbehr, 518 U.S. 668 (1996).

Bowler, Sean & Todd Donovan. 2002. Democracy, Institutions and Attitudes about Citizen Influence on Government. *British Journal of Political Science* 32: 371.

Bowsher v. Synar, 478 U.S. 714 (1986).

Brown v. Thomson, 462 U.S. 835 (1983).

Brunell, Thomas L. 2008. *Redistricting and Representation: Why Competitive Elections Are Bad for America*. New York: Routledge.

Buckley v. Valeo 424 U.S. 1 (1976).

Bullock, Charles S., M.V. Hood III, & Richard Clark. 2005. Punch Cards, Jim Crow, and Al Gore: Explaining Voter Trust in the Electoral System in Georgia, 2000. *State Politics and Policy Quarterly* 5: 283.

Bullock v. Carter, 405 U.S. 134 (1972).

Bush v. Gore, 531 U.S. 1046, 1047 (2000).

Bush v. Vera, 517 U.S. 952 (1996).

California Democratic Party v. Jones, 530 U.S. 567 (2000).

Canache, Damarys, Jeffrey J. Mondak, & Mitchell A. Seligson. 2001. Meaning and Measurement in Cross-National Research on Satisfaction with Democracy. *Public Opinion Quarterly* 65: 506.

Chanley, Virginia A., Thomas J. Rudolph, & Wendy M. Rahn. 2000. The Origins and Consequences of Public Trust in Government. *Public Opinion Quarterly* 64: 239.

Chappelle v. Greater Baton Rouge Airport Dist., 431 U.S. 159 (1977).

Cipriano v. City of Houma, 395 U.S. 701 (1969).

Citrin, Jack. 1974. Comment: The Political Relevance of Trust in Government. *American Political Science Review* 68: 973.

City of Phoenix v. Kolodziejski, 399 U.S. 204 (1970).

Cook, Timothy E. & Paul Gronke. 2005. The Skeptical American: Revisiting the Meanings of Trust in Government and Confidence in Institutions. *Journal of Politics* 67: 784.

Craig, Stephen C., Michael D. Martinez, Jason Gainous, & James G. Kane. 2006. Winners, Losers, and Election Context: Voter Responses to the 2000 Presidential Election. *Political Research Quarterly* 59: 579.

Crawford v. Marion County Election Board, 128 S.Ct. 1610 (2008).

Davis v. Federal Election Commission, 128 S.Ct. 2759 (2008).

DeLaney, Andrew N. 2008. Note, Appearance Matters: Why the State Has an Interest in Preventing the Appearance of Voting Fraud. *New York University Law Review* 83: 847.

Dorn, David, Justina A. V. Fischer, Gebhard Kirchgässner, & Alfonso Sousa-Poza. 2007. Direct Democracy and Life Satisfaction Revisited: New Evidence for Switzerland. *Journal of Happiness Studies* 9: 227.

Dyck, Joshua J. 2009. Initiated Distrust: Direct Democracy and Trust in Government. *American Politics Research* 37: 539.

_____ & Edward L. Lascher Jr. 2009. Direct Democracy and Political Efficacy Reconsidered. *Political Behavior* 31: 401.

Elmendorf, Christopher S. 2010. Refining the Democracy Canon. *Cornell Law Review* 95: 1051.

_____. 2008. Undue Burdens on Voter Participation: New Pressures for a Structural Theory of the Right to Vote? *Hastings Constitutional Law Quarterly* 35: 643.

_____. 2007. Structuring Judicial Review of Electoral Mechanics: Explanations and Opportunities. *Pennsylvania Law Review* 156: 313.

_____ & Edward B. Foley 2008. Gatekeeping vs. Balancing in the Constitutional Law of Elections: Methodological Uncertainty on the High Court. *William and Mary Bill of Rights Journal* 17: 507.

Ely, John Hart. 1980. *Democracy & Distrust: A Theory of Judicial Review.* Cambridge, MA: Harvard University Press.

Erber, Ralph & Richard R. Lau. 1990. Political Cynicism Revisited: An Information-Processing Reconciliation of Policy-Based and Incumbency-Based Interpretations of Changes in Trust in Government. *American Journal of Political Science* 34: 236.

Eule, Julian N. 1990. Judicial Review of Direct Democracy. *Yale Law Review* 99: 1503.

Fallon, Richard. 2006. Judicially Manageable Standards and Constitutional Meaning. *Harvard Law Review* 119: 1274.

Frey Bruno S. & Alois Stutzer. 2004. Beyond Outcomes: Measuring Procedural Utility. *Oxford Economic Papers* 57: 90.

Gardner, James A. 1997. Liberty, Community, and the Constitutional Structure of Political Influence: A Reconsideration of the Right to Vote. *University of Pennsylvania Law Review* 145: 893.

Gerken, Heather K. 2002. The Costs and Consequences of Minimalism in Voting Cases: Baker v. Carr and Its Progeny. *North Carolina Law Review* 80: 1141.

Gonzalez, Celia & Tom R. Tyler. 2008. The Psychology of Enfranchisement: Engaging and Fostering Inclusion of Members through Voting and Decision-Making Procedures. *Journal of Social Issues* 3: 447.

Hall, Thad E., Quinn Monson, & Kelly Patterson. 2009. The Human Dimension of Elections: How Poll Workers Shape Public Confidence in Elections. *Political Research Quarterly* 62: 507.

Harman v. Forssenius, 380 U.S. 528 (1965).

Harper v. Virginia State Board of Elections, 383 U.S. 663 (1966).

Hero, Rodney E. & Catherine J. Tolbert. 2004. Minority Voices and Citizen Attitudes about Government Responsiveness in the American States: Do Social and Institutional Context Matter? *British Journal of Political Science* 34: 109.

Hetherington, Marc J. & Thomas J. Rudolph. 2009. Priming, Performance, and Political Trust. *Journal of Politics* 70: 498.

Hibbing, John R. & Elizabeth Theiss-Morse. 2002. *Stealth Democracy: Americans' Beliefs in How Government Should Work*. London: Cambridge University Press.

Hill v. Stone, 421 U.S. 289 (1975).

Hunt v. Cromartie, 526 U.S. 541 (2002).

Issacharoff, Samuel. 2010. Constitutional Courts and the Boundaries of Democracy. In *Race, Reform, and Regulatory Institutions: Recurring Puzzles in American Democracy*. Heather K. Gerken, Guy Uriel E. Charles, & Michael S. Kang, eds. New York: Cambridge University Press.

Karp, Jeffrey A. 2007. Reforming the Electoral College and Support for Proportional Outcomes. *Representation* 43: 239.

Klarman, Michael J. 1997. Majoritarian Judicial Review: The Entrenchment Problem. *Georgetown Law Journal* 85: 491.

Kramer v. Union Free School District No. 15 395 U.S. 621 (1969).

LaFree, Gary D. 1998. *Losing Legitimacy: Street Crime and the Decline of Social Institutions in America*. Boulder, CO: Westview Press.

League of United Latin American Cities v. Perry, 548 U.S. 399 (2006).

Lenz, Gabriel S. 2009. Learning and Opinion Change, Not Priming: Reconsidering the Evidence for the Priming Hypothesis. *American Journal of Political Science* 53: 821.

Levi, Margaret. 1997. *Consent, Dissent, and Patriotism*. New York: Cambridge University Press.

Llewellyn, Morgan H., Thad E. Hall, & R. Michael Alvarez. 2008. Voter Confidence in Context and the Effect of Winning. *Caltech/MIT Voting Technology Project Working Paper* #68.

Lubin v. Panish, 415 U.S. 709 (1974)

Miller v. Johnson, 515 U.S. 900, 910–15 (1995).

Miller, Arthur H. 1974a. Political Issues and Trust in Government, 1964–1970. *American Political Science Review* 68: 951.

———. 1974b. Rejoinder to 'Comment' by Jack Citrin: Political Discontent or Ritualism? *American Political Science Review* 68: 989.

Mistretta v. United States, 488 U.S. 361, 407 (1989).

Mobile v. Bolden, 446 U.S. 55, 79 (1980).

Muller, Edward N. & Thomas O. Jukam. 1997. On the Meaning of Political Support. *American Political Science Review* 71: 1561.

Munro v. Socialist Workers Party, 479 U.S. 189, 195 (1986).

In re Murchison, 349 U.S. 133, 136 (1955).

Nadeau, Richard & André Blais. 1993. Accepting Election Outcomes: The Effect of Participation on Losers' Consent. *British Journal of Political Science* 23: 558.

Ortiz, Daniel R. 2004. Got Theory? *Pennsylvania Law Review* 144: 459.

Pacific States Telephone & Telegraph Company v. Oregon, 223 U.S. 118 (1912).

Persily, Nathaniel & Kelli Lammie. 2004. Perceptions of Corruption and Campaign Finance: When Public Opinion Determines Constitutional Law. *Pennsylvania Law Review* 153: 119.

Pildes, Richard H. 2002a. *Constitutionalizing Democratic Politics*. In *A Badly Flawed Election: Debating Bush v. Gore, the Supreme Court, and American Democracy*. Ronald Dworkin, ed. New York: The New Press.

———. 2002b. Is Voting-Rights Law Now at War with Itself? Social Science and Voting Rights in the 2000s. *North Carolina Law Review* 80: 1517.

_____. 2001. Judging "New Law" in Election Disputes. *Florida State University Law Review* 29: 691.

_____. 1998. Why Rights Are Not Trumps: Social Meanings, Expressive Harms, and Constitutionalism. *Journal of Legal Studies* 27: 725.

_____ & Richard G. Niemi. 1993. Expressive Harms, "Bizarre Districts," and Voting Rights: Evaluating Election-District Appearances after Shaw v. Reno. *Michigan Law Review* 92: 483.

Primo, David M. & Jeffrey Milyo. 2006. Campaign Finance Laws and Political Efficacy: Evidence from the States. *Election Law Journal* 5: 23.

Purcell v. Gonzalez 549 U.S. 1, 6 (2006).

Quinn v. Millsap, 491 U.S. 95 (1989)

Randall v. Sorrell, 548 U.S. 230, 248–9 (2006)

Rosenson, Beth Ann. 2009. The Effect of Political Reform Measures on Perceptions of Corruption. *Election Law Journal* 8: 31.

Rosenstone, Steven J. & John Mark Hansen. 1993. *Mobilization, Participation, and Democracy in America*. New York: Longman Press.

Roth, Randolph. 2009. *American Homicide*. Cambridge, MA: Belknap Press.

Rutan v. Republican Party, 497 U.S. 62, 107 (1990).

Scheb, John M. & William Lyons. 2001. Judicial Behavior and Public Opinion: Popular Expectations Regarding the Factors That Influence Supreme Court Decisions. *Political Behavior* 23: 181.

_____. 2000. The Myth of Legality and Public Evaluation of the Supreme Court. *Social Science Quarterly* 81: 928.

Scholz, John T. & Mark Lubell. 1998. Trust and Taxpaying: Testing the Heuristic Approach to Collective Action. *American Political Science Review* 42: 398.

Scholz, John T. & Neill Pinney. 1995. Duty, Fear, and Tax Compliance: The Heuristic Basis of Citizenship Behavior. *American Journal of Political Science* 39: 490.

Schlozman, Daniel & Ian Yohai. 2008. How Initiatives Don't Always Make Citizens: Ballot Initiatives in the American States, 1978–2004. *Political Behavior* 30: 469.

Lee Sigelman, Carol G. Sigelman, & Barbara J. Walkosz. 1992. The Public and the Paradox of Leadership: An Experimental Analysis. *American Journal of Political Science* 36: 366.

Shaw v. Reno 509 U.S. 630 (1993).

Smith, Daniel A. & Caroline Tolbert. 2007 The Instrumental and Educative Effects of Ballot Measures: Research on Direct Democracy. *State Politics and Policy* 7: 416.

_____. 2004. *Educated By Initiative: The Effects of Direct Democracy on Citizens and Political Organizations*. Ann Arbor, MI: University of Michigan Press.

Stein, Robert M., Greg Vonnahme, Michael Byrne, & Dan Wallach. 2008. Voting Technology, Election Administration, and Voter Performance. *Election Law Journal* 7: 123.

Charles Stewart III. 2009. Election Technology and the Voting Experience in 2008, Caltech/MIT Voting Technology Project, Working Paper #71.

Storer v. Brown, 415 U.S. 724 (1974).

Sunshine, Jason & Tom R. Tyler. 2003. The Role of Procedural Justice and Legitimacy in Shaping Public Support for Policing. *Law and Society Review* 37: 555.

Tashjian v. Republican Party of Conn., 479 U.S. 208, 224 (1986).

Turner v. Fouche, 396 U.S. 346 (1970).

Tyler, Tom R. 2006. *Why People Obey the Law*. Princeton, NJ: Princeton University Press.

Vermeule, Adrian. 2009. The Parliament of the Experts. *Duke Law Journal* 58: 2231.

Vieth v. Jubelirer 541 U.S. 267 (2004).

Weatherford, M. Stephen. 1992. Measuring Political Legitimacy. *American Journal of Political Science* 86: 149.
Weatherford, M. Stephen. 1984. Economic 'Stagflation' and Public Support for the Political System. *British Journal of Political Science* 14: 187.
Williams v. Rhodes, 393 U.S. 23, 31 (1968).
Zaller, John. 2002. *The Nature and Origins of Mass Opinion*. New York: Cambridge University Press.

7

Judging Democracy's Boundaries

Samuel Issacharoff

The modern American experience with judicial oversight of the political process approaches the half-century mark. In that time, the discomfort with judges supplanting the decisions made through the political process has waned. Except in extraordinary times, such as the election of 2000 or when the Supreme Court assumed active vigilance over racial representation in the 1990s or in the current controversies over corporate expenditures on political campaigns, the idea that courts have a role in superintending the functioning of the electoral process no longer triggers grave constitutional concern. It may be that the American legal system has shed its concerns over the countermajoritarian dilemma, to invoke Alexander Bickel's timeless formulation (Bickel 1986). More likely, however, is that there is now a sense of the familiar about the idea of judicially enforceable rights in the political process, the concept that took hold starting with the reapportionment cases of the 1960s (see *Baker v. Carr* 1962; *Reynolds v. Sims* 1964). Just as likely, this comfortable sense of familiarity is the result of the ability of the Supreme Court to package questions about the integrity of the democratic process within the safe confines of individual rights.

Thus, when Justice Brennan, in *Baker v. Carr* (1962) proclaimed malapportionment justiciable, he did so within the "familiar" confines of equal protection law (226), rather than the more searching inquiry offered by the Republican Guarantee Clause (218).[1] Grounding judicial intervention in the protection of the rights-based claims of classes of deprived voters landed the new political cases within the safe harbor of *Carolene Products* and the justification for judicial solicitude for the discrete and insular outcasts from the broader polity. Even John Hart Ely's pioneering work on the distinct need for process protections, *Democracy and Distrust* (1980), joined the debate in defense of the Warren Court as a byproduct of the perceived need to justify judicial review.

Reiss Professor of Constitutional Law, New York University School of Law. Matthew Brown, Andrew Furlow, Laura Miller, and Peter Ross provided indispensable research assistance.

In this chapter, I want to take a different look at the American experience. It may well be that the particular form in which American courts were able to engage the political thicket required reasserting the rights jurisprudence that swept the world after World War II. However, focusing on the form in which courts framed their doctrines may not well capture the role that such intervention played. As I have argued for many years now, it is hard to look across the sweep of American constitutional law governing the political process – from minority electoral prospects, to campaign finance, to gerrymandering, and so forth – and not be impressed by the transformative role that law has played in shaping American politics. For purposes of this chapter, I want to suggest, without further elaborating, that much of our contemporary dialogue about rights versus structures and process versus substance is an artifact of the path-dependent byways that brought us to a robust body of law governing the political process. Our constitution is conspicuously silent on the contours of democracy, and many of our subsequent doctrinal developments are the consequence of a perceived need for judicial backfilling. While these are important ongoing sources of debate and elaboration, they are by this point more familiar, and I want perhaps to illuminate these issues by looking away from the American experience.

The focus of this chapter will instead be the central role assigned in recently formed democracies to constitutional courts and to the fact that these courts appear to be a required element for the creation of these new democracies. Invariably, these courts are established with the primary purpose of ensuring the constitutional pedigree of the actions of the new political orders, a charge that leaves them unencumbered by the American fixation with the source of the authority for judicial review and the accompanying hand-wringing over countermajoritarianism. If we were to look at the role of these courts as a common enterprise – leaving aside the structural and political differences within the varying new democracies – the question could become one of defining the role that these courts are expected to play under the broad rubric of constitutional democracy. Specifically, the inquiry is twofold: First, how should we understand the role of these courts? And second, how do these courts discharge that role?

THE DEMOCRATIC MOMENT

Beginning roughly with the fall of the Soviet Union, the "third wave" of democratization has swept across the globe. There are more governments that would be termed "democratic" in place today than at any point in human history, and it is likely that a broader percentage of humanity has a democratic say in the elections of its governors than at any time in the past. Most of these new democracies stretch across the boundaries of the former Soviet empire, but not exclusively. Over the past twenty years, democracies have taken hold in formerly autocratic states, such as South Africa, Mexico, South Korea, Thailand, and Taiwan, to mention some of the more prominent ones.[2]

New democracies face characteristic challenges. Some are external, as with the likelihood that they will face military confrontation with neighbors. Most, however, are internal. Of the internal challenges, there are two that are most prevalent. In fractured societies, emergent democracies confront the risk of historic enmities defined by race or religion or ethnicity being redirected to political mobilizations vying for state power. Too often, the battle for power is simply the struggle for the ability to carry out the conflicts of the past in the name of state authority. Alternatively, an unstable democracy may see its first officeholders claim the authority of political processes to ensure their continued rule, the process that Richard Pildes and I describe in the American context as a "lock-up" of democratic politics. In either case, the object (and the corresponding threat) is to prevent the entrenchment of a ruling group increasingly beyond democratic accountability.

One of the interesting developments in this third wave of democratization is the actual form that democracy takes. Almost all regimes import some notion of proportional representation in order to give broad representational opportunities to all social groups. No new democracy has adopted a Westminster-style system of absolute parliamentary sovereignty. All new democratic regimes have specified many of the conditions and limitations of democratic rule in strong constitutional texts. And all the new democracies – with the exception of Estonia – have either created constitutional courts or endowed supreme courts with ample power of judicial review to enforce the democratic commands of the constitution.

It is the last feature that is the subject here. An examination of the post-Soviet democracies, particularly those that seek admission to the European Union, reveals that the newly created constitutional courts are a centerpiece of the effort to comply with rule of law requirements. These constitutional courts are central actors in securing a claim to democratic status for these states, a sine qua non for compliance with the Copenhagen criteria for accession to the EU.[3]

In previous writing, I have focused on the need for all democracies to police their boundaries. My central piece in this area, *Fragile Democracies* (Issacharoff 2007), is an effort to draw out the types of and justifications for the suppression of antidemocratic groups seeking to use the instrumentalities of democracy to overthrow it. In this piece, I want to turn to the complementary risk of what I will term "one-partyism" – the effort to centralize power so as to undermine democratic accountability. It is possible to think of *Fragile Democracies* as having addressed the threats to unstable democratic rule from without, and the new project as looking to the threats from within. In each case, I would suggest, constitutional courts may be called upon to play a limiting role to protect the vitality of democratic competition for office and the ability of the political process to dislodge incumbents.

In almost every one of these new democracies, courts have had to review deeply contested claims of improper internal lock-holds on power. A ready example would be the Ukrainian constitutional court in 2004 derailing efforts to close off the electoral process in that country, ordering a revote, and allowing for election of the opposition candidate, Viktor Yushchenko. While subsequent developments in

Ukraine have shown the vulnerability of democratic gains (Myers 2007), the role of an independent tribunal in at least providing the space for democratic challenge was critical. A similar example – not quite through the courts – would involve the role of independent election authorities with a constitutional mandate creating the pathways for the ultimately successful termination of decades of one-party rule by the PRI in Mexico (see Preston & Dillon 2004). Cases of this sort are common enough in these new democracies to allow some generalizations from the historical examples and to develop a normative framework for assessing the justification for and role of constitutional courts in checking the threats posed when the first holders of power attempt to become the last.

The aim here is not to explore the world of judicial review as such, or to reexamine the debates on constitutional constraints on democratic politics. Both are important considerations. Without the organizing role of structural constitutional limitations on majority processes, democracy threatens to consume itself. Similarly, without some form of independent arbiter of those constitutional limits, democratic politics may fail to protect minorities or allow for political competition. The historic judgment of the third wave of democratization is that the role of independent arbiter is best played by courts, and generally by specialist courts devoted exclusively to constitutional matters.

Instead, this chapter – and the larger project that underlies it – is an examination of how such constitutional courts face these "political questions" and the jurisprudential tools they use to resolve them. To give meaning to cases from dispersed courts, it is critical to address in broad strokes the institutional prerequisites for democratic competition to exist or survive. Almost all new democracies emerge from a civil law system that, to greater or lesser extents, has rejected the common law role of precedent. In the transition to a constitutional regime premised on judicial review, these countries turned to constitutional courts, in part so as not to empower the normal judicial structure with common law authority, including the right of constitutional review. The result, paradoxically, is often a more interventionist form of judicial review by courts not empowered with limiting tools (see Comella 2004),[4] such as the American doctrine of not reaching a constitutional question in a case that can be decided on statutory grounds (*Ashwander v. Tennessee Valley Authority* 1936).

The underlying normative thesis develops from the observation that in the new democracies of the third wave, the most typical scenario is an ethnically riven society emerging from the collapse of authoritarianism or, less frequently, a post-conflict society with the same defining characteristic of a gaping social divide. In these circumstances, a constitution needs to be drafted to bridge the divide to democratic rule. The problem is that the constitutional negotiations take place against the backdrop that one party to the negotiations will hold power over the other. Further, under the press of time, uncertainty, and distrust, the parties are poorly positioned to work out all the details of the constitutional compact – even leaving aside the strategic obstacles always attendant to such enterprises.

In such circumstances, the parties have to get the basic blueprint of governance in place, understanding that many of the critical terms – including the explosive issue of the exercise of emergency powers – will likely be impossible to specify. Viewed in this light, constitutions emerge as a species of underspecified contracts. In mature commercial settings, most countries provide principles of contract law that facilitate the realization of the basic contours of the parties' intent and aspirations, even when time or unforeseen circumstances compel agreement beyond that which was specified at the time of contract formation. The argument, therefore, is that the turn to constitutional courts plays in part a similar role to that of common law courts seeking to realize the intent of the parties in a long-term relational contract. The ability to put off the subsequent interpretation and application takes pressure off the original political contracting parties to specify all the restraints on the exercise of majoritarian political power following the first democratic election. The corresponding move is to insist that courts approach such constitutional cases with a commitment to shoring up the fundamental commitment to majoritarian rule, subject to contestation by hopefully shifting political majorities.

COURTS AND CONSTITUTIONAL TRANSITIONS: THE EXAMPLE OF SOUTH AFRICA

The constraints of the chapter format do not allow an elaboration of the nuanced settings in which constitutional courts will have to address the need to prevent democracy from collapsing into the permanent one-party rule of the initial holders of governmental power. But the contract analogy, though limited, allows some general outlines that can be illuminated through a specific example from South Africa. The basic proposition is that countries emerging from conflict or authoritarian rule are likely to have to formalize a transition to a new order long before any conditions of trust or solidarity will carry them through the formal processes of creating a stable constitutional order. At the same time, such countries desperately need to establish political institutions that can mediate power and provide some legitimacy to the new governmental order. The need for political stability is unlikely to be met through any plebiscitary elections, since this will likely reproduce the divisions of old across a direct (and likely final) struggle for state power. Democracy needs the assent of the people, but – as we note in opening our casebook on the Law of Democracy – there is "no 'We the People' independent of the way the law constructs democracy" (Issacharoff, Karlan & Pildes 2007). The paradox, of course, is that there needs to be some legitimacy for the institutions that will then claim popular assent as their source of legitimacy. The result is that, as Kapstein and Converse (2008) conclude in their study of nascent democracies, "when effective checks and balances are missing from institutional arrangements, even rapid economic growth may not save a democracy from reversal."

South Africa provides a wonderful example of the process of constitutional formation, and then perhaps a sobering cautionary note. In the first instance, nowhere was
the question of limitations on state power through constitutional compromise more
directly posed than in South Africa. The accords that paved the way for the transition
from apartheid were the product of a long, multiparty negotiation. The central issue
was how to provide for a transition to democratic governance with power no doubt
exercised by the black majority, while providing some assurance that what would
follow would not be retribution against the former white rulers.

The process of a negotiated transition from a repressive regime included two
steps, largely innovative, that shape the discussion here. First, the negotiations would
yield only an interim constitution, with fixed representation for the various political
groups, but with a mandate to use the ensuing legislative arena to negotiate a
permanent constitution. Despite the inability to create a full constitutional order
in the transition period, the negotiations did yield an immutable set of thirty-four
Principles that were required to form the basis for a final constitution.[5] Under the
negotiated provisions of the Interim Constitution, the final Constitution could not be
adopted unless it faithfully adhered in its implementation to the negotiated general
principles set out in the Interim Constitution (Gloppen 1997). Most novel was that
the task of ensuring compliance was given in its entirety to the Constitutional Court.
Thus, the Constitutional Court was created not to interpret a constitutional text –
most evidently, since none existed – but to guarantee that the structures and limits of
democratic rule would be honored. In accordance with that mandate, in July 1996,
the proposed permanent constitution was submitted for review to the Constitutional
Court, which rendered its decision two months later (*In re Certification Decision*
1996).

The ruling in what is known as the *Certification Decision* is highly instructive.
The South African Constitutional Court was particularly attentive to structural restraints on the centralization of power, reaffirming limitations on government and
striking down provisions that may be termed an excess of majoritarianism. Specifically, the Court reaffirmed the importance of checks and balances across the
branches of government (776, 788)[6] and strictly enforced the commitment in the
Principles to federalism, ensuring that the national government would not encroach
on the powers of the provinces (South Africa Constitution 1993, sched. 4 princ. 22).[7]
The Court also strictly construed the requirement of "special procedures involving
special majorities" for constitutional amendments (sched. 4 princ. 15). According
to the Court, the purpose of this provision was to secure the Constitution "against
political agendas of ordinary majorities in the national Parliament" (*In re Certification Decision* 1996, 821). Various provisions of the proposed constitution requiring
supermajoritarian action were nevertheless struck down for failing to create special
procedures outside the framework of ordinary legislation (822).[8] For example, the
Court found that allowing the Bill of Rights to be amended by a two-thirds majority

of the lower House failed the "entrenchment" requirement of Principle II (South Africa Constitution 1993, sched. 4 princ. 2), which, the Court ruled, required "some 'entrenching' mechanism . . . [to give] the Bill of Rights greater protection than the ordinary provisions of the [Constitution]" (*In re Certification Decision* 1996, 822–3). The Court also found that the rejection of judicial review for certain categories of statutes violated the commitment to constitutional supremacy and the jurisdictional guarantees for judicial power contained in the Principles (820). The Constitutional Assembly then revised the constitutional draft to meet the Court's concerns in October 1996, and following a second round of judicial scrutiny, the new Constitution was signed and implemented by President Nelson Mandela in December 1996.

Of particular note, however, is the Court's broad interpretation of constitutional protections for minority parties, a check even in the early days of post-apartheid governance against the possibility of one-party domination. I want to focus here on a relatively secondary provision among party protections that, although not one of the decisive issues of post-apartheid South Africa, is nonetheless significant here. As part of the *Certification Decision,* the Court had to address various constitutional provisions protecting minority parties. Beyond the protections of proportional representation, the Constitution contained an "anti-defection" principle in which a member of Parliament would have to resign if he or she attempted to switch parties (*In re Certification Decision* 829n136). The provision was an express subject of negotiations in the transition from apartheid, reflecting fears that the likely parliamentary majority of the African National Congress could be used to woo minority legislators and overconcentrate political power. South Africa joined other countries that formalized such anti-defection concerns through legal prohibitions on what is known as "floor walking."[9]

Although such provisions may restrict expression of beliefs by legislators, there is an overriding concern that minority legislators could be induced to sway from their constituents' interests to support majoritarian policies. Since by definition there are fewer minority representatives than majority ones, any single minority defection would have a more severe impact on the representation of the minority population than the defection of a majority legislator would have on the representation of the majority. Such defection to the majority is not only more costly, but also more likely. Minority caucuses are unlikely to be able to offer the same sort of inducements in terms of personal advancement or choice legislative programs as is the majority. In rejecting the civil liberties challenge to the anti-defection clause, the Court noted that anti-defection clauses were found in the constitutions of Namibia and India and were therefore entirely consistent with democratic governance (Palmer 2006, 790–1).[10]

However, this did not end the debate over floor-crossing in the South African parliament. Once in office and once its political power was consolidated, the ANC used its legislative supermajority to repeal the anti-defection provision. Under the new law, defection was permitted so long as the defecting group constituted at

least 10 percent of the party's legislative delegation. This did little to placate critics because this would pose a very large hurdle to defections from the ANC but
leave defection an individual choice for any party with fewer than ten members of
parliament.

The constitutional amendment prompted a second constitutional challenge, this
time a claim that the amendment would violate the principles of party integrity and
separation of powers inherent in the entire constitutional structure (*United Democratic Movement v. The President of the Republic of South Africa* 2003). Although not
an issue of overriding historical significance, the anti-defection question nonetheless challenged the Constitutional Court's role in guaranteeing the structures of
democracy. The *Certification Decision* had been noteworthy precisely for its attentiveness to the problem of structural limitations on the exercise of political power,
something that was certainly in the air in the immediate aftermath of the South
African negotiations. The question was whether the Court would continue to use
the democracy-promoting metric as the analytic foundation for evaluating efforts by
the ANC to consolidate power.

Viewed after the passage of apartheid, and after the first generation of leadership
left office, the anti-defection question could have been a watershed moment in
the history of South Africa under the ANC. The robust political exchange at the
time of transition assumed that there would be black majority rule, assumed that
the ANC would emerge as the dominant political actor, and further assumed that
constitutional guarantees would serve as a bulwark against the overcentralization of
power. The political shakeout of post-apartheid politics had not yet occurred and
even the ascension of the ANC into increasing political hegemony was tempered
by the calibrated leadership of Nelson Mandela. As the founding generation moved
off the historic stage, however, and as less broad-minded functionaries took the reins
of power, the heroic ANC emerged as the head of an increasingly one-party state,
with all the attendant capacity for antidemocratic abuse. From this perspective, the
question of the day is whether the ANC will turn into the PRI, the Mexican Institutional Revolutionary Party that was similarly the inheritor of a romantic revolutionary
struggle but then imposed one-party rule to suffocate Mexico for almost the entirety
of the twentieth century.[11]

Translated into the context of constitutional adjudication, the anti-defection issue
offered the Court the ability to reassert the structural underpinnings of the *Certification Decision*. Instead, the Court retreated to a formalist account of the Constitution
as guaranteeing primarily procedural norms and individual rights. Thus, the Court
rejected the challenge both on the procedural ground that the mechanisms of constitutional amendment had been adhered to, and on the grounds that no individual
voter could claim a right of faithful representation after the election:

> The rights entrenched under section 19 [of the Constitution] are directed to
> elections, to voting and to participation in political activities. Between elections,

however, voters have no control over the conduct of their representatives. They cannot dictate to them how they must vote in Parliament, nor do they have any legal right to insist that they conduct themselves or refrain from conducting themselves in a particular manner (*United Democratic Movement v. The President of the Republic of South Africa* 2003, 49).

The Court perhaps could have drawn deeper structural authority not only from the negotiated history of South Africa's transition from apartheid, but from the text of the South African constitution. The South African constitution contains a unique provision guaranteeing some form of effective minority party participation consistent with the aims of democracy. As set out in the Constitution, the rules and orders of the National Assembly must provide for "the participation in the proceedings of the Assembly and its committees of minority parties represented in the Assembly, in a manner consistent with democracy" (South Africa Constitution 1996, sec. 57[2][b]) Within the sections establishing the structure of the legislative bodies, at the various levels of the federal system, parallel language requires that the rules for the National Assembly, the National Council of Provinces (sec. 70[2][c]),[12] and the provincial legislatures provide for minority party participation "in a manner consistent with democracy" (sec. 116[2][b]).[13] These provisions provide a potential structural lever for evaluating the effect of party controls. The Constitutional Court recognized this potential tacitly in identifying these provisions as constitutional obligations, subject to judicial control, in the *Certification Decision* (1996, 129). The consequences for South Africa remain an act in progress.

FOUNDATIONAL CONSTITUTIONAL ADJUDICATION

Despite the legacy of apartheid, South Africa had the good fortune of a sophisticated legal elite and a highly transparent process of negotiating the emergence of genuine democratic governance. Most of the countries that emerged from the fall of the Soviet Union had neither the political and intellectual sophistication witnessed in South Africa nor the existence of legal institutions that served as incubators for the new regime. Nonetheless, these countries quickly confronted legal challenges to the core functioning of democracy, in their way as dramatic and momentous as the Certification Decision was in South Africa.

Let me give some examples of the scope of constitutional cases that arise in new democracies. I present these cases not so much to assess whether the resolution was correct – something that is quite often a difficult undertaking from afar. Rather, I want to show that the courts rise to fill a gap in the governing political structure that cannot easily be repaired within an emergent democracy. These cases present a distinct jurisprudential problem in which the courts cannot pretend to find an agreed-on controlling societal organizing principle, as my colleague Ronald Dworkin (1986) would demand. Nor, given the frailty of political structures, do they offer an opportunity for legislative resolution of fundamental contestations of power, as another esteemed colleague, Jeremy Waldron (1999, 82–90), would have it.

If one looks at the role quickly assumed by the new constitutional courts, what emerges immediately is the lack of hesitation over any notion of a political question. For example, it is hard to imagine a more central political issue in the life of a country than the possible removal from office of the president by the legislature. In older constitutional arrangements, as in the United States, the judiciary is given no formal role in the decision-making process, save for the ceremonial role of presiding over the actual impeachment session. In a number of more recent democracies, however, the constitution explicitly gives the constitutional court (or analogous body) the authority to render final judgment by way of appellate review of the parliamentary decision to impeach. This is true in Hungary and the Czech Republic,[14] as well as in South Korea, where this power was dramatically used in 2004 (Lee 2005, 407). At issue in South Korea was the increasing antagonism between President Roh Moo-Hyun and the National Assembly, which finally voted to impeach Roh by a vote of 193–2, with Roh's supporters either abstaining or being barred from the vote. The Constitutional Court of South Korea found that Roh had indeed violated the law in three of the ways alleged by the National Assembly,[15] but that when weighed against the consequences of removing him from office, the impeachment should be dismissed and he should be reinstated as President. The costs of removal, as determined by the court, included prematurely ending the term of a democratically elected official and the political chaos that would be caused by requiring the election of a new president. The court held that "[t]he acts of the President violating the laws were not grave in terms of the protection of the Constitution to the extent that it would require the protection of the Constitution and the restoration of the impaired constitutional order by a decision to remove the President from office" (*Impeachment of the President* 2004).

Alternatively, and more customarily, constitutional courts have had to deal with the mechanics of the election system. Perhaps following the lead of the German Constitutional Court in directing attention to electoral opportunity, this has been a fertile area of judicial engagement. Even among the active Eastern European constitutional courts, the leader is probably the Hungarian Constitutional Court, which has also been among the most receptive to emerging international standards of democratic intervention (see Dupre 2003, 13–16). The Hungarian Court was one of the first to begin work and has been handing down important decisions since the early 1990s (see Jackson 2008, 1266). Having had an early start, it also has been unusually successful in gaining widespread legitimacy despite (or perhaps as a result of) striking down one-third of all legislation passed between 1989 and 1995, according to one estimate (see Scheppele 2005, 44).[16] The Court has policed eligibility for office, striking down, for example, a proposed amendment to the electoral law stating that elected representatives of the "social security self-governments" could not be put forward as candidates at the parliamentary elections (*Decision no. 16/1994*

1994, 245–6). For democracies emerging from extended periods of authoritarian rule – the Soviet example dominates, but it is not significantly different from post-Nazi Germany or post-apartheid South Africa, or even post-Saddam Iraq – coming to terms with the monopoly of technical expertise by those compromised by association with the prior regime is invariably a dominant social and political issue. The difficult line between accountability and revenge is all too often policed by the newly created constitutional courts, as presented in Romania (Sadurski 2005, 156),[17] Ukraine (*Decision nos. 03/3600–97, 03–3808-97* 1998),[18] Macedonia (*Decision no. 16/97* 1997),[19] and, perhaps most notably, Poland (*Judgment no. K.2/07* 2007).[20] Even more troubling is the prospect that lustration laws take a form that sweeps in an ethnic group compromised by association with the old regime but now subject to recriminations by resurgent ethnic claims, as in Moldova (see Agence France-Presse 2002; Wines 2002) or the Baltics (see Skucas 2004, 411).[21] Particularly in the Baltics, the presence of a Russian population associated with Soviet occupation provided an almost irresistible target for xenophobic retribution, even though the Russian population by the end of the Soviet era had had a generations-long presence in the region.

   A particularly striking example is found in Mongolia, where a newly created Constitutional Court waded into the very heart of the political thicket in the first election that successfully displaced the embedded Mongolian People's Revolutionary Party, the long-standing communist rulers. The Court in 1996 interpreted the new constitutional order, ruling that Members of Parliament could not hold cabinet positions in the new coalition government.[22] The question before the Court was in fact framed by a first-order dispute as to whether Mongolia was a presidential or parliamentary system. Perhaps surprisingly (then again, perhaps not), this question had apparently not been specified in the multiparty and broadly participatory Mongolian constitutional design. To strike down the proposed dual role of ministers, the Court first had to decide that Mongolia was constitutionally obligated to adhere to a presidential system, and then conclude that a division of functions between members of parliament and members of the executive was necessary to maintain both separation of powers and political competition between the branches. In effect, the Constitutional Court undertook a multiyear – and eventually unsuccessful – effort to thwart a power grab by a majority faction in parliament.

   More common are cases confronting minimum thresholds for parliamentary office under proportional representation elections. The issue of exclusion thresholds has a rich history, drawing, most notably, from Germany's Federal Constitutional Court (*Bundesverfassungsgericht*). The German court has pursued a functional balance in this area, recognizing that high thresholds can be a barrier to political choice while also recognizing that low thresholds risk impotent governance because representation is fractured among minor parties. The Court repeatedly upheld challenges to thresholds of 5 percent by recognizing that there was a compelling governmental interest in effective governing bodies and that this in turn required avoiding the splintering of parties, "which would make it more difficult or even impossible to form a majority" (Kommers 1997, 187) It has also been vigilant in overturning partisan capture of the political process. Most interestingly, the Court struck down the same 5 percent threshold after German reunification on the grounds that it could not guarantee a sufficient level of representation for the former East Germany, whose nascent political actors were unlikely to forge sufficiently strong national lists for the first postunification elections (188–89, translation of the 1990 National Unity Election Case). The Bundestag then amended the election law in accordance with the Court's suggestions, and in the ensuing elections, some groups from the former East Germany did manage to achieve representation (191).

Following the German lead, the constitutional courts of the Czech Republic and Romania similarly upheld 5 percent thresholds for election against constitutional challenges. In each case, the claim was that the threshold violated a constitutional commitment to proportional representation and to a minimum access to electoral office (Sadurski 2005, 154–5). In each case, the Court weighed the claimed right of representation against the "excessive splintering of the political process" (*Decision Pl. US 25/96* 1998) and the need for efficient political decision making (*Decision 2/1992* 1992).

Alternatively, some countries, particularly in Latin America, have established specialized electoral courts, designed to keep oversight of the political process removed from direct partisan or legislative control. The model draws its inspiration from a 1924 Uruguayan reform that established a stand-alone electoral court with plenary power of administration of the electoral system (Lehoucq 2002, 36),[23] as well as serving as the supreme electoral court (López-Pintor 2000, 153). That court is widely seen as having stabilized democratic governance, save for a tragic decade of dictatorship in the 1970s. Even so, with the reestablishment of democratic rule in 1984, the court again began serving as the anchor for renewed electoral integrity (Espiell 1990, 10).[24]

The Uruguayan model was adopted in the 1920s in both Chile (Gil 1966, 225; Caviedes 1991, 27–8)[25] and Costa Rica[26] – together with Uruguay, the three countries with the most sustained history of democratic governance in Latin America. Of greater interest here, however, is the role that independent electoral tribunals have played in the reemergence of democratic governance starting in the 1980s, most notably in Mexico. The Mexican Supreme Electoral Tribunal today hears over 8,000 cases a year (Magdo 2009) on matters ranging from local electoral practices, to party finance issues, to politically freighted presidential election challenges.

A FRAMEWORK FOR CONSTITUTIONAL COURTS

The wave of newly constituted democracies allows reflection on the dynamics of the process of creating a constitutional pact and the role that an independent judiciary might play in it, regardless of the specific doctrines that define its jurisprudence (Vachudova 2005). If we generalize across the many national settings in which new democracies have emerged, certain common features do stand out, even if the fit may be imperfect to any particular national events. First, the new democracies tend to emerge in countries bearing the deep fractures of prior, often violent, divisions. These can take the more familiar form of racial/ethnic/religious strife, ranging from post-apartheid South Africa to the explosive divisions in Iraq, to the smoldering hatreds in Moldova and the Balkans. But these divisions emerge even in the seemingly more homogeneous populations of the Baltics, with its generations-old Russian population that must now be integrated into a post-occupation role in a functioning democracy.

Second, the process of constitutional negotiation is unlikely to yield a completely realized set of agreements. The romantic view of constitutional design assumes a Rawlsian baseline of dispassionate founders, deeply immersed in the political theory of the day. But constitution making – the act of actually getting a political accord that will provide the foundations of a democratic state – is more likely a rhapsodic event. The precommitment process of constraining future actors to an elaborated political design – termed "Peter sober binding Peter drunk" (Holmes 1995, 135)[27] – may very well get one critical detail quite wrong. Reviewing the political tensions and accompanying forms of social release that accompany actual constitutional negotiations, Jon Elster (2003, 1768, 1768n51) provocatively claimed the precommitment to be Peter drunk binding Peter sober.[28]

Even Elster's less ennobling account fails to give full force to the modern constitutional settings. In less divided societies, it is possible to ratify a constitution through relatively unrepresentative proceedings, or even by fiat, as with the American imposition of a new constitutional order on militarily defeated Japan. But a constitution is fundamentally a social compact, one that has long been recognized as a political resolution of the competing claims for power in the particular society:

> Politics has to consider which sort of constitution suits which sort of civic body. The attainment of the best constitution is likely to be impossible for the general run of states; and the good law-giver and the true statesman must therefore have their eyes open not only to what is the absolute best, but also to what is the best in relation to actual conditions (Aristotle, 181).

The fractured settings for the newly emergent democracies require a process of negotiation that can create an enduring form of governance but must do so through accommodation reached by parties or groups with oftentimes long-standing historic grievances against each other. This generally means two things. First, the process will take time, what Ruti Teitel (2000, 196) terms the "fits and starts" of constitutional negotiation. As a result, any rush to "premature constitutionalization" threatens the ability to form a political consensus over what can be agreed to and, just as centrally, what the parties are not able to agree to (Feldman 2005, 870–2).[29] Here again, the two-stage process of constitutional negotiation in South Africa provides a helpful model. Second – again as in South Africa – the resulting agreement is likely to leave critical issues unresolved.[30] Vicki Jackson (2008, 1265–8) refers to the resulting process as yielding either incremental constitutionalism or even an interim constitution. In either case, the immediate task of the constitutional process is to signal a clear break from the prior regime, even if the precise terms of the new constitutional order are left to another day or another actor. Most significantly, leaving some matters unresolved avoids forcing the parties "into a negotiation 'for all the marbles' in a zero-sum environment" (Rasoul al-Istrabadi 2009, 1627).

Unfortunately, the incompleteness of the constitutional commitment can have fatal consequences for nascent democracies. Some 40 percent of proto-democracies in postconflict countries revert to violence within a decade, suggesting the fragility of these accords. In such circumstances, it is hard to avoid the conclusion of Paul Collier (2009, 75) that the press for elections to consolidate democratic rule actually exacerbates the risk of violence, because competing factions see the election as simply a way to continue the civil war with the authority of state power. To give but one example, the early election in Burundi in 2005 resulted in victory by the Hutu forces, with a return to political repression almost immediately, including the expulsion of UN peacekeepers (78).

Here we may suggest that when viewed as a complex, cross-temporal compact, the incompleteness of constitutional accords and the need for institutions to fill the gaps in the underlying accords are not surprising. Indeed, this conception of constitutionalism shares much in common with conventional accounts of gap filling in private contracts, and with the use of courts as independent institutions tasked with honoring the generalized but incomplete intentions of the parties. Further, the typical incompletely realized constitutional compact will require separation of powers among different institutions of government in order to limit the reach of the first group to hold office. As political scientist Martin Shapiro (1993, 49) notes, "[w]henever a constitution divides powers, it almost always necessitates a constitutional court to police the boundaries."

But if constitutions are anticipated to be incompletely realized agreements, then courts are unlikely to find fully satisfactory guidance within the four corners of the text. This places a distinct institutional pressure on constitutional courts in new democracies to act as common law rather than civil law institutions, ones attendant to the incremental realization of constitutional arrangements through the accretion of decisional law. For jurists largely trained in the civil law tradition of close-quartered exposition of textual commands, the transition is challenging. The divide between the common law demands of constitutional adjudication and the civil law tradition for nonconstitutional cases reproduces the divide in the European Union. There too, a largely common law set of practices has emerged in the European Court of Justice and the European Court of Human Rights, which in turn have to be translated into national law by national courts limited to the civil law tradition.

Viewed in this light, there is an inevitable tension in the role to be assumed by constitutional courts. Since the ultimate authority of these courts comes from the fact of a constitutional accord, courts will likely succeed in helping forge a constitutional order to the extent that they honor the intentions of the parties. And the intention to be bound by the agreement is best revealed by definiteness of terms, in constitutions as in ordinary contracts (see Farnsworth 2004, sec. 3.1). But contract law teaches that for a variety of reasons, including imperfect knowledge of future conditions and strategic withholding of private information, parties to a contract frequently fail to specify all of the relevant terms, leaving the contract incomplete (see Barnett 1992, 821–2). Modern contract law has generally abandoned formalist rules that rendered contracts unenforceable when significant gaps in material terms existed in favor of a more liberal rule that permits courts to serve a gap-filling role (Ben-Shahar 2004, 389).[31] The *Uniform Commercial Code* (2002, sec. 2–204[3]), for instance, expressly accepts as enforceable a "contract with open terms" that allows gap filling with reasonable or average terms.[32] Similarly, the *Restatement (Second) of Contracts* (1981, sec. 33) also favors liberal application of incomplete contracts when it is clear that the parties intended to be bound by the agreement.

There are at least two arguments for gap filling sounding primarily in efficiency (Ayres 1998, 585), each of which has some implication for the role of courts addressing constitutional compacts. The first theory is based on the idea that it is inefficient for parties to invest in discovering and negotiating all of the details and contingencies that might arise in their agreement. If the transaction costs of forming a full contract exceed the benefits, it makes sense for some terms to remain open and to allow a court to fill in the gaps as the necessity arises. In these situations, the commonly accepted remedy is for the court to fill in the missing terms as they believe the parties would do themselves under costless bargaining (Ben-Shahar 2004, 397–8). This method of gap filling is described as "majoritarian" because it seeks to provide terms that most parties would have endorsed under the circumstances (Ayres 1998, 585).

The second theory for efficient gap filling is based on informational asymmetries or other strategic obstacles to full disclosure between the parties that prevent the optimal contract from being formed (Ayres & Gertner 1989, 91; Bebchuk & Shavell 1991, 286). "Information-forcing" default rules can induce the contracting parties to reveal private information by providing terms that would be unfavorable to the better informed party.[33] So, for instance, if one party values performance more than would be ordinarily assumed by the other party, it is efficient for this information to be communicated to the other party so that he might take the necessary precautions to ensure performance. If the default rule sets damages at the average or ordinary cost of nonperformance, the party with the idiosyncratically high valuation will have the incentive to reveal his private information during bargaining.[34] Further, the knowledge that courts will enforce incompletely realized agreements itself provides incentives for the parties to negotiate as many terms as they can, knowing they may be held to a less desirable outcome by an independent adjudicator.

Translated to the context of constitutional bargaining, constitutional courts may facilitate the transition to democracy in two ways. The first is by permitting the parties a quick transition to basic democratic governance before they are capable of full agreement. The second has more to do with the specifics of constitutional compromise, recognizing in the spirit of John Marshall that "it is a Constitution we are expounding" (*McCulloch v. Maryland* 1819).[35] Unlike parties in conventional contracts, the harm in constitutional breach is not retrospective but prospective. Parties to a constitutional compact do not so much fear that their expectations at the time of contracting will not be realized, as that the powers they are creating will be used prospectively against them. At the heart of any constitutional compromise lies the brutish fact that some of the parties to the pact will soon hold state power over their erstwhile fellow negotiators.

From this perspective, constitutional courts play the role of an "insurance policy" against forms of power grabs that cannot be specified or negotiated at the outset of the constitutional process. The term is from Tom Ginsburg, who attributes to the courts the power both to cement the terms of the bargain and to provide for an acceptable response to conditions subsequent to the negotiations:

> [U]ncertainty increases demand for the political insurance that judicial review provides. Under conditions of high uncertainty, it may be especially useful for politicians to adopt a system of judicial review to entrench the constitutional bargain and protect from the possibility of reversal after future electoral change (Ginsburg 2003, 30–1).

This argument may be pushed even further, perhaps by extension of Richard Pildes's (2008) caution against excessive rigidity in initial constitutional design, to say that the prospect of active superintendence of the constitutional pact by courts may allow for greater experimentation and flexibility in the initial institutional design under the constitution.

Whereas American constitutional law remains excessively focused on the powers of judicial review, the prevalence of constitutional courts indicates at least a tacit recognition that court review may indeed be indispensible to the establishment of a functioning constitutional democracy. Indeed, the creation of these constitutional courts is typically accompanied by what may be termed "ancillary powers" beyond simply the ability to submit legislation to judicial oversight. Most common among these additional functions is some form of oversight over the electoral process itself, reaching in many cases to election administration, the subject matters of elections, the eligibility of parties to compete in the elections, and electoral challenges. Indeed, 55 percent of constitutional courts hold specific powers of either administration or appellate review over the election process (Ginsburg & Elkins 2009, 1440–1).

The combination of constitutional review of legislation affecting the political process and administrative oversight of elections appears particularly fortuitous. Both afford constitutional courts the ability to check efforts to close the political process to challenge. More centrally, both correspond to a vision of strong constitutional courts as a necessary check on excessive concentration of political power under conditions that are unforeseeable at the time of constitutional ratification or whose terms cannot be specified under the strategic uncertainties of the installation of democracy.

Here, an American example may be helpful. In a fascinating critical account of the process of Iraqi constitutional formation, Ambassador Feisal Amin Rasoul al-Istrabadi (2009, 1630) recalls how the American constitution was forged in the face of the Framers' inability to resolve the fundamental question of slavery. Whether explicit (as in the recognition of a time limit for the slave trade) or implicit (as with the absence of federal involvement in the internal political affairs of the states), much of the constitutional structure was delicately balanced around a recognition that to address the question of slavery was to call the Union into issue. Moreover, once the Supreme Court removed the capacity for further political accommodations of the slave issue (*Dred Scott v. Sandford* 1857), an explosive Civil War ensued. The question for new constitutional regimes is whether the sources of political accommodation unavailable at the founding may be developed over time.

Although the contract analogy helps explain how courts can fill the breach in nascent democracies, it is by its nature a limited analogy. There are inherent difficulties in fashioning any comprehensive theory of interpretation, even at the level of commercial contracts (Schwartz & Scott 2003).[36] Once the move is made to the realm of statutes, the difficulties of interpretation are compounded by the institutional capability of courts to apply any canons of interpretation consistently and accurately. As Elizabeth Garrett (2009, 2137; review of Ehauge 2002) argues, many canons of statutory interpretation falter precisely because of the limited "institutional capacity of judges" to apply the canons. Moved one step higher to the plane of constitutional interpretation, the difficulty is again compounded. Unlike contracts, there is not a relatively accessible economic presumption that the parties seek to maximize their joint welfare. And unlike statutory interpretation, the canons of construction do not operate against the customary presumption – even if difficult to realize in practice – that the legislature in its continuing capacity is free to override improper court interpretations of its objectives. Even in the context of legislation, there are critiques of the ability of courts to construct a "democracy-forcing statutory interpretation" (Vermeule 2006, 132) Yet that is the task with which constitutional courts are charged.

THE STRUCTURAL ROLE OF COURTS

The object thus far has been to signal the centrality of constitutional courts in constitutional democracies of recent vintage, and to try to give some theoretical grounding to why courts may serve as important guarantors of democratic integrity in conflicted societies. In this regard, constitutional courts serve to refract the exercise of political power in ways that may complement the proportional representation systems and the use of federalism that characterize the recent constitutional democracies. The surmise is that this ability to cabin the exercise of majoritarian prerogatives in the early stages of new democracies permits the realization of a constitutional pact in countries without well-developed political institutions or conditions of trust among rival groups.

Courts that are created exclusively for the purpose of constitutional review of subsequent governmental action are unconstrained by subsequent questions on the legitimacy of judicial review. At the same time, that special role in the process of constitutional formation should lend greater saliency to the democracy-reinforcing steps that these courts must take. One of the objects of this inquiry is to place in different relief the decisions of the U.S. courts since the reapportionment cases of the 1960s, perhaps allowing an examination of the American law of democracy outside its immediate doctrinal moorings.

To return to the American parlance, the ability to cabin excesses of majoritarian power by these courts sounds a great deal like countermajoritarianism. The reason is quite simple: These courts are assuming the role that so bedeviled American constitutional law when the Court engaged these issues nearly fifty years ago. These foreign cases help explore a deeper understanding of the relationship between judicial oversight and protections against the inherent frailties of democracy. They do so not because their jurisprudence is in any fashion binding on American courts, nor even because how they resolve particular cases may or may not be instructive. Rather all democracies need checks on the potential tyranny of majority power. In many instances, these checks are provided by separation of powers, federalism, independent administrative officials, political parties, and the complicated patterns of voting for multiple elective offices. Repeatedly across democratic states, courts emerge as front-line players in policing the boundaries of democracy, regardless of the specific doctrinal mechanisms that any particular political order might specify.

NOTES

1 For an argument in favor of utilizing the Republican Guarantee Clause in redistricting cases (rather than the "embarrassingly standardless" Equal Protection Clause doctrine currently used), see McConnell (2000).

2 Parts of this chapter are drawn from the longer work, "Constitutional Courts and Democratic Hedging," which will appear in the *Georgetown Law Journal*.

3 One of the three governing Copenhagen criteria: "political: stability of institutions guaranteeing democracy, the rule of law, human rights and respect for and protection of minorities," http://ec.europa.eu/enlargement/enlargement_process/accession_process/criteria/index_en.htm.

4 Comella argues that specialized constitutional courts will tend to be relatively less deferential because "[a] constitutional court is not likely to earn its own space in the institutional system if it regularly upholds the statutes that are challenged before it" (1730).

5 The thirty-four Principles contained a number of antimajoritarian protections. As a general matter, these take three forms: 1) an elaborate set of rights guarantees that extends to the confiscation of property; 2) limitations on the exercise of government

power through a balancing of powers within the national government and principles of federalism; and 3) protections provided by the supermajority processes needed to amend the Constitution that require not only a two-thirds vote in the upper house of the national Parliament, but approval by a majority of provincial legislatures. For a more thorough discussion of these provisions, see Issacharoff (2004).

6 The Court pointed specifically to the creation of an upper house (the National Council of Provinces) that would not be based on equipopulational voting, but on the election of ten representatives from each of the nine provinces (865–6). This has great practical significance because one of the provinces is majority Zulu (hence outside the political orbit of the ANC) and two others have large concentrations of white and colored voters. See Gloppen (204, 222–3).

7 The Court found unconstitutional those provisions that failed to provide the required "framework for LG [local government] structures," as well as the failure to ensure the fiscal integrity of political subdivisions (*In re Certification Decision* 996, 861, 911). For the Court, the South African Constitution should provide only those powers to the national government "where national uniformity is required," and only economic matters and issues of foreign policy met this restrictive definition (845–6, 849).

8 The court struck down a provision which required approval of a two-thirds majority of the lower House for any constitutional amendment for failing to dictate "special procedures" for ratification in addition to supermajoritarian assent.

9 New Zealand similarly prohibited party switching by members of parliament in the Electoral (Integrity) Amendment Act 2001, but the prohibition was statutory and sun-setted in 2005 (see Palmer 2006, 610n64).

10 The minority party protections of the anti-defection mechanism were subsequently repealed by constitutional amendment. The repeal is troubling for three reasons. First, the anti-defection principle was a significant subject of debate and compromise in the creation of the overall constitutional framework (see Spitz & Chaskalson 2000, discussing the origins of the anti-defection clause). Second, the proponent of the repeal was the ANC, clearly the majority party least at risk to suffer defection. Third, on my reading of the *Certification Decision*, the structural minority protections provided the central analytic framework for compliance with the interim principles. Although troubled, the Constitutional Court held the repeal to apply only to the procedural requirements of constitutional amendment. The Court did not attempt to impose a doctrine of structural integrity of minority protections to prevent the amendment, which perhaps signifies a retreat from the role the Court assumed in the *Certification Decision* (*United Democratic Movement v. The President of the Republic of South Africa* 2003, 532).

11 I am indebted to Pablo de Grieff for the analogy to the PRI.

12 The rules and orders of the National Council of Provinces (NCOP) must provide for "the participation in the proceedings of the Council and its committees of minority parties represented in the Council, in a manner consistent with democracy...." In addition, the allocation of delegates to the NCOP "must ensure the participation of minority parties in both the permanent and special delegates' components of the delegation in a manner consistent with democracy" (South Africa Constitution 1996, sec. 61[3]).

13 The rules and orders of a provincial legislature must provide for "the participation in the proceedings of the legislature and its committees of minority parties represented in the legislature, in a manner consistent with democracy."

14 Apparently, this is quite common in the post-soviet states (see Ginsburg 2004, 225–44).

15 Roh transgressed the law in the following ways: 1) violating a statute that required the political neutrality of officials during elections (Roh publicly stated his preference for the newly formed Uri Party prior to the parliamentary election); 2) not demonstrating proper respect for the Constitution and constitutional bodies by challenging the National Election Commission's ruling that he had violated political neutrality and illegally called a national referendum; and 3) illegally calling a national referendum to assess the nation's confidence in his leadership.

16 Pogany (1993, 341) also describes Hungary's court as pursuing its mission with "remarkable vigour."

17 Sadurski reviews the decision of constitutional court upholding time-limited exclusion of prefects and other police officials from presenting themselves as candidates in first post-communist election.

18 The Constitutional Court's invalidation of categorical ban on persons from candidacy because of former role as judges, public prosecutors, or state employees.

19 The Constitutional Court's invalidation of exclusion from election to local councils or mayoral office of members of armed forces, police and intelligence officers.

20 The court struck down sweeping disqualification of former "collaborators" as being of such scope as to render "the principle of the sovereignty of the Polish people . . . illusory."

21 Arias-King (2003, 619) describes Western groups' condemnation of Estonia's lustration laws as a type of apartheid. See also Ellis (1996, 181).

22 The account that follows is derived from Ginsburg (2003, 158–205).

23 Per Lehoucq, a "stalemate between *colorados* and *blancos* [in the Uruguayan government] led to depoliticization of electoral governance" in 1924 (37). For additional discussion of the early political history of Uruguay, see Gonzalez (1991).

24 For a more critical account, including laying some of the blame for the 1973 coup on the electoral court, see Weinstein (1975, 127).

25 Federico G. Gil, *The Political System of Chile* 225 (1966); César N. Caviedes, *Elections in Chile: The Road Toward Redemocratization* 27–8 (1991).

26 Lehoucq and Molina (2002, 195) describe the creation of the National Electoral Tribunal (TNE) for the 1946 elections. Wilson (1998, 45) relates the transformation of the TNE into the Supreme Tribunal of Elections (TSE) by constitutional amendment in 1975, and the subsequent role of the TSE as effectively the fourth branch of government.

27 Rubenfeld (2001, 176–77) focuses on intertemporal cooling off as central to constitutional order.

28 Elster (2000, 159) recites historic examples of constitutions drafted against backdrop of social disruptions.

29 Feldman chronicles risks associated with imposed constitutional timetables and conditions in context of multilateral Iraqi negotiations.

30 An older example is the inability of the Israeli founding generation to agree on formal terms on such questions as the extent of religious influence in the new state (see Jacobsohn 1993, 102–3).

31 Although there has been a general shift toward a lax application of the indefiniteness doctrine, the common law rule has not completely fallen by the wayside (see Scott 2003).

32 It states: "Even if one or more terms are left open, a contract for sale does not fail for indefiniteness if the parties have intended to make a contract and there is a reasonably certain basis for giving an appropriate remedy."

33 These "penalty" default rules have been shown to produce more economically efficient outcomes than the alternatives (see Ayres & Gertner 1989).

34 This example comes from *Hadley v. Baxendale* (1854; see Ayres & Gertner 1989, 101; Bebchuk & Shavell 1991, 284–5).

35 "[W]e must never forget, that it is *a constitution* we are expounding" that must "endure for ages to come, and, consequently, to be adapted to the various *crises* of human affairs."

36 Schwartz and Scott argue that modern contract law has neither a descriptive nor normative theories that are sufficiently complete to apply across the spectrum of private contracts.

REFERENCES

Agence France-Presse. 2002. Moldova: Setback for Russian language. *New York Times*, Feb. 22, A6.

Arias-King, Fredo. 2003. Estonia: The little country that could. *Demokratizatsiya* 11: 619.

Aristotle. 1948. *The Politics*. 2nd ed. Trans. Ernest Barker. Oxford: Clarendon Press.

Ashwander v. Tennessee Valley Authority, 297 U.S. 288 (1936).

Associated Press. 1996. *Constitution signed. Winnipeg Free Press*, Dec. 11, B1.

Ayres, Ian. 1998. Default rules for incomplete contracts. In *The new Palgrave dictionary for economics and the law*, ed. Peter Newman, 1: 585.

Ayres, Ian & Robert Gertner. 1989. Filling gaps in incomplete contracts: An economic theory of default rules. *Yale Law Journal* 99: 87.

Baker v. Carr, 369 U.S. 186 (1962).

Barnett, Randy E. 1992. The sound of silence: Default rules and contractual consent. *Virginia Law Review* 78: 821.

Bebchuk, Lucian A. & Steven Shavell. 1991. Information and the scope of liability for breach of contract: The rule of Hadley v. Baxendale. *Journal of Law, Economics & Organization* 7: 284.

Ben-Shahar, Omri. 2004. "Agreeing to disagree": Filling gaps in deliberately incomplete contracts. *Wisconsin Law Review* 2004: 389.

Bickel, Alexander M. 1986. *The least dangerous branch: The Supreme Court at the bar of politics*. 2nd ed. New Haven, CT: Yale University Press.

Caviedes, César N. 1991. *Elections in Chile: The road toward redemocratization*. Boulder, CO: Lynne Rienner Publishers.

Collier, Paul. 2009. *Wars, guns & votes: Democracy in dangerous places*. New York: Harper.

Comella, Victor Ferreres. 2004. The consequences of centralizing judicial review in a special court: Some thoughts on judicial activism. *Texas Law Review* 82: 1705.

Converse, Nathan & Ethan B. Kapstein. 2008. *The fate of young democracies*. Cambridge: Cambridge University Press.

Decision no. 03/3600–97. 1998. 1–12/98, January 26. (summarized in *Bull. Constit. Case Law* 1998 (1): 146–48).

Decision no. 03–3808-97. 1998. 1–12/98, January 26. (summarized in *Bull. Constit. Case Law* 1998 (1): 146–48).

Decision no. 16/1994 1994. *East Europ. Case Rep.* 1 (1994), March 25.

Decision no. 16/97. 1997. March 2. 1997. http://www.cecl.gr/RigasNetwork/databank/Jurisprudence/FYROM/Jur_fyrom.htm.

Decision 2/1992. 1992. June 30, In European Case Reporter 2 (1995) (Romania).

Decision Pl. US 25/96. 1998. In European Case Reporter 5 (1998) (translated).

Dillon, Samuel & Julia Preston. 2004. *Opening Mexico: The making of a democracy.* New York: Farrar Strauss & Giroux.

Dred Scott v. Sandford, [1] 60 U.S. (19 How.) 393 (1857).

Dupre, Catherine. 2003. *Importing the law in post-communist transitions.* Oxford: Hart.

Dworkin, Ronald. 1986. *Law's empire.* Cambridge, MA: Belknap Press.

Elhauge, Einer. 2008. *Statutory default rules: How to interpret unclear legislation.* Cambridge, MA: Harvard University Press.

Ellis, Mark S. 1996. Purging the past: The current state of lustration laws in the former communist bloc. *Law & Contemporary Problems* 59: 181.

Elster, Jon. 2000. *Ulysses unbound.* Cambridge: Cambridge University Press.

————. 2003. Don't burn your bridge before you come to it: Some ambiguities and complexities of precommitment. *Texas Law Review* 81: 1751.

Ely, John H. 1980. *Democracy and Distrust: A Theory of Judicial Review.* Cambridge, MA: Harvard University Press.

Espiell, Héctor G. 1990. *La corte electoral del Uruguay.* San José, Costa Rica: Instituto Interamericano de Derechos Humanos, CAPEL.

Farnsworth, E. Allen. 2004. *Contracts* sec. 3.1, 4th ed.

Feldman, Noah. 2005. Imposed constitutionalism. *Connecticut Law Review* 37 (Summer): 857.

Garrett, Elizabeth. 2009. Preferences, law, and default rules. *Harvard Law Review* 122: 2104.

Gil, Federico G. 1966. *The political system of Chile.* Boston: Houghton Mifflin.

Ginsburg, Tom. 2003. *Judicial review in new democracies: Constitutional courts in Asian cases.* Cambridge: Cambridge University Press.

————. 2004. Ancillary powers of constitutional courts. In *Institutions and public law: Comparative approaches.* ed. Tom Ginsburg and Robert A. Kagan. New York: Peter Lang Publishing.

Ginsburg, Tom & Zachary Elkins 2009. Ancillary powers of constitutional courts. *Texas Law Review* 87: 1431.

Gloppen, Siri. 1997. *South Africa: The battle over the constitution.* Aldershot, UK: Ashgate.

González, Luis E. 1991. *Political structures and democracy.* Notre Dame, IN: Notre Dame University Press.

Hadley v. Baxendale, 9 Ex. 341, 156 Eng. Rep. 145 (1854).

Holmes, Stephen. 1995. *Passions and constraint: On the theory of liberal democracy.* Chicago: University of Chicago Press.

In re Certification of the Constitution of the Republic of South Africa (Certification Decision). 1996. (4) SA 744 (CC) (S. Afr.).

Issacharoff, Samuel. 2004. Constitutionalizing democracy in fractured societies. *Texas Law Review* 82: 1861.

————. 2007. Fragile democracies. *Harvard Law Review* 120: 1405.

Issacharoff, Samuel, Pamela S. Karlan & Richard H. Pildes. 2007. *The law of democracy: Legal structure of the political process.* 3rd ed. New York: Foundation Press.

Impeachment of the President. 2004. 2004 HunNa 1, May 14 (South Korea). http://english.ccourt.go.kr/.

Jackson, Vicki. 2008. What's in a name? Reflections on timing, naming, and constitution-making. *William & Mary Law Review* 49: 1249.

Jacobsohn, Gary J. 1993. *Apple of gold: Constitutionalism in Israel and the United States*. Princeton, NJ: Princeton University Press.

Judgment No. K. 2/07, 2007. May 11 (translated into English and excerpted by the Court).

Kommers, Donald P. 1997. *The constitutional jurisprudence of the Republic of Germany*. 2nd ed. Durham, NC: Duke University Press.

Lee, Youngjae, 2005. Law, politics, and impeachment: The impeachment of Roh Moo-hyun from a comparative constitutional perspective. *American Journal of Comparative Law* 53: 403.

Lehouq, Fabrice E. 2002. Can parties police themselves? Electoral governance and democratization. *International Political Science Review* 23: 29.

Lehoucq, Fabrice E. & Iván Molina. 2002. *Stuffing the ballot box: Fraud, electoral reform, and democratization in Costa Rica*. New York: Cambridge University Press.

López-Pintor, Rafael. 2000. Electoral Management Bodies as Institutions of Governance. New York: United Nations Development Programme, Bureau for Development Policy.

Magdo, Salvador. Interview by Samuel Issacharoff. April 24, 2009. Madrid, Spain.

McConnell, Michael W. 2000. The redistricting cases: Original mistakes and current consequences. *Harvard. Journal of Law & Public Policy* 24: 103.

McCulloch v. Maryland, 4 Wheat. 316 (1819).

Myers, Steven L. 2007. Stalled by conflict, Ukraine's democracy gasps for air. *New York Times*, June 1, A4.

Palmer, Mathew S. R. 2006. Using constitutional realism to identify the complete constitution: Lessons from an unwritten constitution. *American Journal of Comparative Law* 54: 587.

Pildes, Richard H. 2008. Ethnic identity and the design of democratic institutions: A dynamic perspective. In *Constitutionalism in divided societies*, ed. Sujit Choudhry. Oxford: Oxford Unversity Press.

Pogany, Istvan. 1993. Constitutional reform in Central and Eastern Europe: Hungary's transition to democracy. *International & Comparative Law Quarterly* 42: 332.

Raskin, Jamin. 2004. A right-to-vote amendment for the U.S. Constitution: Confronting America's structural democracy deficit. *Election Law Journal* 3: 559.

Rasoul al-Istrabadi, Feisal A. 2009. A constitution without constitutionalism: Reflections on Iraq's failed constitutional process. *Texas Law Review* 87: 1627.

Restatement (Second) of Contracts. 1981.

Reynolds v. Sims, 377 U.S. 533 (1964).

Rubenfeld, Jed. 2001. *Freedom and time: A theory of constitutional self-government*. New Haven, CT: Yale University Press.

Sadurski, Wojciech. 2005. *Rights before courts: A study of constitutional courts in postcommunist states of Central and Eastern Europe*. Dordrecht, Netherlands: Springer.

Scheppele, Kim L. 2005. Democracy by judiciary: Or, why courts can be more democratic than parliaments. In *Rethinking the Rule of Law after Communism*. ed. Adam W. Czarnota, Martin Krygier, & Wojciech Sadurski. Budapest: Central European Univ. Share Co.

Schwartz, Alan & Robert E. Scott. 2003. Contract theory and the limits of contract law. *Yale Law Journal* 113: 541.

Scott, Robert E. 2003. A theory of self-enforcing indefinite agreements. *Columbia Law Review* 103: 1641.

Shapiro, Martin. 1993. The globalization of law. *Indiana Journal Global Legal Studies* 1: 37.

Skucas, Tomas. 2004. Lithuania: A problem of disclosure. *Demokratizatsiya* 12: 411.

South Africa Constitution of 1993 (interim). 1993.

South Africa Constitution. 1996.

Spitz, Richard & Matthew Chaskalson. 2000. *The politics of transition: A hidden history of South Africa's negotiated settlement*. Oxford: Hart.

Teitel, Ruti G. 2000. *Transitional justice*. Oxford: Oxford University Press.

Uniform Commercial Code. 2002.

United Democratic Movement v. The President of the Republic of South Africa. 2003. (1) SA 495, 532 (CC) (S. Afr.).

Vachudova, Milada A. 2005. *Europe undivided: Democracy, leverage and integration after communism*. Oxford: Oxford University Press.

Vermeule, Adrian 2006. *Judging under uncertainty*. Cambridge, MA: Harvard University Press.

Waldron, Jeremy. 1999. *The Dignity of legislation*. Cambridge: Cambridge University Press.

Weinstein, Martin. 1975. *Uruguay: The politics of failure*. London: Greenwood Press.

Wilson, Bruce M. 1998. *Costa Rica; Politics, economics and democracy*. Boulder, CO: Lynne Rienner Publishers.

Wines, Michael. 2002. History course ignites a volatile tug of war in Moldova. *New York Times*, Feb. 25, A3.

PART III

Election Performance and Reform

Overview: Election Reform

Alexander Keyssar

Anyone who has been engaged in election reform during the last decade has surely noticed that change in this arena does not come rapidly. Even after the dramatic events of 2000, the *annus horribilis* of modern American electoral history, progress has been stubbornly slow. The Electoral College remains in place, despite popular opinion that favors its disappearance; electoral administration by partisan officials remains the norm; the rules governing national elections still vary by state and sometimes by county; registration lists have not yet been fully modernized; and turnout remains low among the poor and the less educated. Many states, aided by federal funds, did succeed in buying new voting machines, but some of those machines have performed so problematically that they too have had to be (or soon will be) replaced.

Numerous factors have contributed to the gelatinous pace of change. Funds for innovation (for new equipment, personnel, or training) have been scarce; election issues lack salience in the general public in the absence of a recent or imminent crisis; and enacting new laws requires the support of legislators who have won elections under existing rules and conditions. Compounding these problems has been the acrimonious partisan environment that has suffused political life for the last decade and that leaves little room to consider "good government" initiatives that might, in the short run, benefit one party rather than another.

Nonetheless, a sizable number of energetic voting rights organizations have continued to promote a wide array of reforms – including facilitating the re-enfranchisement of ex-felons, rationalizing (and even nationalizing) the process of registration, and increasing turnout through a host of different mechanisms (among them election day registration, early voting periods, and holding elections on holidays or weekends.) Scholars too have joined the fray, dissecting the political and legal issues, collecting data, and trying to gauge the utility of different approaches to perceived problems.

The four pieces of writing presented in this section of the current volume exemplify several key strands of that scholarship. Two of these are highly focused empirical studies of specific electoral problems that have attracted the attention of many reformers and political observers. "Partisanship, Public Opinion, and Redistricting," by Joshua Fougere, Stephen Ansolabehere, and Nathaniel Persily (hereafter FAP), examines public opinion regarding the critical process of shaping electoral districts. In most states, most of the time, the boundaries of legislative districts are drawn by legislators themselves, leading unsurprisingly to a high incidence of both partisan gerrymandering and incumbent reelection. Despite the obvious ways in which such a procedure can be (and is) abused (it permits politicians to choose voters rather than the reverse), most states (or state legislators, to be precise) have resisted adopting nonpartisan districting mechanisms, such as independent commissions. Why have politicians been able to get away with that resistance, with perpetuating a system that serves their personal interests more effectively than it serves the public? FAP's analysis of recent public opinion polls points to one key factor: Most citizens have precious little information about how districts are drawn and why it matters. More optimistically, their findings indicate that voters, once informed, believe that politicians should not be able to engage in this type of self-dealing and thus that it would be fairer to have district boundaries drawn in a nonpartisan fashion. The people thus are "not irrational" about politicians and conflicts of interest. This happy conclusion will not shock all observers of American politics, but it does suggest that an educated public will support attempts to wrest control over districting from the hands of politicians.

Alan Gerber's essay is a report on both methodological innovations in political science and on research findings regarding methods of increasing turnout. The new methods are "field experiments," which avoid some of the pitfalls of public opinion surveys while helping scholars (and others) measure the efficacy of different campaign activities. The question undergirding such experiments is: What works? Gerber summarizes the finding of several clever and psychologically nuanced experiments aimed at mobilizing voters. He concludes that turnout can be modestly increased through public information messages to voters, particularly if those messages are tailored to put social pressure on prospective voters. In one experiment, turnout rose 8 percent (a significant figure, given the known difficulties of increasing participation) when voters received messages indicating that information regarding who voted would be publicly distributed in their neighborhoods. Whether such communications would work persistently or in different contexts remains unclear, but research of this type seems likely to become part of the toolkit not only of political managers (who want to elect their candidates) but also reformers who want to know whether particular institutional or procedural changes stand a good chance of working.

Archon Fung is also interested in data collection, and he recounts here his effort to gather real-time information about people's experiences at the polls in 2008 through MyFairElection.com, a platform that permitted voters to report on their polling-place experiences through their cell phones. Fung's foray into popular election monitoring was too experimental to yield reliable conclusions, although he did find that a high proportion of his (admittedly nonrandom) sample had fairly positive and unproblematic experiences at the polls. The pay-off of Fung's (and other) ventures into crowd-sourced election monitoring lies in the future: They could lead to the development of large databases that would permit both scholars and public officials to monitor and pinpoint the strengths and weaknesses of our diverse modes of conducting elections.

Whereas the essays by Fung, Gerber, and FAP are tightly focused on particular issues or methods, the article by law professor Edward Foley is a different animal – as announced by its title, "Democracy in the United States, 2020 and Beyond." Foley's ambitious aims are twofold: 1) proposing an agenda for both near-term (2020) and long-term (2050) reform; and 2) specifying a research agenda that could buttress and illumine those efforts at reform. Few will take exception to Foley's near-term proposal, which focuses on developing a "state-of-the-art" infrastructure for casting and counting ballots within the next decade – although numerous members of the reform community have other fish that they would prefer to fry. In contrast, Foley's long-term vision will surely strike many as problematic. I, for example, would be happy to see the Senate dramatically transformed (so that it would less severely violate the principle of one-person, one-vote), but I have trouble imagining two-thirds of the members of that august body endorsing a constitutional amendment that would do so. (Right now it's hard to imagine two-thirds of the Senate agreeing on anything.) I have even more trouble imagining Foley's proposed national civic education program that would alter our political culture and lead citizens to think and behave in a less partisan fashion.

To focus on such disagreements, however, is to miss Foley's point and obscure the value of his essay. Foley is attempting to launch a conversation, to prod a community of scholars and reformers into discussing a long-term agenda, deciding what is most important, and prioritizing reforms of different types. He is painting with a broad, imaginative brush while also offering a host of specific ideas and proposals that would benefit from thoughtful and careful research. (See the remarkable list at the end of his article.) It would take an ingrate to fault him for that.

Yet it would also take a substantial dollop of optimism to believe that Foley's essay (or any other essay of its type) will spark the conversation that he hopes for. For better or worse (likely better and worse), advocates of election reform are a decentralized lot, both in and out of the academy. Periodically since 2000, advocacy groups have floated the idea of coordinating their agendas, of working together on a sequenced plan of action. In theory it has seemed to be a good idea, but in practice there has been little agreement or coordination. As a result, the election reform community remains loosely knit, offering less an agenda than a smorgasbord of approaches to our electoral problems. Some groups work on districting; others on technology; still others on the Electoral College, registration issues, or implanting a right to vote in the U.S. constitution. The list could (and does) go on.

The scholarly world is even more decentralized. Although individual researchers do build on one another's work, the problems they address reflect not only their own tastes and preferences but also their skills, disciplinary expectations, and career pressures. Despite a welcome increase in interdisciplinary projects, legal academics still tend to focus on court decisions; empirical political scientists gravitate toward issues that can be quantified; psychologists lean toward experiments. As a result, most scholarly work still tends to be fairly narrow, cast in disciplinary molds. That is even true of the work presented here, which – more than most – seeks to respond to real-world issues rather than academic disciplines. Decentralized, individualized, needing strong tugs to move toward collective agendas – the community of election and voting rights scholars is very American. For better and worse.

8

New Directions in the Study of Voter Mobilization

Combining Psychology and Field Experimentation

Alan S. Gerber

One of the most exciting developments in election studies is the increasing use of field experimentation to test insights from psychology and behavioral economics. Field experiments combine the rigorous estimation of causal effects that is the hallmark of experimentation with a more naturalistic setting than is characteristic of the typical social science experiment. Through the use of real-world settings rather than laboratories, field experiments attempt to reproduce the environment in which the phenomenon of interest naturally occurs. This realism is intended to minimize concerns about the external validity, or the generalizability of the experimental results.

There was not a single field experiment published in a major political science journal during the 1990s, but over the past decade, dozens of scholars have performed more than 100 experiments in which the effect of campaign activity is measured in real-world contexts. To date, the vast majority of this work examines political mobilization. In these experiments, subjects are randomly assigned to receive different communications. Early experiments suggested that the mode of contact (whether the potential voter was contacted face-to-face, by mail, or by phone) determined the effectiveness of the intervention, but the message delivered was of minimal importance (Gerber and Green 2000). This early finding was in tension with a large literature in social psychology showing that relatively modest differences in how alternatives are presented can have large effects on behavior. Recent work in political science lends support to the social psychology perspective: It appears that sometimes the message can make a substantial difference. In this chapter, I discuss the methodological importance of field experiments and review a selection of the recent experimental findings regarding the most effective messaging strategies to encourage voter participation. I also provide some suggestions for new approaches to encouraging political participation that might be explored using field experimental methods.

WHAT ARE WE TRYING TO MAXIMIZE?

Prior to considering how we might use academic research to improve our electoral system, we need to address a more basic question: How do we know something is an improvement? Evaluating the performance of various options requires a set of criteria and weights to place on each criterion. Put plainly, we need to know what we are trying to maximize. To be most useful, the criteria should be based on things that can be measured in a straightforward way. Measurement in the political domain is a challenge, because some important concepts, such as "legitimacy" or "fairness," are not easy to measure. Setting weights is also difficult, but is clearly important, because there are trade-offs between goals – among other things, alternatives differ in their costs. For instance, there may be near-universal support for the value of "error free" ballot counting, but there is no consensus over how much to pay for it.

For the remainder of this chapter, I will sidestep the vexing problem of what we want to maximize when designing a political system, and focus on the level of voter turnout. I stipulate that achieving a high level of voter participation is an important goal, and that therefore, the effectiveness of alternative ways to produce greater political participation is something worth understanding.

RESEARCH FRONTIER IN THE STUDY OF VOTER MOBILIZATION: WHY SHOULD WE USE FIELD TESTS?

Randomized trials, in which some people or places are randomly assigned to receive an intervention and others are assigned to control groups, are often referred to as the "gold standard" for evaluating causal effects. Although common in medicine since the 1960s, such real-world experiments were almost entirely absent in political science until recently. Field experiments, however, have increasingly become the preferred method for measuring the effectiveness of campaign activity. The primary appeal of field experiments is that they provide an unbiased measurement of the causal effect of an intervention in a natural setting.

To make this point concrete, suppose we wish to use observational data to understand the effects of campaign mobilization activities on voter turnout. There are two main difficulties to such an enterprise – measurement error and selection bias. Measurement is a problem because in the absence of planned interventions by the researcher, it is difficult for the researcher to learn what campaign activities the individual is actually exposed to. The most common source of information about campaign exposure is a survey respondent's self-report of campaign contact or media exposure. Unfortunately, these self-reports are often highly unreliable (e.g., Ansolabehere and Iyengar 1996; Gerber 2005; Vavreck 2007). The measurement error in a respondent's self-report of campaign contact typically produces an upward bias in estimated mobilization effects, because those with high levels of political engagement are more likely to report campaign contact for a given level of actual campaign contact (Vavreck 2007).

The second key difficulty in assessing the effect of campaign mobilization activities, selection bias, occurs when there are relevant preexisting differences across those who experience a high level versus a low level of campaign exposure. Even if we knew with certainty who was exposed to campaign activity and who was not, it may be the case that those exposed to campaign activity differ from those who are not. There are a number of sources of selection bias, the most important of which stems from campaign targeting decisions. Campaigns typically target those voters who are, for reasons unrelated to the campaign activity, more likely to vote. If the researcher is attempting to gauge the turnout effects from campaign exposure, this selection bias creates a spurious positive correlation between turnout and mobilization activities.

Most of what we currently know about campaigns and elections comes from survey data. Survey methods rose to prominence in political science in the 1950s and 1960s and are frequently used to assess mobilization effects from campaigns. To illustrate the measurement and selection issues in the context of a study that employs survey data, consider the leading example of survey-based estimation of campaign mobilization effects, the influential work by Rosenstone and Hansen (1993). Rosenstone and Hansen's work is essential reading for students of American politics and is an exemplar in many respects, providing valuable insights on the patterns of political participation over the past several decades. Rosenstone and Hansen use forty years of data from the American National Election Studies (ANES) and estimate that those who report that they have been contacted by a campaign or party are approximately ten percentage points more likely to vote. However, the measurement of campaign exposure they employ is a self-report of campaign contact, which, as previously noted, may be unreliable and biased. Rosenstone and Hansen acknowledge that campaign targeting may cause selection bias, because those who are exposed to campaigns are different from those who are not exposed. To address possible selection problems, the statistical model used by Rosenstone and Hansen employs all of the variables from the ANES that are available and thought relevant to voter turnout. Unfortunately, the ANES does not have the data from the state voter files commonly used by campaigns to target voters for campaign appeals. In particular, there are no control variables for voter history.[1]

Field experimentation, in contrast, avoids the endemic measurement and selection difficulties of standard observational research. First, randomized experimentation addresses the most important inferential difficulties in observational research. To illustrate this, suppose a candidate or organization wishes to measure the effect of its get-out-the-vote mailings on turnout. To test the effectiveness of the mailing, the organization selects at random a set of households to exclude from its mailings (a control group), and after the election uses the voter records to compare the turnout level of those who are "treated" to those in the control group. There is no measurement problem, given that the organization knows which households were sent the mailings.[2] Further, because random assignment ensures that the treatment and control group each have the same background characteristics (subject to variation caused by chance), this design also eliminates the selection problem. These benefits underscore one of the main advantages of field experimentation: Subject to some regularity conditions, random experiments produce unbiased estimates of causal effects, even when there are issues of failure to treat some of those chosen for the treatment group (Angrist, Imbens, and Rubin 1996). For a discussion of the statistical assumptions for unbiased estimation using political science experiments as examples, see Gerber and Green (2008).[3]

A second advantage of field experimentation is that, in contrast to observational methods, which are limited to studying things that naturally occur, experimental intervention allows testing of "treatments" that have never been tried. There may be novel communications strategies that are either completely untested or not widely known and reported. There might be groups – such as voters with a poor track record of participation – that are ignored by campaigns. What data could researchers use to project how innovative communications strategies or communications outreach to ignored groups would perform if they were integrated into a campaign plan? In cases like this, any attempt to estimate causal effects from existing observational data will be mostly guesswork based on extrapolation. In contrast, experimental investigation is straightforward, because the novel treatments can be the object of analysis.

RECENT MOBILIZATION EXPERIMENTS TESTING THE EFFECT OF ALTERNATIVE MESSAGES ON TURNOUT

The earliest experimental studies of campaigns did not find substantial differences in the effectiveness of alternative messages. The mode of campaigning was highly consequential (face-to-face was far more effective than mail and phone), but the script used in phone calls or face-to-face visits, or pictures and text presented in mailings, were of minor importance (Gerber and Green 2000). For mailings, this conclusion appears quite plausible, given that most political mail has the look and feel of junk mail, and most junk mail goes from the mailbox to the garbage without a second thought. Despite its plausibility, however, recent work has begun to challenge the view that the message is unimportant. Social psychology research suggests that certain messages might be especially effective at persuading citizens to participate. Recently, political scientists and psychologists have begun testing some of these ideas (for a survey of such efforts, see Rogers, Fox, and Gerber 2010). After providing some background, I present results from a few of the recent lines of research. In contrast to the early evidence, recent work finds that which message is used can have a substantial impact on the effectiveness of mobilization appeals.

Background

Over the past decade, there have been dozens of studies evaluating the effect of both partisan and nonpartisan political communications. For a summary of this literature through 2008, see the quadrennial literature review of turnout related field experimental work, *Get Out the Vote* (Green and Gerber 2008). The existing experiments show positive treatment effects from campaign mailings in many, but by no means all, cases. It is typical for the increase in turnout resulting from a single piece of mail to be less than one percentage point, and it is quite rare to observe a two-percentage-point increase in turnout. Often, multiple pieces of mail fail to increase turnout appreciably; in the studies reviewed by Green and Gerber (2008), in two of the three cases where eight or more pieces of mail were sent, there was no measured increase in turnout. A meta-analysis of all existing mail experiments as of spring 2008 estimated that nonpartisan mail produces a .5-percentage-point increase in turnout per piece of mail (95 percent confidence interval for this estimate ranges from -.01 to .995 percentage points, Green and Gerber [2008]). The meta-analysis confirms the results from the first modern field experiment, the 1998 voter mobilization experiments in New Haven, Connecticut, regarding the relatively modest size of the mobilization effect from mailings.

Experimental Studies of Voter Mobilization: Psychology and Voter Turnout

Can Pressure to Conform to Social Norms Increase Turnout[4]

Prior to the November 2008 election, the *Tennessee Tribune*, a Nashville-area newspaper with a circulation of approximately 150,000, published the names of those subscribers who did not vote in the 2004 presidential election. This created some controversy, but the publisher, who had done something similar prior to a 2006 Senate election, responded that "Sometimes when you embarrass people they do the right thing."[5] In a similar spirit, the penalty for not voting in Italy was once a form of social sanction whereby nonvoters had their names posted outside a town hall (Seton-Watson 1983: 111; Jackman 1987: 409; Lijphart 1997: 9). Mild social pressure is commonly employed to encourage contributions to public goods, such as charitable contributions to a church or synagogue; the church collection plate or an appeal for pledge cards during the Jewish High Holidays is a familiar institution to many. Tactics such as the public display of whether a citizen fails to vote may attract attention, but is there any evidence they are effective? Do they enhance participation? Or do they "backfire" and discourage participation?

Voting is a social norm, which suggests that social pressure may be effective in increasing political participation. There is an extensive social psychological literature showing that norms have a powerful effect on behavior, and that people are especially likely to follow social norms when they believe they are being watched or their behavior will be disclosed (Rind and Benjamin 1994; Posner and Rasmusen 1999; Schultz 1999; Whatley et al. 1999; Webster et al. 2003). However, there is also evidence that social pressure tactics may be counterproductive. For example, Brehm and Brehm (1981: 333) found that telling people "don't you dare litter" increased littering.

A field experiment conducted in Michigan prior to the August 2006 primary election investigated the effect of social pressure on turnout (Gerber, Green, and Larimer 2008). Registered voters were assigned to a control group (that received no mailing) or one of four treatment groups, which each received a different mailing (subjects assigned to the treatment groups each received one piece of mail). All four treatment mailings carried the message "Do you civic duty – vote." The first type of mailing included this civic duty message (the "Basic" mailing) and served as a control group for the other treatments, as each of the other three mailings contained the civic duty message as well as additional text. The second type of mailing added a bit of social pressure to the civic duty message. Households receiving the "Hawthorne effect" mailing were told "YOU ARE BEING STUDIED!" and informed that their voting behavior would be monitored using public voting records. It was also stated that the recipient would not be contacted by the researchers. The third type of mailing (the "Self" mailing) added more social pressure. The mailing not only informed the subjects that voting is public record, but also listed the recent voting records of those in the household. The fourth mailing (the "Neighbors" mailing) employed the greatest social pressure. In addition to the recipients own vote history, the mailing presented the voting records of those living in the recipient's neighborhood.[6]

The turnout effects for the mailings with a substantial social pressure component (i.e., "Self" and "Neighbors") were quite large. The "Neighbors" mailing (which showed the recipients and the neighbors vote record) boosted turnout by eight percentage points (compared to the control group, 29.7% to 37.8%, $p < .01$), and the "Self" mailing (which showed the recipients voting record only) raised turnout by almost five percentage points (34.5% versus 29.7%, $p < .01$). These treatment effects were several times the effects found from the typical mailing, providing strong evidence that the message makes a difference, and that an appeal generating social pressure can produce very large behavioral responses. As a point of comparison, recall from the discussion of prior results of voter mobilization mailings that the typical nonpartisan mailing produces an increase in turnout of less than one-half of a percentage point. There have been several follow-up studies investigating social pressure and turnout, which have confirmed the basic findings of the initial social pressure experiment (Davenport 2008; Gerber, Green, and Larimer 2010; Grose and Russell 2008; Panagopoulos 2010; Mann 2009).

The Gerber, Green, and Larimer (2008) study was primarily aimed at understanding the motivation for voting and exploring the effect of social influence on behavior, not to devise mobilization techniques or campaign strategy. However, the findings suggest that social pressure may be an important factor in explaining participation. Indeed, during the previous century – an era that witnessed higher turnout levels than recent decades – voting was much more of a public spectacle, and there was likely far greater social accountability for failure to participate. The most general interpretation of the Gerber, Green, and Larimer study is that it suggests a heightened sense of accountability can have a very large effect on an individual's willingness to conform to a social norm.

Government Outreach and Default Values[7]

Default rules and inertia have a powerful effect on decision making. This influence persists even when the consequences of choosing well, rather than simply adopting the default option, are substantial (Johnson and Goldstein 2003; Thaler and Sunstein 2008; Goldstein, Cialdini, and Griskevicius 2010). After setting an initial investment allocation or savings rate for 401(k) plans, people rarely revisit this decision. Furthermore, the default allocations or savings rates have a large effect on the choices people make (Choi, Laibson, and Madrian 2004). People use default rules in part because it is the path of minimum effort. People do not revisit these initial choices because this requires time for reflection, effort to evaluate the alternatives, and time to implement a new choice.

Many states ask those who register to vote if they also wish to make an additional choice and select a party with which to affiliate. In the context of voting, especially for those without a clear party preference, when confronted with an additional choice, the simplest thing to do is to decline and instead register as "unaffiliated." In some states, however, unaffiliated voters are not permitted to participate in party primary elections. The logic of default rules suggests that many of those who initially register as unaffiliated may find themselves subsequently interested in a party primary election, but lacking sufficient motivation or the information regarding how to change their affiliation status.

In Connecticut, unaffiliated voters cannot vote in either the Democratic or Republican presidential preference primary without first formally registering with the respective party. A recent study by Gerber, Huber, and Washington (2010) investigated whether reducing the barrier to participation in a closed primary for these unaffiliated voters had any effect on turnout. All of the subjects in the sample were initially ineligible to participate in the February 2008 primary.[8] The sample consisted of three separate groups. For one group, the researchers conducted a pretreatment survey. For a second group, the researchers attempted to conduct a pretreatment survey, but the subjects refused the survey. A third group consisted of those who could not be reached or were not called for the survey.

The researchers sent a treatment letter to a random subset of each of the three groups of voters. Mailed a few days prior to the deadline to register with a party prior to the primary election, these letters reminded the recipient of the upcoming election, explained the law regarding the need to affiliate with a party in order to participate in the party's presidential primary, and were accompanied by a blank party affiliation form. The letter provided voters with information about their registration status and the need to register with a party to participate in the primary. The treatment, therefore, lowered the cost to changing one's party affiliation, made individuals aware of the impending primary, and provided information about a potential benefit of party affiliation. Even though the letter was nonpartisan, as a result of receiving the letter, a portion of treated respondents decided to affiliate with a party and also participated in the presidential primary.[9]

The researchers used the post-election Connecticut voter file to obtain an accurate measure of subject registration and turnout behavior. They found that, while treatment effects varied across the three groups described earlier, the letters did increase both party registration and, according to preliminary calculations, turnout. For instance, among those who were not contacted to take the survey, the informational letter caused an additional five percentage points of those in the group that received the letter to affiliate with a party and raised their participation in the primary election by three percentage points. The boost in affiliation and participation are both statistically significant at the 1 percent level. It appears that reminding people (or informing them) about the law and making it just a little easier to participate can substantially improve participation rates.

Descriptive Social Norms: Everybody Is Voting and So Should You[10]

In an effort to boost the participation of single women in the 2004 presidential election, Women's Voices Women Vote (WVWV), a leading political organization, sent out approximately one million mailings built around one important fact about turnout in the prior presidential election: "4 years ago, 22 million single women did not vote." WVWV used a familiar strategy for encouraging turnout. Pointing out that many citizens neglect their civic duty is a common approach to prodding citizens to participate. But does this message actually increase participation?

A growing literature in social psychology on social norms shows that there is a tendency for people to behave in a way that conforms to their beliefs about how most people act in a given situation. These beliefs about what behavior is typical are known as "descriptive norms." Contrary to the intention of the WVWV (and others who convey a similar message), when a citizen is told that millions fail to vote, it is possible that she will form the impression that *not* voting is the descriptive norm and consequently decide *not* to participate. An alternative strategy to increase turnout is to employ a "high turnout" message emphasizing instead that millions of people vote, thereby inducing a belief that *participation* is the descriptive norm.

Researchers recently investigated this question by comparing the effect of alternative messages on voting intentions (Gerber and Rogers 2009). Subjects were called on the phone and exposed to one of two naturalistic get-out-the-vote scripts in the days prior to the November 2005 general election in New Jersey and the June 2006 primary election in California. The scripts presented either a glass half-full or glass half-empty view of turnout to influence participants' perceptions of whether voter turnout in the upcoming election would be high (a high turnout script emphasizes how many people are expected to vote) or low (a low turnout script emphasizes how many people will likely fail to vote). After hearing either the low turnout (LTO) or high turnout (HTO) scripts, respondents were asked if they intended to vote.

If descriptive social norms work in the voting domain as they do elsewhere, the HTO scripts should increase turnout intention relative to the LTO scripts. The results of the Gerber and Rogers study suggest that, consistent with previous research on descriptive social norms, reported intention to vote is significantly higher in the treatment groups exposed to the HTO scripts than among those exposed to the LTO scripts. Gerber and Rogers also examine the effectiveness of the HTO script relative to the LTO script conditional on previous participation rates. They find that citizens with a history of low rates of participation in prior elections respond most positively to the HTO appeal versus the LTO appeal. In contrast, for those with a history of regularly voting, the LTO script proves just as effective as the HTO script.[11] These results suggest that a shift from an LTO to HTO message may be a strategy for increasing the relative rate of participation among those groups that often fail to vote. To be clear, a significant limitation of this research is that it measures the effect of messaging on vote intention and not actual turnout. Experiments with samples large enough to detect effects on actual turnout are a priority.

Some Unanswered Questions

There is substantial evidence that some voter mobilization tactics and messages are more effective than others.[12] A few general questions not answered by the studies reviewed here are: First, what is the most cost-effective way to increase political participation overall and how might this vary across groups or political contexts? Second, what are the tradeoffs associated with various tactics? For example, the "social pressure" tactics are fairly strong. Is there a related method that might tap voters' "pride" that would be less abrasive but equally effective? Finally, what are the collateral benefits to participation for the individual and the group? Does voting, or interventions to increase voting, create a more politically active citizen more generally? Although this is a very important question, I am aware of only limited evidence that voting leads to greater political awareness and involvement. Correlations between participation and political engagement are suggestive, but are ambiguous regarding the direction of causality. Experimental evidence would be especially welcome.

WHAT ARE SOME FURTHER DIRECTIONS FOR EXPERIMENTAL RESEARCH?

Academics are now working with foundations, interest groups, government offices, and political campaigns to design and run experiments that measure the effects of various election-related communications. What is the next step in applying experimental methods to understand how political participation can be increased? There are many other questions beyond the effectiveness of alternative voter mobilization messages that might be investigated using experimental methods. Perhaps the most important new direction would be to begin to concentrate effort on understanding the effects of institutional reforms.

Again, by way of illustration, researchers and municipalities could test the effects of a range of other interventions designed to encourage participation, including small incentive payments for citizens to participate, voter training sessions in community centers and schools, supplementary "advisory" ballot questions to give voters a chance to express their opinions on a range of issues, varying levels of pre-election public service voter communication (such as sending out public notices of the upcoming election), pre-election notice of registration status, travel vouchers for free rides to the polls, real-time internet reporting of Election Day cross-off lists, and permitting parties to concentrate efforts on those who have yet to vote. Outcomes to measure for these eight additional interventions would include turnout as well as survey-based measures of civic satisfaction and confidence in elections and government.

CONCLUSION

The first experimental studies of campaign effects suggested that the type of message used was of little consequence. Recent work shows that the message conveyed in an appeal does, in fact, sometimes make a large difference. Studies have shown, for example, that even a small amount of social pressure can lead to a very substantial increase in voter turnout. To put the magnitude of the mobilization effects described in this chapter into perspective, there is an approximately ten percentage point increase in turnout from midterm to presidential elections. The difference between the presidential years and midterms is enormous; presidential elections typically feature nonstop media attention, a riveting story line, and billions of dollars in campaign spending. By way of comparison, a single social pressure mailing was found to increase turnout by about eight percentage points.

The experimental results suggest two further conclusions. First, framing and presentation may be critical when attempting to affect political behavior. A piece of mail encouraging participation may ordinarily have only a miniscule effect, but a brief letter of encouragement with a specific reminder about a deadline and a requirement may produce a large increase in turnout. Second, experiments are a powerful tool for investigating the effectiveness of alternative interventions. Given the amount of money spent on political campaigns, it might be expected that there is nothing left to learn about political communications. The wave of recent field experimentation has shown that this is not the case. All the experimental studies described and cited in this paper did not exist fifteen years ago; in all likelihood, this work is merely the beginning. If experimentation is embraced, it is reasonable to expect that our understanding of how we might encourage political participation, and more generally, how we might structure our elections, will be transformed over the coming decades.

NOTES

1 Researchers are typically well aware of the threats to inference from measurement and selection problems and sometimes take steps to address them. The measurement problem is often ignored, though in recent years for some forms of campaign activity, especially broadcast advertising, objective measurement of local ad buys has replaced self-reported campaign contacts. Similarly, scholars have begun asking households to collect their political mail. The main approach to solving the selection problem is to include control variables that account for the factors related to both campaign mobilization targeting and voter turnout probability.

2 If all the households assigned to the treatment group do not get the mailing due to incorrect addresses or other issues with experimental administration, the analysis will need to be adjusted accordingly. For a discussion of how "compliance" affects the analysis and interpretation of experimental results, see Angrist, Imbens, and Rubin (1996) or Gerber and Green (2008).

3 Angrist and Pischke (2008) also offer an accessible and engaging discussion of strategies for conducting observational research that deals with, among many other things, strategies for approaching selection problems.

4 This discussion draws heavily on Gerber, Green, and Larimer (2008).

5 The publication of the names of nonvoters was reported by a local television station: http://www.newschannel5.com/Global/story.asp?s=9184672

6 For a fuller description of the mailings, see Gerber, Green, and Larimer (2008).

7 This discussion draws heavily on Gerber, Huber, and Washington (2010).

8 For a discussion of the sample frame and the details of the mailings, see Gerber, Huber, and Washington (2010).

9 In Connecticut, voters who chose to affiliate with a party could do so in person up to the day before the election, or by January 31 if doing so by mail.

10 This discussion draws heavily on Gerber and Rogers (2009).

11 See Gerber and Rogers (2009) for a fuller description of the sample, treatments, and results.

12 A comprehensive survey of recent and potential applications of social psychology to voter mobilization is found in Rogers, Fox, and Gerber (2010).

REFERENCES

Angrist, Joshua D., Guido W. Imbens, and Donald B. Rubin. 1996. "Identification of Causal Effects Using Instrumental Variables." *Journal of the American Statistical Association* 91: 444–55.

Angrist, Joshua D., and Jörn-Steffen Pischke. 2008. *Mostly Harmless Econometrics: An Empiricist's Companion.* Princeton, NJ: Princeton University Press.

Ansolabehere, Stephen, and Shanto Iyengar. 1996. *Going Negative: How Political Advertisements Shrink and Polarize the Electorate.* New York: The Free Press.

Brehm, Sharon S., and Jack W. Brehm. 1981. *Psychological Reactance: A Theory of Freedom and Control.* New York: Academic Press.

Choi, James J., David Laibson, and Brigitte C. Madrian. 2004. "Plan Design and 401(k) Savings Outcomes." *National Tax Journal* 57: 275–98.

190   *Alan S. Gerber*

4

Davenport, Tiffany. 2008. "Public Accountability and Participation: The Effects of a Feedback Intervention on Voter Turnout in a Low Salience Election." Yale University, Typescript.

Gerber, Alan. 2005. "Can Campaign Effects Be Accurately Measured Using Surveys? Evidence from a Field Experiment." Working paper, ISPS Yale University.

Gerber, Alan S., and Donald P. Green. 2000. "The Effects of Canvassing, Telephone Calls, and Direct Mail on Voter Turnout: A Field Experiment." *American Political Science Review* 94: 653–63.

Gerber, Alan S., and Donald P. Green. 2008. "Field Experiments and Natural Experiments." In Janet M. Box-Steffensmeier, Henry E. Brady, and David Collier, eds., *Oxford Handbook of Political Methodology*. New York: Oxford University Press, 357–81.

Gerber, Alan S., Donald P. Green, and Christopher W. Larimer. 2008. "Social Pressure and Voter Turnout: Evidence from a Large-scale Field Experiment." *American Political Science Review* 102: 33–48.

Gerber, Alan S., Donald P. Green, and Christopher W. Larimer. "An Experiment Testing the Relative Effectiveness of Encouraging Voter Participation by Feelings of Pride or Shame." Inducing *Political Behavior* 32: 409–22.

Gerber, Alan S., Gregory A. Huber, and Ebonya Washington. 2010. "Party Affiliation, Partisanship, and Political Beliefs: A Field Experiment." *American Political Science Review*. Forthcoming.

Gerber, Alan, and Todd Rogers. 2009. "Descriptive Social Norms and Motivation to Vote: Everybody's Voting and So Should You." *Journal of Politics* 71: 178–91.

Goldstein, Noah, Robert B. Cialdini, and Vladas Griskevicius. 2010. "A Room with a Viewpoint: Using Norm-based Appeals to Motivate Conservation Behaviors in a Hotel Setting." *Journal of Consumer Research* 35: 472–82.

Green, Donald P., and Alan S. Gerber. 2008. *Get Out The Vote: How to Increase Voter Turnout*, 2nd ed. Washington, DC: Brookings Institution Press.

Grose, Christian R., and Carrie A. Russell. 2008. "Avoiding the Vote: A Theory and Field Experiment of the Social Costs of Public Political Participation." Available at SSRN: http://ssrn.com/abstract=1310868

Jackman, Robert W. 1987. "Political Institutions and Voter Turnout in the Industrial Democracies." *American Political Science Review* 81: 405–24.

Johnson, Eric J., and Daniel Goldstein. 2003. "Do Defaults Save Lives?" *Science* 302: 1338–9.

Lijphart, Arend. 1997. "Unequal Participation: Democracy's Unresolved Dilemma." *American Political Science Review* 91: 1–14.

Mann, Christopher B. 2009. "Reducing the Downside of Social Pressure to Increase Turnout: A Large Scale Field Experiment." Ph.D. dissertation. Yale University.

Panagopoulos, Costas. 2010. "Affect, Social Pressure, and Prosocial Motivation: Field Experimental Evidence of the Mobilizing Effects of Pride, Shame and Publicizing Voting Behavior." *Political Behavior* 32: 369–86.

Posner, Richard A., and Eric B. Rasmusen. 1999. "Creating and Enforcing Norms, with Special Reference to Sanctions." *International Review of Law and Economics* 19: 369–82.

Rind, Bruce, and Daniel Benjamin. 1994. "Effects of Public Image Concerns and Self-Image on Compliance." *Journal of Social Psychology* 134: 19–25.

Rogers, Todd, Craig R. Fox, and Alan S. Gerber. "Rethinking Why People Vote: Voting as Dynamic Social Expression." In Eldar Shafir, ed., *The Behavioral Foundations of Policy*. Russell Sage Foundation and Princeton University Press.

Rosenstone, Steven J., and John Mark Hansen. 1993. *Mobilization, Participation, and Democracy in America*. New York : Macmillan.

Schultz, P. Wesley. 1999. "Changing Behavior with Normative Feedback Interventions: A Field Experiment on Curbside Recycling." *Basic and Applied Social Psychology* 21: 25–36.

Seton-Watson, Christopher. 1983. "Italy." In Vernon Bogdanor and David Butler, eds., *Democracy and Elections: Electoral Systems and Their Political Consequences.* Cambridge: Cambridge University Press.

Thaler, Richard H., and Cass R. Sunstein. 2008. *Nudge: Improving Decisions about Health, Wealth, and Happiness.* New Haven, CT: Yale University Press.

Vavreck, Lynn. 2007. "The Exaggerated Effects of Advertising on Turnout: The Dangers of Self-reports." *Quarterly Journal of Political Science* 2: 325–43.

Webster, J. Matthew, Jamieson Duvall, Leslie M. Gaines, and Richard H. Smith. 2003. "The Role of Praise and Social Comparison in the Experience of Pride." *Journal of Social Psychology* 143: 209–32.

Whatley, Mark A., J. Matthew Webster, Richard H. Smith, and Adele Rhodes. 1999. "The Effect of a Favor on Public and Private Compliance: How Internalized Is the Norm of Reciprocity." *Basic and Applied Social Psychology* 21: 251–9.

9

Popular Election Monitoring

How Technology Can Enable Citizen Participation in Election Administration[1]

Archon Fung

INTRODUCTION

In just the past few years, "crowd sourcing" – highly decentralized monitoring and information processing – has emerged as an important technique. Private sector and civic entrepreneurs have developed numerous Internet-based platforms to elicit information and utilize those data to construct knowledge that would otherwise be more costly or less trustworthy. Wikipedia, "a free encyclopedia that anyone can edit," is perhaps the most prominent of these efforts. Similar approaches are used to produce reviews and ratings of books, movies, hotels, disease, and many consumer products.[2]

Crowd-sourcing approaches have also been applied to develop knowledge in the natural and medical sciences. In ornithology, for example, the 2009 *State of the Birds* reports the status of bird populations in the United States based on professional monitoring databases and tens of thousands of "citizen-scientists" who file their own observations.[3] Google has developed an algorithm to track patterns of influenza infection all over the world based on analysis of Internet users' search behavior.[4] For the United States, Google Flu Trends indicators track flu indicators produced by the Centers for Disease Control and Prevention (CDC) very closely. Google results have the advantage of being available two weeks before CDC data.[5]

Though policy makers and social scientists have been slower to exploit the possibilities of crowd-sourced monitoring, several innovations have emerged. A nongovernmental organization called Ushahidi, for example, has developed a crowd-sourced crisis reporting system that has been used to track incidents of post-election violence in Kenya, violence in the Gaza Strip, and most recently highly localized needs in the 2010 Haiti earthquake.[6] Less dramatically, other crowd-sourcing platforms allow urban residents to document, report, and visualize neighborhood problems such as broken traffic lights, potholes, and vandalism.[7]

These developments in information technology and crowd-sourcing methods have the potential to improve the quality of election monitoring by complementing existing approaches. As with bird migration and the formation of potholes in large cities, the reality of elections in the United States and elsewhere is the sum of processes that unfold in tens of thousands of far-flung places.

In the United States, the problem of ensuring that polls are open and accessible on election day is compounded by the extensive decentralization of election administration. But even if, as some election reform advocates argue, election administration were to become centralized in a single federal agency, the problem of ascertaining the facts-on-the-ground on election day would remain daunting. The resources required to observe every polling place in a large country like the United States exceed the grasp of any imaginable electoral regulatory body. Consequently, it is difficult to know exactly how fair and open any particular election really is, much less respond to problems on election day. This chapter examines the potential for popular, crowd-sourced monitoring methods to improve the fairness of political elections. In the 2008 U.S. presidential elections, several organizations fielded experimental projects in this type of monitoring. A survey of those experiences reveals attractions and potential drawbacks of such systems. It raises important questions regarding how this method might be used and improved in the future.

THE POTENTIAL OF POPULAR ELECTION MONITORING

There are two general reasons to pursue popular election monitoring in the United States in the future: because it is "cool" and because there are reasons to think that it can work well.[8]

By cool, I mean that popular election monitoring utilizes an increasingly common social practice of content creation through large-scale user input. Many people, especially the young and tech-savvy, have come to find peer-provided and widely sourced information entertaining, engaging, and occasionally informative. Examples include video production and sharing through YouTube, Amazon.com book ratings, flyertalk.com or tripadvisor.com sharing of travel and airline rankings and reviews, IMDb.com movie ratings, flikr photo sharing, and Facebook.com.

Election administration and regulation, on the other hand, generally is far from cool. Introducing crowd-sourced popular participation may make the issue more appealing and understandable to many citizens, help educate them about the importance and dimensions of the problem, engage them in efforts to address it, and increase the attention of journalists and public officials.

Popular election monitoring also has the potential to improve the quality and scope of election administration in several ways:

Monitoring capacity would be dramatically expanded by inviting anyone who cares to issue a report to do so. It would aim not just to randomly or strategically sample polling places, but to generate multiple reports about every polling place in the country. For very little investment, TwitterVoteReport produced some 12,000 observations. With moderate advertising, almost 100,000 people called in to the CNN problem hotline. These numbers could be much larger with the support of government and other major media organizations.

Real time. Data generated by popular election are available in real time rather than being stored in reports issued weeks or months later. Such real-time access enables responses to problems as they develop. Media audiences are also much more easily engaged through real-time data, on election day, rather than follow-up studies.

Civic engagement. Currently, citizens participate in elections by casting a vote (or attempting to). Popular election monitoring allows them to participate also by sharing their experiences, observations, and assessments in engaging and entertaining ways.

Legitimacy. Properly implemented, popular election monitoring can have greater legitimacy as a trusted source for some audiences who perceive reports from NGOs, political campaigns, and even some professional media to be flawed. One clear objection is that the quality of reports in popular election monitoring is inevitably uneven. Still, some people prefer Amazon.com ratings to consumer reports, and vice versa.

Vivid depictions in an updated medium. Data generated by popular election monitoring can be very vivid – not just text but also pictures and videos. Popular election monitoring platforms can depict the election using maps, pictures, videos, and text for contemporary news hounds, politicos, and other citizens. Display will only improve in the future.

Transparent analysis and accessibility. Once reports are collected, data gathered by popular election monitoring can be made available for anyone to analyze in any way they like. To the extent there is hand waving in any interpretive exercise of assessment, others can easily check and verify.

Benchmarking best practices, levels of voter satisfaction. Popular election monitoring will allow electoral reform groups, election officials, and citizens themselves to compare the levels of satisfaction and the problems encountered across states and counties with very different voting schemes. These constructive comparisons may help identify best practices that should be more generally adopted.

POPULAR ELECTION MONITORING IN THE 2008 ELECTIONS

Let us define popular, or crowd-sourced, election monitoring as a system in which:

1. Any individual can
2. register an observation about an election and
3. that observation is pooled with other individuals' observations

Project	Organization	Total Reports
TwitterVoteReport	TechPresident, National Public Radio, large coalition	*12,000*
CNN Voter Hotline	CNN	*96,351*
OutVoteLive	Election Protection	*10,428*
MyFairElection	Author, Russell Richardson, ABC News	*1,824*
Polling Place Photo Project (2006 & 2008 election)	New York Times	*6,000*
Video the Vote	YouTube	*1,022*

FIGURE 9.1. Participation in 2008 Popular Election-Monitoring Projects

4. to create a public depiction of the reality of the election
5. that is offered back to the public and to election officials in real-time on election day.

Based on this definition, there were many crowd-sourced projects in the 2008 elections. The largest of these was probably twittervotereport.com.[9] The effort, led by TechPresident and joined by many others, allowed individuals to report voting problems through the twitter communication platform and then displayed the most recent of those reports on Google Maps. The twitter project was implemented in conjunction with National Public Radio (NPR). The author of this chapter worked with San Francisco developer Russell Richardson to create MyFairElection.com – which is described more extensively below.

The Cable News Network (CNN) operated a problem-reporting hotline and then displayed reported problems on a map on its website.[10] Election Protection operated OurVoteLive,[11] which collected reports from its field observers and hotline and then displayed those reports on an electronic map. Several projects, such as YouTube's VideoTheVote and the *New York Times* Polling Place Photo Project, used crowd sourcing to create a more qualitative and entertaining picture of the election.

Figure 9.1 shows these projects and the number of reports submitted to them in the 2008 elections.

MYFAIRELECTION.COM

As of this writing, I did not have access to data from other crowd-sourced election-monitoring projects. Therefore, I will use MyFairElection.com[12] as a brief case illustration of how popular election monitoring can operate and describe the picture of the election that emerged from this monitoring effort.

BASIC CONSTRUCTION AND DESIGN

I initially developed the concept for MyFairElection.com in July 2008. Software engineer Russell Richardson offered to develop the software platform in early September 2008. The platform was fully functional by October, in time for Election Day. Conceptual and engineering labor was provided *gratis*. The only substantial cost was hosting. ABC News provided funds of approximately $10,000 for EngineYard.com, a very-high-bandwidth Internet service provider (ISP), to host the platform in the period immediately before and after the election. These operational details demonstrate that the barriers to entry for constructing crowd-sourced election-monitoring platform are quite low. For this reason, among others, we are likely to see many more popular election monitoring efforts in future elections.

MyFairElection.com allowed users to rate their voting experience. After voting (either by mail or at a polling location), individuals could file a report containing: (1) the location of their polling place; (2) experiences of typical problems such as long lines, broken voting machines, or lack of ballots; (3) positive experiences such as short waits or accessible polling locations; (4) a general rating of their experience, from one to five stars; (5) other comments; and (6) photos. Figure 9.2 presents this simple rating form.

The MyFairElection.com platform aggregated and then displayed the data through a Google Maps mash-up. We thought that the most familiar and therefore accessible kind of data display would be a geographic "heat map," analogous to the ubiquitous weather map. Individual rankings of experiences (one to five stars, per individual) were thus aggregated up to the state level and displayed on an interactive map. On this web page (Figure 9.3), a user could click on any state to see the number of ratings and their average.

The map also allowed users to select any particular state and see ratings at the county level (Figure 9.4).

Finally, users could click on a county and view all of the reports for that county (Figure 9.5). There were two critical design choices in the initial conceptualization of MyFairElection. First, almost all of the other popular election-monitoring platforms collected only problem reports rather than good voting experiences as well. There are two reasons to collect good as well as bad experiences. First, if the data from MyFairElection are any indication of the reality of voting in the United States, the vast majority of voters experience the process as quite satisfactory. A monitoring system (or at least some monitoring systems) should reflect this reality. Second, less controversially, collecting only problems makes it quite difficult to compare polling places, counties, or even states to one another. The OurVoteLive map colored places according to the number of problem reports that they received. But the total number of problem reports will likely correlate to the population of a place; thus, the most "red" states on the OurVoteLiveMap were New York and California. The CNN map colored places according to the number of problem reports divided by

Address (if known): [   ] | **Where was your poll located?**

Country: [Brookline   ]

City, State, Zip: [Cambridge   ] [MA ⬍] [02446]

Which of the following problems did you experience?

☐ Long lines (more than 2 hour wait)
☐ Long lines (1–2 hour wait)
☐ Long lines (30 min –1 hour wait)
☐ Long lines (15–30 minute wait)
☐ Poll place hard to find
☐ No parking at poll place
☐ Someone (3rd party) challenged my right to vote
☐ My name wasn't on registration list
☐ Poll workers did not verify voter identities
☐ I was told that I had improper ID
☐ They ran out of ballots
☐ Ballots were confusing
☐ Voting machines were broken
☐ Voting machines didn't record my vote correctly
☐ Poll workers were confused or incompetent
☐ Unable to cast vote

Which of the following positive experiences did you have?

☐ Poll workers were courteous and friendly
☐ Wait was very short
☐ Poll place was easy to find
☐ Poll place was very accessible
☐ Poll workers solved my problems

How would you rate the polling station?

⊙ Excellent ★★★★★
○ Good ★★★★
○ Fair ★★★
○ Difficult ★★
○ Terrible ★

Any general comments?

[   ]

If you took any photographs, please share them with us

(Choose File) no file selected

photo caption: [   ]

Take more than one photo? Add another

(Submit)

FIGURE 9.2. MyFairElection.com Rating Form

population. Still, the difficulty with that index is that the number of calls is always a tiny percentage of population (nationwide, CNN reports 8,220 calls for registration problems, out of some 150 million voters). That aggregate figure is likely to be much "noisier" than individual rankings.

FIGURE 9.3. National Heat Map of Electoral Ratings

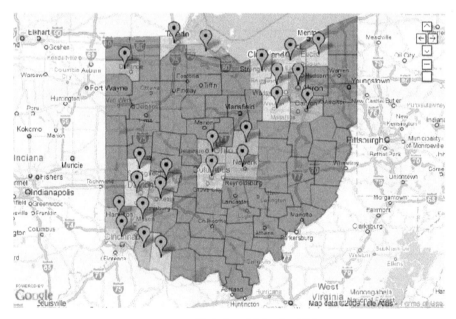

FIGURE 9.4. State Level Map for Ohio

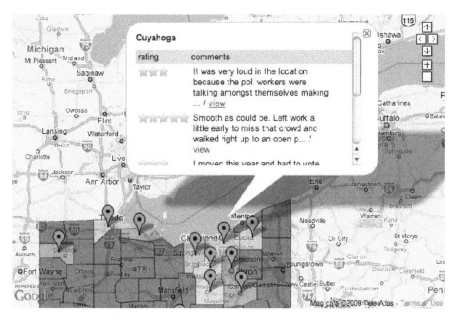

FIGURE 9.5. County level reports for Cuyahoga county

The second important design choice was to display the data in an aggregated heat map. Several popular election-monitoring projects chose this path – such as CNN and OurVoteLive. The TwitterVoteReport project chose instead to display a map with a moving window of live reports that were cluster-mapped (Figure 9.6). These display alternatives merit a sustained discussion among platform designers and users

FIGURE 9.6. TwitterVoteReport data display

Archon Fung

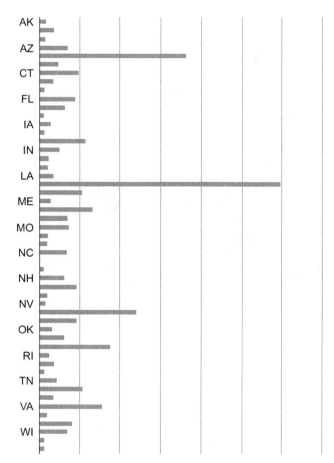

FIGURE 9.7. Number of Reports by State

about the comprehensibility and other advantages of the available options. In 2008, most of us were simply struggling to get a reasonable platform up and running.

OUTREACH AND USAGE

The success of popular election monitoring depends on substantial participation in these platforms. The relatively greater participation in the CNN project is probably attributable to that mass media organization's publicity powers and to the use of telephone rather than web technology. Projects like MyFairElection would benefit from major media partners in the future to compliment the publicity efforts through social networks (such as Facebook) and occasional press coverage. MyFairElection was developed in partnership with ABC News as just such a media partner. However, doubts within the news organization about the reliability of crowd-sourced

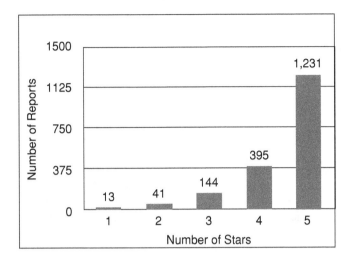

	Yes	Percent
Poll workers courteous and friendly	1,527	83.72
Wait was short	1,152	63.16
Easy to find poll place	1,503	82.40
Poll place accessible	1,390	76.21
Poll workers solved my problems	388	21.27

FIGURE 9.8. Frequency Distribution of Vote Ratings

information created a reluctance to promote the effort. NPR featured and promoted the TwitterVoteReport effort on its sight. This divergence indicates uncertainty on the part of professional journalists regarding the place of this new, technologically enabled method in particular and of citizen journalism more broadly.

Nevertheless, as a prototype and proof of concept, MyFairElection.com did receive substantial usage. Over the life of the site, it has received 17,571 visits, of which 9,369 occurred on Election Day. The vast majority – 14,920 visits – occurred in the days surrounding the election, between October 24, 2008 and November 24, 2009.

Over the life of the site, 1,824 voting experience reports were filed. As Figure 9.7 shows, the distribution of reports was nonrandom. A disproportionately high number of reports came from Massachusetts, probably due to awareness flowing through this author's social networks.

RESULTS

Overall, people reported being highly satisfied with their voting experiences. As Figure 9.8 below shows, 89 percent of users rated their voting experience as four

	Yes	Percent
Poll workers courteous and friendly	1,527	83.72
Wait was short	1,152	63.16
Easy to find poll place	1,503	82.40
Poll place accessible	1,390	76.21
Poll workers solved my problems	388	21.27

FIGURE 9.9. Good Experiences

(395 reports) or five (1,231 reports) stars, whereas slightly less than 3 percent of users reported having one- or two-star voting experiences. A star rating is highly subjective, and we offered little guidance regarding what would count as a one-star or five-star experience. But we also asked users to report whether they had particularly good experiences or encountered specific problems in the course of trying to vote.

Most respondents reported positive experiences at their polls, such as courteous poll workers, short waits, and easy-to-find polling places (Figure 9.9). However, a substantial minority of respondents reported encountering specific problems at the polls. As Figure 9.10 indicates, the most common problems were lines. Twenty percent of respondents reported encountering waiting lines between fifteen minutes and one hour. The third most commonly reported problem was that poll workers did *not* verify identities as required by law. Fortunately, some of the more severe problems – such as names not on registration lists, third-party challenges, and generally the inability to cast a vote – were encountered less frequently.

The frequency of problems is one measure of the adequacy of a voting system. Quite a different measure is the severity of those problems. MyFairElection.com

	Number "Yes"	Percent
Lines 15–30 minutes	189	10.36
Lines 30 minutes–1 hour	184	10.09
Did not verify my identity	164	8.99
Lines 1–2 hours	135	7.4
No parking at poll place	103	5.65
Lines 2+ hours	42	2.3
Ballot confusing	39	2.14
Voting machines broken	32	1.75
Poll place hard to find	27	1.48
Name not on registration list	27	1.48
Improper ID	8	0.44
Machine did not record my vote	7	0.38
Unable to cast vote	5	0.27
Right to vote challenged	4	0.22
Ran out of ballots	2	0.11

FIGURE 9.10. Specific Problems

	Rating of those who encountered problem	Rating of those who did not	Difference	Number Reporting Problem	Percent of Reports
Unable to cast vote	1.00	4.54	3.54	5	0.27
Right to vote challenged	2.00	4.53	2.53	4	0.22
Improper ID	2.75	4.53	1.78	8	0.44
Lines 2+ hours	3.00	4.50	1.50	42	2.30
Voting machines broken	3.28	4.55	1.27	32	1.75
Name not on registration list	3.40	4.53	1.13	27	1.48
Machine did not record my vote	3.42	4.53	1.11	7	0.38
Ballot confusing	3.66	4.50	0.84	39	2.14
Poll place hard to find	3.74	4.50	0.76	27	1.48
Lines 1–2 hours	3.88	4.58	0.70	135	7.40
No parking at poll place	3.95	4.56	0.61	103	5.65
Ran out of ballots	4.00	4.53	0.53	2	0.11
Did not verify my identity	4.11	4.57	0.46	164	8.99
Lines, 30 mins – 1 hour	4.16	4.57	0.41	184	10.09
Lines 15–30 mins	4.39	4.55	0.16	189	10.36

FIGURE 9.11. Mean Satisfaction for Those Experiencing Problems

data captures the subjective severity of a problem in its star rankings of voting experience satisfaction. A rough measure of the severity of a problem is the difference in satisfaction between those who report that they encountered a particular problem and those who did not. These differences in satisfaction are reported in Figure 9.11.[13] The table is sorted in such a way as to have the problems causing the greatest dissatisfaction appear at the top and less severe problems at the bottom. Note that all differences in means are quite significant statistically. For all the problems encountered, the probability of the mean value of satisfaction for those encountering the problem being equal to or greater than for those not encountering the problem is less than 0.005 using two-sample t-tests.

Only five people (one-third of 1 percent) reported being completely unable to cast their vote; unsurprisingly, all five rated their experience as low as possible – one star. Four people reported that their right to vote was challenged, and they rated their voting experience two and a half stars below those who did not report being challenged. Those who waited in line for more than two hours rated their voting experience less than one and half stars below those who did not wait as long. Interestingly, those who had to wait from fifteen minutes to one hour reported being less satisfied than those who did not report such waits, but only slightly so.

COMPARING STATES

As a proof-of-concept project, MyFairElection.com did not receive sufficient usage to allow meaningful state-by-state comparisons. With a larger number of user reports, however, such comparisons would be possible and informative. Such comparisons cut against the fundamental impulse of many election reformers who seek to impose uniform standards everywhere. These comparisons are "experimentalist" in that they treat states as literal laboratories of democracy.[14] Rather than presuming to know the most effective or just method of administering elections, Popular Election Monitoring makes possible empirical comparison of varied experiences from across the country in order to ascertain which practices actually create efficient, equitable, and satisfying elections. Such rankings might thus help feed projects like Heather Gerken's democracy index.

CHALLENGES TO POPULAR ELECTION MONITORING

Though promising, platforms that were deployed in the 2008 U.S. elections were but a beginning. None of them achieved the ambitious potential outlined earlier in the chapter. Future elections will certainly be accompanied by many forms of technologically enabled popular election monitoring. Hopefully, research can help future efforts address some of the main challenges facing popular election monitoring: participation bias, gaming, constructive comparison, and integration with regulatory and news organizations.

PARTICIPATION BIAS AND OUTREACH BIAS

Almost certainly, 2008 popular election-monitoring platforms were much more widely used by some population groups – the more affluent, better educated, computer savvy, socially connected – than others. Future research should seek to establish the extent and character of this participation bias. Though there is a premium on short forms and data submissions (otherwise considerably fewer people would participate), a social-science component might be incorporated whereby a certain percentage of users is asked to complete an extensive demographic survey to determine the character of users, among other things.

Popular election-monitoring platforms should also investigate methods and designs – including the use of mobile phones, text messaging, call centers, and interactive voice mail – that may increase the engagement of underrepresented groups.

SIGNAL-TO-NOISE, SPOILING

Every crowd-sourced or collaborative production effort faces problems of noise from low-quality reports and spoiling from those who intentionally submit erroneous or irrelevant reports. In the future, those who develop popular election-monitoring platforms should coordinate their efforts with more traditional survey researchers to assess the extent to which noisy reports and spoilers create a picture of the election that is substantially different from that created through more conventional methods. We do not know what the underlying signal-to-noise ratio is for popular election-monitoring methods, but we should endeavor to find out. Second, popular election monitors should develop and share methods to increase the quality of reports and so improve signal-to-noise ratios.

Such measures should assure data quality without erecting undue barriers to participation. Systems might create two tiers of users – with the first tier consisting of trained election monitors – which will allow users to see just reports from quasi-professional monitors, if they like (i.e., reports will allow second-tier user data to be filtered out). An open research question is whether the reports of first- and second-tier monitors will be materially different. Registration systems – requiring users to provide an email address – will deter some portion of spammers. Popular election monitoring platforms might also employ real-time human moderation and filtering, as well as systems that allow users to mark other comments as offensive or extraneous. Finally, those who use the data should be able to audit it post hoc to search for indications of spamming, such as multiple posts from the same user or IP address in short time periods.

GOAL: DEPICTING THE ELECTION OR IDENTIFYING PROBLEMS?

One central question for those who build popular election-monitoring platforms is whether such efforts should aim to identify problems only – and so whether users should only report negative experiences – or whether they should also report positive experiences and rate their voting experience overall. Different organizations and developers will choose different goals, depending on their missions and agendas.

Most of the 2008 projects collected problem reports rather than overall experiences. The main reason to focus on problems is to heighten public attention on the voting system's defects. This focus is also appropriate for those who focus mainly – or solely – on addressing obstacles to voting in real time.

One of the advantages of the MyFairElection approach, which allows users to report good as well as bad experiences, is that it allows more direct comparison across counties and states and subsequent benchmarking. Second, it creates a more comprehensive depiction of how Americans experience their elections. As millions of Americans express what they like and dislike about their elections, one research task will be to understand their subjective priorities. We may find that there is a gap between voters' priorities and those of policy makers and voting-rights lawyers.

ORGANIZATIONAL SYNERGIES: COMPETITION, COORDINATION, AND MEDIA

The quality of election monitoring and effect of that monitoring on the integrity of the electoral machinery results from complex formal and informal interactions between many entities including federal and state regulators, individuals who staff polling places, political campaign organizations, individual journalists, mass and new media organizations, fair-voting advocacy groups, and ordinary voters who pull "fire alarms" when they witness voting problems.

One important general question, therefore, is how various popular monitoring efforts should relate to each other and to these various civic, campaign, advocacy, journalistic, and governmental entities. To date, the relationship has been ad hoc. Popular election-monitoring projects have developed in such short time frames that the imperative of developers has been to get systems up and running and get the word out rather than to develop the more complex set of relationships that would maximize the salutary impact of popular election monitoring.

The continuation of this trajectory – letting a thousand flowers bloom, so to speak – is one possible future. In this scenario, various election-monitoring projects would continue to evolve in informal competition with one another. Some would develop ad hoc partnerships with media organizations and others would be projects of media organizations (such as the CNN hotline). There would be little relation to election administrators and regulators.

This scenario would constrain the benefits of popular election monitoring in two ways. First, different projects would compete for users. The success of a popular election-monitoring program depends in large measure on having a very large user base. In the competitive scenario, each organization competes for a fixed base of voters who are willing to file reports. The second problem is that these efforts may remain disconnected from organizations who have the short-term (deploy lawyers and other staff to fix voting problems as they appear) and long-term (reform voting practices) capabilities to improve our voting system.

A second possible future is for separate projects to combine forces in an attempt to create One Big Project in popular election monitoring. Such a project might be sponsored and organized by a new organization, a civic coalition, or even a governmental body such as the Federal Election Commission (FEC). The difficulty with this trajectory is that it would stifle innovation. There are many design choices (about data collection, display, input methods, etc.) and many more implementation strategies. There is no right answer, and compelling platforms will be the product of innovation. Innovation occurs more quickly when there are parallel and independent efforts aiming toward the same general end.

A third possible future is for these independent efforts to create common standards that allow them to share user data with one another. Think of this possibility as the second-order pooling of crowd-sourced data. So, various popular election-monitoring platforms should create data feeds that allow anonymized reports (ratings, specific problems, comments, photos, geo-codes, etc.) to be used by other developers. This way, popular election-monitoring effort could both use data from other projects and create its own channels of recruiting and publicity, methods of data input, moderation and filtering, displays, and analysis. If each of these efforts treated its own user reports as a public good, popular election monitoring efforts in future presidential elections could easily draw hundreds of thousands of reports.

Advocacy and democracy reform organizations could create monitoring platforms that tap into these data streams to pick out their variables of interest (only this state, only problem reports and not good reports, only reports from these sources but not others, etc.), which will differ depending on the agency. Regulators would gain an enormous amount of information about election conditions that they would not otherwise possess.

Mass and new media organizations should themselves create popular election-monitoring platforms and publicize them to their audiences. This trajectory would of course require two changes in the culture of professional journalism. First, these organizations would have to recognize the power of crowd-sourced, citizen-generated information and its contribution to their social mission of helping Americans understand their political reality. Second, these organizations would have to relax their proprietary impulses and realize that they themselves stand to gain by pooling the reports they gather.

There is little doubt that the future will bring more, perhaps many more, popular election-monitoring projects in the United States and abroad. One important task is to improve the quality of these projects and knit them together so, combined with election officials and journalists, they contribute to the fairness and integrity of electoral systems everywhere.

NOTES

1 I would like to thank Russell Richardson for his generous, tireless, and incredibly talented efforts to develop MyFairElection.com from a crude idea into an elegant software platform. It still boggles my mind that someone could make sushi by day, do software engineering by night, and move so far in so few nights. Reynolds Holding and Elizabeth Tribolet of ABC News supported MyFairElection.com from the beginning; they get it. Toshiro Sugihara and Ginny Hunt of Google.com and Conor Kenny at the Center for Media and Democracy provided critical advice, support, and connections that made MyFairElection.com possible. Finally, the project benefitted from the sage advice of Joshua Cohen (Stanford), Heather Gerkin (Yale), Jonah Goldman (Lawyers Committee for Civil Rights), and David Dill (Stanford). Jerry Cohen and Robert Plotkin covered our legal backs, and they did it for free! No more lawyer jokes from me.

2 See amazon.com, imdb.com, tripadvisor.com, patientslikeme.com, and epinion.com.

3 See http://www.stateofthebirds.org/, accessed January 8, 2010.

4 See http://www.google.org/flutrends/, accessed January 8, 2010.

5 For a visual demonstration, see: http://www.google.org/flutrends/about/how.html, accessed January 8, 2010.

6 "Ushahidi" means "testimony" in Swahili. See http://www.ushahidi.com/, accessed January 21, 2010.

7 See http://www.fixmystreet.com/ and http://www.seeclickfix.com/, both accessed January 21, 2010, and http://www.citysourced.com/, accessed May 15, 2010.

8 There is a third reason to pursue PEM in developing-country contexts. It is cheap, and there may be no other way to establish comparable levels of monitoring.

9 http://blog.twittervotereport.com/.
10 http://www.cnn.com/ELECTION/2008/voter.hotline/.
11 http://www.ourvotelive.org/home.php.
12 http://www.myfairelection.com/.
13 Note that the figures reported below are uncontrolled bivariate tabulations. This discussion does not contain multivariate analysis.
14 Dorf, Michael C., and Charles F. Sabel. "A Constitution of Democratic Experimentalism." *Columbia Law Review* 98.2 (1998): 267–473.

Democracy in the United States, 2020 and Beyond

How Can Scholarly Research Shape a Vision and Help Realize It?

Edward B. Foley

"Democracy 2020" expresses the idea of a decade-long initiative to design and implement an electoral process of which our nation can be proud in time for the presidential election that year. The objective is not to rush a half-baked reform for 2012 or even 2016, but to take a decade to do it right. It would be a nice gift to the children born in the year of *Bush v. Gore*, the dawn of the new century, as it will be the first year in which they are eligible to vote in a presidential election.

At first, a decade seemed enough time for major reform. "If we can put a man on the moon in a decade . . . " was how the thinking went. But now I believe that we should strategize in two stages. The year 2020 should still be a target for significant "mid-range" reform, and we should develop a process that uses the time until then to maximum feasible effect. Yet we should also recognize what is not feasible in a ten-year timeframe, and defer for a later date – and an even more ambitious agenda – truly long-term reforms that would take a quarter-century or longer to develop.

DEMOCRACY 2000–2008: A RETROSPECTIVE

What has our nation accomplished since 2000 in terms of electoral reform, and what can we realistically expect to accomplish by 2020?

The answer to this question is quite sobering. In the aftermath of our electoral disaster in 2000, we have: (1) purchased new voting machines that we largely don't like, yet haven't figured out what to replace them with, and at what cost; (2) adopted

I wish to thank for their very helpful comments on earlier drafts: Stephen Ansolabehere, Bruce Cain, Nathan Cemenska, John Fortier, Gordon Gee, Heather Gerken, Stephen Huefner, Alex Keyssar, Alan Michaels, Molly Reynolds, Dan Tokaji, and Laura Williams. I especially thank the Tobin Project, the American Law Institute, and Duke Law School for their sponsoring and hosting the conference at which this paper originally was presented, as well as the editors of the volume in which it now appears. All errors, of course, are my own.

the worthwhile insurance of provisional voting, but with unintended consequences that we haven't figured out how to solve; (3) attempted to modernize voter registration only to discover that we can't yet competently do it; (4) created a new federal agency (the Election Assistance Commission) that is essentially impotent and disliked left and right; and (5) done absolutely nothing to change the procedures for resolving disputes over the counting of votes cast for president – procedures that transformed the *problem* of "hanging chads" into the *calamity* of a Court-ordered halt to a recount for lack of time.

The news has not been all bad, however. The expansion of early voting has been a promising development – although it is uneven throughout the nation, has had hiccups of its own, and (especially regarding its mailed-in version) has some latent vulnerabilities that could surface in another close presidential election. The U.S. Senate election in Minnesota between Norm Coleman and Al Franken exposed these vulnerabilities.

The sheer attention paid to the voting process since 2000 is a good thing. It has raised public awareness about the need for a civilian corps of competent poll workers. It has caused citizens to begin to think about how they want their democracy to function, and about what trade-offs they are willing to make. Transparency, for example, seems to have emerged as an important public value, both in terms of VVPATs[1] and the inspection of ballots in a recount (see Minnesota again), but the public seems unsettled about how to balance accuracy versus speed or cost. Some wonder whether the public interest in issues concerning the voting process can remain sustained during the decade of 2010–2020 if another 2000-like debacle does not occur. But research should move forward on what might be done in the public interest during that period, including on how best to harness (or perhaps even sidestep) potentially declining public attention.[2]

TOO AMBITIOUS FOR 2020

The year 2020 is undeniably too soon for some democracy-enhancing measures. The biggest deficit in American democracy is the U.S. Senate: specifically, the constitutional requirement that each state have an equal vote there regardless of population, combined with the morphing of the filibuster rule into a practical requirement of sixty votes to pass legislation. It would be possible within the next decade to adopt reforms aimed at eliminating the misuse of the filibuster, and this would be a significant benefit for democracy. However, it is not remotely realistic to eliminate the equal-vote-per-state requirement: It would require replacing the current U.S. Constitution with a new one, something for which the cultural groundwork has not been prepared even if it were theoretically desirable (which is debatable).[3]

Nor is it realistic to expect by 2020 the elimination of the Electoral College or other major structural reforms of the way in which we elect our President. The National Popular Vote plan is an effort to end-run the constitutional rules regarding the Electoral College: Under this plan, if states having a majority of Electoral College votes pledge to support the presidential candidate with a majority of the national popular vote, then these states can use their Electoral College power to defeat the Electoral College's design.[4] But the National Popular Vote plan does not account for the possibility of a significant three-way split in the popular vote (for example, 41 percent, 40 percent, 19 percent), with the leading candidate's support coming exclusively from one region of the country. In that situation, if the close runner-up in the popular vote garners a decisive majority of Electoral College votes (under its original design), that candidate would actually reflect broader national support that the bare plurality-vote winner.[5] True constitutional reform designed to replace the Electoral College with a national popular vote to elect the President would include some sort of national run-off if the popular-vote plurality fell below a certain threshold (say 45 percent). But constitutional reform of this magnitude is too ambitious to achieve by 2020.

There is one constitutional reform regarding presidential elections that is especially pressing and much narrower in scope than the debate over the Electoral College versus a national popular vote. This pressing reform concerns the technical procedures under the Twelfth Amendment for counting the votes in Congress that come from the states. The Twelfth Amendment, in its crucial language, is written in the passive voice, leaving entirely unclear who has the ultimate authority to count a state's presidential votes in the event of a dispute: "[T]he President of the Senate shall, in the presence of the Senate and the House of Representatives, open all the certificates [from the states] *and the votes shall be counted.*" Does the President of the Senate have the ultimate constitutional authority to decide which certificate from a state to accept? What if the Senate and the House of Representatives, as bodies, disagree? Can the President of the Senate then constitutionally break the tie between the two chambers? What if the House of Representatives refuses to vote, claiming under the Twentieth Amendment that no President or Vice-President has been elected (and therefore the Speaker of the House serves as Acting President), but the outgoing President of the Senate before noon on January 20 insists on resolving the dispute in favor of counting a certain set of votes and thus declares that a new President of the United States indeed has been elected?

The Constitution is unacceptably unclear on what to do in these kinds of situations. It would be highly advisable to amend the Constitution on just this point, without wading into a controversy over anything else. But as a practical matter, I suspect that any effort to correct this single constitutional problem by 2020 would get bogged down by proposals and counterproposals concerning broader reforms of the presidential election process (Colvin and Foley 2010).[6] Thus, improvements in the procedures for counting presidential votes – which are, indeed, necessary – should be pursued through statutory reform between now and 2020, even though doing so leaves the defect of the Twelfth Amendment in place (to be corrected as a part of a more comprehensive package further on down the road).

A "STATE-OF-THE-ART" VOTING INFRASTRUCTURE FOR 2020

So, what is a realistic agenda for electoral reform between now and 2020? Notwithstanding the sobering lesson of the last decade, I do think it would be realistic for the nation to develop a "state-of-the-art" voting infrastructure for the process of casting and counting ballots. We've learned from the false starts and related mistakes associated with HAVA.[7] Even though it still would be a major challenge and involve potentially contestable value judgments, it can be conceived of largely as an engineering project and *relatively* nonideological – at least when compared to reforms like eliminating the Electoral College. The new (post-2008) congressional efforts to reform voter registration and overseas absentee and military voting are promising first steps along these lines.[8]

The project would require collaboration among computer scientists, other systems engineers, and political scientists, lawyers, and other policy-oriented professionals who would develop the design criteria for the new infrastructure. (The "Open Source Digital Voting Foundation" is a nonprofit organization of computer scientists devoted to collaborative reform along these lines.[9])

Choices would need to be made about the extent to which the system would be designed for early voting – perhaps an Election Week, rather than Election Day – and whether no-excuse, on-demand mail-in voting would be an option. Would there be a single unified system for federal elections, or would states still be permitted a range of alternatives within federal constraints?

A major lesson to be learned from 2008 is the problem of rejected absentee ballots. Minnesota has highlighted the problem, but it is hardly confined there. The rates of rejecting absentee ballots in 2006 were astonishingly high in many states, to the extent that the data is available and trustworthy (another source of concern).[10] Significant scholarly attention needs to be devoted to developing ways to reduce these rejection rates: perhaps better notice procedures for absentee voters, or better graphic design on voter instructions for submitting their ballots, or improved procedures for election officials in reviewing these submissions.[11]

Mail-in ballots present other problems, some well known (increased risk of fraud through vote buying), others coming to light under the glare of Minnesota's recount. Technologically, at present, mail-in ballots must be optical scan and thus have the inevitable "costs" associated with recounting optical scan ballots: (1) It takes a relatively long time for humans to eyeball each oval in a statewide recount; and (2) there is inevitable interpretative subjectivity in this eyeballing process. It is also true that voters who mail their ballots often lack the opportunity to correct overvoting and undervoting errors, which is available to in-precinct voters.

Perhaps, however, a concerted technological effort over the next decade (subsidized by Congress or a nonprofit consortium) could develop new alternative voting methods that would avoid some of these problems. Although Internet-based voting is still a scary prospect to many right now, a decade of well-structured development might not be too short a time to design and implement encryption techniques with sufficient transparency to instill public confidence. If so, it might be possible for citizens to email a vote, either from home or perhaps from specially equipped computers in public libraries, post offices, and other especially convenient locations. This computer-based email voting would avoid the problem of reviewing optical scan ballots. Perhaps, too, it would be technologically feasible to give each voter some kind of verification (analogous to a VVPAT), so that the voter could trust that the computerized system counted the vote correctly while at the same time not permitting that verification to serve as an easy way for voters to sell their votes.

Science fiction? Maybe. But there is no way of knowing without a concerted and collaborative effort to explore the technological possibilities in relation to the normatively appropriate design criteria. Those collaborative conversations should start happening now, pursuant to a systematic process that envisions a schedule for the rollout of the new, state-of-the-art technology in time for field-testing at the latest in 2019 non-federal elections. (It would be preferable, if feasible, to field-test in increasing amounts from 2017 through 2019 in order to be as ready as possible for the presidential election of 2020.)

THE LIFESPAN OF A VOTING TECHNOLOGY

As part of the design or planning process, the research community should step back and ask a larger question: What is the appropriate lifespan of a nation's voting technology, and how can a nation rationally plan for technological upgrades of its voting process over time? It is a question analogous to similar questions the government might ask about technological upgrades in other areas of its responsibility: How long will a new telecommunications infrastructure last, and when should it be replaced? What about a new spy satellite? A new computer system for the IRS? For the FBI?

Some kind of comparative study on the lifespan of public technological systems might be helpful. If the nation did build a state-of-the-art voting infrastructure for 2020, how long could it reasonably be expected to last? Until 2060? Or only half that long? Or possibly twice that long? What was the reasonable lifespan of the lever voting machine, and is it relevant that New York is only now replacing them?

It is impossible to know what will be the rate of technological change in the future. Therefore, is it necessary to adopt some kind of ongoing technological review process to monitor potential innovations? In other words, if Congress sets up a mechanism to implement a state-of-the-art voting infrastructure in 2020, should it also set up some kind of committee to review periodically what other nations do thereafter, with the view of recommending to Congress when it will become time for another decade-long "new state-of-the-art voting infrastructure" development process?

Maybe it is too much to expect the government to deliberate rationally about any public policy question that concerns long-term planning, like environmental or energy policy. Even so, public policy analysts should model good behavior in this regard, so that there is at least a benchmark by which to judge the government's efforts.

TECHNOLOGY AND VOTER ID

Planning for 2020, rather than sooner, may also give us a wider range of options regarding the tired debate over voter identification. If we take a decade to develop a "state-of-the-art" universal voter registration system, it may be possible to incorporate ID information into the registration process in a way that avoids the necessity of voters bringing ID with them when they vote. For example, if the registration record for a voter includes a digital photo, and that registration record is available to the poll worker at the time of voting – or perhaps available to the public librarian who assists a voter emailing a vote from a library kiosk – then the ID comparison is between the voter's actual face and the photo already on file, not with a photo ID card that the voter carries in a wallet. Or it might be possible for a voter to have a choice of equally valid forms of ID. For example, the registration record might include – as other systems do – a special personal identifying question (mother's maiden name, place of birth, etc.) that would authenticate the voter upon casting the ballot. The point isn't to settle on an answer to the ID issue now, but to use the decade-long process with the possibility of technological innovation to develop a "win-win" solution that meets the professed policy concerns of both sides of the debate.

TROUBLESHOOTING – AND "WAR-GAMING" – EVEN THE STATE-OF-THE-ART" INFRASTRUCTURE

Whatever voting infrastructure ends up in place in 2020, it will be imperative to have mechanisms and procedures for troubleshooting that system. One of the most important lessons learned over the last few years is that not enough attention has been given to back-up systems, contingency planning, and rapid-response procedures when things do go wrong in the voting process. More research can be done on how to assist states and localities with "emergency preparedness," especially the need for continual updating of these protocols in light of intervening changes in law and practices since the previous election. A different kind of audit can, and should, be designed to identify *before* each election the gaps in a state's preparedness plan (to supplement, not supplant, the postvoting audits that are starting to occur in many states).[12]

One promising idea that has emerged in 2008 along these lines is the value of "war-gaming," in advance of an election, scenarios that could occur if things go wrong. The *McCain v. Obama* simulation conducted in 2008 is an example: The scenario involved a heavy winter storm in Denver, the possibility of outcome-determinative provisional ballots cast as a result of extending polling hours, and conflicting positions taken by state and local officials on whether to count those ballots.[13] Election officials, both from Colorado and elsewhere, have expressed appreciation for the value of the exercise: It focuses the mind to see potential weaknesses of a state's rules or procedures when they are examined in the context of a specific scenario.

The *McCain v. Obama* simulation was designed to examine how a specially structured court would handle the constitutional questions arising out of that particular
scenario. But different war-gaming exercises could be designed with different institutional actors in mind. How might a state's Secretary of State respond if presented
with a certain situation? What would a poll worker do if confronted with a particular
problem? Indeed, some election analysts have expressed an interest in re-running
the Colorado snowstorm scenario with the point of focusing on the decision whether
to extend the polling hours, rather than on the consequence of what to do with the
provisional ballots once the polls are extended. (A great idea, in my judgment.)

An ambitious, but extremely useful, research agenda would be to design an array of
war-gaming scenarios for a series of key states – as many as the research project could
afford. The goal would be to identify vulnerabilities in each state's electoral system
and then war-game what would happen if events put pressure on those vulnerabilities.
A limited version of this project would start with just one scenario for each selected
state. This more modest version might design a range of different types of scenarios,
each one tailored to the specific circumstances of each target state. For example,
a scenario that focuses on no-excuse absentee voting for a state with that feature;
a scenario on "super-precincts" or "vote centers," for a state that has experimented
with this reform; a scenario involving malfunctioning voting machines that lack
any kind of paper trail where this situation might affect the result of a presidential
election, perhaps in Pennsylvania. Although a variety of scenarios (a different one in
each separate state) would reduce the ability to make direct comparisons between
the war-gaming exercises – it's a bit "apples and oranges," unless one tests multiple
scenarios in a single state or a single scenario in multiple states – this kind of
experimental diversity might still be instructive, and represents the best way to make
use of limited funds. If different types of scenarios or different states seem to show
promise, the experiment might be expanded – and made more systematic – based
on the preliminary findings.

This kind of war-gaming exercise would have helped in Minnesota to avoid some
of the issues that emerged there in the recount and court contest. The state could
have war-gamed what would happen if the number of rejected absentee ballots
was larger than the margin of victory. The exercise would have exposed that the
administrative recount process was not designed to consider this issue, as the State
Canvassing Board and Minnesota Supreme Court ultimately concluded. The law
could have been amended to empower the administrative recount process to review
rejected absentee ballots (a legislative proposal for future elections that has already
been made since the problem surfaced), thereby avoiding the need for a separate
subsequent judicial contest of the recount result. Streamlining the process in this
way would have permitted the dispute over this Senate election to end in early
January rather than in late June.

Similarly, war-gaming the issue of rejected absentee ballots would have exposed
in advance the fact that different localities within Minnesota handled identical

absentee ballots differently: Some localities would count, while other localities would reject, ballots with identical deficiencies. The statutory and constitutional issues triggered by this administrative disparity could have been avoided before Election Day if, on being made aware of this disparity, election officials had adopted uniform procedures. But one cannot assess the need for uniform procedures if one is unaware of the disparity in the first place. A war-gaming scenario in which each Minnesota locality is asked specific questions – for example, "How do you handle the situation in which an unregistered voter accidently receives a registered voter's ballot and therefore submits the ballot without an accompanying new registration form? Do you reject the ballot on the ground that registration is a prerequisite, or do you count the ballot on the ground that the voter's lack of registration in this instance was partially induced by official error?" – would have raised awareness that different counties within the state were prepared to give diametrically opposite answers in this situation. This awareness would have allowed the state to settle on a policy, weighing the value of statewide uniformity against the value of local control in this particular context, rather than just stumbling into protracted high-stakes litigation over this issue.

A similar war-gaming exercise on the issue of potential double-counting of dupli-cate ballots could have helped clarify Minnesota's rules for handling that issue as well. The issue was what to do when ballots have been duplicated because the orig-inal ballots cannot be fed through the machines, but in the administrative recount, there is evidence – but not definitive proof – indicating that the duplicates accidently became detached from the originals, and both were counted. In this situation, should state law err on the side of double-counting to avoid the possibility of zero-counting of a valid vote and hence disenfranchisement of an eligible citizen? Or should the sys-tem err on the side of discarding a valid vote to make sure that no ballot is wrongfully counted twice? When this issue arose during the recount of the 2008 Senate election, Minnesota law was not absolutely clear on how to resolve it; a war-gaming exercise might have exposed this uncertainty, enabling it to be remedied before Election Day.

Hindsight, of course, is always 20–20, and the challenge of this war-gaming project would be to develop techniques so that foresight in designing the scenarios would come as close to matching 20–20 hindsight as possible. At least the exercise would assess risks intelligently and thus war-game the most significant risks, even if it turns out that a less significant risk is the one that materializes. In any event, the creation of a well-designed war-gaming project should be on the nation's election reform agenda.

LESSONS FROM LOOKING IN THE "ELECTRON MICROSCOPE" OF THE ELECTORAL PROCESS[14]

There is much more to be learned from Minnesota's experience in resolving its 2008 U.S. Senate election. It is startling that in a state with a well-deserved reputation for relatively high quality of election administration, officials were still discovering misplaced ballots more than three months after Election Day. On February 6, while on the witness stand during the trial over who won the Senate seat, Rachel Smith – then the elections director of Anoka County, who subsequently spearheaded the University of Minnesota's efforts to develop a program for training election administrators, and who embodies the kind of fair-minded conscientiousness that a state should want in its local elections officials – announced that she had just discovered twelve more previously uncounted ballots. Another county administrator made a similar announcement the next day.

How could this happen, after the umpteen reviews of the ballots that had already occurred? Could it have been prevented by putting different systems and procedures in place ahead of time? Even if an entirely error-free election is impossible, is error-reduction reasonably achievable?

These questions raise a broader point. I have written elsewhere that "optimality," not perfection, should be the goal of election administration, and have begun a process of thinking about how to define "optimality" and what it would entail (Foley 2007). But this line of inquiry needs to be pursued much further. As a nation, we remain schizophrenic about how to think about an unusually close election. In part, we are enamored with the concept of "statistical tie," thinking that we should just flip a coin in certain circumstances, but without ever bothering to define the precise narrowness of result that would call for a coin toss. At the same time, however, we remain beholden to our democratic rhetoric that "every vote counts," and thus we must reserve the coin toss for an actual tie and otherwise figure out how to get it right in our counting of ballots. No other field of inquiry would settle for the underdeveloped and internally inconsistent standards for performance evaluation that our voting process has. We have no way of assessing, for example, whether Minnesota's electoral system fell short of objective quality standards and thus exposed itself to protracted litigation when a close election resulted; or instead, whether Minnesota officials did all that could reasonably have been expected of them ahead of time, and what we see now is just the inevitable result of an extraordinarily close election even in a state that meets specified standards of optimality.[15]

Research on how to define and measure optimality in the performance of election administration would be valuable no matter what else happens over the next decade, but it would be particularly valuable if it were incorporated into a systematic effort to decide a state-of-the-art voting infrastructure by 2020 (as described earlier in the chapter). Developed early in the planning process, the optimality standard would become the overarching criterion by which technological alternatives and their costs could be judged. If the infrastructure were built to the specified optimality standard, then its implementation could be assessed by whether it successfully performed as intended.

OPTIMALITY AND THE RESOLUTION OF POST-VOTING DISPUTES:
A MODEL CODE

A well-developed optimality standard would recognize the inevitable need for procedures to handle postvoting disputes that might arise in a close election. Even
if a state-of-the-art voting infrastructure is employed for the casting and counting
of ballots, an optimality standard is "self-aware" that it is not perfection and thus
has a built-in mechanism for best handling this kind of dispute. (A well-designed
ocean liner has enough lifeboats if, despite its optimal design, it unexpectedly hits an
iceberg.) The experience of Washington in 2004 (in its gubernatorial election) and
Minnesota in 2008, as well as the "near miss" in Ohio's presidential election in 2004
and related dispute-resolution problems in Ohio in both 2006 and 2008 concerning
congressional races, all indicate that we are far from having an optimal system for
resolving these disputes. Nothing has been done since 2000 to fix this particularly
flawed aspect of our electoral process, one that comes into play when the stakes are
the highest.

I have come to believe that, at a minimum, we should develop a Model Code
for the resolution of disputes regarding the counting of ballots cast for presidential
electors. Congress could make a state's adoption of this Model Code a condition of
obtaining "safe harbor" status during the congressional review of Electoral College
votes submitted by each state. ("Safe harbor" status means, as widely discussed
during *Bush v. Gore*, that Congress will not second-guess a state's declaration of
its Electoral College winner if the declaration satisfies the "safe harbor" conditions.
Currently, the "safe harbor" conditions concern timing and fidelity to the state's own
rules. There is no reason, however, why the "safe harbor" conditions could not be
modified to include additional substantive criteria that the state's dispute-resolution
mechanism must follow.[16]) States could choose whether they wanted to adopt the
Model Code for other elective offices, like Governor or U.S. Senate. Indeed, they
would be free to reject the Model Code even for presidential elections if they were
willing to avoid the benefit of "safe harbor" status. But adoption of the Model Code,
with this "safe harbor" inducement, would go a long way to developing for the nation
a rational and fair method of handling disputes over the counting of votes.

Developing this Model Code would take considerable work. But it would draw
upon the *McCain v. Obama* simulation and the insights developed from that exercise regarding the method of selecting judges that is best calculated to achieve an
impartial tribunal.[17] A Model Code, in addition to structuring the dispute-resolution
tribunal to be impartial, would also specify a timetable that (contrary to current
procedures in Minnesota) would permit a fair resolution of the dispute in time for
the President to take office on January 20.

A necessary adjunct to the creation of this Model Code would be an amendment
to the federal Electoral Count Act to provide clearly that if a state satisfies the new
"safe harbor" requirement, as determined by a special nonpartisan congressional

panel (designed also with the insights of the *McCain v. Obama* exercise in mind), then it would take a vote of *both* Houses of Congress, not just one, to reject the Electoral College votes submitted by the state in a way consistent with the Model Code. This statutory amendment is, for the reasons stated earlier, the best one can do in the absence of a constitutional fix to the Twelfth Amendment itself. But it would be a highly desirable component of any "Democracy 2020" project to put in place this Model Code as a "safe harbor" provision in time for the 2020 presidential elections. No state-of-the-art voting infrastructure developed for 2020 would be complete without this Model Code and the necessary implementing amendments to the congressional Electoral Count Act.

PRE-ELECTION LITIGATION

Although the just described Model Code would address only postvoting disputes, some thought should be given to possibility of reform aimed at the litigation over the voting process that increasingly occurs in the run-up to Election Day. The year 2008 saw a large dose of this litigation, as did 2004 and even 2006, and there is every reason to believe it will continue in both 2010 – a crucial election year for control of the redistricting process – and 2012, our next presidential election.

There is an active debate about how undesirable – or, just the opposite, beneficial – this pre-election litigation is procedurally, apart from the signal it sends about the inadequacy or ambiguity of the rules governing the voting process. (If these rules were absolutely comprehensive and clear, there would be no point in litigating about them.) Advocates of the "undesirability thesis" focus on the complaints of state and local election officials, who see these "last-minute" lawsuits as disruptive and destabilizing. They argue that these lawsuits inject more confusion into the voting process, and thus are more likely to induce poll worker error, than leaving an imperfect set of rules in place. No time for new poll worker training, they point out, if the rules are changing right before the ballots are cast.

By contrast, believers in the "benefit thesis" see pre-election litigation on balance as doing more good than harm, tending to clear up problems more than causing them, and therefore putting in place a better electoral system before the ballots are cast than otherwise would exist. These folks acknowledge that pre-election litigation is less disruptive and thus more beneficial the earlier it occurs, but assert that even new lawsuits in the final weeks, days, or even hours before actual voting begins can be advantageous to avoid potential disenfranchisement. They cite lawsuits that caused polls to stay open longer, or more backup ballots to be supplied, or new protocols to be promulgated for administering voter ID or provisional voting rules, as examples where the net effect was more voter protection.

It would be worthwhile to commission scholarly research that would undertake a systematic analysis of the relevant data that would shed light on this debate. The research could also consider ways in which the procedures for conducting this kind of pre-election litigation could be improved, so that whatever the current cost-benefit ratio, in the future the net balance would be more favorable. In 2008, there was a belated and largely unsuccessful attempt to use mediation and other Alternative Dispute Resolution" (ADR) techniques to handle this pre-election litigation more efficiently. The nature of these lawsuits may not lend themselves to ADR-type interventions. But it is premature to say that nothing can be done to make this litigation less chaotic and more rational, and research could examine just what sort of alternatives might be developed.

One concern that has emerged with regard to pre-election litigation, as well as with postvoting disputes, is the fear that these lawsuits are being decided on the basis of the partisan leanings of the judges who hear them, not an impartial effort to judicially discern what the law requires in the given situation. The 2–1 split of the Eleventh Circuit panel that decided Florida's "no match, no vote" case fueled that fear (*Florida NAACP v. Browning* 2008), as did the Sixth Circuit's 10–6 en banc ruling in Ohio's "database mismatching" lawsuit – although the Supreme Court's unanimous reversal of the Sixth Circuit's decision helped restore some measure of confidence in the judiciary (*Ohio Republican Party v. Brunner* 2008). But several 4–3 outcomes of the Ohio Supreme Court, although not a strictly partisan divide (as that court has seven Republican members), added to the fear that the judicial reasoning is more arbitrary than objective.[18]

One possible solution would be to replicate the model of an impartial tribunal developed for the *McCain v. Obama* simulation. Although that model was developed for postvoting disputes, it could be employed in a pre-election context. Indeed, special election courts based on this model could be created by state or federal statutes to handle pre-election lawsuits that otherwise would be filed in conventional state or federal courts. Additional research could be conducted on the desirability of this potential reform for pre-election litigation. Research could also consider potential methods of implementation, including how best to secure sufficient support for adoption of any concrete piece of reform legislation along these lines.

Compared with postvoting disputes, these pre-election lawsuits seem even more fast-paced and idiosyncratic in their lifecycle from complaint to appeal to ultimate resolution. They do not follow a standard, methodical schedule. This fact makes it more difficult to implement in this context the idea of an "amicus court," or "shadow court" – a private-sector advisory tribunal designed to model impartial judicial deliberation over the election-related issue pending before the actual court.[19] Even so, further research might suggest modifications to the amicus court idea that would be more useful in this pre-election context. For example, war-gaming some pre-election litigation scenarios might yield much of the benefit of the shadow court concept in a controlled, manageable timeframe in advance of the actual pre-election litigation later in that same election year.

One legal issue worth investigating is whether Congress has the constitutional power to create a special elections court with exclusive jurisdiction over any pre-election litigation concerning the voting process for federal elections. Could Congress "remove" any such case to this new court, even if the case were filed in state court on state law grounds? With regard to presidential elections, it would seem too much of a stretch of the "safe harbor" concept to say that a state must relinquish control to a federal forum for disputes that occur even before ballots for presidential electors are cast. But since those same ballots also include congressional elections, it might be possible for Congress to use its Time, Place, and Manner power to say that any litigation over the casting of those ballots – or the registration rules that entitle eligible citizens to cast those ballots – must be resolved in a forum that Congress has created to assure a nonpartisan treatment of the case.

NONPARTISAN ELECTION ADMINISTRATION BY 2020

The whole issue of partisan bias in the administration of the voting process has been a repeated refrain over the last decade. Katherine Harris, of course, kicked off this conversation with her performance during the dispute over Florida's votes in the 2000 presidential election. Then it became Ken Blackwell's turn in Ohio, during the 2004 presidential election. It continued in Ohio with Jennifer Brunner in 2008, although she was from the opposite party than Blackwell. Nor has the topic been limited to these two states. There have been similar allegations of partisan abuse by elected Secretaries of State over the last decade in Indiana and Minnesota, among other places.

Given all these complaints, is it possible to put in place a decade-long reform process so that "Democracy 2020" includes nonpartisan election administration at the state and local level – as well as an effective nonpartisan institution at the federal level? Could Congress be convinced to use its Spending Power to entice states to adopt this reform as a condition of receiving funding for the state-of-the-art voting infrastructure to put into operation by 2020? Alternatively, would – or should? – the state-of-the-art voting infrastructure be designed so that it is implemented for federal elections by nonpartisan federal employees, rather than relying on state and local employees? (Perhaps federal administration of federal elections could be modeled on the Census, another temporary federal effort, although there have been recent fears of partisan manipulation of the Census process.)

This reform seems such a heavy lift politically that one wonders whether it is worth the effort. Like the potential elimination of the Electoral College, perhaps it should be consigned to the category of longer-term reform.

My initial inclination would be to be cautious and tentative on this one, so that it does not derail the "Democracy 2020" effort. There might be hybrid, interme-diary solutions that could be explored once it becomes clearer in the decade-long design process exactly what role state government would have in implementing the Democracy 2020 infrastructure. If in 2020 we will continue to rely on local and state officials to count the ballots – even ballots cast for federal office – then we might want to assure a measure of nonpartisanship in the counting process. But there may be ways to do that without requiring the elimination of partisan Secretaries of State altogether. For example, federal law might insist that the local election officials who tally initial results operate in some form of nonpartisan canvassing board (a practice which already exists in a number of states), and might even require that the certification of results in federal elections be conducted by a nonpartisan state-level canvassing board (on which a partisan Secretary of State could sit but not be the exclusive member).

Minnesota's successful experience with its State Canvassing Board in conducting the administrative recount portion of the disputed U.S. Senate election can serve as a model for this type of reform. Mark Ritchie, an elected Secretary of State from Minnesota's version of the Democratic Party (Democratic-Farmer-Labor, or DFL), chaired the State Canvassing Board. Before the Board began its duties in this recount, there were widely voiced fears among Republicans that Ritchie would abuse his position to tilt the process in favor of Franken. But sitting with Ritchie on the Canvassing Board were two members of the Minnesota Supreme Court with solid Republican credentials, including the Chief Justice recently appointed by Republican Governor Tim Pawlenty. Ritchie was thus structurally constrained by their presence from favoring Franken.

To be sure, Ritchie deserves partial credit for putting these two Republicans on the Board; state law did not require him to do so. Any use of this Minnesota experience as a model for law reform in other states would want to include some sort of statutory guarantee of bipartisan neutrality in the composition of the State Canvassing Board, rather than relying on a fortuitously fair decision by an elected Secretary of State. (Imagine Katherine Harris entrusted with the same appointment power as Ritchie? Would she have been as impartially fair-minded? Unlikely.) Still, the Minnesota experience shows that it is not entirely necessary to eliminate elections for Secretary of State in order to have that office serve on a nonpartisan State Canvassing Board.

In other words, nonpartisan election administration is not an all-or-nothing proposition, and federal law over the next decade should look for ways of being opportunistic in increasing the degree of nonpartisanship in the process without expecting to achieve perfection in this regard by 2020. Given the general public expectation that judges are the most nonpartisan of government officials, nonpartisanship in the judicial consideration of any lawsuits over the voting process might be considered a key component of this opportunistic incrementalism. Meanwhile, federal law could put its own house in order by replacing, at least in time for the 2020 election, the inadequate Election Assistance Commission with a well-designed nonpartisan Federal Election Administration Agency. A valuable area of research would be to flesh out various options worth considering under this "opportunistic incrementalism" rubric (Tokaji 2009).

ASSESSING PRIORITIES

I started this chapter by distinguishing the mid-range horizon of 2020 from a longer-term timeframe suitable for an even more ambitious reform agenda. If one is careful about which goals one puts in the mid-range category and which, by contrast, one leaves for the longer term, then one should be able to accomplish all the mid-range goals. One should not need to prioritize among them in terms of what is most important to accomplish by 2020. In principle, precisely because they are in the mid-range rather than longer-term category, one should be able to achieve them all.

Still, it is prudent to be pragmatic. The reform agenda I have outlined for 2020 is plenty ambitious enough, and if we end up unable to complete every element, we should not give up on those we can accomplish. Therefore, it is worth keeping in mind which ones are most important and deserve our strongest efforts and sharpest attention over the next ten years.

Of those I have mentioned as feasible for 2020, my top three priorities are as follows: first, developing the state-of-the-art voting system; second, instituting the systematic practice of war-gaming as part of election preparedness to troubleshoot the state-of-the-art system or, if necessary, whatever suboptimal system we still happen to have; and third, adopting a Model Code, at least for resolving disputed presidential elections but perhaps more broadly. If we could adopt only these three measures during the next decade, there would still be plenty of democracy-enhancing work remaining for the future. With these three reforms in place, however, we could truly tell the children born in the year of *Bush v. Gore*, who will have now come of age to cast their first presidential ballots, that we have finally learned the lessons of that debacle and put in place a voting process of which they – and we – can be proud.

NOTES

1　VVPAT stands for Voter Verified Paper Audit Trail, which permits voters using touch-screen voting technology to verify that the vote recorded by the computer is what they intended.
2　I leave aside developments in areas of election law besides election administration. Regarding campaign finance, the last decade produced a major piece of legislation ("McCain-Feingold," officially entitled the Bipartisan Campaign Reform Act) that, although initially upheld by the Supreme Court, is now in the process of being dismantled by a Court that for the foreseeable future will be controlled by a majority hostile to such laws. The Court's decision to reargue in *Citizens United v. Federal Election Commission* is the most recent indication of the Court majority's hostility to McCain-Feingold. (This paper was written while *Citizens United* remained pending before the Court; but, as this book goes to press, the Court has now confirmed the expectation that it would overrule its 2003 decision *McConnell v. FEC*, which had upheld key provisions of that statute.)
3　Article V of the U.S. Constitution stipulates that "no state, without its consent, shall be deprived of its equal suffrage in the Senate." Thus, even the ordinarily difficult

means of amending the Constitution (a two-thirds vote in each house of Congress, followed by ratification in three-fourths of the states) cannot be used to change this equal-vote-per-state requirement. Since Wyoming, for example, is not going to consent to a change (despite being sixty times smaller than California, a margin much larger than the Founders faced), it will take a new Constitution to formulate a more democratic basis of representation in the upper house of our nation's legislature.

4 For details, see http://www.nationalpopularvote.com/.

5 One can imagine a Northeastern liberal eking out a plurality of votes in New York and adjacent states, whereas a moderate from Missouri comes up just short in the national popular vote but wins an impressive Electoral College victory with California, Texas, Florida, Illinois, and the rest of the Midwest (with a very conservative candidate coming in third). Conversely, one could imagine a Southern conservative with a popular-vote plurality but winning Electoral College votes only in the South, whereas a Midwestern moderate wins a decisive Electoral College majority by strongly defeating a Northeastern liberal in non-Southern states.

6 I discuss this problem in more detail in other work. Suffice it to say here that the neither the Electoral Count Act of 1887 nor the Twentieth Amendment have adequately solved the institutional uncertainty perpetrated by the Twelfth Amendment. *Bush v. Gore*, or more precisely Al Gore's acquiescence in that 5–4 ruling, prevented the defects of the Twelfth Amendment from becoming operative in determining the outcome of the 2000 presidential election. But there is no guarantee that the Supreme Court will be able or willing to exercise a similar process-terminating role if and when there is another disputed presidential election of the kind that occurred in 1876.

7 HAVA is the Help America Vote Act of 2002.

8 Electionline's weekly report for October 29, 2009, contains an initial explanation of the new Military and Overseas Voter Empowerment (MOVE) Act: see http://www. pewcenteronthestates.org/uploadedFiles/wwwpewcenteronthestatesorg/Reports/ Electionline_Reports/electionlineWeekly10.29.09.pdf.

9 See http://www.osdv.org/.

10 In the Election Day Survey data that the Election Assistance Commission reported for the 2006 general election (the most recent year available when this work was written), Indiana rejected 14.5% of absentee ballots cast in the state. California rejected 4.1%, amounting to 163,747. Three other states rejected more than 5% of their absentee ballots cast: North Carolina (9.1%), Nevada (6.1%), and Kentucky (5.6%). Nationwide, 346,612 absentee ballots were rejected (almost 3% of all absentee ballots cast nationwide), but this figure is inaccurately low, because seven states – including Minnesota – did not report to the EAC the number of absentee ballots they rejected.

Moreover, as disturbing as the overall volume of rejected absentee ballots is, perhaps even more troubling is the widespread variation among states concerning the rates at which they rejected absentee ballots. Ten states reported rates of rejecting absentee ballots at less than 1 percent. Some of these states had relatively large numbers of absentee ballots cast. For example, New Mexico rejected only 0.2% of its absentee ballots, which amounted to 23% of is total vote; likewise, 20% of Michigan's ballots were absentee, but the state rejected only 0.9% of those. Obviously, the states where high rejection rates had the biggest disenfranchising effect on the overall electorate were those that rely heavily on absentee voting. California's 4.1% rejection rate is especially troubling because 35% of all California ballots were absentee. The interactive effect of these percentages means that almost 1.5% of the entire California electorate that turned out to vote in 2006 had their ballots discarded; many close races (and not just Minnesota's U.S. Senate seat) could be affected by this level of ballot nullification.

11 My own forthcoming scholarship on lessons learned from the disputed U.S. Senate election in Minnesota will address some of these matters.

12 Additionally, the "ecosystem approach" of *From Registration to Recounts* could be extended to the forty-five states not covered in this book to identify the ecological factors that would help each state improve its electoral preparedness plan (see Huefner et al. 2007).

13 Information about the *McCain v. Obama* simulation, including the final opinion released by the distinguished three-judge panel that decided the hypothetical case, can be found at this page of the *Election Law @ Moritz* website: http://moritzlaw. osu.edu/electionlaw/electioncourt/index.

14 "Electron microscope" is a phrase that Minnesota Secretary of State Mark Ritchie has used to describe the extraordinarily intense scrutiny under which an election system is placed when a major statewide recount, like the Coleman-Franken one, occurs.

15 The fact that Minnesota did not submit to the Election Administration Commission data for the 2006 election on the number of rejected absentee ballots is, however, a sign that the state was giving insufficient administrative attention to this issue – and this administrative deficiency was glaringly exposed two years later.

16 Congressional compliance with its own "safe harbor" rules – meaning that Congress itself will honor its commitment to accept whatever results are obtained if a state meets the "safe harbor" conditions – assumes that no breakdown occurs because of the ambiguity of the Twelfth Amendment (as described earlier in the chapter). If the two chambers of Congress disagree on whether a state has met the "safe harbor" conditions, or if the President of the Senate asserts unilateral authority to break an impasse on this issue, then no amount of statutory reform can avoid the deficiency of the existing constitutional text.

17 The Model Code project would also draw on a long-term project on the history of disputed elections in the United States (a project that I am undertaking with Steve Huefner, my *Election Law @ Moritz* colleague). The first major disputed election, New York's 1792 race for governor, in which John Jay was attempting to unseat George Clinton, raised the same basic issues that were central to *Bush v. Gore*. For a preliminary discussion of that dispute, see Foley (2009).

18 See, e.g., *State ex rel. Stokes v. Brunner* 2008 (ordering Secretary of State to permit observers at early voting locations); *State ex rel. Colvin v. Brunner* 2008 (upholding Secretary of State's decision to permit a five-day period in which previously unregistered voters may simultaneously register and cast an early ballot); *State ex rel. Summit County Republican Party v. Brunner* 2008 (ordering Secretary of State to appoint to statutorily bipartisan local elections board the person recommended by the local Republican party, rather than her own nominee, for a Republican-designated slot).

19 For further discussion of the "amicus court" (or "shadow court") idea, see Foley (2008, 62); *A Model Court for Contested Elections (Or, the "Field of Dreams" Approach to Election Law Reform)*, Free & Fair Commentary (June 19, 2007), available at http://moritzlaw.osu.edu/electionlaw/comments/articles.php?ID=157 (containing a link to the Tobin Project paper).

REFERENCES

Colvin, Nathan & Edward B. Foley. 2010. The Twelfth Amendment: A Constitutional Ticking Time Bomb. *University of Miami Law Review* 64: 475.

Florida NAACP v. Browning, 522 F.3d 1153 (11th Cir. 2008).

Foley, Edward B. 2007. The Analysis and Mitigation of Electoral Errors: Theory, Practice, Policy. *Stanford Law & Policy Review* 18: 350.

————. 2008. Let's not repeat 2000: A special political tribunal could help resolve election conflicts without mistrust. *Legal Times* (April 21). http://moritzlaw.osu.edu/library/documents/Foley-LegalTimes-4–21-08.pdf (accessed April 10, 2010).

————. 2009. The Original Bush v. Gore: An Historical Perspective on Disputed Elections. Oct. 14. http://moritzlaw.osu.edu/electionlaw/docs/post_lecture_draft05march09.pdf (accessed April 7, 2010). A revised version of this lecture will be published in the Indiana Law Review with a new title: *The Founders' Bush v. Gore: The 1792 Disputed Election and its Continuing Relevance*.

Huefner, S., D. Tokaji, E. Foley, and N. Cemenska. 2007. *From Registration to Recounts: The Electoral Ecosystems of Five Midwestern States*. Columbus, OH: Ohio State University.

Ohio Republican Party v. Brunner, 544 F.3d 711 (6th Cir. 2008), *order vacated by* 129 S.Ct. 5 (2008).

State ex rel. Colvin v. Brunner, 120 Ohio St. 3d 110, 896 N.E.2d 979 (2008).

State ex rel. Stokes v. Brunner, 120 Ohio St. 3d 250, 898 N.E.2d 23 (2008).

State ex rel. Summit County Republican Party v. Brunner, 118 Ohio St. 3d 515, 890 N.E.2d 888 (2008).

Tokaji, Dan. 2009. The Future of Election Reform: From Rules to Institutions. *Yale Law & Policy Review* 28: 125.

11

Partisanship, Public Opinion, and Redistricting

Joshua Fougere, Stephen Ansolabehere, and Nathaniel Persily

INTRODUCTION

When the Supreme Court first entered the political thicket with the "one person, one vote" cases of the 1960s, contemporaneous polls showed the Court to be on the right side of public opinion. In 1966, 76 percent of Americans called the Supreme Court decision "rul[ing] all Congressional Districts had to have an equal number of people in them so each person's vote would count equally" "right" (Louis Harris and Associates Poll, The Roper Center for Public Opinion Research).[1] Few, if any, innovations from the Warren Court years met with such deep approval by the public or have had comparable staying power. Indeed, majorities continue to support redistricting based on population equality (see Ansolabehere and Persily 2009).[2]

Beyond the easy-to-grasp concept of "one person, one vote," however, the public has little knowledge or opinion concerning the redistricting process. Polling on redistricting has been done sporadically and locally.[3] As a consequence, only a few published articles attempt to describe or account for public attitudes concerning the complicated and low salience modern controversies surrounding redistricting on such issues as partisan or incumbent protecting gerrymandering.[4]

This chapter analyzes survey data with the hope of gauging where Americans stand on various controversies surrounding the redistricting process. The first part briefly presents the public opinion surveys utilized and the questions most central to the analysis. The second part begins by examining the extent to which the public is uninformed and lacks opinions about redistricting. In short, Americans exhibit both characteristics – they have not heard much about the debate as a whole and therefore most do not have opinions about it. The third part then analyzes the structure of public opinion where it does exist. We begin by considering the impact of demographics on public opinion. Breaking up our discussion into subsections on fairness, satisfaction, and institutional actors, we then analyze variables related to partisanship and incumbency protection.[5] We ask, for instance, whether respondents feel differently about the process if their party controls their state's government or if they identify with the party out of power. We look at whether, in states with divided government, respondents are any more likely to view the results of the redistricting bargain as fair or satisfactory than in states with unified governments. We also distinguish between states with maps that are biased in one party's favor and those that are not. Overall, we find that respondents hold rational opinions. Winners are happier than losers, and voters generally desire a fair process achieved through methods muting the potential influence of partisanship in the line-drawing process. The third part of this chapter concludes by briefly illustrating the strong relationship that opinion on redistricting has with opinions about politicians more generally.

SURVEY METHODOLOGY AND DATA

Our study focuses on two surveys conducted in 2006. The Pew Research Center, in association with the Brookings Institution and the Cato Institute, conducted a survey in October 2006 on "Electoral Competitiveness."[6] The survey consisted of 2,006 adult respondents nationwide, with an oversample of respondents from districts with competitive U.S. House races in 2006.[7] Four of the questions asked bear directly on the redistricting issue. In addition to the Pew survey, we employ data from a poll conducted as part of the Cooperative Congressional Election Studies (CCES) designed by a team from MIT (2006).[8] One thousand respondents were asked various questions related to the 2006 elections, four of which were about redistricting.

The questions in both studies track opinions on two general issues. First, several questions address basic opinion with and knowledge about drawing voting districts. Second, each survey contains a question about who is or should be responsible for drawing district lines. The precise wording of the CCES questions considered here is as follows (2006):

Every ten years states have to draw new Congressional and state legislative district boundaries.

Q30. Do you think districting in your state is done fairly?

    Yes
    No
    Not Sure
    No Opinion

Q31. Would you prefer that redistricting in your state was done by the state legislature or by an independent commission?

    Legislature
    Commission
    Not Sure
    No Opinion

Q32. Occasionally the courts have to settle disputes about redistricting. Do you think that courts in your state do a very good job in deciding questions about election districts, a good job, a poor job, or a very poor job?

The Pew Center asked the following questions (Pew Research Center 2006, 10):

Q50. As you may know, states with more than one seat in the U.S. House of Representatives redraw their congressional district boundaries from time to time. How much, if anything, have you heard or read about the debate over how these boundaries should be drawn – a lot, a little, or nothing at all?

Q51. Thinking specifically about [INSERT STATE], as far as you know, who is normally in charge of how congressional district lines are drawn . . . is it . . . [9]

Elected officials such as the state legislature
A nonpartisan committee or panel
Don't know/Refused

Q52. Just your opinion, are you satisfied or dissatisfied with the way congressional district lines are drawn in your state, or don't you have an opinion about it?

Q53. What in particular are you dissatisfied about regarding the way [STATE]'s districts are drawn?

[Answer given]
Don't know/Refused

In addition to these studies, our discussion is supplemented with data from a Democracy Corps Poll in 2006,[10] 2005 and 2008 polls from the Field Research Corporation (DiCamillo and Field 2005a, 2005b, 2005c, 2008a, 2008b), and 2005 surveys from Ohio and California (see Tolbert, Smith and Green 2009).

In each of the following sections, our dependent variables take two forms – ordered and binary. For ordered variables, we present coefficients from linear regressions to facilitate interpretation, but we have also performed ordered probits and multinomial logits.[11] For binary variables, we use probit regressions. We also provide crosstabs of the data.

THE LOW LEVEL OF KNOWLEDGE AND INFORMATION

Any account of public opinion and redistricting must begin with a discussion of the low level of knowledge and information most respondents demonstrate when asked about the subject.[12] We present here the data on the lack of information and knowledge from respondents about districting, and then look at the structure of non-opinion.

TABLE 11.1. *Uncertainty by question*

	Not Sure	No opinion	DK/refuse	Total
Pew Center				
Who is in charge of drawing districts?			47%	47%
Satisfied with the way districts are drawn?		70%	3%	73%
CCES				
Districting done fairly?	36%	14%		50%
Prefer districting done by legislature or independent commission?	27%	14%		41%
How well do courts do in districting cases?	52%			52%

For the precise wording, see the first part of the chapter. Data are weighted. The question from the Pew Survey that asks those who said they were dissatisfied with the process what in particular they were dissatisfied about is not reported for the obvious reason that it is only asked to a subset of respondents who had already reported having an opinion. Fourteen percent of those 294 individuals did not know or refused to answer.

Low Information and Knowledge

The most direct evidence of low levels of information is from the Pew Center survey[13] and the Field Research Corporation. Respondents in the Pew Survey were explicitly asked how much they had heard about the debate over redrawing congressional district boundaries. Only 10 percent of all respondents and 12 percent of registered voters stated that they had heard "a lot." Among those same groups, 38 percent and 41 percent, respectively, had heard "a little" about the issue. The largest number of respondents answered that they knew nothing about the debate – 51 percent of all respondents and 47 percent of registered voters. Similarly, in the run-up to a 2005 ballot initiative on redistricting reform in California, Field asked voters how much they knew about redistricting. Just 11 percent answered "a great deal" and 27 percent said "some". By contrast, the majority of respondents had only seen, read, or heard "a little" (34 percent) or "nothing at all" (28 percent) (DiCamillo and Field, 2005c, 2).

Even when questions are not directly about awareness of the issue, responses reflect the low levels of knowledge people have about the subject. Table 11.1 presents the "not sure," "no opinion," and "don't know" responses for the other questions from Pew and CCES. The data add further support to the previous finding that only one-tenth of Americans reported knowing a lot about the debate. Indeed, in both surveys, the largest levels of uncertainty correspond to questions about the respondents' opinion on the issue – whether they are satisfied (73 percent), whether they think the process is done fairly (50 percent), and how well they think the courts do in settling disputes (52 percent). With little or no knowledge about redistricting in general, we should expect to find few opinions on the substance of the matter.

Americans reveal a similar lack of knowledge about who is responsible for drawing districts. Forty-one percent are not sure or have no opinion on whether they would prefer redistricting to be done by the legislature or by an independent commission. Likewise, when asked not about their opinion but the factual question – "Who is in charge of drawing congressional districts in your state?" – 47 percent did not know. In addition to the high percentage who answered "Don't know" to this question, several of those who did answer had incorrect information. Specifically, 21 percent of the respondents who answered the question were wrong about who actually drew the congressional districts in their state.[14] These misinformed individuals comprised 11 percent of all respondents, therefore yielding a total of at least 58 percent of Americans who do not know what body is responsible for redistricting.[15]

Structure of Non-Opinion: Breaking Down the Likelihood of Having an Opinion

With these general trends as the backdrop, we proceed to analyze low information and knowledge, first considering demographic characteristics and then asking if other factors help explain where Americans do and do not have opinions on redistricting. Table 11.2 presents the responses to Pew's direct question about awareness, and Table 11.3 gives figures for the remaining questions by variable.

DEMOGRAPHICS AND OTHER INDIVIDUAL CHARACTERISTICS

We begin by considering three immutable demographic characteristics: race, gender, and age. With respect to race, there is considerable consistency among African Americans, Hispanics, and whites on most questions, including Pew's direct question about knowledge, and no one group is always most or least informed. On questions about the fairness of redistricting or satisfaction, racial groups do not differ much, with single-digit percentage points separating the most and least likely to express an opinion. When asked about who draws the districts, whites were less likely to respond to the factual question, and Hispanics had an opinion about who should draw districts more often than whites or African Americans. Regression analyses support these findings of nondifferentiation: Race is never a significant predictor of the likelihood a respondent has an opinion or is knowledgeable about redistricting (see Appendix A).

With respect to age and gender, there appears to be some distinction based on the survey. In both, women are significantly more likely than men to be unsure or to have no opinion, sometimes by twice as much.[16] This effect is, however, more pronounced in the CCES survey than in the Pew study. That said, the regressions in Appendix A show that gender is a significant predictor of non-opinion for all questions. Age cohorts track a consistent pattern in the Pew survey – younger respondents are less knowledgeable than older ones in each question. In the CCES questions, on the

TABLE 11.2. *Pew Center question 50 by demographics*

| | How much, if anything, have you heard or read about the debate over how congressional districts are drawn? | | | |
	A lot	A little	Nothing	Don't Know
Race				
Black	9%	46%	45%	1%
Hispanic	8%	40%	49%	3%
White	10%	38%	52%	1%
Gender				
Men	13%	39%	48%	1%
Women	7%	38%	54%	1%
Age				
18 to 29	4%	31%	64%	1%
30 to 49	10%	36%	53%	1%
50 plus	13%	43%	43%	2%
Education				
No HS	4%	38%	54%	4%
HS Diploma	6%	38%	55%	2%
Post-HS Study	9%	38%	53%	0%
4 Yr College	12%	38%	50%	0%
Post-Grad	26%	42%	32%	0%
Partisanship				
Republican	9%	39%	51%	0%
Democrat	10%	46%	43%	1%
Independent	10%	32%	57%	1%
In Party	10%	44%	44%	2%
Out Party	14%	40%	46%	1%
News attention				
Very closely	24%	46%	30%	0%
Fairly closely	8%	42%	49%	1%
Not too closely	7%	34%	58%	1%
Not at all close	3%	31%	66%	0%
Geography				
Recent Issue St	14%	40%	46%	1%
Other States	7%	37%	54%	1%

Data are weighted. Note further that the Pew Study follows the census categories for race. Accordingly, for Pew questions here and in subsequent Tables, Hispanic includes Hispanic Whites, and White includes Non-Hispanic Whites.

other hand, there is little evidence of any pattern. In line with this, age behaves differently in the regressions based on the survey. It is statistically significant in regressions for almost all Pew questions but never so for CCES.

Education generally yields predictable results. On Pew's question about how much respondents knew of the redistricting debate, for example, an increase in

TABLE 11.3. *Demographics of no opinion*
Total of "No Opinion," "Not Sure," and "Don't Know/Refuse"

	Opinion about the process			Who draws districts	
	CCES 30	CCES 32	Pew 52	CCES 31	Pew 51
Race					
Black	54%	48%	72%	46%	37%
Hispanic	46%	48%	78%	35%	40%
White	50%	55%	73%	42%	50%
Gender					
Men	38%	41%	68%	28%	41%
Women	61%	63%	77%	54%	53%
Age					
18 to 29	43%	56%	83%	35%	56%
30 to 49	49%	51%	76%	45%	48%
50 plus	51%	52%	65%	39%	42%
Education					
No HS	79%	67%	78%	55%	52%
HS Diploma	62%	61%	76%	56%	51%
Post-HS Study	46%	48%	71%	36%	47%
4 Yr College	39%	48%	73%	38%	42%
Post-Grad	38%	42%	60%	18%	37%
Partisanship					
Republican	47%	50%	72%	43%	50%
Democrat	56%	60%	69%	46%	40%
Independent	47%	50%	76%	36%	48%
In Party	49%	50%	71%	46%	48%
Out Party	51%	51%	72%	41%	42%
News attention					
Very closely			53%		30%
Fairly closely			71%		41%
Not too closely			82%		56%
Not at all close			85%		57%
Geography					
Recent Issue St	46%	54%	74%	40%	42%
Other States	53%	46%	73%	43%	49%

Data are weighted. The question wording is as follows: CCES 30 ("Do you think districting in your state is done fairly?"), CCES 32 ("Occasionally the courts have to settle disputes about redistricting. Do you think that courts in your state do a very good job in deciding questions about election districts, a good job, a poor job, or a very poor job?"); Pew 52 ("Just your opinion, are you satisfied or dissatisfied with the way congressional district lines are drawn in your state, or don't you have an opinion about it?"), CCES 31 ("Would you prefer that redistricting in your state was done by the state legislature or by an independent commission?"), and Pew 51 ("Thinking specifically about [INSERT STATE], as far as you know, who is normally in charge of how congressional district lines are drawn . . . is it Elected officials such as the state legislature or a nonpartisan committee or panel?") (see CCES 2006; Pew Research Center 2006).

education level corresponds with a greater number of respondents who know "a lot." Similarly, higher education attainment is associated with fewer "not sure" or "no opinion" responses on all other questions. Likewise, it is significant in several regressions presented in Appendix A.

The impact of partisanship, like age, differs between the two studies. In the Pew Study, Democrats were consistently the most informed respondents about redistricting as compared to Republicans and Independents. "Only" 43 percent of Democrats reported having heard nothing about the issue, compared to 51 percent and 57 percent in the other two groups, respectively. In line with that response, Democrats had the highest response rate to questions about satisfaction and redistricting authority. By contrast, Democrats were consistently the *least* knowledgeable and expressed the *fewest* opinions in the CCES survey. They had the highest rate of "not sure," "no opinion," or "don't know" responses among the three groups on all questions. And for two questions – about fairness and satisfaction with the courts – about 10 percent more Republicans than Democrats gave substantive answers or opinions.

Partisanship, however, was generally not significant in the regressions presented in Appendix A after controlling for other demographic variables.[17] In Pew's direct question about awareness, being a Democrat was a significant predictor of a greater likelihood to have heard more about the debate. The only other question for which partisanship was statistically significant was the Pew survey question concerning who draws the lines in the respondent's state. Again, Democrats were more likely to give an answer. All other political orientation variables[18] were insignificant.

Finally, we note an entirely unsurprising result from the Pew data.[19] That is, respondents reporting that they follow news about candidates and elections more closely in their state or district were also more likely to have heard more about the redistricting debate, more likely to have an opinion about how lines are drawn, and more likely to know who is in charge of drawing district lines in their state. This variable is strongly significant in all of the regressions presented in Appendix A.

State-Based Explanations?

Here we look at an additional variable for its effect on the likelihood that Americans have an opinion or are knowledgeable about redistricting. Specifically, we consider geography,[20] separating out respondents from states in which redistricting has been more "in the news."[21] We define that category to include states where redistricting has been subject to an initiative since 2000[22] and states in which there was substantial and controversial litigation this decade.[23] Our list of such states is: Arizona, California, Colorado, Georgia, Michigan, Ohio, Pennsylvania, and Texas.[24]

As with many other predictors, we find somewhat mixed results in the Pew and CCES data. In response to Pew's question about awareness of the redistricting debate, respondents in these states are considerably more aware. Table 11.2 shows higher percentages of those knowing "a lot" and "a little" as opposed to "nothing," and this variable is strongly significant in the regressions presented in Table A1, even after controlling for demographics and partisanship.[25] By contrast, the variable is insignificant in almost all other regressions displayed in Tables A2 and A3. While Table 11.3 illustrates some interesting results – a higher rate of opinions on fairness of the process but not on the performance of courts, for instance – any such associations are not statistically significant in our regressions.

Exposure has a limited effect on awareness of the redistricting authority. When Pew asked respondents which authority draws the lines in their states, 82 percent of those who answered the question identified the correct authority in states with more recent redistricting action, whereas 77 percent were correct in other states. Moreover, people in states with a recent redistricting initiative or litigation responded that they knew who was in charge of redistricting at a higher rate than did people in other states, and this result was significant in the regression (see Table A3).[26]

Surveys conducted prior to the initiatives in California and Ohio track these results with added detail.[27] We see, for example, that poll timing matters as voter awareness starts off low even in these states but grows, as one would expect, closer to election day. In California's 2005 election, only four in ten voters had heard of redistricting in February (DiCamillo and Field, 2005c, 2). By June, 50 percent of registered voters and 60 percent of likely voters were aware of Proposition 77 (DiCamillo and Field, 2005b), and on the eve of the election, approximately 10 percent more voters knew about the proposal (see Tolbert, Smith and Green 2009, n. 10). Similarly, in Ohio in 2005, only one-third of respondents had not heard of or did not have an opinion on the reform measure shortly before the election (*Id.*, 98). The low level of information and opinions nonetheless remains high relative to other topics. A few months before California's second reform attempt in 2008, for instance, only 23 percent of respondents had heard of Proposition 11, whereas 45 percent had heard of a measure concerning abortion (DiCamillo and Field, 2008b).

STRUCTURE OF OPINION: SATISFACTION AND CONCERNS
IN DRAWING DISTRICTS

We turn to the structure of public opinion among individuals who gave substantive responses. We begin by considering how demographic variables help explain beliefs about redistricting. Finding mixed results, we then move to the crux of our findings, discussing how partisanship, incumbency, and institutional responsibilities affect voters' perceptions. Finally, we observe that distaste for politicians generally correlates with opinions about redistricting.

Demographics and Individual Characteristics

Tables 11.4a and 11.4b present the breakdown of opinions by demographics and political party. Table 11.4a gives percent positive and negative responses from all

TABLE 11.4A. *Demographics of opinion (all respondents)*

	Think districting done fairly		Satisfied with the way lines drawn		Courts do a ___ job settling disputes		Prefer an indep. commission or legislature	
	Yes	No	Yes	No	Good/V good	Poor/V poor	Comm.	Leg.
Race								
Black	11%	36%	11%	17%	30%	22%	46%	8%
Hispanic	11%	42%	11%	11%	30%	22%	52%	13%
White	21%	29%	13%	14%	19%	26%	49%	10%
Gender								
Men	21%	41%	17%	16%	24%	35%	58%	14%
Women	17%	22%	10%	13%	18%	18%	40%	6%
Age								
18 to 29	26%	31%	8%	9%	26%	18%	52%	13%
30 to 49	21%	30%	11%	13%	23%	26%	46%	9%
50 plus	16%	33%	17%	18%	19%	30%	51%	10%
Education								
No HS	17%	4%	8%	14%	9%	25%	32%	13%
HS Diploma	18%	20%	11%	13%	17%	22%	36%	8%
Post-HS Study	22%	34%	12%	16%	26%	26%	51%	12%
4 Yr College	20%	49%	18%	11%	24%	33%	67%	9%
Post-Grad	14%	48%	19%	21%	24%	34%	72%	10%
Partisanship								
Republican	31%	23%	17%	11%	23%	27%	42%	15%
Democrat	14%	29%	13%	18%	19%	21%	45%	9%
Independent	13%	39%	10%	14%	21%	29%	56%	7%

Questions, respectively, are: CCES 30, Pew 52, CCES 32, and CCES 31. Data are weighted.

TABLE 11.4B. *Demographics of opinion (respondents with opinions)*

	Think districting done fairly	Satisfied with the way lines drawn	Courts do good/v good job settling disputes	Prefer an independent commission
Race				
Black	23%	41%	57%	86%
Hispanic	21%	50%	58%	81%
White	42%	47%	43%	83%
Gender				
Men	34%	52%	41%	80%
Women	44%	42%	50%	87%
Age				
18 to 29	46%	46%	59%	80%
30 to 49	41%	46%	47%	84%
50 plus	32%	48%	39%	83%
Education				
No HS	80%	36%	26%	72%
HS Diploma	47%	46%	43%	81%
Post-HS Study	42%	43%	50%	81%
4 Yr College	32%	62%	43%	88%
Post-Grad	23%	48%	42%	88%
Partisanship				
Republican	57%	62%	46%	73%
Democrat	33%	42%	48%	83%
Independent	26%	41%	43%	89%

Questions, respectively, are: CCES 30, Pew 52, CCES 32, and CCES 31. Data are weighted.

respondents, and Table 11.4b displays opinions only among those with responsive answers.

As before, we begin by considering race. Overall opinion on the redistricting process again differs between the two surveys. When CCES asked whether respondents thought districting is done fairly, whites were twice as likely as African Americans and Hispanics to answer yes. Likewise, though not as starkly, a higher percentage of minorities than whites stated that the process was not fair. In the Pew study, by contrast, only small differences existed between racial groups as to their satisfaction with the way congressional districts are drawn. Race was never statistically significant in our regressions on trichotomous ordered variables (see Appendix B)[28] for fairness or for satisfaction when controlling for other demographic characteristics (see Tables B1 and B3).

On specific aspects of the process, no consistent patterns emerged between racial groups. Although African Americans display slightly more distaste for legislatures drawing the lines, preferences on the best line-drawing authority are largely the same across races. Our regressions support this finding, showing no significance for racial variables in Tables B2 and B4. There is, however, greater variation in opinion on the courts' involvement in dispute settlement. Blacks and Hispanics were eight percentage points more likely to think the courts do a good or very good job than a poor or very poor job – 30 percent versus 22 percent of all respondents. Whites, on the other hand, exhibit greater distrust for the courts. Twenty-six percent of all respondents believe that they do a poor or very poor job, compared to 19 percent who answered good or very good. Again, our regressions back up these results, finding some significance in race variables when testing respondents' opinions on the courts' work in redistricting disputes (see Appendix B).[29]

As to remaining demographic characteristics – age, gender, and education – the data show some variation but not much. Because of the overwhelming percentage of females who did not express an opinion, their response percentages are lower across the board. As such, any gender differences are difficult to perceive. Age categories reveal some distinctions. Among CCES respondents, older respondents are less likely to find the process fair. Again, however, Pew's question about satisfaction yields more opinions with age, but an equal split in satisfaction and dissatisfaction at all ages. Older respondents are more likely to express negative views of courts' handling of redistricting disputes, but opinions on line-drawing authority do not vary much. Finally, with respect to education, more educated CCES respondents find redistricting to be unfair, whereas among Pew respondents, satisfaction levels are mostly even at all levels. Higher education attainment is also associated with a greater preference for independent commissions drawing district lines.

Regressions displayed in Appendix B support these findings. Gender is generally insignificant. As the tables suggest, age is significant and negative in regressions testing views on fairness and the courts, but is insignificant with respect to satisfaction and line-drawing authority. Lastly, more educated respondent are more likely to view the process as unfair and more likely to prefer commissions.

Partisanship is associated with divided opinion along all metrics about redistricting. In general, Republicans are more likely to think the process is done fairly and to be satisfied with the way in which district lines are drawn. For non-Republicans, the opposite pattern holds. Twice as many Democrats and Independents believe that redistricting is not done fairly than think it is fair.[30] Democrats and Independents are also somewhat less satisfied with the way lines are drawn, in contrast to Republicans who are somewhat more satisfied. Moreover, slightly more Democrats and Independents prefer that lines be drawn by an independent commission than do Republicans, and Republicans prefer a legislative body about twice as often as Democrats and Independents.[31]

Partisanship and Incumbency

We now turn to the heart of our analysis concerning the influences of partisanship and incumbency protection on the redistricting process. The redistricting process is carried out by legislatures in most states (National Conference of State Legislatures

2009, 178–179). Unsurprisingly, criticism of the process reflects concerns about partisan or self-interested gerrymandering of districts. In this section, we attempt to gauge the pervasiveness of this concern among the general public.

At the outset, we make a few observations. First, the strong lack of opinion described in the second part of this chapter implies that what we observe in substantive opinions here is leveraged off the very few respondents who actually have opinions about redistricting. Second, although we consider several variables separately, many are closely related. Whether a state has a divided government, for instance, is highly correlated with whether its redistricting plan is biased in favor of one party. Whether a state's plan is biased is also closely tied to whether partisan or nonpartisan institutions were responsible for drawing district lines (see Note 42). Not only should such variables be interpreted together, but many variables for which we observe differences in the tables do not show up as significant in our regressions because their impact is likely being captured by other variables.

Finally, although closely related, we consider opinions on fairness, satisfaction, and institutional responsibility separately below. This facilitates the discussion and accounts for the fact that our questions come from two different surveys. The CCES survey, for example, asks just about redistricting whereas Pew explicitly refers to U.S. congressional districts. To the extent that some variables described below are more applicable to state district lines, this might explain some differences between the surveys.[32] Furthermore, fairness and satisfaction are distinct: A voter might be generically "satisfied" with a redistricting outcome while nonetheless finding the process unfair. For all that, however, the issues certainly parallel one another in many respects, and this should be clear in our discussion and results.

On the whole, we find that people's opinions are not irrational. Success at the polls affects opinions. Moreover, voters appear to desire fairness, which, along with satisfaction, is best achieved by dividing parties and institutions to mitigate self-interest in the redistricting process.[33]

For the variables discussed in the following three subsections, Tables 11.5a and 11.5b present percentages for all respondents and among those with an opinion.

Fairness

We begin with fairness. Overall, when asked by CCES if they thought redistricting was done fairly, 31 percent of all respondents and 62 percent of those giving an answer said "No." Only 19 percent of all Americans and 38 percent of those with an opinion thought it was carried out fairly in their state. Moreover, respondents in states in which there was a recent redistricting initiative or protracted litigation (see Notes 22 and 23) were much less likely to believe that the redistricting is done fairly – a result that was strongly significant in our regressions (see Tables B1 and B2). A Field Poll conducted in one such state (California) prior to a 2005 initiative revealed similar feelings in response to a more loaded question. Asked "do you feel that the way the state's district lines were redrawn after the last census was generally fair and balanced, or were they redrawn to give the incumbent party an unfair advantage

TABLE 11.5A. *Geography-based opinion (all respondents)*

	Think districting done fairly		Satisfied with the way lines drawn		Courts do a __ job settling disputes		Prefer an indep. commission or legislature	
	Yes	No	Yes	No	Good/V good	Poor/V poor	Comm.	Leg.
Recent Controversy								
Yes	14%	41%	12%	15%	19%	33%	51%	11%
No	22%	26%	14%	14%	22%	23%	48%	10%
Partisanship								
In Party	34%	18%	15%	15%	25%	24%	34%	21%
Out Party	16%	34%	10%	18%	20%	30%	49%	10%
State Control								
Republican	25%	24%	9%	16%	24%	25%	47%	12%
Democrat	12%	40%	11%	16%	19%	33%	47%	11%
Split	19%	32%	16%	13%	22%	25%	51%	9%
State Bias								
States with bias	13%	36%	10%	16%	18%	31%	53%	10%
States without bias	20%	32%	14%	13%	22%	25%	50%	10%
Final Line Drawer								
Legislature	13%	38%	10%	16%	18%	30%	50%	11%
Partisan Comm.	16%	37%	14%	14%	20%	34%	53%	12%
Commission	22%	26%	12%	14%	25%	19%	55%	6%
Courts	24%	25%	13%	12%	25%	24%	45%	7%

Questions, respectively, are: CCES 30, Pew 52, CCES 32, and CCES 31. Data are weighted.

TABLE 11.5B. *Geography-based opinion (respondents with opinions)*

	Think districting done fairly	Satisfied with the way lines drawn	Courts do good/v good job settling disputes	Prefer an independent commission
Recent Controversy				
Yes	26%	44%	37%	82%
No	45%	49%	50%	84%
Partisanship				
In Party	65%	50%	51%	62%
Out Party	33%	35%	39%	83%
State Control				
Republican	51%	36%	49%	80%
Democrat	24%	39%	37%	81%
Split	38%	55%	46%	85%
State Bias				
States with bias	26%	38%	37%	84%
States without bias	38%	52%	47%	84%
Final Line Drawer				
Legislature	25%	39%	38%	82%
Partisan Comm.	30%	51%	36%	82%
Commission	45%	46%	57%	90%
Courts	49%	52%	50%	87%

Questions, respectively, are: CCES 30, Pew 52, CCES 32, and CCES 31. Data are weighted.

when running for election in each district?", 43 percent of registered voters stated that the lines gave an unfair advantage to incumbents whereas only 18 percent found them to be fair and balanced (DiCamillo and Field 2005c, 2).

We also see significant divergences in opinion on various metrics of partisanship. First, in states where one party controls the government, we observe striking differences based on party. We code respondents of the same party that controls the government as the "in-party" and those of the opposite party as "out-party."[34] Asked whether they believe redistricting is done fairly, respondents from the in-party were about twice as likely to say "Yes" than "No." Conversely, respondents from the out-party answered "No" about twice as often as "Yes." This result was occasionally significant in our regressions (see Tables B1 and B3).[35]

These variables should be interpreted alongside another – whether a state has a unified or divided government – because "in" and "out" parties only exist where there is a unified government.[36] In states where the governor and the legislature are divided in some way, the two parties may need to strike a deal to pass a redistricting plan. If a state government is entirely controlled by the same party, however, there is no need to bargain for a fairer map. That said, it is also possible that the bargaining process itself results in a more raucous debate, which displeases voters.[37] On this metric, we find that respondents from Republican-controlled states were twice as likely as those in Democratic states to think that the process was fair, and people in states with divided government were in between the two.[38]

Relatedly, we ask if partisan bias in the resulting district maps affects public opinion. We have bias data for only twenty-six states and accordingly, our number of observations (N) decreases significantly for this analysis. Our measure of bias represents the expected number of seats that Democrats would win with exactly 50 percent of the vote.[39] For instance, a bias measure of 6 percent means that if Democrats receive 50 percent of the vote, they would be expected to capture 56 percent of the legislative seats. The plan is biased by 6 percent. A negative value means that the bias favors Republicans. To account for noise in the estimates, we code states as "biased" if both houses[40] were biased in either direction by 5 percent or more.

With respect to perceptions about fairness, Table 11.5a shows that voters in states with biased plans were somewhat less likely to find the process fair – 13 percent versus 20 percent in other states – and were more likely to label it as unfair. These differences were not statistically significant in regressions displayed in Appendix B. Bias, however, is highly correlated with the previous variable (whether a state has a divided government) because states with divided government are much less likely to show bias. Accordingly, the impact of bias, if any, may be captured elsewhere in the regressions.

Finally, for the same subset of twenty-six states, we have data on which body was responsible for drawing the final plan – the legislature, an independent commission, a bipartisan commission,[41] a partisan commission, or the courts (see Ansolabehere, Fougere, and Persily 2010). Table 11.5a shows that in states with nonpartisan line drawers – that is, where done by the courts or a commission – more people found the process to be fair and fewer found it to be unfair than in states utilizing the legislature or a partisan commission.[42]

Satisfaction

Satisfaction with the redistricting process is related, but not identical, to whether the process is perceived as fair. It is, therefore, not surprising that here we find many parallels with the prior section, but also some differences and fewer distinctions among voters. To begin, when the Pew Center asked if people were satisfied or dissatisfied with the way district lines are drawn overall, responses were basically split. Thirteen percent of respondents were satisfied and 14 percent were not.

We first consider expressions of satisfaction. Most significantly, we find greater evidence of a division between respondents in unified versus divided government states. In particular, in states where both parties control at least one branch of the government, Americans report higher satisfaction with the redistricting process. This result is statistically significant in regressions in Tables B1 and B3.[43] Similarly, we see greater satisfaction among members of the in-party as compared to the out-party,[44] among respondents in states without biased maps, and among those in states where a body other than the (self-interested) legislature drew district lines. Because these variables are all related to whether there is a unified government, it is again not too surprising that the latter observations were not significant in the regressions. The story, however, is the same: Respondents appear more satisfied with redistricting when they are on the winning side and when partisanship is less likely to dominate the process.

With respect to dissatisfaction, the same metrics yield opposite results. Pew followed up with the 294 individuals who expressed dissatisfaction with the process by asking the particular reason for that feeling. The question was open-ended, with questioners allowed to probe only for clarity. Pew then coded twelve responses. Similar to other responses, dissatisfied respondents blamed gerrymandering generally (6 percent), incumbency protection (10 percent), and too much partisanship (10 percent). An additional 2 percent stated that an independent panel was needed to draw districts. Remaining answers were quite broad.[45]

These general findings continue with our more specific variables. First, we again find frustration among minority party members: Members of the out-party are more dissatisfied than satisfied and considerably more dissatisfied than members of the in-party. Moreover, respondents in states without a divided government were more likely to be dissatisfied.[46] People from states with biased maps also reported a higher level of dissatisfaction. Finally, looking at the institution responsible for redistricting, the greatest level of dissatisfaction (and the greatest disparity between dissatisfaction and satisfaction) came from states where the legislature drew the lines.

Although evidence of dissatisfaction largely parallels our other findings, one group that found redistricting to be unfair did not report significantly different levels of satisfaction. In particular, people in states experiencing a recent redistricting initiative or controversy were only slightly more likely to be dissatisfied with the redistricting process, and this variable was not significant in the regressions. Accordingly, the data indicate that although controversial or high-profile redistricting caused respondents to find the process more unfair, they were not significantly less satisfied with the end result.[47]

Our findings track those reported by others analyzing the Pew data, especially with respect to electoral winners and losers. Bowler and Donovan find that Americans who hope their members of Congress are reelected are more satisfied with districting. On dissatisfaction, differences were stark but not surprising: Respondents who hold no unfavorable views about politics, live where their party usually wins, and do not think elected officials draw lines were not likely to be dissatisfied with the redistricting process. In contrast, respondents with the opposite responses on all three questions were much more likely to be dissatisfied (Bowler and Donovan 2009, 12, 17). In a cut of the data that we do not replicate, McDonald considers winners and losers in the high-profile states of California, Ohio, Texas and finds that 21.6 percent of those on the losing side expressed dissatisfaction compared to just 9.1 percent of the winners (McDonald 2007, 15).

Attitudes Toward Institutions

As should be clear from the previous two sections, attitudes toward institutions involved in redistricting are closely related to perceptions about the process more generally. People are more likely to report fairness and satisfaction where disinterested actors are in charge and where some bargaining should occur. Here, we consider opinions about institutions specifically.

First, CCES asked respondents whether they would prefer that redistricting be done by a legislature or an independent commission. Overall, paralleling their perception that the process is not fair, people expressed strong disapproval of legislative control of the redistricting process. Although most states entrust legislatures with line-drawing authority (National Conference of State Legislatures 2009, 178–9), only 10 percent of Americans would prefer that redistricting be done by that body. By contrast, 49 percent would prefer that an independent commission were in charge.

A closer look at partisanship reveals somewhat predictable feelings on this question. Members of the in-party preferred an independent commission considerably less often than the average American and reported a preference for the self-interested legislature at a rate twice that of the general population. Respondents from the out-party, by contrast, shared the same opinion as most Americans, with 49 percent preferring an independent commission and only 10 percent preferring the legislature. Thus, even though the surveys were taken several years after the lines were drawn in most states, we find some fairly strong evidence of both approval from winners and bitterness among losers about the process in states with a unified government.[48]

These data parallel analyses of initiatives in California and Ohio in 2005 to move line-drawing authority from the legislature to a commission. In a recent study, Tolbert, Smith and Green seek to explain why both initiatives lost despite seemingly strong support for independent commissions in postelection surveys. At least part of the explanation, they argue, is that self-interested voters act strategically, and winners prefer the status quo even if they like the idea of commissions in the abstract. Most voters are "winners" at the district level and, as such, are more likely to favor the status quo.[49] Losers at both the state and district level (so-called "dual losers") were most likely to support reform, but they only constitute a minority of voters (Tolbert, Smith and Green 2009). Likewise, Field Polls conducted in California throughout 2005 show that Democrats and liberals (the winners) opposed reform whereas Republicans and conservatives (the losers) were consistently in favor of divesting the legislature of its authority (DiCamillo and Field, 2005a, 2005b, 2005c). In 2008, California considered another redistricting initiative, and Republicans and conservatives again favored the reform more than Democrats and liberals (although the latter group now expressed plurality support) (DiCamillo and Field 2008a).[50]

Other variables in the Pew and CCES surveys, however, do not add much to the analysis of attitudes toward commissions and legislatures. Respondents in states with a divided government and states with a biased plan showed only a slightly higher preference for independent commissions than did those in states with a unified government or a non-biased plan. Similarly, and somewhat surprisingly, states experiencing a recent controversy or initiative did not correlate with a significantly stronger preference for independent commissions over legislatures.

With respect to the courts, of course, partisanship and incumbency issues are more complicated. Some states that elect judges do so in nonpartisan elections, which might be thought to diminish fears of partisan plans.[51] On the other hand, in states that hold partisan elections for judges, one might expect some concerns about partisanship affecting courts' role in the redistricting process. Reflective of this more nuanced picture, the data reveal more satisfaction with the courts as opposed to the process overall. CCES survey respondents, of whom a strong majority felt that redistricting was not done fairly, were split on their satisfaction with the courts' job in settling disputes. Twenty-one percent thought the courts did a good or very good job (19 percent and 2 percent, respectively), whereas only slightly more – 27 percent – found that the courts do a poor or a very poor job (18 percent and 9 percent, respectively).

Only a few variables help explain opinions about the courts and the redistricting process. First, in states where redistricting was controversial or the subject of an initiative, CCES respondents exhibited a much lower opinion of courts' involvement in redistricting disputes. Second, opinions of the courts are somewhat lower in states with biased redistricting plans. This may reflect a general distaste for the redistricting process more than a specific concern about the courts.

Finally, we find that in the twenty-six states for which we know the final line-drawing authority, respondents prefer the authority with which they are familiar. In states where courts drew the final lines, opinion was split on whether the courts did a good or poor job. Compared with partisan-controlled states, in which more voters stated that the courts do a poor job, this provides some evidence that the courts were able to win over some support where they participated directly in redistricting.[52] Analogously, Table 11.5b shows that, among those with an opinion, respondents in states where commissions control the process are more likely to prefer a commission.[53]

Related Distaste: Politicians

As a final matter, we consider the relationship between voters' opinions on politicians generally and their attitudes concerning the redistricting process. As redistricting implicates issues of partisanship and incumbency, we ask to what extent low public opinion can be explained by less favorable attitudes toward politicians (Persily 2002; Persily and Lammie 2004).[54] To test this idea, we look at approval levels for Congress and the President, as well as opinions of political independents.[55] Tables 11.6a and 11.6b give the percentages.

As expected, the tables reveal a strong relationship between public attitudes toward politicians and redistricting. Although this trend is observable for each variable presented,[56] it is most noticeable with respect to approval of the legislature – the

TABLE 11.6A. *Correlation with opinion about politicians (all respondents)*

	Think districting done fairly		Satisfied with the way lines drawn		Courts do a __ job settling disputes		Prefer an indep. commission or legislature	
	Yes	No	Yes	No	Good/V good	Poor/V poor	Comm.	Leg.
Congress Approval								
Approve Strongly	47%	0%	20%	16%	11%	36%	0%	54%
Approve	38%	17%	17%	9%	39%	21%	40%	13%
Neither	18%	20%	6%	7%	18%	14%	31%	8%
Disapprove	18%	31%	11%	17%	19%	31%	52%	11%
Disapprove Strongly	13%	51%	8%	30%	21%	36%	69%	9%
Presidential Approval								
Strongly Approve	34%	21%	16%	12%	20%	34%	37%	14%
Somewhat Approve	25%	27%	16%	12%	26%	23%	43%	14%
Somewhat Disapprove	17%	23%	12%	18%	22%	27%	40%	11%
Strongly Disapprove	12%	41%	12%	18%	20%	27%	61%	6%
Not sure	5%	14%	8%	7%	3%	0%	9%	4%
Partisanship								
Independents	13%	39%	10%	14%	21%	29%	56%	7%

Questions, respectively, are: CCES 30, Pew 52, CCES 32, and CCES 31. Data are weighted. For Pew Center poll, the precise wording of responses on congressional approval is Very Favorable, Mostly Favorable, Can't Rate, Mostly Unfavorable, Very Unfavorable. In the CCES survey, the responses "Approve Strongly" under congressional approval and "Not Sure" under presidential approval represented very small percentages of the sample, which explains the odd figures. With respect to presidential approval, Pew only gives two possible responses, Approve or Disapprove. Accordingly, those percents are duplicated twice under Strongly and Somewhat. With the exception of the respective questions from the studies, these facts hold true for Table 11.6b as well.

TABLE 11.6B. *Correlation with opinion about politicians (respondents with opinions)*

	Think districting done fairly	Satisfied with the way lines drawn	Courts do good/v good job settling disputes	Prefer an independent commission
Congress Approval				
Approve Strongly	100%	56%	24%	0%
Approve	69%	67%	65%	76%
Neither	47%	50%	57%	79%
Disapprove	37%	39%	37%	82%
Disapprove Strongly	20%	21%	36%	89%
Presidential Approval				
Strongly Approve	62%	58%	37%	72%
Somewhat Approve	48%	58%	53%	75%
Somewhat Disapprove	43%	39%	45%	79%
Strongly Disapprove	23%	39%	42%	90%
Not sure	25%	55%	100%	67%
Partisanship				
Independents	26%	41%	43%	89%

body directly affected by redistricting plans. As approval levels decrease, so too do opinions that redistricting is fair or done in a satisfactory way. Further, as opinions of Congress decrease, voters were steadily more likely to prefer that an independent commission, and not the legislature, be responsible for drawing election districts. Indeed, in each of the regressions presented in Tables B1, B2, and B3, the variable for congressional approval is a statistically significant predictor of these opinions. Thus, on top of prior explanations given in this part, we find that views about politicians generally are a strong indicator of views on redistricting.

CONCLUSIONS

Our look at public opinion and redistricting has occurred in several stages. We began with the overwhelmingly low salience of redistricting in general. Although some factors help explain these data – voters in states where redistricting initiatives and controversies were more high-profile, for instance, are more knowledgeable – there is no escaping that one of the primary takeaways from our study is that Americans are not well-informed and do not often have an opinion when it comes to drawing election districts.

Analyzing the structure of public opinion where it does exist, we find a little something for everyone (or every theory). Demographic characteristics tell part of the story, with minorities less likely than whites to label the redistricting process as fair, for example. Opinions also differentiate along partisan and ideological lines.

And of course, opinions on drawing district lines to elect members of Congress are strongly related to opinions about Congress itself.

Our primary focus was on partisanship and incumbency protection, and on that topic, we found that Americans think rationally about redistricting. Those who identify with the party in control of a state's government are more likely to be satisfied and consider fair the redistricting process. A divided government also left voters more satisfied. Respondents were, however, less likely to view the redistricting process as fair or to express satisfaction with it if they lived in states where final district lines were drawn by a partisan body or in states where the map itself is biased in one party's favor. Opinions about institutional actors paralleled these observations, leading us to conclude that voters generally favor a redistricting process that requires bargaining and is run by disinterested actors.

APPENDIX A: REGRESSIONS TESTING LACK OF OPINION

TABLE A1. *Pew study question 50*

Variables	Saturated	Pared down
Demographics		
White	0.01 (0.11)	0.02 (0.11)
Black	−0.05 (0.14)	−0.04 (0.14)
Hispanic	0.09 (0.14)	0.09 (0.14)
Female	0.15 (0.05)*	0.15 (0.05)*
Age	0.00 (0.00)*	0.00 (0.00)*
Education	−0.08 (0.02)*	−0.08 (0.02)*
Income	0.00 (0.01)	
Geographic Variables		
Recent Issue State	−0.21 (0.05)*	−0.21 (0.05)*
Census Region	−0.01 (0.02)	
Political Orientation		
Democrat	−0.09 (0.06)	−0.10 (0.05)*
Republican	0.01 (0.07)	
Ideology	0.00 (0.03)	
In Party	−0.04 (0.07)	
Out Party	0.03 (0.07)	
News Attention		
Elections	0.16 (0.03)*	0.16 (0.03)*
R^2	.13	.12
N	1,268	1,268

The dependent variable, how much respondent has heard about the redistricting debate, is ordered: a lot (equal to 1), a little (equal to 2), and nothing (equal to 3). Thus, a negative relationship corresponds to a greater likelihood respondent has heard more about the debate as the independent variable increases. Coefficients are from a linear regression to facilitate interpretation, but order probits were also run. Coefficients are significantly different from zero at $*p < .05$.

TABLE A2. *Questions regarding fairness and satisfaction*

Variables	Done Fairly?	Satisfied?	Courts' Job
Demographics			
White	−0.16 (0.21)	−0.07 (0.21)	0.30 (0.21)
Black	−0.57 (0.32)	−0.17 (0.26)	0.07 (0.33)
Hispanic	−0.48 (0.29)	−0.13 (0.31)	0.24 (0.30)
Female	−0.55 (0.12)*	−0.24 (0.10)*	0.43 (0.12)*
Age	0.00 (0.00)	0.01 (0.00)*	0.00 (0.00)
Education	0.24 (0.06)*	0.07 (0.05)	−0.10 (0.06)
Income	0.04 (0.02)*	0.01 (0.03)	−0.04 (0.02)
Geographic Variables			
Recent Issue State	0.10 (0.12)	−0.01 (0.10)	−0.09 (0.12)
Region	0.11 (0.05)	0.06 (0.05)	−0.10 (0.06)
Political Orientation			
Democrat	0.10 (0.17)	0.14 (0.14)	0.19 (0.18)
Republican	0.09 (0.17)	0.00 (0.14)	0.00 (0.17)
Ideology	−0.04 (0.06)	−0.04 (0.06)	−0.03 (0.06)
In Party	0.22 (0.20)	−0.01 (0.15)	−0.21 (0.19)
Out Party	−0.09 (0.20)	−0.10 (0.15)	−0.10 (0.20)
News Attention			
Elections	N/A	−0.30 (0.06)*	N/A
Log Likelihood	−481.6	−724.2	−499.3
Pseudo R²	.09	.07	.06
N	764	1,279	764

For the first and second columns, probit regressions were run on a binary variable where respondents express a positive or negative opinion (value 1) or do not (value 0). Conversely, for the third column, probit regressions were run on a binary variable where respondents express a positive or negative opinion (value 0) or do not (value 1). Coefficients are significantly different from zero at *$p < .05$.

TABLE A3. *Questions regarding line-drawing authority*

Variables	Preferred Authority?	Know Who Draws?
Demographics		
White	−0.20 (0.24)	0.00 (0.20)
Black	−0.55 (0.34)	−0.28 (0.27)
Hispanic	−0.33 (0.33)	−0.13 (0.29)
Female	−0.47 (0.12)*	0.32 (0.09)*
Age	0.01 (0.00)	0.00 (0.00)
Education	0.32 (0.07)*	−0.02 (0.05)
Income	0.02 (0.02)	−0.01 (0.02)
Geographic Variables		
Recent Issue State	0.05 (0.13)	−0.27 (0.10)*
Region	0.07 (0.06)	−0.01 (0.05)
Political Orientation		
Democrat	0.09 (0.18)	−0.25 (0.13)*
Republican	−0.11 (0.18)	−0.01 (0.13)
Ideology	−0.03 (0.07)	0.00 (0.06)
In Party	0.13 (0.20)	0.15 (0.14)
Out Party	0.17 (0.20)	0.12 (0.14)
News Attention		
Elections	N/A	0.21 (0.05)*
Log Likelihood	−458.2	−810.6
Pseudo R²	.09	.05
N	764	1,279

For the first column, probit regressions were run on a binary variable where respondents express a preference for a commission or a legislature (value 1) or do not (value 0). For the second column, probit regressions were run on a binary variable where respondents do not know or refuse to answer (value 1) or give a substantive response (value 0). Coefficients are significantly different from zero at $^*p < .05$.

APPENDIX B: REGRESSIONS TESTING OPINIONS ON REDISTRICTING

Our data on state bias and line-drawing authority only covers twenty-six states. As such, many observations drop out when we include these variables in our regressions. We therefore present results for regressions with all variables except state bias and final line-drawing authority first in Tables B1 and B2. Tables B3 and B4 (with smaller N) then give results from the same regressions with variables for state bias and for who drew the plan added.

Two additional notes are necessary. First, in Tables B1 and B3, we include "No opinion" respondents in our analysis to achieve a higher N. The regressions were also run on ordered variables excluding those individuals and the results did not materially change. Second, F tests were run to test whether variables could be dropped from the pared-down models presented.

TABLE B1. *Questions regarding fairness and satisfaction (no bias data)*

Variables	Done Fairly		Satisfied with Process?	
	Saturated	Pared down	Saturated	Pared down
Demographics				
White	0.02 (0.11)	0.03 (0.11)	−0.04 (0.07)	−0.03 (0.07)
Black	−0.10 (0.16)	−0.08 (0.16)	0.01 (0.09)	0.00 (0.08)
Hispanic	−0.15 (0.15)	−0.11 (0.15)	−0.01 (0.10)	0.01 (0.10)
Female	0.10 (0.06)	0.10 (0.06)	−0.08 (0.04)*	−0.08 (0.03)*
Age	0.00 (0.00)	0.00 (0.00)	0.00 (0.00)	
Education	−0.05 (0.03)	−0.05 (0.03)*	0.03 (0.02)	0.03 (0.02)
Income	0.00 (0.01)		0.00 (0.01)	
Geographic Variables				
Recent Issue State	−0.23 (0.06)*	−0.25 (0.06)*	0.00 (0.04)	
Split State	0.09 (0.08)		0.14 (0.06)*	0.10 (0.03)*
Region	−0.01 (0.03)		0.01 (0.02)	
Political Orientation				
Democrat	0.07 (0.10)		0.04 (0.05)	
Republican	0.07 (0.10)		0.06 (0.06)	
Ideology	0.00 (0.03)		0.00 (0.02)	
In Party	0.36 (0.13)*	0.35 (0.08)*	0.08 (0.08)	
Out Party	−0.04 (0.13)		0.03 (0.08)	
Political (Dis)taste				
Congress Approval	−0.12 (0.04)*	−0.12 (0.03)*	−0.08 (0.02)*	−0.09 (0.01)*
Pres. Approval	−0.06 (0.04)	−0.06 (0.03)*	0.02 (0.04)	
Awareness				
Heard of Debate	N/A	N/A	0.02 (0.03)	
R^2	.16	.15	.06	.06
N	732	732	1,461	1,461

Dependent variables are ordered. For the first column, coded responses are "Yes" (equal to 1), "Not sure" or "No opinion" (equal to 0), "No" (equal to −1). For the second, coded responses are "Satisfied" (equal to 1), "Don't Know/Refuse" or "No opinion about it" (equal to 0), and "Dissatisfied" (equal to −1). Coefficients are from linear regressions to facilitate interpretation, but order probits were also run. Coefficients are significantly different from zero at $*p < .05$.

TABLE B2. *Questions regarding courts and line-drawing authority (no bias data)*

Variables	Courts' Job		Preferred Authority	
	Saturated	Pared down	Saturated	Pared down
Demographics				
White	0.35 (0.15)*	0.35 (0.15)*	0.04 (0.24)	0.01 (0.24)
Black	0.46 (0.27)	0.46 (0.26)	−0.17 (0.37)	−0.19 (0.35)
Hispanic	0.50 (0.20)*	0.49 (0.20)*	−0.24 (0.34)	−0.28 (0.33)
Female	0.06 (0.08)	0.07 (0.08)	−0.06 (0.13)	−0.08 (0.13)
Age	−0.01 (0.00)*	−0.01 (0.00)*	0.00 (0.00)	
Education	−0.01 (0.04)		0.15 (0.07)*	0.14 (0.07)*
Income	−0.02 (0.01)	−0.02 (0.01)	0.05 (0.02)*	0.05 (0.02)*
Geographic Variables				
Recent Issue State	−0.23 (0.08)*	−0.26 (0.08)*	−0.05 (0.13)	
Split State	0.03 (0.13)		0.05 (0.18)	
Region	−0.02 (0.04)		0.00 (0.06)	
Political Orientation				
Democrat	0.01 (0.15)		−0.05 (0.21)	
Republican	0.02 (0.13)		0.05 (0.21)	
Ideology	−0.01 (0.05)		−0.11 (0.08)	−0.10 (0.08)
In Party	0.05 (0.20)		−0.31 (0.27)	
Out Party	−0.19 (0.18)		0.19 (0.27)	
Political (Dis)taste				
Congress Approval	−0.11 (0.05)*	−0.09 (0.04)*	0.16 (0.07)*	0.16 (0.07)*
Pres. Approval	0.03 (0.05)		0.14 (0.08)	0.13 (0.07)
Log Likelihood			−400.9	−404.9
Pseudo R²			.10	.09
R²	.08	.07		
N	732	732	665	665

Dependent variables are ordered or binary. For the first column, coded responses are "Very Good" (equal to 2), "Good" (equal to 1), "Not sure" (equal to 0), "Poor" (equal to −1), and "Very Poor" (equal to −2). Coefficients are from linear regressions to facilitate interpretation, but order probits were also run. For the second, coded responses are "Commission" (equal to 1) and "Legislature" or "Not Sure" (equal to 0). "No opinion" responses are excluded. Probit regressions were run on this binary variable. Coefficients are significantly different from zero at *p < .05.

TABLE B3. *Questions regarding fairness and satisfaction (with bias data)*

Variables	Done Fairly		Satisfied with Process?	
	Saturated	Pared down	Saturated	Pared down
Demographics				
White	−0.03 (0.13)	−0.03 (0.12)	−0.09 (0.08)	−0.08 (0.07)
Black	−0.01 (0.18)	−0.01 (0.18)	0.00 (0.10)	−0.02 (0.09)
Hispanic	−0.19 (0.17)	−0.19 (0.16)	−0.03 (0.11)	−0.01 (0.11)
Female	0.02 (0.07)	0.02 (0.07)	−0.07 (0.04)	−0.06 (0.04)
Age	−0.01 (0.00)*	−0.01 (0.00)*	0.00 (0.00)	
Education	−0.06 (0.04)	−0.07 (0.03)*	0.02 (0.02)	
Income	0.00 (0.01)		0.00 (0.01)	
Geographic Variables				
Recent Issue State	−0.14 (0.10)	−0.13 (0.07)	0.00 (0.06)	
Split State	0.02 (0.10)		0.17 (0.07)*	0.12 (0.04)*
State Bias	−0.01 (0.12)		0.02 (0.06)	
Commission	0.26 (0.14)	0.23 (0.09)*	0.02 (0.08)	
Courts	0.25 (0.13)	0.23 (0.13)	0.09 (0.07)	0.06 (0.06)
Partisan Commission	0.06 (0.13)		0.06 (0.07)	
Region	−0.02 (0.04)		0.01 (0.02)	
Political Orientation				
Democrat	0.06 (0.12)		0.03 (0.07)	
Republican	0.02 (0.11)		0.07 (0.07)	
Ideology	0.01 (0.04)		−0.03 (0.02)	−0.03 (0.02)
In Party	0.32 (0.16)*	0.33 (0.11)*	0.09 (0.09)	
Out Party	−0.02 (0.15)		0.05 (0.09)	
Political (Dis)taste				
Congress Approval	−0.09 (0.04)*	−0.09 (0.04)*	−0.07 (0.02)*	−0.07 (0.02)*
Pres. Approval	−0.08 (0.04)	−0.07 (0.03)*	0.03 (0.05)	
Awareness				
Heard of Debate	N/A	N/A	0.03 (0.03)	
R^2	.17	.16	.07	.06
N	537	537	1,155	1,155

Dependent variables are ordered. For the first column, coded responses are "Yes" (equal to 1), "Not sure" or "No opinion" (equal to 0), "No" (equal to −1). For the second, coded responses are "Satisfied" (equal to 1), "Don't Know/Refuse" or "No opinion about it" (equal to 0), and "Dissatisfied" (equal to −1). Coefficients are from linear regressions to facilitate interpretation, but order probits were also run. Coefficients are significantly different from zero at $*p < .05$.

TABLE B4. *Questions regarding courts and line-drawing authority (with bias data)*

	Courts' Job		Preferred Authority	
Variables	Saturated	Pared down	Saturated	Pared down
Demographics				
White	0.31 (0.18)	0.30 (0.18)	0.22 (0.29)	0.23 (0.29)
Black	0.48 (0.32)	0.48 (0.31)	−0.12 (0.43)	−0.12 (0.43)
Hispanic	0.50 (0.23)	0.49 (0.22)*	−0.16 (0.39)	−0.11 (0.37)
Female	0.05 (0.10)	0.05 (0.09)	−0.17 (0.15)	−0.18 (0.15)
Age	−0.01 (0.00)	−0.01 (0.00)*	0.00 (0.01)	
Education	−0.02 (0.05)		0.16 (0.08)	0.14 (0.08)
Income	−0.02 (0.01)	−0.03 (0.01)*	0.06 (0.02)*	0.06 (0.02)*
Geographic Variables				
Recent Issue State	−0.25 (0.15)	−0.18 (0.10)	−0.32 (0.22)	−0.24 (0.17)
Split State	−0.13 (0.17)		−0.03 (0.25)	
State Bias	−0.06 (0.17)		0.62 (0.26)*	0.65 (0.23)*
Commission	0.24 (0.18)	0.23 (0.11)*	0.54 (0.29)*	0.58 (0.27)*
Courts	0.04 (0.21)		−0.12 (0.28)	
Partisan Commission	0.14 (0.18)		0.74 (0.27)*	0.69 (0.25)*
Region	0.00 (0.05)		0.05 (0.08)	
Political Orientation				
Democrat	0.15 (0.17)		0.10 (0.25)	
Republican	0.16 (0.16)		0.09 (0.24)	
Ideology	0.00 (0.06)		−0.04 (0.09)	
In Party	−0.20 (0.23)		−0.46 (0.32)	−0.41 (0.22)
Out Party	−0.31 (0.20)	−0.17 (0.13)	−0.01 (0.32)	
Political (Dis)taste				
Congress Approval	−0.11 (0.06)	−0.09 (0.05)	0.12 (0.08)	0.12 (0.08)
Pres. Approval	0.05 (0.06)		0.20 (0.09)*	0.22 (0.07)*
Log Likelihood			−284.8	−286.1
Pseudo R²			.12	.12
R²	.08	.07		
N	537	537	490	490

Dependent variables are ordered or binary. For the first column, coded responses are "Very Good" (equal to 2), "Good" (equal to 1), "Not sure" (equal to 0), "Poor" (equal to −1), and "Very Poor" (equal to −2). Coefficients are from linear regressions to facilitate interpretation but order probits were also run. For the second, coded responses are "Commission" (equal to 1) and "Legislature" or "Not Sure" (equal to 0). "No opinion" responses are excluded. Probit regressions were run on this binary variable. Coefficients are significantly different from zero at *$p < .05$.

NOTES

1   And in 1969, 52% of all respondents and 69% of those with an opinion favored "continuing with the present equal districting plan" (Gallup Poll, The Roper Center for Public Opinion Research).The 1966 survey conducted by Louis Harris & Associates was based on personal interviews with a national adult sample of approximately 1,250. The 1969 survey conducted by Gallup Organization was based on personal interviews with a national adult sample of 1,551.

2   The 2009 poll, designed by Ansolabehere and Persily, first asked "Do you think all legislative districts in your state should have the same number of people per district or is it okay for some to have more people than others?" 32% answered that districts should have equal populations, 53% stated that it is okay for district populations to differ somewhat, and only 12% thought that it is okay for some districts to have many more people than other districts. A substantial share of Americans, however, supports the "federal" model allowing for county representation in one house of a legislature. Fifty-four percent answered that it is better to have districts with equal populations in both chambers, but 40% preferred one seat for each county in one chamber and equal population districts in the other chamber.

3   In addition to the two surveys central to our study, some private polls have been conducted on redistricting. They are often state-specific and tied to a particular reform initiative (see, e.g., DiCamillo and Field 2005a, 2005b, 2005c, 2008a, 2008b; Tolbert, Smith, and Green 2009).

4   We are aware of only a few such studies. Two brief papers on public attitudes toward redistricting both analyze the same dataset (see Pew Research Center 2006; McDonald 2007; McDonald 2008). Another study using Pew data considers attitudes toward redistricting as they relate to general perceptions about politics, electoral winners and losers, and line-drawing authority (Bowler and Donovan 2009). A fourth focuses on unsuccessful initiatives in California and Ohio to analyze the effects of self-interested, strategic voting among so-called representational winners and losers (Tolbert, Smith, and Green 2009).

5   As discussed in more detail below, we observe a significant difference in overall responses to the CCES question about fairness and Pew's question about satisfaction. The results do not necessarily contradict. A population may, for example, find the process to be unfair on average while nonetheless splitting on satisfaction and dissatisfaction. The disparity is, nonetheless, significant enough to warrant acknowledgment and even a question about the extent to which the polls are consistent.

6   The data can be downloaded at http://people-press.org/dataarchive/.

7   For this and additional details about the study methodology, see the study by the Pew Research Center (2006) and 26069.Methodology.doc, available for download with the study.

8   For general information about the study, see http://web.mit.edu/polisci/portl/cces/commoncontent.html and the essay by Stephen Ansolabehere and Nathaniel Persily, *Vote Fraud in the Eye of the Beholder: The Role of Public Opinion in the Challenge to Voter Identification Requirements* (2008).

9   The study clarifies that "Montana, North Dakota, South Dakota, Vermont, and Wyoming each have only one Congressional district. Respondents from these states were not asked questions 51 through 53" (Pew Research Center 2006, 10 n. 2).

10 The survey by Democracy Corps was conducted by Greenberg Quinlan Rosner Research based on telephone interviews with a national likely voters sample of 1,005 (The Roper Center for Public Opinion Research 2006).

11 Results are on file with the authors. The significance of variables did not materially change.

12 The results in this section track those in the literature finding that the public is poorly informed or pays little attention to process issues like redistricting (see, e.g., McDonald 2007, 14).

13 McDonald reports the same low information results from the Pew study (McDonald 2007; McDonald 2008).

14 A list of redistricting authorities by state for congressional districts and state legislative districts is kept by the National Conference of State Legislatures (see National Conference of State Legislatures 2009). The correct authority for congressional districts was matched up with a table of weighted responses to Question 51 from the Pew Study by state. The percentages of Correct and Incorrect answers were then calculated.

15 We say "at least" because presumably an unknown number of respondents were guessing. Those who guessed incorrectly are included in the 58% while those who guessed correctly, despite not knowing who draws the lines, are not captured in that figure.

16 This result tracks a well-known phenomenon that women are more likely to say "not sure" or "don't know" than men, even when they have an opinion.

17 All regressions were also run using a continuous variable for party identification instead of binary variables for Republican and Democrat, as reported in the appendices. Because differences were very slight and did not materially change our results, we use party dummies to facilitate our discussion and comparisons with the tables.

18 In addition to dummies for Republicans and for ideology, we include dummies for whether the respondent was a member of the party in control in her state (the "in-party") or a member of the party out of control (the "out-party"), if her state's legislature and governorship were all of the same party. It is not entirely obvious why this would predict likelihood to have an opinion, but it was included on the possible theory that a respondent may be more or less motivated to stay informed of the issue if his party was in or out of power. Nonetheless, as Appendix A reveals, the variables were not significant.

19 We did not find the same variable in the CCES study.

20 Census region was also included in our regressions but was not significant.

21 McDonald performed a similar analysis just on the Pew Study data and just for three states: California, Ohio, and Texas (2008, 156–7).

22 For a list of redistricting initiatives, see Nicholas Stephanopoulos, *Reforming Redistricting: Why Popular Initiatives to Establish Redistricting Commissions Succeed or Fail* (2007).

23 For a list of redistricting cases by state in the 2000s, see http://www.senate.leg.state. mn.us/departments/scr/redist/redsum2000/redsum2000.htm.

24 We also split up states with litigation and those with initiatives but the pattern did not change. In analyses where the variable was significant grouping the two together, both remained significant when separated. Similarly, where the grouped variable was not significant, splitting up litigation and initiative states did not result in either becoming significant on its own.

25 McDonald also reports that voters "learn" when exposed to the issue, and thus our findings track his on this metric despite considering more states (see McDonald 2007, 14).

26 Although not reported in Appendix A, we also ran probit regressions testing whether another geographic variable was a significant predictor of respondents' likelihood to know who was responsible for district lines. Specifically, we used dummies for states where the final lines were drawn by a commission, partisan commission, or courts (Ansolabehere, Fougere, and Persily 2010). We did not find significance, indicating that knowledge does not shift based on the different authorities for drawing lines in a given state. Moreover, running the same regressions against a dependent variable equal to 1 if the respondent states that she "knows" a commission drew the lines in her state (based on Pew question 51) further highlights the low levels of awareness. There, the flag for partisan commission states was significant but negative. Thus, people in those states were *less* likely to report knowing that a commission drew their lines.

27 In 2005, California's Proposition 77 proposed turning redistricting authority over to a panel of retired judges. Ohio similarly proposed that an independent commission draw its lines. In 2008, California's Proposition 11 proposed shifting redistricting authority to a non-partisan, fourteen-member commission.

28 Responses were ordered as follows: yes/satisfied, not sure/don't know/no opinion, no/dissatisfied.

29 Specifically, both Hispanic and White are significant in Table B2, while Hispanic is significant in Table B4. In Table B2, White has a positive sign, indicating an increase in appreciation for the courts for white respondents. Though this sounds odd in light of Table 11.4a, the magnitude of the white coefficient is smaller than that for Black or Hispanic. As such, whites are less likely than minorities to support the courts, which accords with the description above.

30 Californians are no different. In February 2005, more California Democrats felt that the process was unfair than did Republicans. Majorities of all party identifiers considered the process unfair. Question wording may explain why, as the question appears biased toward negative responses. The poll asked "do you feel that the way the state's district lines were redrawn after the last census was generally fair and balanced, or were they redrawn to give the incumbent party an unfair advantage when running for election in each district?" (DiCamillo and Field 2005c).

31 The partisanship variables – that is, party, ideology, and in- and out-party membership – do not achieve statistical significance in the regressions reported in Appendix B.

32 Of course, it is also quite possible, given their general lack of information, that voters do not perceive any differences between state legislative and congressional redistricting.

33 Another survey, which is not considered in detail due to its strong bias in question wording, reveals a similar distaste for drawing districts that result in strong partisanship. A January 2006 Democracy Corps Poll asked how a proposal to "require that Congressional districts be drawn to encourage competitive elections to reduce the number of extreme partisans in Congress" would affect their likelihood to support the candidate. A strong majority (68%) stated that their support would increase, with 28% answering "much more likely," 29% "somewhat more likely" and 11% "a little more likely" (Democracy Corps Poll, The Roper Center for Public Opinion Research 2006).

34 State party control is based on post-2000 election results from http://www.ncsl.org/programs/legismgt/statevote/statevote2000.htm (state legislatures) and http://www.ncsl.org/programs/legismgt/statevote/govParty_post2000.htm (state governorship). These data were then combined with respondent's party to create flags for in- or out-party. We do not consider Independents or minor parties here.

35 "In party" is significant.

36 We use data about partisan composition following the 2000 election, which is the time when most district lines were drawn following the census. Legislative data by state are from http://www.ncsl.org/programs/legismgt/statevote/statevote2000.htm and governorship data are from http://www.ncsl.org/programs/legismgt/statevote/govParty‗ post2000.htm. Though not reported here, we have also gathered data about state government composition in 2005, immediately preceding the surveys.

37 In light of this thinking, our regressions only employ a flag for whether the state has a divided government or not. In other words, we do not include a flag for either Republican-controlled or Democrat-controlled states despite presenting percentages for these states in Tables 11.5a and 11.5b. Here, we are most interested in whether any required bargaining results in a redistricting map that voters perceive as fairer. Accordingly, we only include a flag for so-called split states in our regressions.

38 A dummy variable for states with divided government was never significant in the regressions reported in Appendix B for CCES's question on fairness (or CCES questions about the courts and preferred line drawing authority). We also ran the same regressions from Appendix B with "split state" as the only geographic variable, and the results were the same. It was not a significant predictor of opinion.

39 Our measure of bias is based on 2002 estimates produced by Bruce Cain and John Hanley (see Ansolabehere, Fougere, and Persily 2010).

40 We also have coded a bias variable if only one house is biased and the other is not. Here, we display results for bias in both houses so as to capture more extreme instances of bias. Running the same regressions in Tables B3 and B4 with the more mild bias measurement, it was not significant for any regressions on CCES or Pew data.

41 We group independent and bipartisan commissions together.

42 These variables are not significant in Table B3, but their impact may again be captured elsewhere. As with the variable for divided government, these institutional variables capture bias because bias is lower in states where the legislature is not the final authority for redistricting. Out of the twenty-six states for which we have data, eight of the eleven exhibiting bias were states where the legislature drew the final lines.

43 The variable is labeled as "Split State".

44 Like the average respondent, a respondent identifying with the in-party was equally likely to be satisfied as he was to be dissatisfied.

45 They were: too complicated/unclear process (4%), other (misc) (15%), other (misunderstood question) (13%), everything (12%), unfair distribution of resources (6%), the public has no say (2%), don't know/refused (14%). Six percent cited the use of racial criteria.

46 As noted above, the variable for divided government ("Split State") was strongly significant in the regressions in Appendix B.

47 Our expanded list of states again yields results analogous to McDonald's in this regard (see notes 20–25; McDonald 2007, 14).

48 Despite the strong differences in Tables 11.5a and 11.5b, the variables "In Party" and "Out Party" are not significant in our regressions on preferred authority in Tables B2 and B4.

49 District-level losers are defined as individuals whose party identification does not coincide with at least two of her three representatives (state House, state Senate and U.S. Congress).

50 Proposition 11 barely succeeded, and there are many possible explanations for why it passed this time. Perhaps the most straightforward is that 2008 was a general election year and 2005 was not. Turnout for the presidential election and the controversial Proposition 8 may have favored Republicans and conservatives as compared to Democrats by just enough. It is, however, unclear why Democrats shifted from strong disapproval in 2005 to plurality support for reform shortly before Election Day in 2008. These may have been some spellover from voters' increased frustration with the Democratic legislative over the budget crisis or rising frustration with the government overall or simply a slightly different subset of the electorate voting.

51 For specific information about the methods of selecting appellate and trial court judges by state, (see Rottman and Strickland 2006, 25–8, 33–9).

52 In Table B4, however, only the flag for "Commission" is significant in the refined regression.

53 Table B4 shows that partisan commission and commission were significant in the regressions on preferred authority.

54 Using the same Pew data, Bowler and Donovan analyze how attitudes toward redistricting relate to negative attitudes toward politicians generally and "instrumental evaluations." They find, for example, greater dissatisfaction among respondents who dislike politics, whose party generally loses, and who think that elected officials draw district lines (Bowler and Donovan 2009).

55 Because a lack of party affiliation is a strong indicator of distaste for politicians, we include these percentages in Tables 11.6a and 11.6b. A dummy variable is not, however, included in the regressions in Appendix B. This was done because (1) when included, it was insignificant and (2) including it had an effect on Republican and Democrat dummies given that there were few respondents in nontraditional parties.

56 Despite the indication in Tables 11.6a and 11.6b that lower presidential approval is associated with lower opinions about redistricting, this variable is rarely significant in the regressions in Appendix B.

REFERENCES

Ansolabehere, Stephen, Fougere, Joshua and Persily, Nathaniel. 2010. bias_resp_better_040507.xls (Data on file with authors).

Ansolabehere, Stephen and Persily, Nathaniel. 2008. Vote Fraud in the Eye of the Beholder: The Role of Public Opinion in the Challenge to Voter Identification Requirements. *Harvard Law Review*. 121: 1742–4.

———. Public Opinion and Election Law Controversies Past and Present. http://volokh.com/2009/11/17/public-opinion-and-election-law-controversies-past-and-present/.

Baker v. Carr. 1962. 369 U.S. 186.

Bowler, Shaun and Donovan, Todd. 2009. Voter Perceptions of Elections and Electoral Competition. (Manuscript prepared for Midwest Political Science Association 2009 Conference, on file with authors).

Colegrove v. Green. 1946. 328 U.S. 549.

Cooperative Congressional Election Studies (CCES). 2006. http://web.mit.edu/polisci/portl/cces/commoncontent.html.

———. 2006. MIT_CCES_v4. doc (Data on file with authors).

DiCamillo, Mark and Field, Mervin. 2008a. The Field Poll, Release # 2292. http://field.com/fieldpollonline/subscribers/Rls2292.pdf.

————. 2008b. The Field Poll, Release # 2280. http://field.com/fieldpollonline/subscribers/Rls2280.pdf.

————. 2005a. The Field Poll, Release # 2168. http://field.com/fieldpollonline/subscribers/RLS2168.pdf.

————. 2005b. The Field Poll, Release # 2159. http://field.com/fieldpollonline/subscribers/RLS2159.pdf.

————. 2005c. The Field Poll, Release # 2153. http://field.com/fieldpollonline/subscribers/RLS2153.pdf.

Issacharoff, Samuel et al. 2007. *The Law of Democracy: Legal Structure of the Political Process*, 3rd ed. (132–3).

McDonald, Michael P. 2008. Legislative Redistricting. In *Democracy in the States: Experiments in Election Reform*, ed. Bruce E. Cain et al., 147. Brookings Institution Press.

McDonald, Michael P. 2007. Where the Ivory Tower Meets the Road: Voter Perceptions of Electoral Competition. (Manuscript prepared for "2008 and Beyond: The Future of Election and Ethics Reform in the States" conference, on file with authors).

National Conference of State Legislatures. 2009. Redistricting Law 2010, 178–9. http://www.senate.mn/departments/scr/redist/Red2010/Redistricting_Law_2010.pdf.

Persily, Nathaniel. 2002. In Defense of Foxes Guarding Henhouses: The Case for Judicial Acquiescence to Incumbent-Protecting Gerrymanders. *Harvard Law Review* 115: 593.

Persily, Nathaniel and Lammie, Kelli. 2004. Perceptions of Corruption and Campaign Finance: When Public Opinion Determines Constitutional Law. *University of Pennsylvania Law Review* 153: 119.

Pew Research Center. 2006. Most Have Heard Little or Nothing About Redistricting Debate: Lack of Competition in Elections Fails to Stir Public (October 27). http://people-press.org/dataarchive/.

————. 2006. 26069. Methodology.doc.

Roper Center for Public Opinion Research, The. http://www.ropercenter.uconn.edu/data_access/ipoll/ipoll.html.

Rottman, David B. and Strickland, Shauna M. 2006. U.S. Dep't of Justice, State Court Organization 2004, 25–8, 33–9. http://www.ojp.usdoj.gov/bjs/pub/pdf/sco04.pdf.

Stephanopoulos, Nicholas. 2007. Reforming Redistricting: Why Popular Initiatives to Establish Redistricting Commissions Succeed or Fail. *Journal of Law and Politics* 23: 331.

Tolbert, Caroline J., Smith, Daniel A. and Green, John C. 2009. Strategic Voting and Legislative Redistricting Reform: District and Statewide Representational Winners and Losers. *Political Research Quarterly* 62(1): 92–109.

PART IV

Conclusion

12

More or Less

Searching for Regulatory Balance

Bruce E. Cain

The existence of a broad consensus about core democratic features and values creates a basic reform template for democratizing authoritarian regimes and dictatorships. But because there is far less theoretical or political agreement about the relative merits of different forms of democratic representation and governance, there is no simple guide for improving established democracies. Democratic political institutions and practices have changed considerably over time and vary widely beyond the most basic attributes. Consequently, there is no international consensus about which country is the most democratic, which means that there are several perfectly acceptable alternative paths for emerging democracies to follow. This poses no serious problem for world peace and harmony, but it greatly complicates political reform in the United States. Simply put, it is difficult, if not impossible, to evaluate purported reform efforts absent a single, agreed-on democratic ideal form.

All democracies are based on the principle of popular sovereignty (i.e., that power resides in the people), but there is no universal consensus in the United States or internationally about what this means. Is direct voter control more democratic than representative government? Do less restrictive voter eligibility rules always make a system more democratic? Which rule for collective decisions is best: unanimity, supermajority, or a mere plurality of citizens? Are proportional seat allocation rules superior to single-member, simple plurality rules? Should popular sovereignty be limited for the sake of minority rights and fairness?

Most Americans at least agree on the importance of such democratic values as freedom of choice, transparency, equality of voice, full participation, and the like. Real-world political reform discussions (as opposed to academic debates) are rarely, perhaps never, about the validity of these abstract values per se. Rather they focus more practically on deciding which aspects of representation and governance should be covered by these values, which rules and processes best achieve those ends, and which part of the polity should decide and referee reform disagreements (i.e., the courts, elected officials, or the public). Transparency, for example, is widely acknowledged as essential for democracy, but exactly how much is needed and in which parts of the government is a matter for debate. Another question is whether transparency a fundamental right defined by the courts or a politically constructed response to modern public demands. Similar questions arise from other core values. Equality of voice is also a critical democratic value, but should it extend beyond the electoral arena to other forms of speech and influence, such as political campaign contributions or lobbying activities? Popular sovereignty and citizen participation are democratic cornerstones, but does this imply that the most advanced democratic governments should rely on more direct popular control and less on representative government?

It is only a slight exaggeration to say the central dividing line in U.S. reform debates is between more democracy and less, more being the almost teleological belief in the expansion of basic democratic values into new practices and realms of government, and less being the idea that even widely accepted democratic values have practical limits. The proponents of more democracy place greater faith in individual citizen capacity, downplay the role of intermediaries, and prefer fewer checks on the majority will. The proponents of less take the opposite view on all three points and focus more on ensuring democratic capacity and effective governance. They do not want democratic governments to be procedurally pure in a majoritarian sense, but to be as legitimate and inclusive as possible.

Trends in recent years have favored the proponents of more democracy over less. Many people naturally assume that maximizing a given democratic value – more participation, transparency, freedom of choice/contestation or equality – will necessarily mean a better democracy. Often coming from a populist or economic tradition, they seek a process that is purer by the criteria of one or more core democratic values. If core democratic values are good, then applying them further must be better. Skeptics, usually from a pluralist or Madisonian tradition, argue for limitations and balance. As a consequence, there are two competing visions of reform: more (i.e., maximized majoritarianism) and less (i.e., restrained democracy).

The purpose of this chapter is to explore the divisions between the more and less democracy positions, and in the end to relate these to the current state of election law and political regulation scholarship as reflected in this volume. In the sections that follow, I will first argue that beyond the threshold values of freedom, transparency, equality, integrity, and participation underlying any true democratic system, there are tradeoffs between and limits to these democratic goals. Consequently, sometimes providing more democratic opportunities can lead to less democratic outcomes. Maximizing a particular democratic value can lead to implicit adverse trade-offs with other democratic values that might, in total, diminish the democratic character of a society. Just as importantly, modern reforms can also fail when they make naïve and unrealistic assumptions about human capacities and prejudices, the role of intermediaries, and the need for checks on the majority. Several of the chapters in this book demonstrate the persistence of racial prejudice in the Obama era.

Removing legal and institutional protections for historically discriminated groups because they offend the principle of pure majority rule and are "apparently" no longer needed could plausibly set back the cause of racial justice and inclusion in America. A balanced theory of reform makes more realistic assumptions about citizen capacity and assesses the value of democratic systems by their effectiveness, stability, and legitimacy, not just the democratic purity of their processes. There is also a growing appreciation in the field of political regulation for the dynamic between elected officials, the courts, and the public. Many of the chapters in this book demonstrate a convergence in law and political science toward a new regulatory institutionalism that relies less on the single contributions of political self-correction, constitutional intervention, or plebiscite control, and more on studying and fostering positive interactions between these three reform mechanisms.

THRESHOLD DEMOCRATIC VALUES

Democratic systems vest sovereignty in the people. On a practical level, this means holding periodic elections that allow qualified members of the population to choose their representatives, policies, or both. To have these critical democratic moments, however, there must be specific rules and procedures governing them. The design of these institutional processes is usually guided at least implicitly by democratic values, but because they also have important political consequences, intentionally or unintentionally conferring advantages to some individuals or groups over others, the underlying motivation for reform often operates at multiple levels simultaneously. This muddies the waters of democratic design because it can and often does mean that support for a particular reform measure is at least partially based on strategic or tactical advantage, not on fidelity to some set of coherent democratic principles.

Core democratic values support the proper functioning of these processes. Some values govern the conditions necessary for people to make decisions (transparency/freedom of information, free choice/contestation). Others dictate the way preferences are aggregated (equality of voice, fairness in allocation, full participation) or implemented (integrity/nondistortion). Both those who hold the more- and the less-democracy positions acknowledge the necessity of core democratic value thresholds, but the former argues for maximization and the latter for restraint.

To better understand this point, consider the linkages between core democratic values and the proper functioning of a democracy. First, citizens cannot make meaningful choices unless they are properly informed. A government that withholds large amounts of information about conditions in the country and its performance from its citizens, or that systematically interferes with the free distribution of information, undercuts the ability of its citizens to form preferences and make decisions. The threshold value of transparency in contemporary democracies is therefore measured by such indicators as the existence of a free press (i.e., not controlled by the government), access to information about policies and performance through freedom of information laws, the ability to observe government proceedings (e.g., open meeting laws), and the like. But how far does that right to know extend? How soon and how much information can citizens require of their governments? How far do transparency considerations extend beyond the electoral phase?

Adequate citizen capacity also requires free choice/contestation. The will of the majority cannot be truthfully assessed if citizens are coerced into decisions, or if choices are choked off before they make their way to the ballot box. The secret ballot and nonintimidation laws protect voters from those who would commandeer their decisions. But a free choice also implies alternatives and hence the norm of contestation. At a minimum, democracy requires contestation for critical offices, meaning that voters get a choice and can hold office holders accountable for their actions and decisions by voting them out of office.

The jump from having no choice to having at least one other alternative is a fundamental shift in a democratic direction. The movement beyond two to having multiple choices is less fundamental. Proponents of proportional representation systems nonetheless argue that voters should be given many choices, believing in essence that more choices equal more democracy. Federalists maintain that having many elections at more levels furthers democracy. Initiative advocates argue the same for putting multiple policies up to a vote. And so forth. How many alternatives should citizens have? Is more always better? At what point does the number of choices exceed citizen capacity to evaluate them adequately?

Elections are a defining democratic moment, and how votes are counted and winners are determined matters greatly to the fate of policies and candidates. A critical electoral design question is who gets to participate. The modern norm has increasingly evolved in the direction of full participation. Most basically, this has meant expanding the franchise to include women and minorities, and more recently, eliminating discriminatory barriers to the full enjoyment of those rights. The Courts through application of the Fourteenth and Fifteenth Amendments and the Congress by passing the Voting Rights Act of 1965 removed institutional barriers (first poll taxes and literacy tests, and then later redistricting, at large and multimember districts, annexations, etc.) that suppressed voting among African Americans and Latinos. Unbiased – or at least minimally biased – electoral participation is an important goal for a democracy for several reasons: First and foremost, because a proper gauge of the electorate requires representative turnout, and secondly because participation per se can be educative. Recent reforms have aimed beyond voting for candidates to other forms of voting and nonelectoral forms of political participation and civic engagement. In some parts of the country, this has meant voting to decide policies and constitutional issues increasingly through direct democracy, not just electing representatives. The meaning of participation has also expanded horizontally to the implementation of laws, with citizens demanding and receiving the right to observe and participate in administrative decision making. Is more opportunity to participate necessarily more democratic?

Beyond the growing number of opportunities to participate, participation has been redesigned to be more equal. Since the 1962, the settled U.S. doctrine has shifted toward the "one person, one vote" principle that an individual's vote should be equally weighted, which means as a practical matter that districts should be equally populated. The basic theoretical intuition is one of equal influence: That every person in a democracy should have approximately the same chance to influence the outcome of an election, even if that probability is very small to begin with. If we analogize an election to performing a utilitarian calculus of the greatest good for the greatest number, voting equality is potentially problematic, as Robert Dahl (1956, Chapter 4) noted. Whereas the Benthamite utilitarian calculus gives more value to those with strong preferences, modern voting processes tend to assign equal weight to every vote, thereby factoring out the intensity of feelings. The intuition that voting equality does not adequately reflect people's preferences may explain why turnout or campaign contributions are sometimes framed as revealing intensities of preference. By that reasoning, it is a virtue of the American system that people have to care enough to overcome the inconveniences of voting or the costs of making a contribution to a candidate. Even so, the notion of equal voice is more widely accepted in the United States than in other democracies.

However, maximizing the goal of equal voice and applying it to other realms of participation is more controversial. Some reformers, for instance, extend the logic of an equally weighted vote to an equal right to cast a winning vote. In short, they argue that a vote is not truly equal, even in an equally populated district, if the chances of casting a winning vote or a decisive vote are not equal as well. So members of a group or party by this reasoning would have an unequal right if a districting arrangement was biased against them such that their votes did not yield a proportionate share of seats, or if their opportunity to cast a decisive vote in a competitive race was lessened by an incumbent plan that made all but a few seats noncompetitive. Taken to a logical conclusion, this implies that proportional systems are more democratic than district-based, simple-plurality ones. But how far should the quest for equality go? Supporters of plurality rules believe that they further the goal of governance by creating larger, artificial majorities that are more stable and less vulnerable to party coalition defections. Is this consideration less democratic than proportional outcomes?

The last group of core democratic values concerns the translation of electoral outcomes into policy and government actions. The integrity of the system matters because the popular will can be thwarted by powerful individual incentives such as self-enrichment, favoritism, and the like. High levels of corruption or incompetence can undermine the legitimacy of and public confidence in a democratic political system. Bribery and extortion prohibitions, or conflict of interest restrictions, for instance, protect democratic representation from distortions caused by self-interested material gain. Since the desire to acquire personal wealth can cloud a representative's judgment and disrupt the electoral connection between public actions and constituent preferences, anticorruption regulations are almost universally regarded as foundational reforms for a democracy.

The recent trend in the United States has been to shift from quid pro quo corruption to a conflict-of-interest paradigm. The latter differs from the former in the sense that it is preventative (removing officials from situations that might induce corruption) and aims to lessen not just the incidence of corrupt acts, but the appearance of corruption as well (Stark 2000; Trost and Gash 2008). The movement toward greater reliance on conflict-of-interest logic is evident in both the McCain-Feingold campaign finance and the new lobbying restrictions adopted by Congress in 2006. As compared to the bureaucratic or judicial arenas, there is greater room for partiality with elected officials (i.e., favoring the groups and organizations that helped put the elected official in office) and more ambiguity about the ethical justification of quid pro quo trading for the sake of reaching consensus.

Bias and incompetence can also undermine the integrity of democratic electoral systems, as the administration of recent elections has amply demonstrated. The failure to accurately tally the votes in an election, or to register and enfranchise voters, can undermine confidence in the system and skew results unfairly. The partisan bitterness engendered by the controversy over Florida's ballot and recount procedures in 2000 or Ohio's provisional ballot problems in 2004 persist to this day. The ensuing paranoia over the potential for stealing elections forced many states to pay for expensive changes in election machinery and paper ballot options, and precluded for the moment any attempt to move to Internet voting.

But as with the other values, the critical question is how far to take the pursuit of integrity, specifically how far to extend the notions of corruption and conflict of interest into legislative behavior. Legislatures are supposed to represent interests, including their own. Because the U.S. state and national governments decentralize legislative powers to committees and allow for bills to be proposed and amended by individual members, U.S. governments have tended to have stricter bribery and conflict-of-interest regulations than parliamentary systems that give little or no power to backbenchers. In the last thirty years, pay-for-play and earmarking scandals had the effect of encouraging stronger disclosure rules and more prohibitions. But again, the question is how far the regulatory scheme should go in limiting the possible effects, or appearance thereof, of corrupting interests that might distort the majority will?

THE IMPULSE FOR MORE DEMOCRACY: MAJORITARIANSIM

Many contemporary reform advocates are at least implicitly majoritarian in their orientation. Evidence of this abounds in the election law field. For instance, the "politics as market" school, championed most prominently by Rick Pildes and Sam Issacharoff, posits competition as the critical feature in democratic representation (Issacharoff and Pildes 1998). According to this view, just as well-functioning markets promote the efficient production of private goods for consumers, vigorous competition between political parties and candidates encourages fairer and more representative outcomes for voters, leading ultimately to policies that better reflect the preferences of the many without the distortion of the powerful and rich few. More choice is assumed to be better than limited choice, especially given the propensity for duopoly lock-up and incumbent retrenchment in the American system. This leads them to recommend such measures as redistricting reform, loosened ballot access restrictions, and open primary laws in order to lower barriers to entry for new candidates, parties, and groups.

Another variant of academic majoritarianism is the median voter school, exemplified by scholars such as Rick Hasen, Elizabeth Gerber, and Elizabeth Garrett. Less explicitly linked to the market analogy, they lean heavily toward political changes that produce or enhance median voter results. So, for example, Professor Hasen favors campaign finance reforms that lessen differences in influence caused by inequities of wealth through contribution caps, targeted prohibitions, and a voucher system that lets voters participate in campaign finance on an equal footing (Hasen 2003, 2008). Garrett, one of the foremost defenders of the initiative process, sees direct democracy as a tool for strengthening the majority voice in an otherwise representative democracy system (Garrett 2005).

Both the market and median voter perspectives at least implicitly assume that a truly democratic majority is built on a foundation of individual equality. Both also take citizen preferences as a given and do not dwell on worries about false or rash citizen opinions. Their primary focus is to end democratic distortion and to achieve an accurate and fair reflection of constituent preferences, whether well considered or not. Anything in the electoral realm that deviates from the majority will is a democratic flaw in need of mending.

Majoritarianism in its various guises feeds into the logic that more democracy is the solution for all that ails democracy. More transparency leads to greater citizen knowledge and engagement, and to fuller participation. More competition will motivate greater numbers of voters to pay attention to politics and go to the polls. Expanded choices will draw in voters who currently find the alternatives of a two-party system too limited. The meta-assumption behind this thinking is that if a threshold level of a core democratic value like competition is good, then more is better. In the language of mathematical social science, the majoritarian position assumes a monotonically increasing function between core democratic values such as competition or realizing the will of the majority and the welfare of its citizens. In the end, however, this belief is an assumption, not a known fact, and a suspicious one at that: The functions of political design cannot be counted on to be either monotonic or simple.

There are other questionable assumptions behind the majoritarian viewpoint. First and foremost, it rests on faith in the expanded capacity and willingness of citizens to take on the additional burdens of citizenship offered by more choices, participation opportunities, and information. The optimistic view holds that higher education levels and the Internet have decreased the costs, cognitive and otherwise, of becoming informed and getting involved in public affairs. If it is easier to get information or to give input to the government, then surely more citizens will avail themselves of those resources and opportunities. Moreover, the theory goes, giving citizens more opportunities should further their sense of efficacy, encouraging more citizen effort and engagement. Proponents of proportional representation (PR), for instance, often argue that the lack of meaningful choice inhibits public interest and diminishes electoral turnout, and that the presence of a more diverse set of candidates would spur an increase in citizen involvement.

Arranged against this optimism is a large body of public opinion research that suggests that there are serious limits to the willingness and ability of citizens to learn and participate, let alone take on added responsibilities. The Columbia University's seminal studies in upstate New York started from the premise that voters would act like rational consumers shopping for the best price but discovered instead that partisan attachments were much more rooted and fixed in contextual sociology (Berelson et al. 1954). The so-called Michigan studies followed with further evidence that the American voters' level of civic knowledge was far from perfect and complete (Campbell et al. 1976). This view was later somewhat modified by issue voting modelers in the 1970s, but despite these shifts in the weight of judgment about voter capacity, no serious political science study has ever claimed that average voters are well informed about the details of government processes or national, state, and local policies, particularly the more technical and complex ones. Citizens may know enough to judge candidates or even to vote their interests on complex initiatives by relying on cues and cognitive rules of thumb, but there is no evidence that voters are less prone to error, emotional judgment, or plain indifference than in the past. The debates on Iraq involvement in 9/11 or over the so-called death panels in the Health Care bills serve as sober reminders of this. The Internet has indisputably increased the amount of almost costless information, but it has also brought us blogging, the decline of the print media, and more rash, unverified rumor mongering. Local TV and talk radio thrive, but at best (and even that not too frequently), they provide short bits of shallow analysis of critical issues and political races. There is more than enough serious information on the Internet about government and critical policies of the moment, but only a minority of Internet users will even try, let alone succeed, in finding it.

Another important limit to citizen capacity is the degree to which prejudices persist despite rising levels of education and information. Several of the studies in the volume reinforce this point. After the election of Barack Obama as President in 2008, there were many who asserted that this was proof that America was postracial, and that the voting-rights protections of the civil rights era were no longer needed. In fact, white racial attitudes have not progressed since 1988, even among younger cohorts, and racial reaction likely explains why Obama ran behind Kerry in several states in 2008 (Cain, Douzet, and Lefebvre 2009). White conservative voting may be ideological to some significant degree, but it is also motivated in part by racial stereotypes and sentiment toward blacks. The chapter by Hutchings, Wong, Jackson, and Brown demonstrates that even in a multicultural American society, white-nonwhite threat perceptions are the strongest and seemed to be based on the dominant position of the in-group feeling that it is losing ground to an out-group (Hutchings, Wong, Jackson and Brown, this volume p. 71). It is a reminder that identity politics is a persistent feature in politics, something that Marxists overlooked when they assumed that class would supercede religion, ethnicity, and race. The design of political institutions in the United States must assume that racial prejudice is deep-seated and compensate accordingly to ensure that the dominant racial group is not consistently winning at all levels of government, leaving minorities permanently out in the cold. Naïve majoritarian design could unintentionally exacerbate racial tensions and minority alienation.

Related to the citizens' knowledge and cognition is their capacity and willingness to participate in public affairs. The amount of total electing continues to rise, not just in the United States, but also in other Organization for Economic Cooperation and Development (OECD) countries (Dalton and Gray 2003). In addition, there are more opportunities to participate in administrative hearings, citizen commissions, neighborhood councils, and the like. The opportunities to participate have spread from the electoral moment to almost every phase of a democracy's existence. However, this impressive proliferation of democratic opportunities has not brought about a corresponding increase in participation rates: U.S. voting rates have nudged up in the last two Presidential elections but are still low by international and historical standards (Jackman 1987).

Similarly in OECD countries, participation rates are down even as the amount of electing has increased (Dalton and Gray 2003). Why? In the end, participation, even in occasional events like elections, is costly, and time is scarce. The amount of time the average citizen wants to or can devote to such duties is limited, and as opportunities increase, citizens act more strategically, picking and choosing their spots. If this is correct, it has implications for democratic design and what reformers should expect when the number of participation venues proliferates. Who will take advantage of these new participation opportunities – the average citizen or "interested" persons and affected interest groups? And if the latter, whose interests are then furthered?

All of this is relevant to a second assumption underlying the more-democracy position: that citizens would be better off with fewer intermediaries. In a highly complex political system, such as the United States, formal rules abound, unlike the Westminster model. But this formal complexity breeds an abundant amount of informal norms and behavior. Among other functions, political parties, interest groups, the media, and opinion leaders play a critical role as boundary spanners for the formal institutions of government, coordinators of individual actions, and transmission belts delivering political information to citizens.

The presence of intermediaries also increases the ultimate uncertainty about the outcomes of institutional change; if not properly accounted for, it can lead to unintended consequences for well-meaning reforms. This is true not only because intermediaries are necessary and therefore arise to fill the void sometimes created by institutional change, but also because intermediaries can thwart the intent of reforms by adjusting their strategies. This point is nicely illustrated by the history of U.S. party reform. American political parties, it has been widely observed, are coalitions of groups and interests. Their ultimate goal is to select candidates for elective offices and to win elections. When a party's constituency is broad and diverse, the structure of the party itself must evolve to take that into account. Thus, the Democratic Party became the party of loose coordination; the Republican Party the party of tighter and more disciplined organization. Whereas both parties had their factions, Democrats had to be more accommodating to diverse interests. Thus, they had no choice but to figure out how to reach mutual accommodation in order to win in November.

In the end, the Democrats' party reforms weakened many of the myriad ties that connected its national leadership to the precinct level, a natural consequence of the expanded and democratized primary system and an increasing resort to plebiscitarian tactics ultimately orchestrated by special interests (Polsby 1983). As a result, the role for party insiders and other elites with institutional loyalty diminished. Instead, the media, driven by their entertainment imperative, and interest groups tied to specific policies and ideology rose up to replace the party leaders and bosses. Conflict could no longer be managed or quietly resolved behind the scenes. Given the incentives and constituent bases of the new media and interest groups, disagreements became public and then hardened, sometimes even before the causes and dimensions of the disagreements were fully known.

The corollary of the theory of intermediaries is the iron law of oligarchy: that democratic reforms intended to give power to the people often shift it from one set of elites to another. In Nelson Polsby's critique of party reform, it shifted power from the somewhat accountable party leaders to a predominantly unaccountable media whose main motive was not the public interest or even winning voters, but rather driving up ratings and providing entertainment. As he wrote:

> ...elites do not disappear or become less significant in governing under a mass persuasion system. They are, however, less accountable to one another and more subject to the constraints of popular fashion. They must learn to feed the mass media successfully, to cultivate different virtues, e.g., less patience of the sort employed over the bulk of his career by Richard Daley, more indignation a la Ralph Nader.

Interest groups that organize themselves around such anachronisms as state and local party systems are bound to lose out to those that are skilled in packaging their ideas in ways that appeal to reporters and news media gatekeepers (Polsby 1983: 148).

There are other examples in which populist reforms gave rise to new intermediaries, or to old ones in new guises. The campaign finance changes in the 1970s, for instance, gave rise to political action committees (PACs) and the McCain-Feingold regulations to bundlers and independent nonprofits.

A key assumption of majoritarianism is the supremacy of the electoral majority along with a corollary skepticism about the wisdom of checks and balances in the modern era. The U.S. Constitution – a product of the eighteenth century – was founded on skepticism about unchecked power, including that of the majority. By dividing government functions between separate branches and across different levels of government, the American design made it practically impossible for any party or faction to have unchecked power. As a result, policy responses to electoral shifts are often dampened, and the majority can get frustrated with the institutional obstructions thrown in their path.

At the state level, the suspicion of unchecked executive power led to a "plural executives" design in many states, dividing the Governor's duties between numerous separately elected statewide officials (e.g., Lt. Governors, Attorney Generals, Superintendent of Schools, Treasurers, Controllers, Secretaries of State, and the like). Given the malleability of state constitutions, they track public attitudes toward political power much the same way that rings in a tree reveal historical climate changes. Legislatures were initially the most powerful branches of state governments, but as they became visibly captured by "special interests" in the second half of the nineteenth century, the reform reaction moved in two directions. One, the Progressive, sought to consolidate executive power and to establish more neutral government expertise. The other, the Populist, sought to take power away from elected officials by means of constitutional limitations and the popular initiative.

The populist impulse has proved to be particularly enduring, partly because it has the "more democracy" allure. Representative government, even with Madisonian checks and balances (most states mimic the federal government's structure with the exception of direct democracy and elected judges provisions) suffers from agency problems: That is to say, representatives can be influenced by party leaders, campaign donations, and interest group lobbyists into taking positions that might ultimately not be favored by the voting majority. Given that repeated waves of campaign finance and lobbying reform efforts have not eliminated these democratic "distortions," the natural reform impulse is to try to limit representatives' power further (i.e., if one cannot trust elected officials then give them less discretion and power) and empower the people to make more decisions directly. This line of thinking then leads to the increasing usage of direct democracy, the demand for expanded opportunities to observe and participate in government decisions, and the questioning of checks on the majority will.

There may be an even deeper democratic problem at the root of this: the difficulty of denying the majority will in a democratic system. The federal courts are arguably the strongest bulwark against majority tyranny, but ultimately, antimajoritarian court decisions issued can exact a high price in terms of institutional prestige and can be overturned subsequently by politically calculated appointments to the bench. However, the choice is not always between a majority and minority, but sometimes between the present majority and the deferred or considered majority will. The distinction between now and later can matter significantly if some majority thoughts are rash or evolve over time. In this sense, advanced democratic reform may often be about choosing between different types of majoritarianism rather than just the balancing of majority and minority rights.

In the end, it is hard to maintain an eighteenth-century belief in inalienable, God-given rights in a predominantly secular, religiously disestablished state, or in braking public governance in the interest of more rational deliberation in the new-media era. The underlying ethic in modern American democracy tends to be utilitarian and in the moment. The democratic purpose is to produce the greatest happiness to the greatest number, and fundamental rights to property or life are defined by the majority (even if modulated by legal precedent and tradition). In the course of U.S. history so far, there is ample evidence on this point in the dramatic reversals and re-reversals in policies related to fundamental rights such as the death penalty, abortion, and taxation.

Although it is hard to argue with the point that democratic legitimacy ultimately rests on majority approval, the flaw in majoritarian reasoning is the conflation of the temporary and considered majority will. The temporary majority is its momentary judgment, subject to the incomplete information and inherent limitations of citizens. The considered majority is majority's judgment when channeled through processes that allow for more time, more debate, and more interim experimentation. In the name of majority supremacy, reform majoritarians and academic populists favor changes that strip away deliberative mechanisms because they appear to erect institutional obstructions on the majority's path. What they fail to ask is whether it is ultimately in the majority's interest to go down the easier, faster democratic path.

A THEORY OF RESTRAINED DEMOCRACY

A theory of restrained democracy has its roots in both Madisonianism and modern-day pluralism. The former posits that the fundamental democratic challenge is avoiding the twin tyrannies of unfettered majority and minority control. This problem is still as relevant as ever, but Madisonianism's deontological assumptions about fundamental minority rights are getting harder to defend in contemporary, secular

American culture. Divine law or pure reason is not likely to be the best public rationale for respecting minority rights in today's political environment. The theory of restrained democracy adopts a more explicitly utilitarian framework.

Pluralism – an offshoot of Madisonianism – describes the ideal sociology of democracy, a world of multiple temporary majorities where at various times and in various domains, individual citizens at least sometimes find themselves in a majority of some sort. The decentralized institutional structure of U.S. government, built on a mistrust of concentrated power, facilitates individual microvictories throughout the system but is designed to prevent the sorts of enduring permanent, entrenched majorities that can ultimately corrode legitimacy and incite alienation among those who regard themselves as permanent losers. Restrained democracy theory extends pluralist logic more explicitly to reform efforts and adapts it to the new realities of modern citizenship.

Pluralism can sometimes be an excuse to do no reform. Extreme pluralism can paint an overly benign picture of the distribution of power in society, allowing inequalities in civil society to reinforce political power imbalances, particularly those driven by wealth. Certain personal attributes such as race and socio-economic status matter more than others politically in America and therefore deserve special consideration in reform design. A pure pluralist might not be comfortable with measures that target particular minorities for special assistance: A poor black man might be disadvantaged with regard to race or income, but not as a male. Multiple identities by this reasoning can become a pluralist excuse to ignore differences in the types and degrees of disadvantage, undermining the goal of creating a supportive democratic culture that promotes government legitimacy.

As noted earlier, restrained democracy theory maintains a judicious skepticism about public opinion and provides for institutional mechanisms to encourage deeper public deliberation before action, especially for decisions with important long-term implications and consequences. It premises reform on the possibility of both indi-vidual and aggregate public misjudgment. Individual citizens can and will make mistakes in their candidate and policy evaluations for many varied reasons, includ-ing incomplete and imperfect information, strong biases and predispositions, and the desire to please and conform to others, just to mention a few. To be clear, mis-takes in this sense mean that given an individual's values and goals, a person chooses in a way that he or she comes to regret in retrospect.

Social psychologists and behavioral social scientists remind us that irrationality can also often be generated and transmitted in groups. Excessive patriotism, widespread fear, and bandwagon effects can move majorities toward collective opinions that they might later regret. The possibility of individual citizen mistakes and aggregate regrets can never be totally eliminated, but representative institutions should be designed to lower the odds of such misjudgments and limit their adverse effects. Indeed, one might argue that the Internet, blogging, talk radio, the prevalence of politics-as-entertainment TV commentary, and the erosion of reporting norms have reinforced the tendency for public misjudgment, creating more, not less, unhelpful democratic noise.

Many American political reforms since the nineteenth century have removed the institutional brakes on public opinion. Revealing and implementing the majority will is the prevailing democratic imperative. Thus, the indirect election of Senators has given way to direct elections, convention nomination has yielded to primaries (some of which are open to all voters from the other parties), and direct democracy mechanisms such as the recall, referenda, and popular initiatives are used more frequently than ever, and not just in the United States (Cain 2003). The majoritarian pressures upon U.S. political institutions persist to this day. In 2005, for instance, the U.S. Senate very narrowly averted abolishing the filibuster rule, a long-standing supermajority mechanism.

Few, if any, would want to restore some of the past braking mechanisms such as franchise restrictions, indirect elections, or malapportionment. But before further brakes are removed in a specific way, reformers need to ask whether the majority interest is served in the long run by some of the existing majoritarian practices. For instance, should states allow constitutional change by a mere majority of those who happen to show up at the polls at a given election, or should judges be elected directly, subjecting them to the hotbed pressures of reelection.

In addition to relying heavily on elections, modern governments are increasingly poll-driven. Media outfits and outside groups run polls constantly on the issues and decisions of the day. The increasing fusion of reelection and governance reinforces hypersensitivity to public opinion, even when the public is clearly not well informed. Restrained democracy reform theory would consider better ways to gauge public opinion, favoring perhaps deliberative polling over the media-financed standard polling (Fishkin 1995). In a deliberative poll, respondents are exposed to opposing points of view before they are asked to give an opinion. Normal polling simply takes views as they are found, however half-baked and ill-informed. Given that reelection is often the modern representative's primary motive, the quality of public opinion matters more than ever. Distinguishing opinions grounded in facts and an appreciation of consequences from prompted attitudes offered solely for the sake of providing an answer to the pesky pollster might help further the deliberative process and increase the odds of the government making better decisions.

An increasingly important democratic challenge in this regard is the absorption of new media and the Internet. The rapidity with which information is shared and the weakening of mediating norms regarding credible sources and factual verification create new opportunities for public misjudgment. Reformers cannot ignore these developments or assume that they will change for the better any time soon. It means considering new methods for extending and broadening public deliberation to counteract the rush to public judgment and the immediate imposition of the majority will. The important point is that restrained democracy theory, unlike academic populism, does not treat public opinion as sacrosanct. Well-functioning democracies do not simply aggregate preferences; they create an environment that nurtures well-considered opinions.

Restrained democracy theory also differs from the more-democracy position with regard to the use of countervailing powers, including those that can counter temporary majorities. As opposed to lifting the restraints on majority power, more in this case means giving voice to countervailing interests. The typical contemporary reform impulse is to limit undesirable activities that might lead to distortion of the majority will. Hence, campaign contributions have to be capped at a certain amount, overall spending on politics should be limited, or actions prohibited that might cause a perceived conflict of interest. Quite apart from whether limitations and prohibitions are the best strategy for accomplishing the goal of more democracy, it is a constitutionally limited option in the United States. As a practical matter, the Supreme Court's strong First Amendment position has created alternative paths for activities that were meant to be limited (i.e., the so-called hydrology principle, see Issacharoff and Karlan 1999). So contribution limits diverted unwanted behavior down alternative, often less transparent paths. The FECA limits of the 1970s led to more PAC activity and eventually party "soft" money. McCain-Feingold opened the doors to more independent expenditures and nonprofit activity. In short, the quest to close all the gates of evasion can end in futility if there are major constitutional limitations.

The pluralist method of dealing with unequal power is "more voice, not less," meaning that another way to neutralize political advantage aside from capping and prohibiting is to support countervailing voices. Building on the Madisonian principle of opposing faction with faction, a pluralist solution expands the number of players in a political area to offset the advantages of the dominant players. Public financing fits into this category. If one intends public money to replace private money, public financing can never succeed. As we have seen at both the federal and state levels, it is hard to substitute public for private money voluntarily, especially when political races for office are highly competitive, and this is impossible to impose nonvoluntarily under current judicial doctrine. Typically, the inducement into public financing fails because the ability to raise more private money with less restriction outweighs the advantages of taking public money. Indeed, there is evidence at the state level that only candidates without realistic chances of winning opt into state public financing schemes (Mayer, Werner, and Williams 2006). But if the public money is viewed only as providing a supplement (not a substitute) to private financing, particularly for first-time candidates, and the goal is to encourage more candidate participation and not to eliminate the taint or inequities associated with private money, public financing can be seen as an instrument of pluralism.

Lobbying reform is another constitutionally protected area of political activity that requires a different approach. The standard populist reforms try to limit lobbyists' influence by restricting their ability to give gifts, regulating official contacts with former government colleagues, or closing off the immediate path for elected officials and staff to well-paying private-sector jobs for a specified period of time. Indeed, some would go so far as to prohibit lobbying entirely were it not a constitutionally protected political activity.

Building again on the principle of countervailing interests, an alternative approach would be to increase the types of lobbyists and other forms of expertise in the political system. A fairly substantial body of political science research reveals that whereas the numbers of lobbyists have increased substantially in recent decades, the mix of lobbyists is still heavily weighted toward business and moneyed interests (Apollonio, Cain, and Drutman 2008). One plausible explanation for this is that concentrated interests can more easily organize themselves to lobby than dispersed interest groups that must overcome inherent collective action and free-rider problems. If this structural explanation is correct, then the "bias" in the country's advocacy system is built in.

The strategy of "less voice," the usual reform move, is more effective with respect to such potentially corrupt aspects of lobbying as gifting, privately funded trips, and the lure of private-sector employment to members and staff (Cain, Gash, and Oleszek 2008). The courts have allowed a larger sphere of regulation when the goal is to reduce quid pro quo corruption and self-enrichment than other goals such as equality. Dealing with bias under such constraints requires a strategy of "more voice." Because the goal of equalizing speech or influence is not recognized as a compelling state purpose (and for some conservative justices, not even a legitimate one), a strategy of countervailing rather than capped or prohibited voice offers a better chance of success.

How might this be done? One might consider creating public lobbyists along the model of public defenders in criminal proceedings. Groups that qualify based on membership could qualify for a public lobbyist to work on their causes and bills. Another option might be to bolster the nonpartisan standing and professionalism of congressional staff. Most congressional staff members do not view their low-paying, untenured positions as long-term careers and therefore typically leave after a short period of service to pursue private-sector jobs. Inducing a longer term of service, a greater sense of professionalism, and a norm of neutral expertise might provide more of a counterbalance to lobbyist influence.

An important principle of restrained design is a more explicit acknowledgment of the role of intermediary groups. The majoritarian, political ideal-based individual citizen equality naively ignores the role that intermediaries play. Changes in rules change the abilities of any given group to influence political outcomes, but not the reality that some intermediaries will be more empowered by a given change than others. The inevitability of intermediaries – a corollary of Michels' Iron Law of Oligarchy – is evident in many facets of modern politics. When freedom of information laws were passed, the expectation was that they would empower individual citizens. In fact, individuals did use the Freedom of Information Act (FOIA) procedures for gaining information, usually about their benefits and personnel records, but it was the press, political and commercial competitors, and opposition researchers who used it to the greatest political and policy advantage.

In general, transparent, accountable, and multiple intermediaries and agents are preferable in a democracy to the opposite. In those instances where there is a choice, democratic design should tip the balance in that direction. In Europe, for instance, the EU has given more power to its unelected bureaucrats than its elected parliament, creating what many lament as a serious democratic deficit (Fabbrini 2007). Frustration with this lack of accountability has been manifest when voters have been given the opportunity to express their sentiments in national referenda in France, the Netherlands, and most recently Ireland. In the United States, recent campaign finance reform deliberately constricted the flow of unlimited, "soft" money into the parties and by so doing encouraged the flow into and out of independent groups and nonprofit organizations, often with nontransparent sources of support and misleading names. There were essentially three ways the reformers could have channeled the flow of campaign funding: through candidates and their organizations, political parties, or outside groups. The first two options were more politically accountable than the third, but the third was chosen because it was popular to restrict money to candidates and political parties (i.e., it seemed more democratic), and the Iron Law of Intermediaries was ignored or downplayed by the reform community.

Similarly, advocates of the popular initiative did not foresee the growth of initiative entrepreneurs and the consultant industry. The myth that popular initiatives arise from the grassroots is belied by California's experience: The public agenda is driven by those with money and expertise to qualify measures for the ballot. That in itself is not a reason to abolish initiatives, but it might be a reason to revise the process by which initiatives get on the ballot to make sure that there is public comment and greater transparency during the qualification stage.

Most importantly, a critical feature of restrained democracy is refocusing reform proposals toward the outcomes of democratic government (stability, legitimacy, efficaciousness) and away from process for its own sake. The more-democracy focus is on maximizing the public's access to and the majority's influence over government. It is a procedural perspective. The restrained democracy perspective looks more explicitly at outcomes and performance. Democratic processes per se may be more inherently appealing than other forms of government, at least in Western culture, but in the end, the dramatic growth in democratic forms of government would not have happened if they did not serve the interests of their populations better as well. Maximizing democratic values without regard for outcomes achieves purity but risks undermining the functioning of democratic government.

Consider some typical requirements for any government. First, it needs to be legitimate; citizens have to believe that their government has the right to make decisions that affect their lives, and that their interests are incorporated into collective decisions. If citizens do not believe that the government serves their interests in the long run, this undermines its stability. If the government teeters on the brink of collapse and chaos, or cannot defend itself from internal or external threats, the citizens will suffer. Similarly, if a democratic government cannot solve problems or govern effectively, procedural purity will matter little.

With respect to reform, this means that if the function of democracy is to further some version of the utilitarian, greatest-good principle, then it is possible that procedural values should be increased at some level but not necessarily beyond. Returning to the example of transparency, there are times when the right to information has to be curtailed in order to protect defense or police secrets because if the information got into the wrong hands, it would harm the interests of the majority. Full participation and observation taken too far might diminish the opportunity for real deliberation among government officials and increase the possibilities of obstruction. This is particularly a problem if one adopts the realistic assumptions that average citizens will not have the energy or motivation to take advantage of all the new avenues of participation, and the intermediaries will fill the void. The irony of democratic opportunity is that groups with concentrated interests and higher resources will have more motivation and means to participate than the average citizen. Instead of lessening bias, more democracy can increase bias by creating opportunities that citizens cannot utilize as effectively as concentrated groups. This means, in effect, that more democratic opportunities can result in less democratic outcomes.

TOWARD A BALANCED REGULATORY APPROACH: THE PROMISE
OF NEW ELECTION LAW INSTITUTIONALISM

Whereas not all, and maybe only a few, of the authors in this volume might agree with a restrained democracy approach (some, after all, favor majoritarian reforms), there may be an emerging consensus around a more balanced approach to political regulation and some moderation in the positions taken by election law scholars with respect to long-standing issues such as the merits of rights-based versus structural frameworks, or the emphasis on political self-correction versus aggressive legal intervention in the name of reform. Whether this will ultimately serve the interests of the more democracy or the restrained democracy school remains to be seen.

Reform measures in the United States can originate with elected officials, the courts, or the public (especially in states with the popular initiative). Reforms of and by elected officials are usually coerced to some degree by circumstance – a scandal, the perception of electoral advantage, and the like – and even then, these changes typically do not go as far as outside reform groups or party opponents would like. Still, there are enough examples of the U.S. Congress passing meaningful reforms – e.g., McCain-Feingold or and the 2007 new ethics rules in the House – to bestow at least partial validity on the idea that the American political system can self-correct. Even though many scholars pay homage to the importance of political self-correction, even the most fervent proponents of this point of view in the past, like Nelson

Polsby and Daniel Lowenstein, recognized the need for some judicial intervention to protect basic voting rights such as the "one person, one vote" principle or the right of political party self-determination (a "negative" right in the sense that it is freedom from excessive state interference).

The U.S. courts provide a second source of reform through constitutional review and interpretation of statutes or direct democracy measures. Among the authors of this volume, Samuel Issacharoff stakes out the strongest position in favor of heavy court involvement in political regulation. Focusing on the danger of politicians locking up the political system to their advantage, he depicts the courts as relatively impartial referees that can fill constitutional gaps and police the boundaries of democratic structures, protecting "the vitality of democratic competition for office and the ability of the political process to dislodge incumbents." Constitutional courts in developing countries extend that role by mediating disputes between ethnic groups and preventing the slide into one party/faction government: "[W]ithout the organizing role of structural constitutional limitations on majority processes, democracy tends to consume itself" (Issacharoff, this volume, p. 153).

Others, shaken by the U.S. Supreme Court's intervention in *Bush v. Gore* and by disturbing studies that reveal how ideology shapes judicial decisions, are more skeptical of the view that courts can serve as neutral referees in political disputes. Richard Hasen's empirical work, for instance, finds that judicial interpretations of the single-subject rule in U.S. states are highly subjective, depending all too often on the judge's view of the underlying policy. With the rise in election law litigation, Hasen wants the courts to be guided by clearer and more specific legislative language and by the influence of outside amicus courts (Hasen, this volume, p. 109).

None of the chapters in this book examine the third path of reform, namely interest group pressure, public opinion at all levels, and direct democracy measures. The latter is a particularly important mechanism for political reform that is normally held up by legislative inertia. Whereas state courts have been very deferential to the public will expressed through initiative reform measures, much of the recent literature on the popular initiative abuses dispels any idealistic notions about whether they represent the public will more purely. Initiatives have become a business run by professionals and funded with substantial sums of special-interest money. Voters do not read measures carefully and rely heavily on cues. Voters tend to reject many of the most extreme reforms, but in an atmosphere of anger and frustration, they can sometimes approve reforms that make things worse (for example, extremely harsh term limits).

All three paths to reform have flaws as well as advantages. The new election law paradigm increasingly looks at how the legal and political reform paths (including new methods of political pressure) can complement and intersect in useful ways. Heather Gerken and Michael Kang, two of this volume's editors, have been leading proponents of what Richard Hasen refers to in his chapter as the new election law institutionalism. Whereas the chapters by Gerken, Kang, and Foley directly reflect this new approach, this interest beyond the courts is also evident indirectly in the work of those who do not consider themselves new institutionalists. Consider the somewhat different takes between Richard Pildes and Pam Karlan on the Voting Rights Act (VRA). U.S. minority voting rights have been strongly shaped by the Supreme Court's interpretation of the Fourteenth and Fifteenth Amendments to the U.S. Constitution, but both Pildes and Karlan view the congressional role in racial progress as pivotal as well. For Karlan, the VRA passed by Congress in 1965 continues to shape the institutional and political context of elections in covered jurisdictions in ways that protect racial minorities from disfranchisement and vote dilution: "[S]ince all political deals take place in the shadow of the law, the negotiations among politicians in covered jurisdictions are inflected by the Act's standards." She argues that the VRA is an "ordinary" legislative act protecting minority citizens' rights, and the Court should treat it not with heightened skepticism but with the presumption that "Congress has legitimately used its enumerated powers" (Karlan, this volume, p. 96). Pildes, although more skeptical of whether the VRA will survive future Court scrutiny, is no less interested in Congressional action: He would prefer that as it did with HAVA and the NVRA, Congress address some of the new infringements on the right to vote with legislation that particularly focuses on the socio-economic inequities associated with voting technology and election administration (Pildes, this volume, p. 24). Their differences aside, the important point is their acknowledgment of a leading role for Congress in framing reform affecting a fundamental political right. Explorations of the dynamic between legislative and judicial action in political regulation are more common and explicit now in election law than they were ten or twenty years ago.

A second aspect of the new election law institutionalism is the interest in alternative methods to incentivize desired political behavior beyond legal prohibitions and rules. This, perhaps more than any other aspect of their work, separates the new institutionalists like Gerken, Kang, and Foley from the previous generations of election law scholars. As agents of reform, judges have more credibility than other public officials because of judicial norms of impartiality and fairness and the limits of precedent on potentially subjective judicial interpretations. Elected officials, particularly those running under partisan labels, are not similarly socialized or constrained. For this reason, many scholars favor taking the supervision of elections out of partisan offices and inculcating judicial-like norms of professionalism and neutrality in election administration officials, redistricting commissions, and others who oversee the conduct of the political system. Rick Hasen, a consistent proponent of this idea, holds out the hope that if there were more nonpartisan election officials, there would be less litigation and pressure on the court to wade into these matters (Hasen, this volume, p. 112).

But new institutionalists like Heather Gerken and Michael Kang are skeptical that a nonpartisan, professional election administration nirvana can be achieved soon (and perhaps ever) and argue for "the development of non-judicial institutions that would deploy politics as the remedy for politics" rather than depending "on the vigilance, good faith and neutrality of courts independent commissions and nonpartisan election overseers." They suggest instead "hard approaches" (i.e., institutional change) like citizen-based districting commissions that would follow baseball-style arbitration rules (i.e., iterative processes that encourage competition between the parties to provide the best plans) and "soft approaches" (i.e., that change the politics but not the institutions) like the democracy index or "shadow institutions" that shame actors into making better, less self-serving choices (Gerken and Kang, p. 91). In the same vein, Ned Foley argues for model codes, war-gaming exercises to explore the weaknesses ex ante in election administration systems, and amicus courts of retired judges to help guide judicial decisions in neutral and fair directions (Foley, this volume, p. 220).

A key element in this approach is the prospect of shaming through transparency and comparison, namely that public officials, including the judiciary, will have a harder time taking the low road when the higher road is made visible by the parallel actions of outside groups and institutions. Some will, of course, question whether shame is a sufficiently powerful motive unless it has serious and demonstrated electoral consequences for legislators, but the case for persuasion by invidious comparison is certainly plausible for commissioners, judges, and nonelected public officials. Alan Gerber's study provides both a degree of validation for the shaming perspective and some perspective on how strong the effects might be. Drawing on the insights of social psychology and the results from field experiments, he finds that voters are more likely to turn out when they believe that others, including neighbors, will be able to know whether the citizen has shirked his or her civic duty and not voted. But the magnitude of the effect is on the order of less than ten-percentage-point difference (Gerber, this volume, p. 184), which is more properly termed marginal than transformative. This caveat aside, Gerber's studies give new institutionalists hope.

The last element of new institutionalism is a heavier emphasis on measurement and empirical evidence. Complementing the new institutionalist emphasis on shaming, Archon Fung argues for new forms of transparency by "popular, or crowd-sourced, election monitoring" and points to efforts using new media, such as TwitterVoteReport, as potentially important new sources of data about the performance of election administration (Fung, this volume, p. 194). Due to its decentralized structure and the low level of funding that election administration often receives, hard data on the performance of election systems and poll workers is difficult to find and unevenly produced. But if democracy indexes and indicators are going to be built in order to benchmark election administration progress, the effort to collect reliable data will be critical. As Persily, Fougere, and Ansolabehere argue, we want ultimately to understand both the total amount of error and whether there is bias in the system. It may not be possible to eliminate mistakes completely, but it should be possible to eliminate bias and to minimize total error to ensure this. As compared to Fung, Persily, Fougere, and Ansolabehere rely on new and more comprehensive voter surveys and aggregate statistics, like the residual vote (Persily, Fougere, and Ansolabehere, this volume, p. 228). Data will also inevitably influence court opinions on election law matters in the future, but Chris Elmendorf argues that the courts may find that there is little or no evidence for the courts' current justifications for regulating aspects of campaign finance and redistricting (Elmendorf, this volume, p. 129). Will this make the courts more skeptical about the purported salutary impacts of reform claims, or will the courts continue to rely on the judges' intuitions about these matters?

I have long thought that the encompassing field for all of this activity should be called political regulation and not election law, precisely because it would better acknowledge the symbiosis between law and social science in this field. But whatever label we stick on this enterprise, the study of political reform will hopefully progress in a more empirically based and integrated direction. The new institutionalists may ultimately be wrong about the power of shaming and external example, but they are certainly not wrong in thinking that political reform requires all kinds of incentives, including the fear of legal penalties, the prospect of electoral advantage, or the humiliation of a bad public image.

CONCLUSION

The demand for more democracy has not been slowed down by the many achievements of the modern era. Questioning the further extension of democratic values into new realms of government risks the reputation of being against reform or worse, permitting corruption. But a closer examination of the premises behind the more democracy reveals that it rests on some very shaky assumptions about individuals and groups. This accounts in part for why modern reforms have not always lived up to expectations. The theory of restrained democracy is no less supportive of democratic values per se, but is skeptical of simple maximization strategies. The ultimate goal should be a democracy that works for the greatest number, and this may mean less emphasis on pure democratic procedures if it leads to better outcomes. The new institutionalism in election law acknowledges that the public needs help and attempts to enlist intermediaries (e.g., scholars formulating indexes, motivated citizens tweeting data, retired judges on amicus courts, etc.) to check and hold accountable public officials. This may be the most promising path for avoiding simple democracy-maximizing reforms that assume too much of average citizens to succeed.

REFERENCES

Ansolabehere, Stephen, Josh Fougere and Nathaniel Persily, "Partisanship, Public Opinion and Redistricting," this volume, p. 228.

Berelson, Bernard, Paul Lazarsfeld and William McPhee, *Voting: A Study of Opinion Formation in a Presidential Campaign*, Chicago: University of Chicago Press, 1954.

Cain, Bruce, "New Forms of Democracy? Reform and Transformation of Democratic Institutions," in Bruce E. Cain, Russell J. Dalton and Susan E. Scarrow, eds., *Democracy Transformed?: Expanding Political Opportunities in Advanced Industrial Democracies*, pp. 1–20, 2003.

Cain, Bruce E., Dorie Apollonio and Lee Drutman, "Access and Lobbying: Looking Beyond the Corruption Paradigm," 36 *Hastings Constitutional Law Quarterly* 13, 2008.

Cain, Bruce E., Frederick Douzet and Hugo Lefebvre, "La Nouvelle Carte Politique des Etats-Unis," *Herodote*, 1, n132, 2009.

Cain, Bruce E., Alison Gash and Mark Oleszek, "Conflict of Interest Legislation in the United States: Origins, Evolutions and Inter-Branch Differences," in *Conflict of Interest and Public Life: Cross-National Perspectives*, Christine Trost and Alison Gash, eds., Cambridge: Cambridge University Press, 2008.

Campbell, Angus, Phillip E. Converse, Warren E. Miller and Donald E. Stokes, *The American Voter*, Chicago: University of Chicago Press, 1976.

Dahl, Robert A. *A Preface to Democratic Theory*, Chicago: University of Chicago Press, 1956, Chapter 4.

Dalton, Russell and Mark Gray, "Expanding the Electoral Marketplace," in Bruce E. Cain, Russell Dalton, and Susan Scarrow, eds., *Democracy Transformed?* New York: Oxford University Press, 2003.

Elmendorf, Chris, "Empirical Legitimacy and Election Law," this volume, p. 129.

Fabbrini, Sergio, *Compound Democracies*, New York: Oxford University Press, 2007.

Fishkin, James, *The Voice of the People: Public Opinion and Democracy*, New Haven, CT: Yale University Press, 1995.

Foley, Ned, "Democracy in the United States, 2020 and Beyond," this volume, p. 220.

Fung, Archon, "Popular Election Monitoring," this volume, p. 194.

Garrett, Elizabeth, "Hybrid Democracy." 73 *George Washington University Law Review* 1096, 2005.

Gerber, Alan, "New Directions in the Study of Voter Mobilization," this volume, p. 184.

Gerken, Heather and Michael Kang, "An Institutional Turn in Election Law Scholarship," this volume, p. 91.

Hasen, Richard L., *The Supreme Court and Election Law: Judging Equality from Baker v Carr to Bush v Gore*, New York: New York University Press, 2003.

Hasen, Richard L., "Beyond Incoherence: The Roberts Court's Deregulatory Turn in FEC v. Wisconsin Right to Life," 92 *Minnesota Law Review*, 2008.

Hasen, Richard L., "Judges as Political Regulators," this volume, p. 109, 112.

Hutchings, Vincent, Cara Wong, James Jackson and Ronald Brown, "Whose Side Are You On? Perceptions of Competitive Threat in a Multi-Racial Context," this volume, p. 71.

Issacharoff, Samuel, "Constitutional Courts and the Boundaries of Democracy," this volume, p. 153.

Issacharoff, Samuel and Pamela S. Karlan, "The Hydraulics of Campaign Finance Reform," 77 *Texas Law Review* 1705, 1999.

Issacharoff, Samuel and Richard H. Pildes, "Politics as Markets: Partisan Lockups of the Democratic Process," *Stanford Law Review*, 643 (1998), 567.

Jackman, Robert, "Political Institutions and Voter Turnout in the Industrial Democracies," *American Political Science Review*, 81, n2 (1987).

Karlan, Pamela, "The Second Reconstruction, the Third Reconstruction and the Reconstruction of Voting Rights," this volume, p. 46.

Mayer, Kenneth, Timothy Werner and Amanda Williams, "Do Public Funding Programs Enhance Electoral Competition?" in Michael P. McDonald and John Samples, eds., *The Marketplace of Democracy: Electoral Competition and American Politics*, Washington, DC: Brookings Institution, 2006.

Pildes, Richard, "Voting Rights: The Next Generation," this volume, p. 24.

Polsby, Nelson, *The Consequences of Party Reform*, New York: Oxford University Press, 1983.

Stark, Andrew, *Conflict of Interest in American Public Life*, Cambridge, MA: Harvard University Press, 2000.

Trost, Christine and Allison Gash, *Conflict of Interest and Public Life: Cross-national Perspectives*, New York: Cambridge University Press, 2008.

Index

Absentee ballots, 212, 215–216, 224–225n
African Americans
  classical prejudice in, 54
  discrimination perceptions, 11–12
  group interests perceptions in, 14–15
  in-group identity in, 56
  linked fate perceptions, 12–13, 56
  population demographics, 52, 72n
  public opinion on redistricting, 231, 236t,
    237–238, 248t, 251t, 252t, 253t, 257n
  racial alienation perceptions, 64t, 64–65, 70–71,
    73n
  racial attitudes, group identity effects on, 64t,
    64–65, 71
  racial clashes generally, 52–53
  voter disenfranchisement historically, 17
  voting rights disfranchisement, 24
  zero-sum competition determinants, 64t, 64–65
  zero-sum competition distribution mapping,
    59–60, 60t, 62
Afro-Caribbeans
  discrimination perceptions, 11–12
  population demographics, 72n
  racial alienation measures, 68–69, 69t, 70–71,
    73n
  zero-sum competition determinants, 68–69,
    69t, 70
  zero-sum competition distribution mapping,
    59–60, 60t, 62
Alabama, 36
Alito, Samuel, 48n
Allport, G., 54
Alt, J. E., 129
Alvarez, R. N., 131
American National Election Studies (ANES), 181
Amicus courts, 83, 92–93, 112–113, 220

Anderson, C. J., 134, 143n
Angrist, J. D., 189n
Angrist and Pischke, 189n
Ansolabehere, S., 4–5, 130–131, 141n, 175–176,
  255n, 283–284
Anti-defection principle, 156–158, 168n
Ashwander v. Tennessee Valley Authority, 153
Asian Americans
  classical prejudice in, 54, 71
  discrimination perceptions, 11–12
  immigration status perceptions, 67t, 68
  linked fate perceptions in, 67t, 68
  population demographics, 52, 72n
  racial alienation perceptions in, 67t, 68, 70–71,
    73n
  racial clashes generally, 52–53
  zero-sum competition determinants, 67t, 68
  zero-sum competition distribution mapping,
    59–60, 60t, 62
Atkeson, L. R., 131, 142n

Baker v. Carr, 123, 150
Ballot access, court rulings on, 106–107, 144n
Ballot counting
  duplicate, 216
  in legitimacy, 131–132
  nonpartisanship in, 221–222
  reform of generally, 177, 211
  voting technology and, 131–132, 142n
Ballot design
  multilingual, 36–37
  in right to vote affirmation, 38
  VRA application to, 23, 24
Bipartisan Campaign Reform Act
  (McCain-Feingold), 223n
Birch, S., 130–131

CPSIA information can be obtained
at www.ICGtesting.com
Printed in the USA
BVHW041331311220
596851BV00002B/6